MOTHERS ON THE MARGIN?

Mothers on the Margin?

*The Significance of the Women
in Matthew's Genealogy*

E. ANNE CLEMENTS

◆PICKWICK *Publications* · Eugene, Oregon

MOTHERS ON THE MARGIN?
The Significance of the Women in Matthew's Genealogy

Copyright © 2014 Elizabeth Anne Clements. All rights reserved. Except for brief quotations in critical publications or reviews, no part of this book may be reproduced in any manner without prior written permission from the publisher. Write: Permissions, Wipf and Stock Publishers, 199 W. 8th Ave., Suite 3, Eugene, OR 97401.

Pickwick Publications
An Imprint of Wipf and Stock Publishers
199 W. 8th Ave., Suite 3
Eugene, OR 97401

www.wipfandstock.com

ISBN 13: 978-1-62564-063-5

Cataloguing-in-Publication data:

Clements, Elizabeth Anne.

    Mothers on the margin? : the significance of the women in Matthew's genealogy / E. Anne Clements.

    xiv + 296 pp. ; 23 cm. Includes bibliographical references.

    ISBN 13: 978-1-62564-063-5

    1. Bible. N.T. Matthew I, 1–17—Criticism, interpretation, etc. 2. Jesus Christ—Genealogy. 3. Women in the Bible. I. Title.

BS2575.52 C57 2014

Manufactured in the U.S.A.

Scripture quotations taken from the New Revised Standard Version Bible, copyright © 1989 the Division of Christian Education of the National Council of the Churches of Christ in the United States of America. Used by permission. All rights reserved.

Scripture quotations taken from the New English Bible, copyright © Cambridge University Press and Oxford University Press 1961, 1970. All rights reserved.

Scripture taken from the Holy Bible, NEW INTERNATIONAL VERSION®. Copyright © 1973, 1978, 1984, 2011 by Biblica, Inc. All rights reserved worldwide. Used by permission.

In memory of my mother
Elizabeth Monica Hancock

Contents

Preface | *xi*
Acknowledgment | *xiii*

Part One: The Five Mothers of Matthew's Genealogy

1   Introduction: The Genesis of a Thesis | 3
        Why Women?
        Hermeneutical Stance and Reading Strategy
        Methodology

2   Matthew's Genealogy | 21
        The Genealogy
        The Women of the Genealogy

3   Tamar | 40
        Preliminary Remarks
        A Narrative Reading of Tamar's Story
        Androcentric and Feminist Perspectives
        Tamar's Inclusion in Matthew's Genealogy

4   Rahab | 68
        Preliminary Remarks
        A Narrative Reading of Rahab's Story—Joshua 2:1–24
        A Narrative Reading of Rahab's Story—Joshua 6:15–25
        The Contrast with Achan
        חסד and חרם
        Feminist Perspectives
        Rahab's Inclusion in Matthew's Genealogy

Contents

5   Ruth | 96
    Ruth, Rahab, and Tamar
    A Narrative Reading of Ruth's Story
    Feminist Perspectives
    Ruth's Inclusion in Matthew's Genealogy
    Tamar, Rahab, and Ruth

6   "She of Uriah" | 121
    Bathsheba in the Old Testament
    Reading the Gaps in the Text: Differing Perspectives
    A Narrative Reading of Bathsheba's Story
    The Inclusion of "She of Uriah" in Matthew's Genealogy

7   Mary | 145
    Mary's Relationship to the Four Foremothers
    A Narrative Reading of Mary's Story
    Feminist Perspectives
    Mary in Matthew's Gospel
    Mary's Relationship with "She of Uriah"
    The Five Women of the Genealogy: Their Relationship to One Another and Matthew's Gospel Narrative

Part Two: The Collective Significance of the Women for the Ongoing Gospel Narrative

8   Tamar, Rahab, and Ruth: Aspects of Matthean Discipleship | 179
    Righteousness in Matthew
    Faith in Matthew
    Mercy in Matthew
    Conclusion

9   Others on the Margin in Matthew's Gospel | 194
    Marginality in Matthew
    The Women as Representative of the Marginalized in Matthew's Gospel
    Outsiders in Matthew's Story
    Marginalized Jews
    The Gentile Outsiders
    Conclusion

10   Women in Matthew's Narrative Life | 231
       A Gendered Reading
       Characters in Matthew's Story
       Matthew 3–25: Women in the Main Narrative Section
       Matthew 26–28: Women in the Passion and Resurrection Narrative
       A Positive Gynocentric Counternarrative

11   Conclusion: Mothers on the Margin? Matthew's Call to Conversion | 271

     Bibliography | 279

Preface

I am delighted that Pickwick Publications have agreed to publish my PhD dissertation. Some minor changes have been made to the original thesis but in the most part it stands in its original form. When writing my thesis, apart from the initial sections on methodology, I consciously chose to write in a style that is accessible to the more general reader since I hope that this book will have an appeal beyond the academic world. I also hope that whoever picks this up and reads it will both enjoy it and be challenged by the radical call to conversion that Matthew's Gospel presents to us all.

E. Anne Clements
Otford, Kent
May 2014

Acknowledgment

I am grateful to Wipf and Stock's editor Robin Parry for his helpful advice in preparing this book for publication.

Sincere thanks goes to my two PhD supervisors, Joy Osgood and John Colwell, who over six years held me to the course and who provided much wisdom, insight, and encouragement. Thanks also goes to David Firth and Stephen Wright for advice on my completed thesis. Over the period of writing I have appreciated the opportunity to present papers at post-graduate seminars at Spurgeon's College, London, and to receive feedback and support from staff and other students. In particular, I am grateful to Judy Powles, Spurgeon's librarian, for her help and friendship.

Thanks also go to my church, West Kingsdown Baptist, for graciously allowing me to take an extended sabbatical in order to write my thesis and to the Baptist Union of Great Britain for providing a scholarship to cover the period.

In addition to my church family, I am indebted to my immediate family. Thanks to my three daughters, Bethan, Emma, and Shona, for their love, prayers and belief in me. In particular, thanks to Bethan, who kindly proofread the text.

However, my greatest thanks goes to my husband, Ronald Clements, who, as well as caring for the church in my absence, cheered me on, helping me in a thousand and one ways to the completion of my PhD and its preparation for publication.

Part One

The Five Mothers of Matthew's Genealogy

1

Introduction

The Genesis of a Thesis

Why Women?

This thesis grew out of an initial observation. Within the first few verses of Matthew's patrilineal genealogy that opens his Gospel, four women are referred to: Tamar, Rahab, Ruth, and "she of Uriah." Why, I wondered, did Matthew choose to include four Old Testament women in the annotations of his genealogy and why these particular four women? This question is not a new one and in part my work is a response to a long-held, traditional view that has collectively labeled these woman as sinners or sexually scandalous. Other explanations have also sought for one denominator common to all four women to explain their inclusion. Invariably one woman does not "fit" and arguments are marshaled to force the women into one category (chapter 2). Unhappy that the reductionist view does not take seriously each woman's narrated history, I have chosen to employ a narrative methodology to discover whether a thorough narrative reading of each woman's individual Old Testament story might indicate why Matthew chose to include each woman within the opening verses of his Gospel (chapters 3–6). This has led to questions concerning the fifth woman of the genealogy: Mary. She is also the first named woman in the narrative of the prologue. How does she stand in relation to the four Old Testament women? Continuing to use a narrative analysis I have sought to establish how she is presented by the Matthean narrator and in what ways she might relate to the other four (chapter 7). Having considered the women's individual significance in part 1, I have then moved on to consider the collective significance of the women for Matthew's Gospel. Sensitivity both to their narratives and their placement within the genealogy has led to three groupings of the women. It is under these three configurations that I have considered their collective significance for the ongoing gospel narrative in part 2.

- The first three women of the genealogy—Tamar, Rahab, and Ruth

    All women were originally outsiders to Israel yet all three exhibit characteristics that are essential to the covenant relationship between YHWH and his people, characteristics that are key virtues of Matthean discipleship (chapter 8).

- Two clusters—
    - Tamar, Rahab, and Ruth
    - "she of Uriah" and Mary

All five women initially occupy places on the margins and consequently represent both those who are outsiders to Israel and those on the margins within Israel. The inclusion of these women serves to signal the importance of those on the margins in the ministry of the Messiah and to anticipate Matthew's rhetoric concerning the broadening of Israel's boundaries to include Gentile outsiders (chapter 9).

- All five women—Tamar, Rahab, Ruth, "she of Uriah," and Mary

    As a gender category it will be argued that these five women are significant in establishing Matthew's rhetoric regarding women. Reading Matthew from a gendered point of view I argue that, in contrast to the dominant male focused narrative, there is a counternarrative that focuses on women. Their inclusion is the first indication of a positive gynocentric[1] counternarrative that, it will be demonstrated, runs throughout the Gospel (chapter 10).

---

1. The adjective gynocentric describes a focus on women.

The Genesis of a Thesis

Hermeneutical Stance and Reading Strategy

Reader response theory has brought to the fore the subjectivity of the individual reader who approaches the text. It is only as readers come to the text that meaning is created. The reading process is complex and multifaceted. Carter provides a helpful summary of what readers do as they formulate meaning from the text:

> We notice features of the text. We construe words and fill gaps. We supply content and understandings that the text assumes of us. We attend to actions, conflicts, characters, setting and point/s of view . . . We discern and evaluate different points of view, different behaviours and values. We link scenes, attend to settings, construct sequences, identify causality, determine temporal relation, and create unity.[2]

No individual is value free; all possess ideologies and adopt particular stances (even if not recognized or acknowledged) as they come to the text. As they read, they create meaning from the text in the light of all that makes them who they are. Consequently, contrary to apparent modernist assumptions, there is no such thing as an interest-free, innocent reading that is completely objective in its interpretation. Individuals make up communities and interpretative communities also determine meaning. Since no reading is innocent, I will start by outlining my position. I come to the biblical text as a reader from within the Christian ecclesial community (I am a Baptist minister) and as a woman. As a woman from within the Christian ecclesial community, I adopt the position of approaching the text not with distrust and suspicion but with an essential trust that desires to be open to the text, alongside an awareness of its patriarchal ideology. I do not accept the position held by many feminist readers, that to engage with the text is to enter a struggle for power between the conflicting ideologies of text and reader, or that one's task is simply to uncover and critique the androcentric[3] language and patriarchal ideology of the biblical stories. Rather the text gives us an invitation to an encounter, to "respond to what is there."[4] I accept Vanhoozer's proposal that we are called to respond to the textual "covenant of discourse" with an ethics that attends "to the text's

---

2. Carter, *Matthew and the Margins*, 2.

3. The adjective androcentric describes a focus on men. By using the term I do not mean a piece of writing is exclusively male but that its main focus is masculine.

4. Vanhoozer, *Is There a Meaning in This Text?*, 395.

overture of meaning."⁵ Vanhoozer argues that "our duty to receive the textual stranger as a welcome guest is an obligation implied in the covenant of discourse."⁶ As a counter to a hermeneutics of suspicion so often employed by feminist critics,⁷ I will employ what I shall call a "hermeneutics of hospitable awareness," a hospitality that welcomes not just the friend but the stranger and even the perceived enemy. By this I am referring to the nature of the biblical text, which, for example, at points portrays the woman as evil.⁸ I come to the text firstly with a desire to understand the illocutionary force of the text. I read the text not in an uncritical way that accepts everything at face value but with a desire for an encounter. My hospitality to the text is not naïve (although in Ricoeur's terms it might be called a second naïveté), but seeks to move beyond a hermeneutics of suspicion, which has a place within the interpretative process but which should not determine the whole.

Beirne expresses this approach well:

> In a broadened feminist exegetical approach, it may be best to avoid starting at the signpost "be suspicious," and adopt instead Ricoeur's recommendation that the first step ought be "a naïve grasping of the meaning of the text as a whole," followed by the critical, interpretative stage, and concluding with a return to the text with what is now a "sophisticated, empathic understanding." Within this process, suspicion may well have a place, especially as a balance to uncritical affirmation of an androcentric text. But, as with all other exegetical tools, it is useful only inasmuch as it contributes to the overall goal of increased understanding.⁹

As a woman, I am aware that the biblical text is both androcentric (the masculine is normative) and patriarchal (the male dominates). Since the ground breaking work of Trible, one of the first to articulate a feminist literary stance in biblical studies, the problems of reading an ancient text shaped so powerfully by patriarchal cultures have been thoroughly highlighted and uncovered by feminist scholars. Many different methodologies

---

5. Ibid.

6. Ibid., 397.

7. Feminists argue that the act of the text being written establishes male dominance and female subjugation and therefore needs to be approached with a hermeneutics of suspicion.

8. See Zech 5:5–8.

9. Beirne, *Women and Men in the Fourth Gospel*, 16, quoting Ricoeur, *Interpretation Theory*, 74, and Lee, "Reclaiming the Sacred Text: Christian Feminism and Spirituality," in Joy and Magee, *Claiming Our Rites*, 83.

have been employed; basic to all has been the recognition that the biblical texts are products of androcentric, patriarchal cultures and history and that women's stories need to be retrieved and reclaimed. The way a text is constructed is intimately connected with its ideology for all texts have a persuasive and transformative power, inviting the reader into the textual world and in so doing offering a model of perceiving things differently. Each narrative has its own rhetorical stance, a means of persuasion. As speech-act theory reminds us, texts have perlocutionary power; they affect us. For many feminist critics to read with the grain of the text presents insurmountable difficulties, for the biblical text assumes a social, economic, and political world where men dominate and subjugate women. To counter this critics such as Fiorenza locate the locus of interpretative authority not with the reader and the text but with the interpretative community, which, in Fiorenza's case, is the "*ekklēsia* of women."[10] She writes, "The locus or place of divine revelation and grace is therefore not the Bible or the tradition of a patriarchal church but the *ekklēsia* of women."[11] Elsewhere, she defines the *ekklēsia* of women more fully as "a rhetorical space from where to assert women's theological authority to determine the interpretation of Christian scripture, tradition, theology, and community."[12] However, I take a more conservative stance, believing the primary locus of interpretative authority lies with the reader and the text. As a reader situated within a Christian reading community that adheres to the boundaries of the canonical text, I believe that since God's revelation is textually mediated through the canonical text, "We are tied to these texts."[13]

Lapsley presents a "crude typology" by dividing feminist interpretation of the Bible into three broad categories.[14]

1. Loyalists—Those who acknowledge the biblically legitimated oppression of women but who locate the problem in the *interpretation* of the Bible, not the text itself.

2. Revisionist—Those who acknowledge the patriarchal aspects of the text but who don't view them as definitive. They look for countertraditions within the Bible, voices that offer alternatives to dominant biblical voices and which must be teased out to be heard.

3. Rejectionists—Those who completely reject the Bible as authoritative.

10. Fiorenza, "Will to Choose or to Reject," 126.
11. Ibid., 128.
12. Fiorenza, *But She Said*, 152.
13. Barth, *Church Dogmatics*, 492.
14. Lapsley, *Whispering the Word*, 3.

My stance is that of the conservative feminist critic. Locating myself within the revisionist camp, I adopt a reading strategy that focuses on stories or voices that are often overlooked. I reject the position of radical feminists such as Fuchs, who argues that the Bible comprises literary texts that are "pernicious" in the way they portray women and their power relations with men.[15] She therefore believes that all pictures of biblical women are male constructs that are used to subvert and subdue women. Because of this, Fuchs concludes that a hermeneutics of resistance is the only way forward because "the Bible's rhetorical art and its patriarchal ideology are inseparable and complementary."[16] However, I consider that dialogue, characterization, plot, timing, point of view, gaps, repetition, and omission are tools of the literary artist (male or female), not hopelessly flawed constructs of a male ideology.

In this thesis I provide a woman's narrative interpretation and in doing so I consciously engage with women scholars, who work from a variety of feminist positions. Although I have learnt much from them, many adopt a position in relation to the text that I do not share. From time to time I engage with feminist viewpoints, critiquing some and incorporating the views of others. Underlying my argument is the view expressed by Watson that a critique of patriarchal ideology often overlooks "the possibility of a *self*-critique within the text or its broader context."[17] That there is an inbuilt critique of patriarchy within the text was first articulated by Trible in her ground-breaking article "Depatriarchalizing in Biblical Interpretation."[18] A number of feminist scholars since Trible have made the same observation; for example, Pardes notes that "while the dominant thrust of the Bible is clearly patriarchal, patriarchy is continuously challenged by antithetical trends."[19] In addition Gunn and Fewell note, "The Bible shows us not merely patriarchy, élitism, and nationalism; it shows us the fragility of these ideologies through irony and counter-voices."[20] A dynamic of self critique, not just of patriarchy but of other dominant ideologies such as Israel's exclusive calling, may be seen to be at work either in the immediate context of a narrative or a broader biblical context. A challenge to patriarchal values comes most fundamentally in the opening

---

15. Fuchs, *Sexual Politics in the Biblical Narrative*, 21.
16. Ibid., 29.
17. Watson, *Text, Church and World*, 178.
18. Trible, "Depatriachalizing in Biblical Interpretation," 30–48.
19. Pardes, *Countertraditions in the Bible*, 51.
20. Gunn and Fewell, *Narrative in the Hebrew Bible*, 204.

The Genesis of a Thesis

chapter of the Old Testament, "So God created humankind in his image, in the image of God he created them; male and female he created them" (Gen 1:26), and provides an alternative vision of the relation of men and women to each other and God than that pertaining in a typical patriarchal culture. The New Testament too contains egalitarian texts that provide a theological critique of patriarchy. Fiorenza considers such texts to be the "tip of the iceberg indicating a possibly rich heritage now lost to us."[21] It is not my purpose to retrieve such a heritage but rather to seek within the text itself countertraditions to dominant themes.

Biblical scholarship of the twentieth century has largely been influenced by the male voice and modernist assumptions. In the search for coherence a premium was placed on discovering the univocal, "true meaning" of the text. Twenty-first-century postmodern approaches have become much more aware of the multi-vocal nature of the biblical texts. It is often the stories of women, those excluded from the public, patriarchal discourse, which challenge the dominant voice of the text. In the past their stories have frequently been overlooked or ignored. Foucault talks of "subjugated knowledges" which he defines as "a whole set of knowledges that have been disqualified as inadequate to their task or insufficiently elaborated: naïve knowledges located low down on the hierarchy . . . a particular, local, regional knowledge."[22]

One could argue that often within the biblical text stories of women are "subjugated knowledges" that have been "insufficiently elaborated" within the larger narrative and are therefore missed within the wider framework of theological discourse. Their stories might appear relatively insignificant, "particular" and "local," confined to the margins, yet by focusing on them one begins to realize their importance within the narrative whole.

My readings within this thesis are not offered as definitive but it is hoped they will shed fresh light on the five women in Matthew's genealogy and their significance for the gospel narrative.

---

21. Fiorenza, *In Memory of Her*, 56.
22. Foucault, *Power/Knowledge*, 82.

Methodology

Narrative Analysis

The use of a literary approach to reading the Bible that involves a narrative analysis of the text has become popular among scholars of both the Old and New Testament. This method does not seek to establish the sources behind the text, or the way in which it was put together, or the setting in which it was written, questions that engaged traditional historical-critical lines of enquiry. Rather, a literary-critical approach is concerned with the text as it comes to us as a finished product; it acknowledges the integrity of the text in its final form. Berlin, among others, has taught us, "If we know *how* texts mean, we are in a better position to discover *what* a particular text means."[23] Throughout this thesis I will use a narrative analysis of both Old and New Testament texts to interpret what the text is saying, because as Firth points out, "attention to the narrative skill employed is a vital interpretative element."[24] This involves consideration of different aspects of the narrative, such as the way it is structured and the effect of repetition and chiasm, the setting of the story, the development of the plot, the means of characterization, the textual time given to different parts of the story, and the point of view of the different characters and the narrator. While on the surface the story might be considered to be primarily about one thing, for example the succession of the line of Judah or the conquering of Jericho, the dramatic and unexpected in the story turns the reader's attention elsewhere. In this context it is important that we "open ourselves to the Bible's irony."[25] In Hebrew narrative it is often the ironic element in a story that provides a subtext, revealing another "take" on what is going on. I am particularly interested in the way the different Old Testament women under consideration are characterized for "we know them only as they are presented in the narratives, and it is to this alone that we can refer."[26] As we shall see, in terms of their characterization, the Hebrew narrative is fraught with ambiguity, yet, it will be argued that there are clear textual pointers that help the reader in evaluating each woman.

The narrative art of the Greek New Testament writers differs in a number of ways from that of the Hebrew Old Testament writers. In some

---

23. Berlin, *Poetics and Interpretation*, 17.
24. Firth, *1 & 2 Samuel*, 22.
25. Gunn and Fewell, *Narrative in the Hebrew Bible*, 205.
26. Bar-Efrat, *Narrative Art*, 47.

The Genesis of a Thesis

senses the Greek text of Matthew is more straightforward, much more compact in its telling, offering less ambiguity with which the reader has to grapple. Yet, there are also similarities, particularly in Matthew's Gospel, where many Hebrew techniques such a repetition, parallelism, and *inclusio* are still in use.[27]

Both Old and New Testament narrative critics have used the literary theorist Chatman's model as a useful tool to describe the structural form of narrative prose. Chatman distinguishes between the story—*what* is told, and the discourse—*how* it is told.[28] The story involves the plot, that is, the actions and happenings, the different characters, and the settings. The discourse describes the way the story is expressed, the rhetoric of the narrative; in other words, how it communicates. Although modern literary terms are used such categories describe the universal features common to stories ancient and modern.

How does the real author, who in this case lived hundreds of years ago, communicate with the real reader who picks up and reads Matthew's Gospel today? Based on Chatman's distinctions, narrative theorists distinguish between the teller of a story (the sending party), the story itself, and its audience (the receiving party). The sending party is not one entity but comprises the real author, the implied author, and the narrator. The receiving party consists of the real reader, the implied reader, and the narratee. The story itself is represented by the narrator and narratee.

THE STORY

real author *implied author* (narrator)	(narratee) *implied reader* real reader
Sending party	Receiving party[28]

The real author (our unknown person situated in first-century Middle East),[30] when writing Matthew's Gospel, made a series of decisions about

---

27. See Anderson, *Matthew's Narrative Web*, for a detailed analysis of Matthew's web of verbal repetitions.

28. Chatman, *Story and Discourse*, 26.

29. Adapted from Chatman, *Story and Discourse*, 151.

30. From the earliest times the Gospel has been attributed to Matthew. In the earliest texts available in Greek or in translation, the Gospel carries the heading "according to Matthew." Around AD 180 Irenaeus is the first to comment that "Matthew also issued a written Gospel." Irenaeus, *Against Heresies*, (*Haer.* 3.1.1). In consequence, church tradition for the majority of the past two thousand years has ascribed the Gospel to the apostle Matthew named in Matt 9:9. Since the rise of historical criticism

the plot, setting, characterization, and rhetorical devices, including the role of the narrator. A sense of the real author's "second self" can be gained in the process of reading and response to the text. This is referred to as the implied author.

The implied author is the closest that real readers can get to the actual author who wrote the text approximately 2,000 years ago, so what can be inferred about the implied author of Matthew's Gospel? There are a number of features in the text that are most easily explained by the supposition that Matthew had strong roots in Judaism. For example, much of the material that is distinctive to Matthew has a strongly Jewish flavor[31] and there is currently general agreement among the majority of scholars that Matthew's Gospel reflects a close relationship with Judaism.[32] The Old Testament scriptures are not only quoted on a number of occasions but the many allusions made to Old Testament stories betray a thorough knowledge of their content.

The implied author of the Gospel incorporates a narrator, who is the story's voice and who guides the reader. Matthew's narrator, the unseen voice who tells the story, is both reliable and ever present. The narrator is closely aligned with the implied authorial point of view that stands behind all that is written. Kingsbury comments, "Matthew as implied author oversees the whole of the story of the life and ministry of Jesus and also involves himself, through his voice as narrator, in every aspect of this story."[33]

I will use "Matthew" when referring to the implied author and the term "narrator" to refer to the guiding voice within the narrative. For ease of reference the masculine pronoun will be used when referring to Matthew and the narrator but with the recognition that female voices would have contributed to the traditions used by the real author when constructing the narrative.

Just as the text conveys a sense of the implied author, a corresponding image is created of the implied reader. The implied reader, like the implied author, is not a flesh and blood person but an imaginary person

---

this has been called into question and ultimately it cannot demonstrated who wrote Matthew's Gospel.

31. Davies and Allison, *Matthew 1–7*, 29; see their extended discussion, 25–58.

32. Recent scholarly discussion has centered around Matthew's love-hate relationship with Judaism and whether the Gospel reflects a separation from Judaism or remains within the Jewish formative tradition of the first century AD. Differing scholarly conclusions on the issue of Matthew's relationship to Judaism are reflective of the tensions within the text that offer both a pro-Jewish and anti-Jewish stance.

33. Kingsbury, *Matthew as Story*, 32.

who is envisaged by the implied author as receiving and responding to the text. The implied author perceives the implied reader to be an idealized recipient, who brings certain skills to the reading of the text. The implied author recognizes that implied readers function at different levels according to their readerly competences. In the case of Matthew's Gospel many of Matthew's original recipients would have heard rather than read the text, therefore aural echoes (for example in the repetition of key words and phrases) are important in the way they contribute to the intertextual web of meaning. The narratee, the third person of the receiving party, is the narrator's counterpart, the one to whom the narrator addresses his remarks within the story. As both Kingsbury and Anderson point out, in Matthew's Gospel there is no clear distinction between the implied reader and the narratee.[34] The narratee is addressed by the narrator and, for our purposes, stands in for the implied reader. The final receiving party, the real reader, mirrors the real author as someone who reads and interprets the text, coming from a viewpoint outside the narrative world. Clearly, the intertextual connections that I perceive as a real reader may differ from those that Matthew's implied readers may have understood.

Since we have no access to Matthew or his original readers and since we have only the text itself, my assertions about Matthew's intention in including the five women in his genealogy are intelligible only as statements about the implied author for whom no absolute claims can be made. I consider that the rhetoric of the text betrays the implied author's intent particularly in passages such as the genealogy, where there is direct commentary from the narrator to the narratee. However, I am making no definitive claims about the implied author's understanding of the intertextual connectedness of the text since I acknowledge that texts can be read in many different ways. Also, the claims I am making for the intertextual connectedness of the text may or may not have been perceived by Matthew's implied readers/hearers. Nevertheless, if it can be demonstrated that the claims I am making as a real reader about Matthew's intertextual connectedness cohere with the text's own rhetoric, themes, and literary structure, then it is a good reading in that it makes sense.

A narrative methodology acknowledges that it is important to read Matthew as Matthew in its final form, for Matthew's story is inherently meaningful regardless of its sources and composition history. Thompson refers to this as reading vertically before reading horizontally.[35] Neverthe-

---

34. Ibid., 38. Anderson, *Matthew's Narrative Web*, 37–38.
35. Thompson, "Reflections," 365–66.

less, the four Gospels invite comparison and it is helpful to look sideways, to practice what Fokkelman refers to as lateral reading since the "*dialectics of similarity and difference* find a unique and powerful application in the New Testament."[36] I do not accept the assumption of redaction critics that Matthew edited Mark in fine detail as the basis for his Gospel, since it is now recognized that the two source theory does not allow for the complexity of the sources Matthew used. However, it seems probable that Matthew made considerable use of Mark both in structuring particularly the latter half of his Gospel from chapter 14 and also in the selection and telling of his stories, including stories about women. When considering Matthew's material, some comparisons will be made with Mark's material (and occasionally Luke and John) since comparison serves to clarify Matthew's emphases and rhetoric but no detailed redactional studies will be conducted.

In adopting a narrative reading of both the Old and New Testament texts, I will mainly confine myself to the world of the text rather than seeking meaning outside the stories themselves within the circumstances in which they were written. Nonetheless, I do not consider that the text is a free floating entity but that behind it lies a historical and theological reality. I do not accept the view that historical reference and narrative form are incompatible and, whilst I choose to focus on the narrative, reference to historiographical elements will sometimes be made.[37]

Intertextuality

Hays et al. note, "Intertextual canonical reading holds great promise as a way for postmodern interpreters to restore lines of conversation with the church's classic premodern traditions of interpretation."[38] Within a theological framework intertextuality is not just a theoretical concept since for hundreds of years it has been recognized that biblical exegetes are working within a web of meaning and that there has always been an important

---

36. Fokkelman, *Reading Biblical Narrative*, 198.

37. Watson comments that Ricoeur's argument that fiction and history are interlaced shows up "a major weakness in contemporary study of the gospels, which assumes that fiction and history are simple opposites . . . Ricoeur enables us to conceive of a historiography enriched by fiction and not subverted by it." Watson, *Text and Truth*, 56–57. Solvang also notes that "Reading the biblical text with narrative technique does not eliminate the need for historical understandings." Solvang, *Woman's Place*, 9.

38. Hays et al., *Reading the Bible*, xiii.

place in Christian tradition for detecting echoes of other biblical texts in a given text. Hays's book *Echoes of Scripture in the Letters of Paul* made a significant contribution to the reception of the paradigm of intertextuality into theological exegesis in the 1990s.[39] The world of biblical semiotics has appropriated the term "intertextuality" from work originally done by the post-structuralist Kristeva.[40] She coined the term to indicate that texts are dynamic; they do not stand in autonomous isolation but stand in dialogical relationship with other texts. Intertextual ways of working involve discerning the relationship one text can have with another and how together they can produce new meaning. The nature of the biblical canon itself is intertextual. It is comprised of a collection of many different writings that are placed alongside each other in the canon so that each text is not read in isolation but exists in relationship with other writings. In consequence, the biblical canon places individual texts in new relationships with other texts. The proximity of one text to another alters the meaning potential of both. The intertextual connectedness of the biblical canon makes it hermeneutically justifiable to read one text in the light of another. In other words all biblical texts have what Alkier refers to as an "intertextual disposition."[41] The term indicates that signals of intertextuality exist in a text which prompts the reader to seek its relation to other texts. An intertextual reading is alert to these signals that draw other texts into play. It provides a way to discern the thematic, literary and theological links between two or more biblical texts that exist in different times and cultures. This continues the long held Christian interpretative strategy of finding continuity within many diverse biblical books. Alkier provides a helpful definition of an intertextual investigation.

> *Intertextual* investigation concerns itself with the effects of meaning that emerge from the references of a given text to other texts. One should only speak of intertextuality when one is interested in exploring the effects of meaning that emerge from relating at least two texts together and, indeed, that neither of the texts considered alone can produce. One must also remember that within the paradigm of intertextuality, that intertextual generation of meaning proceeds in both directions:

---

39. Hays, *Echoes of Scripture*.

40. Moi, *Kristeva Reader*. Kristeva eventually abandoned the term as too narrow to describe the intersubjectivity of human discourse.

41. Alkier, "Intertextuality," 11.

> The meaning potential of both texts is altered through the intertextual reference itself.[42]

Such an investigation can be approached from two different perspectives: the production-orientated perspective and the reception-orientated perspective. At the production level it is recognized that the implied author of the text, Matthew, has used other texts in the writing process. In Matthew's case many of these have been taken from the Old Testament and used both explicitly in quotations and implicitly by allusion. The meaning of Matthew's narrative (the hypertext) is shaped by its relationship to the Old Testament (the hypotext). The text of Matthew's Gospel has been causally determined by historically earlier Old Testament texts. Paying attention to these necessary causal relationships is attending to intertextuality at the production level of the text. A reliable reader will know these texts and read Matthew's text in the light of them. Not to attend to these causal relationships would be to ignore the text's own intertextual connectedness. The production-orientated perspective of an intertextual investigation explores the indices of the text, signs that have been directly determined by earlier texts, and have been put there by the writer in order to draw them into a necessary relationship with his/her text. Working from a production-orientated perspective, Hays argues that intertextual signals in a text can exist on three levels: quotation, allusion, and echo, and may be seen as "points along a spectrum of intertextual reference."[43] My intertextual investigation is prompted by the citing of the names of women in the genealogy that allude to other texts. In fact, the opening verses of Matthew's Gospel immediately invite the consideration of many other texts. Textual worlds within the Old Testament are intertextually inscribed in the names mentioned in Matthew's genealogy, including those of Tamar, Rahab, Ruth, and "she of Uriah." By their inclusion the text itself explicitly invites the reader to consider what relationship might exist between the stories of these women and the story of Jesus as told by Matthew. To put it in Anderson's words,

> Whatever the actual reader makes of the presence of the women will affect how he or she reads the rest of the narrative, especially chapters 1 and 2. Likewise, his or her reading of the rest of the Gospel will affect in retrospect the interpretation of the women's presence in the genealogy.[44]

---

42. Ibid., 9.
43. Hays, *Echoes of Scripture*, 23.
44. Anderson, *Matthew's Narrative Web*, 52.

The citing of their names in each case draws not just a specific verse into play as an intertextual reference but complete narrative stories. With the inclusion of the Old Testament women in the genealogy Matthew is implicitly alluding to their stories and thereby inviting the reader to read the texts of Genesis 38, Joshua 2 and 6:15–25, Ruth, and 2 Samuel 11–12, both alongside one another, since by their naming Matthew draws them into specific intertextual relationship, but also in conjunction with Mary, mother of Christ and the final woman of the genealogy, and the ensuing story of Jesus as told by Matthew. I am particularly interested in the semantic, thematic similarities that might be perceived between the stories of the women and themes running throughout Matthew's Gospel. Read in the light of these texts Matthew's Gospel gains new depth and resonance. It further leads to a consideration of how the interaction of the two might create new meaning.

Having been motivated by Matthew's text, I move beyond the production-orientated perspective to a second important perspective of intertextual study; the reception-orientated perspective. The reception-orientated perspective asks about "the sense effect that results for various readers during the synchronous reading of more texts."[45] The relationship between the two texts is a potential one rather than a necessary one; it is synchronic rather than diachronic, in that the texts can appear to be significantly related but have no discernible causal connections. From this perspective the reader makes the connection between texts; it is an exploration of the similarities between the texts that I discern as a real reader. I am indebted to Wolde for her analysis where she discusses these possible similarities, for ease of reference I list her points as follows:

A. Stylistic and Semantic Similarities

1. Repetition of words or semantic fields. For example, there may be words or themes that appear in two different texts that bring them into relationship.

2. Repetition of larger textual structures. For example, similarities in style or the framework of a narrative, discourses or expressions, and temporal or spatial arrangements.

3. Similarities in genre.

---

45. Schneider, "How Does God Act," 45.

B. Narratological Similarities
 1. Analogies in character descriptions or in character types.
 2. Similarities in an action or series of actions.
 3. Similar narratological representations, i.e., the way the narrator represents the action of a character.[46]

Wolde notes that all these repetitions can be read as iconic pointers to intertextual relationships.[47] On the basis of perceived repetitions I will investigate the relationships that exist both between the five women themselves in terms of recurring themes and narratological presentation, and then move on to consider whether the recurring themes which I identify are also present in Matthew's Gospel. In relating the texts of the women's stories from the Old Testament to Matthew's own story of Jesus the Messiah, the potential meaning of both is altered. As a reader I perceive suggestive and creative thematic parallels between the two. I do not consider the production-orientated perspective and the reception-orientated perspective to be mutually exclusive for "the paradigm of intertextuality involves both perspectives."[48]

I acknowledge that reception-orientated intertextual reference can motivate a number of different readings. I also acknowledge that the intertextual connections in Matthew's text are more obvious in some places than in others. For example, Mary clearly stands in relation to the other four women of the Old Testament because of her placement at the end of the genealogy. The connection between Rahab and the Canaanite woman of Matthew 15 may seem less obvious. It may be argued that the stronger intertextual connections are clearly established by the text itself while others depend on my perceptions as a reader. I realize that my perceptions will be shared by others in some places but not in others. The key question is: What determines a valid reading? Schneider notes, "The multiple perspectives of intertextual readings lead immediately to questions of ethical interpretation and problems of the theological truth claims of specific statements."[49] Does the legitimacy of my intertextual reading depend on its correspondence to Matthew's authorial intention? Alternatively does it need to establish a correspondence with how Matthew's implied readers would have understood the text? My answer to both these questions is

46. Wolde, "Intertextuality," 432–33.
47. Ibid., 433.
48. Schneider, "How Does God Act," 45.
49. Ibid., 46.

"No," since both the author and the original recipients of Matthew's Gospel are only known to us hypothetically. It is impossible to know for certain the intent of the original author in including five women in his genealogy or how his readers/hearers would have understood the text.

Recognizing the difficulty of judging what are legitimate intertextual readings, Hays has established seven tests to identify what he refers to as the "intertextual echoes" of the text.[50] The first, fourth and final tests are relevant to my discussion. Although we can only establish indirectly what might have been in the mind of the author and his readers it is not inappropriate to ask the historical question, as Hays does in his first test, concerning availability. Was the source of the intertextual echo available to the author and the original readers? In Matthew's case it is clear that he was familiar with the Old Testament text (later acknowledged as canonical within Judaism) in both its Greek and Hebrew form and that he expected his implied readers also to be familiar with this text and to acknowledge the text as scripture. Hence we can confidently assume that the Old Testament texts of the women's stories would have been known by Matthew. Hays's fourth test raises the issue of thematic coherence. How well does the intertextual reading fit into the line of argument that Matthew is developing? If an intertextual thematic coherence can be demonstrated, then it is a credible (but not definitive) identification of the implied author's intentionality. It will be argued that the intertextual themes emerging from the stories of the five women are themes that are central to Matthew's rhetoric in three main areas. These three areas are interlinked because all are concerned with establishing a new identity for the people of God: Gentile inclusion into the people of God, the place and priority of the marginalized in the purposes of God, and the role and place of women in the kingdom of heaven that the Messiah inaugurates. Elsewhere Hays notes that intertextual narration is a culture forming practice. "Communities form and maintain their identities through the stories they tell about their origins, history, and future destiny."[51] The inclusion of the five women, the telling of the Messiah's origins and history, anticipates and contributes to Matthew's rhetoric regarding the identity of the community of disciples the Messiah will gather to himself. The recurrence of key themes point back to the stories of these women, indicating that there is thematic intertextual coherence to Matthew's rhetoric concerning the new identity of the people of God. This intertextual coherence argues for the validity of the reading I am proposing.

50. Hays, *Echoes of Scripture*, 29–32.
51. Hays, "Liberation of Israel," 102.

Hays's final test is entitled "Satisfaction."[52] He asks, does the proposed reading illuminate the surrounding discourse, is it a "satisfying account of the intertextual relation?"[53] In other words, does the proposed intertextual reading make sense in terms of the whole? I will demonstrate that my intertextual reading is entirely satisfactory and that the recovery of women's stories from the margins, both from the Old Testament and within Matthew, highlights the radical nature of Matthew's rhetoric running throughout his Gospel concerning the people of God.

The first step in any intertextual study is to acknowledge the integrity and narrative artistry of each story in its own right. Alkier comments, "For methodological reasons and reasons pertaining to the ethics of interpretation, one must perform intratextual analyses of the texts to be brought together before any intertextual work commences."[54] Hence the texts of the five women of the genealogy will be studied in their own right, considered as intratextual structures with their own syntactic, semantic, and rhetorical logic. In part 1 I will investigate the Hebrew stories of Tamar, Rahab, Ruth, and Bathsheba before moving onto Mary as presented by Matthew. In part 2 I will investigate the intertextual themes I discern between their stories, both individually and collectively, and Matthew's gospel narrative as a whole.

Increasing specialization has led to a virtual divorce in Old Testament and New Testament scholarship. In recognizing the intertextual relationships that are invited by the naming of the Old Testament women in Matthew's genealogy I seek to combine the insights of both Old Testament and New Testament scholars. I have made use of the NRSV as base text but on occasions I have freely departed from it and made my own translations from the Hebrew and Greek texts. However, I do not engage with text critical discussions, nor, in the main, do I make any reference to extrabiblical material, Jewish or Graeco-Roman. Interaction with Matthean scholarship in part 2 is relatively limited due to the fact that the majority of Matthean scholarship has been historical-critical and redaction-critical, not narrative-critical.

---

52. Hays, *Echoes of Scripture*, 31.
53. Ibid.
54. Alkier, "Intertextuality," 10.

2

Matthew's Genealogy

The Genealogy

Matthew's narrative tells the story of Jesus. In terms of genre the narrative is an ancient form of biography[1] and the one undeniable feature of the narrative is that it follows a chronological sequence of Jesus' life: birth, baptism, ministry in Galilee, the journey to Jerusalem, death, and resurrection. Like all stories, the structure, which arranges the individual parts so that the story is brought to a satisfying conclusion, has a beginning (Matthew 1–2, the prologue), middle (Matthew 3–25, the central section), and an end (Matthew 26–28, the passion and resurrection).[2]

---

1. Burridge has shown that the Gospels share a sufficient number of features with ancient Graeco-Roman biographies to place them within the overall genre of βίοι. Although Matthew can't be linked to any one strand of the Graeco-Roman biographical tradition his Gospel, along with the others, form a part of that tradition. Burridge, *What Are the Gospels*.

2. Kingsbury has also proposed a simple three-fold structure to the Gospel but he argues that the prologue extends to Matt 4:17. His structure focuses on the way Matthew presents the Christ and the key to his analysis rests on the importance of a repeated phrase "from that time Jesus began" (Matt 4:17; Matt 16:21) that marks a new phase in Jesus' ministry. Matt 4:17 marks the beginning of the middle section and Matt 16:21 marks the start of the final part of the Gospel. Kingsbury, *Matthew: Structure, Christology, Kingdom*, 1–25. This is taken up and defended by his pupil, Bauer. Bauer, *Structure of Matthew's Gospel*.

However, in their commentary, Davies and Allison note no single structural principle can be discerned. Davies and Allison, *Matthew 1–7*, 72. They follow Gundry's conclusion that "the gospel of Matthew is structurally mixed," Gundry, *Matthew*, 11, a conclusion with which Hagner concurs. Hagner, *Matthew 1–13*, liii. The lack of

Where does the story of Jesus begin? A story can begin from any one of a number of places. The choice of a starting point is an important decision because the way a story begins dramatically affects the way readers interpret and understand it. Matera is correct when he comments, "Few things are more essential to appreciating a story than understanding the manner in which the narrator begins."[3] The opening of a story has to set the scene and provide the initial threads that draw the reader into the plot. Importantly it sets up clues as to how to interpret all the information that follows. All four gospel writers are story tellers and all four start at different points. In Matthew's Gospel Jesus is introduced by means of a genealogy that charts his descent from Abraham through three epochs. Matthew opens his tale within the context of a larger text that locates Jesus the Messiah within the generations of Israel, within the story of salvation. No character is introduced and the narrative does not begin until Jesus has been situated ideologically and temporally by the genealogy. The genealogy places Jesus within an Old Testament theological and historical framework essential for understanding the rhetoric of the Gospel as a whole. Jesus is both defined by the ancestors of Israel and defines them as Israel's history reaches its climax in the birth of the Messiah. Among his ancestors in Matthew's genealogy are four women, Tamar, Rahab, Ruth, and "she of Uriah."

The Superscription

The genealogy is prefaced by an introductory verse which states that the following verses describe the "genesis of Jesus, the Christ, the son of David, the son of Abraham" (Matt 1:1). From the opening verse the narrator is making theological claims about the main protagonist within the story; he is the Messiah. Jesus is also identified within the ongoing history of the people of Israel; he is a Jew, the son of Abraham. Thirdly, Jesus is of royal descent, he is a son of David, a Davidic Messiah. The opening words of the gospel, βίβλος γενέσεως, parallel words from Genesis 2:4 and 5:1 and immediately create intertextual links with Genesis. Matthew's genealogy, like that of the genealogies in Genesis, follows the pattern of A begat B, B

---

consensus on the best way to structure Matthew's Gospel indicates the strength of their conclusion. Matthew's many verbal and thematic repetitions, his artistry and skill in the construction of his narrative, ultimately defy definition. Like Kingsbury, I will follow a threefold outline of the Gospel but for the purposes of my thesis place markers at different points from those suggested by Kingsbury.

3. Matera, "Prologue," 3–20.

begat C, and so on but differs from them in one important respect. The genealogies of Genesis are normally introduced with the forefather from whom the descendants follow, for example Genesis 10:1 reads, "These are the descendants (LXX γενέσεις) of Noah's sons, Shem, Ham, and Japheth."[4] By contrast, Matthew's genealogy is not entitled "book of the genesis of Abraham" but rather "book of the genesis of Jesus Christ," in other words the genealogy starts at its end point—Jesus Christ. Bauer comments that this "would [thus] strike the implied reader as remarkable."[5] The unusual introduction highlights the fact the Jesus is unique and that he stands at both the beginning and end of a history that charts the salvation of God's people. The line of descendants starts with Jesus Christ (Matt 1:1) and ends with Jesus, the one called Christ (Matt 1:16), for Jesus has no progeny. Bauer makes the point that entitling the genealogy with the name of the final descendant "subordinates the forefathers to this last descendant and indicates that they gain their meaning and identity from . . . Christ."[6] This is true also of the foremothers of Christ, four of whom are notably mentioned in the patrilineal genealogy.

The Literary Function of the Genealogy

Bauer in his application of narrative criticism to ascertain the literary function of Matthew's genealogy concludes, firstly, that the genealogy "provides the basic orientation to the person of Jesus"[7] and that, secondly, it "indicates that one can understand the story of Jesus only as one comes to it through the flow of salvation history as Matthew presents it in the genealogy."[8] Building on this observation, I argue that the inclusion of four Old Testament women highlights their involvement in the flow of salvation history as Matthew understands it.[9] An analysis of their stories will indicate the roles they played and how they in turn orientate the reader

4. It is generally held that Matthew had access to both the Hebrew MT and Greek LXX forms of the Old Testament.
5. Bauer, *Structure of Matthew's Gospel*, 456.
6. Ibid.
7. Bauer, "Literary Function," 464.
8. Ibid., 467.
9. I use this phrase with caution as I am aware that in the past attempts to chart an abstract theological concept of salvation history in Matthew's Gospel have ignored the complexity of the narrative and sought to impose a synthetic conceptual framework on the text. However, Matthew 1 makes clear that Matthew connects salvation (Matt 1:21) with history (Matt 1:1–18). Cf. Eloff, "Ἀπό . . . ἕως," 85–107.

not only to the person of Christ but also to the ongoing narrative of his life. Bauer goes on to note that conversely the genealogy also signifies that "the history of Israel can no longer be understood on its own terms, but only as it gains meaning and significance from its function within the narrative of Matthew's Gospel."[10] It will be shown that not only do all five women (Mary providing the bridge between the past and present history of Israel) have significance for the ongoing narrative but that also the women's stories gain further significance as they are read in the light of the Gospel. Foundational to my thesis is the view that the literary purpose of the genealogy is to orientate the reader to the gospel narrative as a whole, providing clues as to how it should be read. In Waetjen's words, the genealogy, and in particular these women are a "key" to understanding what follows.[11] As such the intertexts inscribed by the naming of the women act to foreshadow important aspects of the Messiah's ministry and teaching. The five women also serve to represent two groups of people who, it will be argued, are significant in Matthew's narration of the story of Jesus: those on the margins and women.

The Genealogical Annotations

Matthew's genealogy divides Jewish history into three epochs of fourteen generations with David at the transition from the first to second epoch and the deportation to Babylon as the transition from the second to the third. Matthew's genealogy is patrilineal (a straight line of male descendants) but the Matthean narrator goes beyond the bare essentials by adding more than the names of a succession of fathers; the genealogy is annotated.[12]

Matthew 1:2–6a	Abraham to King David, first epoch of 14 generations
Matthew 1:6b–11	David to Jechoniah, second epoch of 14 generations
Matthew 1:12–16	Jechoniah to Joseph, third epoch of 14 generations[13]

10. Bauer, "Literary Function," 467.

11. As per Waetjen's title, "Geneaology as the Key to the Gospel according to Matthew."

12. Bauckham, *Gospel Women*, 18–19.

13. In actual fact there are only thirteen generations listed in the third section

Brown suggests that Matthew's "discovery" of a 3 x 14 pattern in Jesus' genealogy makes the theological point that "God planned from the beginning and with precision the Messiah's origins."[14] Brown also notes that in order to create the three epochs of fourteen generations Matthew has left out names, notably in the second section where he omits four generations and six kings. Wilson has shown that the "telescoping" of ancient genealogies, by leaving out what are considered to be unimportant names, is not unusual.[15] It is therefore all the more notable that, although the Matthean narrator has telescoped the genealogy by leaving out the names of six Jewish kings, he *has* included reference to five women in the annotations.

The Women of the Genealogy

In Matthew's genealogy there are ten annotations. Of these ten, five refer to women. The reader's attention is caught by the five women because their naming interrupts a repeated pattern. These annotations are like additional notes, but for what reason are they included?

The list below indicates the annotations in italics and the reference to women in bold italics.

Matthew 1:1	*Introduction to the book of the genealogy*
Matthew 1:2–6a	*Abraham to King David, first epoch of 14 generations*
Matthew 1:2	Judah *and his brothers*
Matthew 1:3	Perez and Zerah *by **Tamar*** (ἐκ τῆς Θαμάρ)
Matthew 1:5	Salmon fathered Boaz *by **Rahab*** (ἐκ τῆς Ῥαχάβ)
Matthew 1:5	Boaz fathered Obed *by **Ruth*** (ἐκ τῆς Ῥούθ)
Matthew 1:6	David *the king*
Matthew 1:6b–11	*David to Jechoniah, second epoch of 14 generations*
Matthew 1:6b	Solomon *by **she of Uriah*** (ἐκ τῆς τοῦ Οὐρίου)
Matthew 1:11	Jechoniah *and his brothers at the time of the deportation to Babylon*

---

and the first section. Although naming fourteen fathers, Matthew only lists thirteen generations.

14. Brown, *Birth of the Messiah*, 80.
15. Wilson, *Genealogy and History*, 33–34.

Matthew 1:12–16	Jechoniah to Joseph, third epoch of 14 generations
Matthew 1:12	*After the deportation to Babylon* Jechoniah
Matthew 1:16	Joseph *the husband of Mary, of whom* (τὸν ἄνδρα Μαρίας, ἐξ ἧς) was born Jesus, who is called the Christ
Matthew 1:17	*Conclusion noting three epochs of 14 generations culminating in the Messiah*

Mention of the women in Matthew's genealogical annotations draws the reader's attention to their histories. For the competent reader their names will recall Old Testament stories of individual characters, characters and stories the narrator considers important for the reader to bring to mind in preparation for reading *the* story of Jesus the Messiah. It is, therefore important firstly, to establish the Old Testament narratives to which these names refer.

Identifying the Four Women

It is quite clear that the Tamar referred to in Matthew 1:3 is the Tamar of Genesis 38 since Judah is named and she is identified as the mother of Perez and Zerah (cf. Gen 38:29–30). It is also clear that Ruth, mother of Obed, wife of Boaz, is Ruth from whom the book of Ruth is named and that "she of Uriah," mother of Solomon, is the Bathsheba of 2 Samuel 11–12. Tamar and Bathsheba are further identified by their mention in the 1 Chronicles genealogies, "Tamar, Judah's daughter-in-law, also bore him Perez and Zerah" (1 Chr 2:4) and "these were the children born to him [David] there: Shammua, Shobab, Nathan and Solomon. These four were by Bathsheba, daughter of Ammiel" (1 Chr 3:5).

What is not clear is Rahab's identity. Most commentators have identified the Rahab of Matthew 1:5 with the Rahab of Jericho. However, if she is identified as the Rahab of Jericho, there is a problem on three counts: firstly, with the spelling of her name in Matthew, secondly, with her identification as Salmon's wife because of the lack of attestation outside of Matthew's Gospel to her marriage to Salmon, and, thirdly, her identification as Boaz's mother because of the chronological incongruity between Rahab and Boaz. I will briefly review the arguments.[16]

---

16. For an extended discussion, see Bauckham, *Gospel Women*, 34–41.

In a paper entitled "Is 'PAXÁB in Mt 1,5 Rahab of Jericho?" Quinn notes the difference in the spelling of her name.[17] Whereas Matthew refers to Ραχάβ (Matt 1:5) Quinn points out that the name of the Canaanite prostitute of Jericho is transliterated in the LXX as Ραάβ. He concludes that Matthew was not referring to the Rahab of Jericho but "an insignificant woman, mentioned nowhere else in Scripture."[18] However, Brown responds by noting that inconsistency in the spelling of names occurs in Matthew's genealogy a number of times when compared to the LXX.[19] It would also seem strange that Matthew should include an unknown woman alongside three other known women of the Old Testament. Many others have also since concluded that almost certainly the two names refer to the same woman.

The second problem is that neither the Old Testament nor any extant Jewish literature from the period attests to Rahab's marriage to Salmon. It will be argued that Matthew had important reasons for including Rahab in the genealogy and therefore needed to provide Rahab with a husband! Also it is quite possible that, as Bauckham argues, her marriage to Salmon was already an exegetical tradition but one that we do not have access to.[20]

The final problem is the chronological incongruity of her motherhood of Boaz.[21] Salmon (or Salma) is named in Ruth's genealogy (Ruth 4:21) and that of 1 Chronicles (1 Chr 2:11) as the father of Boaz (he is not mentioned elsewhere). If Rahab was the mother of Boaz, according to the genealogies of Ruth 4:18–22 and 1 Chronicles 2:1–15 there is a 200 year time gap. But this is solved when one realizes that, like many genealogies (including Matthew's), the Old Testament genealogies contract time, leaving out generations.[22] I will work on the assumption that the Rahab of Matthew 1:5 is indeed the Rahab of Joshua 2.

---

17. Quinn, "Is 'PAXÁB in Mt 1,5 Rahab of Jericho," 225–28.

18. Ibid., 228.

19. Brown, "Rachab," 79–80.

20. Bauckham ingeniously argues that Matthew, working in Jewish exegetical traditions, could have found a basis for Rahab's marriage to Salmon from 1 Chr 2:54–55. Bauckham, *Gospel Women*, 37–41.

21. Noted by Brown, *Birth of the Messiah*, 60, and Davies and Allison, *Matthew 1–7*, 173.

22. Wilson, *Genealogy and History*, 33–34.

Reasons for the Inclusion of the Women

Why did the Matthean narrator choose to include women in the genealogical annotations and why these particular women? Writing in quite a different context, Gourevitch comments, "So remembering has its economy."[23] We remember the things that are significant, that shape our understanding of reality, that give form to the story so far. A genealogy is an economic form of remembering *par excellence*. Names give rise to stories and the names of Tamar, Rahab, Ruth, and Bathsheba give rise to stories that shaped the history of Israel, a history whose longings and hopes for the future were distilled in the birth of a Messiah born of Mary.

Matthew need not have included these women; a patrilineal genealogy would have been perfectly intelligible without them. Luke's genealogy (Luke 3:23–38) includes no women. Brown notes, "Their presence in a genealogy is unusual according to biblical patterns."[24] More tersely, Hill notes, "The naming of women . . . in a Jewish genealogy is contrary to custom."[25] So why did Matthew, in his economy of remembering, feel it necessary to include five women?

From a feminist perspective the inclusion of all five women significantly enhances the all-male patrilineal genealogy. They and their stories represent the many other mothers in Jesus' lineage who are never mentioned. If one were to include any woman, the inclusion of Mary, the mother of the Messiah, may seem an obvious choice. Clearly, the inclusion of each woman rests on the fact that she bore a male child to a man in the line of Abraham. Are they there because they are mothers of sons in the Messianic line and Matthew wants to acknowledge the importance of motherhood? If this is the case, why not name the four ancestral mothers of the Jewish faith: Sarah, Rebekah, Rachel, and Leah? The four women of the Old Testament named by the narrator are not obvious choices to represent Jewish ancestral mothers, especially since Rahab's Old Testament story makes no mention of motherhood. So why did Matthew include these particular women, what was it about their stories that Matthew wished readers to recall as they came to read about Jesus the Messiah?

Although Mary's presence is explicated in the ongoing narrative, the narrator gives no reasons for the inclusion of the four Old Testament

---

23. The context being that of the Rwandan genocide. Gourevitch, *We Wish to Inform You*, 72.

24. Brown, *Birth of the Messiah*, 71.

25. Hill, *Gospel of Matthew*, 74.

women. The gap that is opened up by their inclusion without explanation has led to a plethora of suggested possibilities as real readers have responded to the text.

Below is a table showing the views of a selection of scholars that I have categorized under six headings. Some scholars have suggested more than one reason for the women's inclusion and therefore their names appear in more than one column.[26]

All sinners	All Gentiles	All foreshadow Mary	Divine irregularity	Polemical	Other
Carson[1]	Albright & Mann[2]	Anderson[3]	Hagner[4]	Johnson[5]	Heil[6]
Johnson	Bauckham[7]	Bauer[8]	Hill[9]	Freed[10]	Levine[11]
Morris[12]	Bauer	Brown[13]	Stendahl[14]	McKay[15]	Nolland[16]
Waetjen[17]	Beare[18]	Davies[19]	Witherington[20]		
	Boring[21]	Davies & Allison[22]	Wright[23]		
	Bredin[24]	Goulder[25]			
	Brown	Hagner			
	Davies & Allison	Hanson[26]			
	France[27]	Harrington[28]			
	Gundry[29]	Jones[30]			
	Hare[31]	Lyke[32]			
	Hauerwas[33]	Schaberg[34]			
	Hendrikson[35]	Scott[36]			
	Hutchinson[37]	Smit[38]			
	Keener[39]	Tatum[40]			
	Luz[41]	Weren[42]			
	Mussies[43]	Wainwright[44]			
	Smit				
	Waetjen[45]				

It is clear from this survey that the two most popular reasons given by scholars today for the inclusion in the genealogy of the four women from the Old Testament is either that they were included because they were

26. Numbered references in the table can be found at the end of this chapter.

Gentiles, or because all four, in a variety of different ways, foreshadow Mary. However, a brief glance at the history of interpretation shows that the earliest suggestion in Christian interpretation, one that has exercised a powerful influence for centuries in the way the four women have been viewed in Christian thought, is that these four women were included because they were "sinners."

a) All were sinners

The suggestion that Matthew included these four women because they are all sinners has a long heritage. Notably, Jerome (d. AD 420) in his *Matthew Commentary* expounds the view that the genealogy includes those women who are considered by scripture to be reprehensible, to demonstrate that Jesus has come on behalf of sinners in order to blot out their sin.

> 1.3. *Judah begot Phares and Zara of Thamar*. In the Savior's genealogy it is remarkable that there is no mention of holy women, but only those whom Scripture reprehends, so that [we can understand that] he who had come for the sake of sinners, since he was born from sinful women, blots out the sins of everyone. This is also why in what follows Ruth the Moabite and Bathsheba, wife of Uriah, are recorded.[27]

Jerome reflects a view that seems to have been the predominant explanation for the women's inclusion among the early exegetes of scripture. Chrysostom (d. AD 407) in his *Homilies on St. Matthew*[28] muses on why Matthew includes only women "that are famed for some bad thing." This theory has dominated interpretation throughout the centuries and is still argued today. For example, Johnson asks whether in including the four women there was good enough reason "for the author to introduce blots into the genealogy of the Messiah."[29] Carson condones the view that at least three of the four women are guilty of "gross sexual sin."[30] Likewise, Morris comments, "Three of the four are of morally dubious reputation. Matthew is surely saying that . . . the gospel is for sinners. It is a sinful world, and Matthew is writing about grace."[31] Critiquing this view,

27. Jerome, *Fathers of the Church*, 59–60.

28. Homily 1.14 concludes "if women were to be mentioned, all ought to be so; if not all but some, then those famed in the way of virtue, not for evil deeds." Chrysostom, *Homilies*, 57.

29. Johnson, *Purpose of the Biblical Genealogies*, 155.

30. Carson, "Matthew," 66.

31. Morris, *Gospel according to Matthew*, 23.

Bauckham comments, "It is remarkable, however, that no commentators seem to notice that, if sin is to be found in the genealogy, there are much more notorious biblical sinners among the men than the women."[32] It is invidious to single out the four women as sinners. The genealogy is full of "blots," all humans lead compromised lives and all need a Messiah to save them from their sins. It will be shown that to characterize these women as sinners distorts the picture painted by their Old Testament stories and says more about the patriarchal interpretation of the Church Fathers (and some modern commentators), which links women with sex and sin, than it says about the purpose of their inclusion in Matthew's annotations. It is particularly true in this case that "Oppression thus attaches not so much to the narratives themselves as to an interpretation."[33]

b) All were Gentiles

My survey shows that a significant proportion of scholars from recent years favor the view that Matthew included the four women because they were all Gentiles. Jesus is the Messiah for Gentiles as well as Jews and this is indicated by the inclusion of Gentile women in his ancestry. That Gentiles, as well as Jews, will be welcomed into God's kingdom is evidenced by Jesus' parting words to his disciples to go "and make disciples of all nations" (Matt 28:19). So, for example, Luz writes, Matthew "was intent on ensuring that four Gentile women appeared in Jesus' line of descent. In doing so he clearly sent a signal. The universalist perspective, the inclusion of the Gentile world, must have been important to him."[34] Similarly, Bauckham considers their Gentile origin to be the primary reason for their inclusion because it is a "convincing element common to all four and also accords well with the overall messianic purpose of the genealogy."[35]

There are three problems with this theory. Firstly, although it can be argued that all four were Gentiles this is not made explicit in all four cases in the text. The texts of Joshua 2 and Ruth clearly establish that originally Rahab was a Canaanite and Ruth a Moabite, their Gentile origins are integral to the plot of their stories. Tamar's Gentile origins, unlike those of Rahab and Ruth, are not made explicit. The setting of her story is in the context of Judah leaving his brothers and travelling into Canaanite territory where the ensuing events take place. Consequently, the text in Genesis

---

32. Bauckham, *Gospel Women*, 25.
33. Watson, *Text, Church and World*, 187.
34. Luz, *Theology of the Gospel of Matthew*, 26.
35. Bauckham, *Gospel Women*, 27.

38 strongly implies that Tamar, like her mother-in-law, was originally a Canaanite.[36] The theory that all four women were Gentiles also relies on the assumption that Bathsheba is a Hittite since she is married to Uriah the Hittite. However, nothing in the narrative in 2 Samuel implies that Bathsheba is a Hittite. In fact, the reverse is the case since her patrimony as daughter of Eliam (2 Sam 11:3) argues for her credentials as an Israelite.[37]

Secondly, since Mary was not Gentile, this theory like the previous one, assumes that the four women are not linked in any way to the fifth woman of the genealogy. Yet the unusual nature of the genealogical inclusion of women naturally links Mary to the Messiah's foremothers.

Thirdly, this theory assumes that as a group their gender is unimportant for Matthew. Since, by default, no man in Jesus' genealogy could be Gentile, in order to include Gentiles Matthew has to name women.[38] I will argue that, on the contrary, their gender is of great importance to Matthew in the telling of the Jesus story.

The merit of the theory lies in its emphasis on the importance of the Matthean vision concerning the Messianic universal mission. It is also commendable because it is the only one of the main theories that looks beyond the immediate context of the genealogy to the wider Gospel in order to suggest reasons for the women's inclusion.

c) All foreshadow Mary

Another proposal is that these four women are included because they *are* linked to Mary. A number of scholars have suggested different theories about ways that all four foreshadow Mary, the fifth woman in the genealogy. The most commonly held view focuses on their inappropriate sexual relationships. Davies and Allison comment on their "irregular and even scandalous" unions.[39] They argue that it is in their unusual, shameful unions with their partners that all four share an element in common with Mary. Similarly, Waetjen calls them "women of various reputations,

---

36. Bauckham examines and dismisses the Jewish tradition that Tamar was an Aramean. Bauckham, *Gospel Women*, 28–30.

37. This assumes a connection between her father Eliam (2 Sam 11:3; Ammiel in 1 Chr 3:5) with Eliam, the son of Ahithophel (2 Sam 23:34), David's counselor Ahithophel was a Gilonite (2 Sam 15:12) from a town near Hebron in the western foothills of Judah and, thus, a true Israelite.

38. It was only at a later point (but still relatively early on, within the era of the Roman Empire) that Jewishness became determined by the female line. See Lucas, *Conflict between Christianity and Judaism*, 91.

39. Davies and Allison, *Matthew 1–7*, 171.

mostly, however, of morally questionable character."[40] Waetjen continues by noting that these women are "indeed, 'irregularities,' 'detours of God's way' who serve as forerunners of Mary."[41] More positively, their unions may appear scandalous but are nevertheless used by God to further his purposes. Davies and Allison also state, that these unions "eventuated, in God's providence, in the Messiah's coming . . . any slanderer would in truth have been depreciating what God has chosen to bless. One can easily see how Matthew might have intended this to prefigure the situation of Mary."[42] Consequently, allied to this view is the argument that the four women demonstrate that God works in unusual ways. First suggested by Stendahl in his paper "Quis et Unde," Hagner summarizes this position, "The sovereign plan and purpose of God are often worked out in and through the most unlikely turn of events, and even through women who, though Gentiles or harlots, are receptive to God's will."[43] The four women are still seen to be problematic but the emphasis in this view is on the God who works in unusual ways. God's dealings are often strange and the way he worked in these women's lives prepares the reader for the unusual way he works in Mary's life to bring about the birth of Christ. As Wright puts it, "If God can work through these bizarre ways . . . watch what he's going to do now."[44] I will examine this view and other theories about how the four women are linked to Mary in greater detail in chapter 7. Although I reject these particular arguments, I will proceed on the assumption that the five women are linked in some way.

d) Polemical reasons for their inclusion

I have listed three scholars who have argued that the women are included for polemical reasons. Johnson argues that inclusion of the four women reveals Matthew's familiarity with the rabbinic polemic of first-century Judaism concerning the ancestry of the Messiah, which, he supposes, must be older than the later rabbinic evidence available. The Sadducees and Essenes, arguing for a Levitical Messiah, were opponents of the Pharisees who supported a Davidic Messiah. Johnson opines that the Sadducees and Essenes "brought into the polemic an emphasis on the four women as blots

---

40. Waetjen, "Genealogy as the Key," 215.
41. Waetjen, "Genealogy as the Key," 216.
42. Davies and Allison, *Matthew 1–7*, 171.
43. Hagner, *Matthew 1–13*, 10.
44. Wright, *Matthew for Everyone*, 4.

in the Davidic ancestry."⁴⁵ Apart from Rahab, the women's presence in the Messiah's ancestry could not be denied by the Pharisees so Johnson argues they "put the most charitable construction on them as was possible."⁴⁶ He notes that in Jewish tradition there is a tendency "to exonerate each of the women and to picture at least Rahab and Ruth as exemplars of conversion and faith."⁴⁷ He puts this down to the Pharisees' attempt to play down the damaging effects of their presence in the genealogy. Johnson goes on to suggest that Matthew (writing after AD 70) is writing his Gospel as an apology for the Christian faith directed toward the Pharisaic element in Judaism. Matthew includes the women "because they had come to occupy a traditional place in the ancestry of the Davidic Messiah, especially in discussions with those who maintained the expectation of a Levitical Messiah."⁴⁸

Freed also thinks the four women are included for polemical reasons. Freed argues that "Matthew uses the genealogy of Jesus and writes the narrative in 1.18–25 to reply to the charge of illegitimacy" leveled against Jesus.⁴⁹ Freed examines the positive stance taken by the rabbis in relation to the women and then considers Jewish writings contemporary with Matthew's Gospel. On the basis of Philo's interpretation of Tamar and Josephus's treatment of Rahab and Ruth as well as later Jewish writings, he concludes that Jewish thought considered that by divine power these women were transformed from "questionable, if not sinful, natures to states of innocence or virtue . . . Mary's behavior, again like that of the four women, is to be explained and accepted as an act of God through the Holy Spirit."⁵⁰ However, chapter 7 will argue that Matthew portrays Mary's non-sexual conception and pregnancy as unique, without comparison.

Feminist writer McKay also contends that the women are included to counter charges of Mary's unsuitability:

> Tamar, Rahab (as Boaz's mother), Ruth and the wife of Uriah, all women of "suspect character" . . . are brought into Matthew's genealogy of Jesus, possibly as a means of lessening the farouche quality of Mary's marital credentials. It is unlikely that women

---

45. Johnson, *Purpose of the Biblical Genealogies*, 139.

46. Ibid., 178.

47. Johnson examines a whole variety of Jewish primary sources relevant to the four women. Ibid., 159–75.

48. Ibid., 209.

49. Freed, "Women in Matthew's Genealogy," 6.

50. Ibid., 15.

Matthew's Genealogy

who had been considered "unsatisfactory" in the Hebrew Bible's telling of their tales would be ushered into pride of place . . . had there not been some compelling reason to include them, such as a means of countering charges of Mary's unsuitability as the mother of the messiah.[51]

McKay's argument rests on the assertion that the women were all of suspect character and that they had been considered "unsatisfactory" in the telling of their tales. She has, in fact, simply accepted the traditional male-dominated scholarly view, stretching back to the Church Fathers, concerning these women. I shall demonstrate that their Hebrew tales do not consider the women to be "unsatisfactory" but quite the opposite.

e) Other suggestions

A number of other suggestions have been made, including those by Heil, Levine, and Nolland.

Heil argues that Tamar begins the line of direct descent to David, which reminds the reader that sinfulness was connected with the Davidic kinship from the beginning with Judah.[52] He argues that the sinless unions of Rahab and Ruth offset the sinful union of Tamar and the reader is given hope for the Davidic line and the fulfillment of the universalistic promises made to Abraham. But Bathsheba then underlines the sinfulness of David and that hope is dimmed. Tragedy is reversed by Mary who bears Jesus, who saves his people from the sinfulness exemplified by Judah and David, which is recalled by Tamar and the wife of Uriah. The birth of Mary's son fulfills the universalistic hope inspired by Ruth and Rahab. This reading is ingenious but is based on Heil's imposed reading of sinful and sinless unions. Nothing is said in the Old Testament text about the sinfulness of Tamar's union and of Rahab's union with Salmon nothing is known at all.

Levine argues that the four women "all demonstrated faith when the men with whom they are associated in the Hebrew narratives did not."[53] Even though this could be argued of three of the four women, she encounters a problem with Bathsheba. Although Levine acknowledges that nothing is said of Bathsheba's faith in 2 Samuel, she unconvincingly appeals to Uriah's faith on the grounds that Bathsheba is in symbolic association with him, but this will not do, Matthew does not refer to Uriah but to Uriah's *wife*.

51. McKay, "Only a Remnant," 52–53.
52. Heil, "Narrative Role of the Women," 538–45.
53. Levine, *Social and Ethnic Dimensions*, 86.

In a study on Matthew's genealogical annotations Nolland notes the parallels to the genealogies in Genesis and 1 Chronicles 1–9, where annotations have also been included. Nolland concludes that the specific roles of the annotations in the Old Testament genealogies serve two functions: firstly, to fit the genealogy into a wider literary context and, secondly, to enhance the capacity of the genealogy to function as compressed tellings of the history that stands behind them.[54] He suggests that given the link to Genesis marked in Matthew 1:1, and the similarities in form between the Genesis genealogies and the Matthean genealogy, Matthew uses his annotations for the same dual purpose: to fit the genealogy into a wider literary context and to enhance the compressed tellings of history that stand behind the names mentioned. For example, in Matthew 1:11 reference is made to Jechoniah *and his brothers at the time of the deportation to Babylon*. This neatly summarizes the downfall of a dynasty. I accept Nolland's first proposal that Matthew's annotations fit the genealogy into a wider literary context. With regard to his second proposal, even although it is quite reasonable to argue that the five annotations not connected with the women are compressed tellings of the wider history that lies behind the names, I do not think this provides a convincing rationale for the inclusion of the women since it is hard to see how each woman represents a significant period of Israel's history.

Furthermore, it should be noted that although there are parallels between Matthew's genealogy and the genealogies of Genesis, significant differences exist. If, for example, a comparison is made with the genealogy of Esau's descendants in Genesis 36:9–43, which is also notable for annotations that highlight the role played by women, mention of the women there serves a clear function. The genealogy of Genesis 36:9–43, unlike Matthew's genealogy is filiated, not linear. Esau had a number of wives and they are singled out in order to introduce the different lines of descent. This is clearly not the function of the annotations of the women in Matthew's genealogy.

In another paper Nolland expands this thesis to comment specifically on the women in Matthew's annotations and contends that each woman represents a significant period in Israel's salvation history.[55] Tamar stands for the role of women in the early patriarchal generations. Rahab evokes the exodus from Egypt and entry into promised land otherwise unmarked in the genealogy. Ruth is a woman outside Israel who comes in, finding

---

54. Nolland, "Genealogical Annotations," 121.
55. Nolland, "Four (Five) Women," 527–39.

refuge with the God of Israel. Bathsheba points to David's sin and God's judgement. Nolland argues that all evoke important aspects of salvation history, as will Mary.

Nolland is correct in noting that Rahab is the only oblique reference in the genealogy to the exodus and entry to the promised land, a key point in Israel's salvation history. However, the appeal that Tamar represents the women of the early patriarchs is unconvincing since allusion could have been made to other mothers. Sarah, Rebekah or Rachel would have provided a more compelling representative and further justification would be needed to support the contention that Ruth's story represents an important period in Israel's salvation history.

Traditionally, following the reductionist view, the assumption, virtually universal among scholars who offer an opinion, is that one common reason must be found as to why all four women are mentioned. The four women are thus characterized under one heading as "all sinners" or in terms of their "irregular and potentially scandalous unions" or as "Gentiles." More contemporary approaches, which have combined one or more of the above reasons for their inclusion, do not significantly mitigate the problem since they still do not respect the women's individual narrated histories. In a more recent paper that reviews much of the literature on this question, Smit suggests one reason for their inclusion; they foreshadow Mary. He then moves towards a slightly more nuanced approach because he argues that they foreshadow Mary in a number of ways. He suggests that their gender, their irregular relationships (divinely vindicated) and their connections to Judah and David, whom, he claims, are the two men with the strongest messianic connotations, all "vindicate in advance the circumstances of Mary's somewhat awkward pregnancy."[56]

But if each individual woman is a character in her own story why does the assumption need to be made that all four are named for the same reason? To characterize all four women on the basis of the same one trait is an inadequate reading of their stories. The impulse that seeks to find a reason for their inclusion in what characterizes them as women is, I believe, correct. However, the scholarly need to force these four/five varied individuals into one mold to provide a neat theory for their inclusion does not do justice to their individuality as women or the variety of their narrated histories. There is a need to reclaim interpretative space for each woman before conclusions can be reached concerning her inclusion in

---

56. Smit, "Something about Mary," 206.

the genealogy and the implications that might have for the ongoing gospel narrative. Consequently, I will take a different approach to this question.

Before going on to propose a number of reasons for their collective significance in part 2, my starting point will be the women as individuals. I will first consider the way each woman, in her own right, is presented by her story teller and from her story suggest conclusions about possible reasons for her inclusion in Matthew's genealogy. The opening of the Gospel with the genealogy highlights the importance of the Old Testament narrative for Matthew, who continues in the infancy narrative and beyond to demonstrate the fulfillment of scripture as the story of Jesus the Messiah is told. Additionally, the Gospel of Matthew is imbued with allusions to the narratives of the Old Testament. Therefore it is appropriate that the primary source to be considered in order to understand the presence and significance of the first four women are their stories as told in the Old Testament. My investigation will demonstrate that the first three women chosen to be included are all initially outsiders to Israel, who demonstrate righteousness, faith, and loving loyalty in the face of rejection, condemnation, and hardship. As a result they find a place within Israel becoming key players in her salvation history as mothers to sons in the Messianic line. Less can be said of Bathsheba but her story also plays a key role in salvation history as does the fifth and final woman of the genealogy, Mary, the mother of the Messiah.

Table References (for p. 29)

1. Carson, "Matthew," 66.
2. Albright and Mann, *Matthew*, 5.
3. Anderson, "Matthew: Gender and Reading," 7–10.
4. Hagner, *Matthew 1–13*, 10.
5. Johnson, *Purpose of the Biblical Genealogies*, 152–78.
6. Heil, "Narrative Role of the Women," 538–45.
7. Bauckham, *Gospel Women*, 17–46.
8. Bauer, *Structure of Matthew's Gospel*, 454–55.
9. Hill, *Gospel of Matthew*, 74.
10. Freed, "Women in Matthew's Genealogy," 3.
11. Levine, *Social and Ethnic Dimensions*, 59–88.
12. Morris, *Gospel according to Matthew*, 23.
13. Brown, *Birth of the Messiah*, 71–74.
14. Stendahl, "Quis et Unde," 74.
15. McKay, "Only a Remnant," 53.
16. Nolland, "Four (Five) Women," 527–39.
17. Waetjen, "Genealogy as the Key," 216.
18. Beare, *Gospel according to Matthew*, 63–64.

19. Davies, *Matthew*, 31.
20. Witherington, *Matthew*, 40–41.
21. Boring, "Gospel of Matthew," 132.
22. Davies and Allison, *Matthew 1–7*, 170–71.
23. Wright, *Matthew for Everyone*, 4.
24. Bredin, "Gentiles and the Davidic Tradition," 110.
25. Goulder, *Midrash and Lection*, 232.
26. Hanson, "Rahab the Harlot," 53.
27. France, *Gospel of Matthew*, 36–37.
28. Harrington, *Gospel of Matthew*, 32.
29. Gundry, *Matthew*, 15.
30. Jones, "Subverting the Textuality," 259.
31. Hare, *Matthew*, 6.
32. Lyke, "What Does Ruth Have to Do with Rahab," 280.
33. Hauerwas, *Matthew*, 32.
34. Schaberg, *Illegitimacy of Jesus*, 33.
35. Hendrickson, *Gospel of Matthew*, 116–17.
36. Scott, "Birth of the Reader," 88.
37. Hutchison, "Women," 152–64.
38. Smit, "Something about Mary," 191–207.
39. Keener, *Matthew*.
40. Tatum, "Origin of Jesus," 527–28.
41. Luz, *Matthew 1–7*, 84–85.
42. Weren, "Five Women," 288–305.
43. Mussies, "Parallels," 38.
44. Wainwright, *Feminist Critical Reading*, 67–69.
45. Waetjen, "Genealogy as the Key," 216.

3

Tamar

Preliminary Remarks

My narrative readings of the four Old Testament women are particularly concerned to discover what characterizes them as women. Therefore some brief comments on characterization in Hebrew narrative will be made. To set the scene it will also be helpful to summarize Israel's social/sexual structures, which form the background to their stories.

Characterization in Hebrew Narrative

The way Hebrew narrative portrays characters has been thoroughly explored by Alter,[1] Sternberg,[2] and Bar-Efrat.[3] Below is a very brief summary of the main points to be noted.

What the reader knows about each of the four women under investigation is controlled entirely by the narrator of their stories. The narrator selects the details that can be known of their characters, brings them in and out of each scene, and controls their relation to the ongoing plot and their relationship with other characters within the story. The Old Testament biblical narrator, whose viewpoint is aligned with the implied author and with God, is all seeing and all knowing (in the same way as is

---

1. Alter, *Art of Biblical Narrative*.
2. Sternberg, *Poetics of Biblical Narrative*.
3. Bar-Efrat, *Narrative Art*.

the narrator of Matthew's Gospel). The Old Testament biblical narrator is therefore reliable in terms of the accuracy of the information given about a character but, by necessity, that information is selective.

The shaping of a character in terms of outward physical description is relatively sparse in Hebrew narrative. Normally there is no description of physique, appearance or even age. Therefore, it is significant to the plot when the reader is told physical details about a person. Of the four women, no physical description is given apart from Bathsheba, who is described from David's point of view as beautiful, an indicator of her sexual desirability.[4] Her beauty is noted because it is central to the plot; it is the motivation for David's consequent shameful behavior. In a similar fashion Tamar's clothing is only mentioned because her change of clothes signifies her change of *persona* and her desire to disguise her identity from Judah.

The name given to a character is significant as it can often tell the reader something about them. For example, the name Tamar, meaning "fruit palm," suggests to the alert reader that her lack of children is not due to her infertility and Rahab, meaning "spacious" or "broad," links her inherently to the broad land of Canaan but also possibly gives hints about her profession as a prostitute.[5]

The Hebrew narrator does not often let the reader into a character's inner personality, their inner speech, thoughts, and mental states. This is not unusual in ancient literature generally.[6] Consequently, little insight is given by the narrator to women's psychological points of view. Very rarely is the implied reader told about a character's internal motives and thus the gaps opened up by the lack of knowledge of motivation invite real readers to form their own conclusions. The one exception in the stories under consideration is that the reader is told that Tamar sees that Shelah has grown up and not been given to her, giving the reader an indication of her mindset and motivation as she sits by the road waiting for Judah.

Character traits noted by the narrator are always important in plot development. Traits may be voiced directly to the reader through the narrator. For example, the reader is told that Boaz is a man of standing.

---

4. Gunn and Fewell note that beauty is the most common description of a character's appearance and the information usually indicates sexual desirability in stories of courtship, seduction, or rape. Gunn and Fewell, *Narrative in the Hebrew Bible*, 57.

5. On the basis of Jewish midrash Brenner suggests "the Broad" (with the same connotations today) was the name given to an unknown woman by Hebrew scribes to indication her profession. Brenner, *I Am*, 83.

6. Burridge notes, "Detailed character analysis and psychological assessment are lacking . . . in the bulk of ancient literature." Burridge, *What Are the Gospels*, 121.

However, characterization usually emerges indirectly, either through the person's own actions and speech, or through the speech of one of the other characters. The main method of characterization is simply to report what an individual does. Their actions, or lack of actions, allow the implied reader to form conclusions about the character involved. The reader is able to construct the character of three of the four women under review through the actions they take, for what is notable is that in three of the four stories the woman is the main protagonist. This is unusual, for Hebrew narrative is decidedly androcentric, mainly focusing on the actions taken by men. Rarely are women given any agency; women seldom have a voice or take independent action and their stories operate against the backdrop of strongly patriarchal societies and values. However, Tamar, Rahab, and Ruth are all women whose actions further the plot and provide the main point of interest. Only in Bathsheba's story does a conscious effort have to be made to shift "from the narrator's eye to the reader's 'I'"[7] since she is almost entirely passive throughout and speaks only two words.

Characters in Hebrew narrative very rarely appear alone and a common technique (known as parataxis) is to place two together and allow the reader to make comparison. This occurs in all four stories: Tamar is contrasted to Judah, Rahab to the spies, Ruth firstly to Naomi and then to Boaz, and Bathsheba to David. One character's speech can be used by the narrator to shape another character. For example, the narrator uses Judah's assessment of Tamar's actions to convey the narrator's evaluation of her character and judgement of her. The same method is used for Ruth when she is evaluated by both the men and women of Bethlehem.

Explicit moral evaluative judgements by the narrator on the actions of a character are relatively rare in Hebrew narrative and therefore all the more significant when provided. No direct evaluative comment is made on any of the four women. However, as we shall see, crucially in two of these stories men are portrayed as having done evil in the Lord's sight.

The Legal Background Underlying the Women's Stories

One further point needs to be addressed that will elucidate the dynamics of each woman's story. It will help to establish in advance the position each woman occupies in relation to Israelite social/sexual structures as

---

7. Bach, "Signs of the Flesh," 63.

defined by the various laws in Leviticus and Deuteronomy. I recognize the difficulty of establishing the relationship between the books of Genesis, Joshua, Ruth, and 2 Samuel and the legal formulations in the books of Leviticus and Deuteronomy. However, when their stories assume a certain cultic legal background then it is not unreasonable to draw parallels between the way characters act and the legal codes preserved in Leviticus and Deuteronomy.

According to the legal institutions enshrined in Leviticus and Deuteronomy, a woman's role was strictly proscribed in ancient Israel (as in other ancient Near Eastern states). Niditch points out that there were only two proper roles for a young girl to occupy. Either she was an unmarried virgin in her father's house, under his authority and protection, or else she was a faithful, child-producing married woman in her husband's or her husband's family's house.[8] In both cases her sexuality was not her own to control but was under the authority of her father as a virgin and her husband as his wife. In either case violation of her position by having sexual relations with a man was deemed extremely serious and the woman was punished by stoning (Deut 22:20–22), although an exception was made in cases of rape (Deut 22:25–28). The male members of society were expected to maintain these socio-structural categories. A father was allowed to give his daughter in marriage but must ensure that she remained a virgin until then and a husband may enjoy his wife but not give her to another man. In contrast, a man's sexuality was his to control but he should take care not to infringe the rights of other men.[9] In the case of adultery with a married woman both the man and woman were punished by death (Deut 22:22). Prostitution was officially not condoned but a husband who had sexual relations with an unmarried woman was not considered to have committed adultery. A father was not to profane his daughter by making her a prostitute (Lev 19:29). However, as Bird has shown, particularly in urban areas of patriarchal societies, prostitution was not uncommon. Since most women were under the protection of their fathers and husbands and were not accessible there was a need for a legitimized "Other" woman.[10] Both Tamar and Rahab's stories indicate an accommodation to prostitution that allowed the man to take advantage of "Other" women.

---

8. Niditch, "Wronged Woman," 145.
9. See Fymer-Kensky, "Deuteronomy," 63.
10. Bird, "Harlot as Heroine," 121.

The married woman who did not bear children was in a "sociologically uncomfortable position,"[11] since her identity and integration into her husband's clan depended on her bearing children. A series of women in the Genesis narratives—Sarah, Rebekah, and Rachel—have difficulty in bearing children and are scorned by others (Gen 16:4). Rachel's outburst to Jacob, "Give me children or I will die" (Gen 30:1), reflects her desperation. Niditch goes on to note the economic implications for the childless widow:

> If her husband dies, the woman must rely on her children for support; for they inherit the father's property. In terms of long-range security in the social structure, it is more important for a woman to become her children's mother than her husband's wife.[12]

According to the law of levirate set out in Deuteronomy 25:5-10, if a husband died without his wife bearing children, his male kin were expected to raise children for the dead man in order to repair the social fabric of the kinship group. Until this happened the woman was in an anomalous position, since she could not fulfill her role as a child bearing wife nor was she able to remarry outside her husband's kinship group.

The narratives of both Tamar and Ruth take for granted a social world in which some form of levirate institution was practiced. Clearly, the Genesis narrative and possibly that of Ruth predate the Deuteronomy text. However, it seems the levirate institution antedated the legislation of the Pentateuch and was widely practiced throughout the surrounding regions.[13] Levirate marriage would ensure the perpetuation of the dead man's lineage as well as providing an heir to retain the family estate, the emphasis being on the former social function. "Properly understood, the levirate in Israel, as in every other culture where it is practised, is primarily a social rather than an economic institution, and has to do with ensuring the continued existence of a unilineal descent group through succeeding generations."[14] The birth of a son would also ensure that a woman would be cared for in old age, though Osgood concludes that, whilst not denying the importance of the practice of the levirate for the woman concerned,

---

11. Niditch, "Wronged Woman," 146.
12. Ibid., 145.
13. See Sarna, *Genesis*, 266.
14. Osgood, "Early Israelite Society," 368-69.

Tamar

"the biblical material makes no mention of concern for the widow being the primary object of the levirate."[15]

As noted, the brother of a deceased, childless man was required to marry his widow in order that his name "may not be blotted out in Israel" (Deut 25:6). The problem in both Tamar and Ruth's stories is that neither Judah nor Boaz are brothers-in-law; therefore are they legitimate *levirs*? In Tamar's case the distinction is crucial because it means the difference between accusations of incest or a legitimate sexual encounter. It is possible that at an earlier stage the custom of levirate marriage was more widely practiced, extending to any male related by kinship descent, and only became limited to brothers-in-law at a later stage. Osgood argues that the popular translation for *yibbum* (יבם), brother-in-law, is mistaken. The masculine form of the Hebrew root יבם carries the meaning progenitor but is translated in English as "the levirate." The word levirate derives from the Latin *levir* which in turn means brother-in-law, hence the misunderstanding that the role of the *levir* was limited to the brother-in-law. Osgood also argues that in fact the levirate was one of the responsibilities of the *go'el* (גאל), extending to any male member of the descent based local group. I argue that both narratives proceed on the assumption that Judah and Boaz are legitimate *levirs*.[16] It explains the dramatic change in Judah's reaction to Tamar's pregnancy. This change is not just because he knows he is the father but because he recognizes he is a legitimate *levir* (Gen 38:26). It is also the rationale Boaz provides for marriage to Ruth (Ruth 4:10).

Questions Informing the Analysis

The questions that will inform my narrative reading of the stories concerning Tamar, Rahab, Ruth, and Bathsheba are: How is each woman characterized? What points of view are presented? How does the construction of the narrative shape the way the reader sees each woman? What role does each woman play in relation to the other characters in the story? Finally, what are the stories of these women doing and saying in the wider narrative context? The answers provided to these questions will be used to suggest reasons for the inclusion of each of these women in Matthew's genealogy.

15. Osgood, "Early Israelite Society," 358.

16. Not all scholars agree that levirate marriage is at issue in Ruth—e.g., Sasson, *Ruth: A New Translation*, 132.

A Narrative Reading of Tamar's Story

Tamar's story is contained within the discrete literary unit of Genesis 38 that forms part of a narrative stretching from Genesis 12–50. Typical of much biblical narrative, the Genesis narrative is constructed from a number of seemingly separate plots that have their own beginning, middle, and ending which, in the past, has led historical critics to suggest independent sources that were put together by a final redactor. This has led to an atomizing of the text so that Genesis 38 has been viewed as a late addition to an already existing text, quite out of place in its present context.[17]

However, in his groundbreaking book *The Art of Biblical Narrative* (1981), Alter challenged scholarly opinion, which had been dominated hitherto by source critical views. Through literary analysis he demonstrated how common motifs[18] and language link Genesis 38 to the larger Joseph cycle, which in turn is a subplot within the larger Genesis story of promised land and nationhood as God's people.

Ostensibly the story in Genesis 38 is about marriage and offspring, particularly the offspring of Jacob's son, Judah. Land and numerous descendants are central to God's promise of blessing; a promise originally made to Abraham and repeated to the patriarchs as the history of God's people unfolds. Such promises "are often depicted as impossible, unlikely, or endangered."[19] Barrenness threatens fulfillment of the promise on a number of occasions. Alter comments that "the Patriarchal Tales . . . make clear that procreation, far from being an automatic biological process, is fraught with dangers, is constantly under the threat of being deflected or cut off."[20] Tamar's story fits into this ongoing theme.

---

17. "The account does not belong to the main thread of . . . the Joseph narrative, but was inserted here only secondarily." Gunkel, *Genesis*, 395. See also, e.g., Brueggemann, *Genesis*, 307, and von Rad, *Genesis*, 356–57.

18. E.g., themes of recognition and deception.

19. Bos, "Out of the Shadows," 48.

20. Alter, *Genesis*, xlvi.

The Narrative Structure of Genesis 38

Although it is now widely accepted there are clear thematic links to the surrounding Joseph story,[21] Genesis 38 stands as a "smaller literary whole"[22] with its own internal narrative form. It has a clear structural design starting with descent and after the turning point of verse 12 ascent. Lambe has shown how, over a period of time, Judah descends from a point of equilibrium, "Judah went down" (Gen 38:1), to a point of disequilibrium (Gen 38:12a) that is only reversed when "he went up to Timnah" (Gen 38:12b).[23] Tamar then takes things into her own hands resulting in the restoration of life and stability for herself and Judah's family (Gen 38:27–30). In other words, Judah's geographical travels act as a metaphor for the fortunes of his family.

Structure of Genesis 38[24]

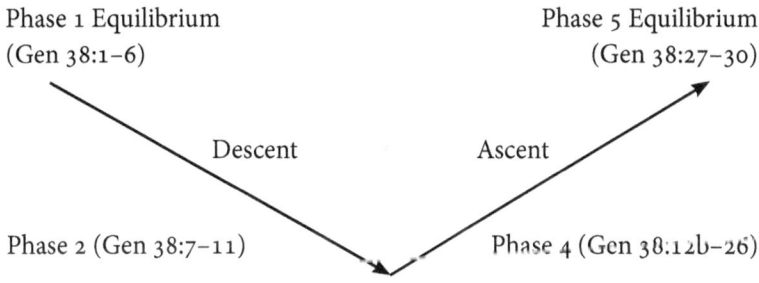

On the surface this is a story about Judah and the establishing and continuance of his family line, providing the framework for Tamar's story. But, as Emerton comments, Tamar "is in a sense the heroine of the story."[25] In the first section (Gen 38:1–11) Judah is the main protagonist, although within his story Tamar suffers from the deceit of both son (Gen 38:9) and father (Gen 38:11). Genesis 38:12 is the turning point, with the lowest

---

21. See, e.g., Bal's feminist analysis of the connections in Bal, *Lethal Love*, 95–103; Wenham, *Genesis 16–50*, 363; and Wilson's more recent exploration of the story's links to the Joseph cycle in Wilson, *Joseph*, 86–92.
22. Bar-Efrat, "Some Observations," 159.
23. Lambe, "Genesis 38," 102–25.
24. Diagram based on Lambe, "Genesis 38," 103.
25. Emerton, "Judah and Tamar," 410.

point in the story being the death of Judah's wife before Judah goes up to Timnah. Tamar becomes the main protagonist in both the next two sections (Gen 38:13–26, 27–30), although the balance of power remains with Judah; as patriarchal head of the family he threatens her life and the life of the children she carries.

Genesis 38:1–11	Judah's Story: Judah establishes and loses a family (Phase 1 and 2)
Genesis 38:12	The turning point (Phase 3)
Genesis 38:13–26	Tamar's Story (Phase 4)
Genesis 38:27–30	The Outcome: The birth of twins, Judah regains a family (Phase 5)

Both Judah and Tamar's stories can be further divided into two parts, the second part of Tamar's story forming the dramatic climax to the whole plot and the outcome providing the epilogue which rounds off the story.

Judah's story

Genesis 38:1–6	Judah takes a wife and has three sons; he takes Tamar for Er
Genesis 38:7–11	Two sons die; Tamar is banished
Genesis 38:12	The turning point

Tamar's Story

Genesis 38:13–23	Tamar poses as a prostitute; the prostitute cannot be found
Genesis 38:24–26	The dramatic climax; Tamar is brought out to be burned
Genesis 38:27–30	The Outcome: The birth of twins, Judah regains a family

Judah's Story

GENESIS 38:1–6 | JUDAH'S FAMILY

The scene, in common with Rahab and Ruth's story, opens with someone going on a journey, a good place for any story to start. It is a story of what happens to Judah when he "went down from his brothers and turned aside to a certain Adullamite" (Gen 38:1). However, immediately there are warning signals that all will not go well. At the outset, Judah intentionally separates himself from his kinship group. His journey from the hill country of Hebron to Adullam on the plain also traces a metaphorical "spiritual removal"[26] as he goes down and turns aside.

Judah sees a Canaanite woman, unnamed but patriarchally defined in terms of her father Shua.[27] Although Abraham and Isaac insist on the importance of their sons not marrying a Canaanite (Gen 24:3; 28:1) Jacob's son Judah does not hesitate. Sternberg comments, "Having distanced himself from his natural environment, he proceeds to sink as low as assimilation . . . to forbidden marriage."[28] Three sequential verbs describe Judah's actions in quick succession "he saw . . . he took[29] . . . and went in to her" (Gen 38:2). She conceives and bears a son whom Judah names Er.[30] The birth of the firstborn son is followed by two more sons whom the nameless woman names Onan and Shelah. Judah appears increasingly disinterested in his family, only bothering to name his first son, leaving his wife to name the other two; the text indicating that Judah was not even present for the final birth but was in Chezib—the place of lies.[31]

As has been noted, there is often little character description in Hebrew narrative, characters normally reveal themselves by what they say and do. In this case it is Judah's actions that indict him from the start of the story. Cotter's comment is perceptive:

> Judah has yet to say anything, but he has done a great deal: left his family, taken a woman apparently in an informal marriage

---

26. Sternberg, "Biblical Poetics," 485.

27. In Gen 38:12 she is Bat-Shua, Shua's daughter. In 1 Chr 2:3 she appears in variant form as "Bath-Shua the Canaanite woman."

28. Sternberg, "Biblical Poetics," 485–86.

29. The Hebrew says he "took" her rather than the more normal biblical phrase "took as wife."

30. Some Hebrew manuscripts read "she named," as do the Samaritan version and Targum Jonathan.

31. Gen 38:5b LXX has "she," the MT "he." The Hebrew root כזב means to deceive.

although she was not within the kinship group, done so without permission, bothered to be present only for the birth of his first son, and not bothered to name the second two. For the birth of his third son he is in a place called "Falsehood." A more suggestive portrait of inappropriate behaviour is hard to imagine.[32]

Although no notice is given, time passes, as in the next verse Judah does not allow the now grown firstborn son Er the privilege he had enjoyed but takes a wife for him. The reader is led to assume this woman is also a Canaanite but no mention is made of her background or origin. It is at this point in the story the woman simply named Tamar enters the scene. She is given to a man who turns out to be "evil (ער) in the Lord's eyes" (Gen 38: 7).

Genesis 38:7–11 | The Death of Judah's Sons and Banishment of Tamar

One of the striking features of this story is the omniscience of the narrator who knows and tells the reader what is in the mind of God (Gen 38:7, 10), Onan (Gen 38:9), Judah (Gen 38:11, 15), and Tamar (Gen 38:14). Acting like a Greek chorus or Shakespearean soliloquy, the narrator informs the reader of things of which the other characters in the story are not aware. This gives the audience a privileged bird's eye perspective on events. Readers sit *with* the gods rather than *in* the gods! The first piece of inside knowledge is unusual. It is not often in Hebrew narrative that the audience is told what God thinks. The narrator gives the reason for Er's untimely death, letting his readers know how God viewed Er. "But Er, Judah's firstborn, was evil in the Lord's eyes, and the Lord put him to death" (Gen 38:7). The reader does not know what Er did to incur God's wrath (although the word ער indicates moral evil) but God's judgement is unequivocal. In contrast to Jacob's grief over the loss of Joseph (Gen 37:34), Judah is not seen in mourning; the text remains silent on the matter reinforcing the reader's negative image of Judah.

Judah then tells Onan, "Go in to your brother's wife and perform the duty of a brother-in-law (יבם) to her; raise up offspring for your brother" (Gen 38:8). Onan dishonors his role as *levir* in refusing to give Tamar a child. The narrator lets the reader know that Onan has no intention of raising offspring for his brother, "since Onan knew that the offspring would not be his" (Gen 38:9). Onan ostensibly obeys Judah but, although

32. Cotter, *Genesis*, 281.

he regularly[33] uses Tamar for sex, he practices *coitus interruptus* to prevent Tamar from having children, letting his sperm "spill on the ground when he went in to her lest he give offspring to his brother" (Gen 38:9). Tamar is used and abused. The reader is not told of Onan's motive and is left to surmise whether his action is due to resentment at being forced to act as *levir*, or selfishness and greed, since he would suffer economic loss if Tamar gives birth to a son.[34] For a second time the narrator reveals that God has seen, "What he did was evil in the Lord's eyes, and he put him to death also" (Gen 38:10). Earlier in the troubled history of this patriarchal family God has acted to defend another foreign woman who has been treated badly; Hagar is the first person in the Genesis text to name God, "You are אתה אל ראי" (Gen 16:13), the God who sees me. The repeated phrase "in the Lord's eyes" in Genesis 38 reminds the reader that YHWH is indeed the God who sees. To outward appearances Onan is fulfilling his levirate duty whilst Tamar seems unable to fulfill hers by bearing a child; the narrator wants the reader to know things were not as they appeared. Even though Tamar remains silent throughout, presumably unaware of the cause of Onan's death, "the reader comes to see what the narrator sees."[35]

Judah, also not party to the inside information the narrator has given readers, banishes Tamar to her father's house. At this point the reader is given his point of view on events, "for he feared he [his son, Shelah] too would die, like his brothers" (Gen 38:11). The implication of Judah's inner speech is that he connects Tamar to the deaths of his sons and sees her as "a jinxed barren wife."[36] He leaves her under his authority, unable to remarry,[37] promising her his youngest son when Shelah comes of age. Yet his deep fear that, linked to Tamar, Shelah too might die without offspring, implies that Judah is simply going to let her languish, giving her father's family the economic responsibility to provide for her. Calvin considers that from the start Judah's intentions are dishonorable, "Judah acted very unjustly in keeping one bound, whom he intended to defraud."[38]

33. The use of the Qal perfect בָּא after the conjunction אִם is a frequentative perfect implying the action took place on more than one occasion.

34. Sarna notes, "With the death of the first-born, Onan inherits one-half of his father's estate. However, should he provide an heir to his brother, his portion would be diminished." Sarna, *Genesis*, 267.

35. Berlin, *Poetics and Interpretation*, 52.

36. Bos, "Out of the Shadows," 47.

37. In later Judaism an ordinary widow was relatively autonomous legally, whereas "the levirate widow is defined by her relationship to a man who has an exclusive claim on her biological function." Wegner, *Chattel or Person?*, 97.

38. Calvin, *Genesis*, 282.

The narrator, having reported both Judah's direct speech to Tamar and his interior speech, records no response from Tamar. Real readers might wonder what she is feeling and thinking behind her silent submission. Not seeking to justify herself or accuse others, Tamar suffers the social and economic disgrace of being sent away. She has not produced children but her partners have died and her father now has to support, feed, and clothe her. The reader is simply told Tamar obeys her father-in-law's instructions, "So Tamar went to live in her father's house" (Gen 38:11). Wenham notes the only verbs she is subject to are "the two verbs of compliance and retreat."[39] Being confined both in her father's house and widow's clothes Tamar apparently no longer has any power to change her situation or honor her dead husband by bearing a son.

Cotter's comment is insightful:

> She is now utterly inside, trapped in structures real and cultural: inside her father's house (while still being legally part of her father-in-law's household), inside the clothing that marks her as a widow and a daughter-in-law (while denied the husband that would provide her income, status, and progeny).[40]

In denying her the right of *levir* Judah not only denies Tamar the right to a child, who will perpetuate her deceased husband's lineage and ensure her place within the clan, he also denies her economic security leaving her socially and economically on the margins.

To summarize: at the end of the first section of the story Tamar has been twice widowed and is left trapped in her father's house as a widow-in-waiting. So far, she has been entirely passive, acted upon by others but having no agency or voice of her own. The story world reflects her situation as a woman within a strongly patriarchal society, apparently powerless to alter her circumstances but waiting patiently for Shelah to be given to her in levirate marriage.[41]

Genesis 38:12 | The turning point

The story, having started with a non-specific reference to time, "It happened at that time" (Gen 38:1), now moves into its second phase with

---

39. Wenham, *Genesis 16–50*, 367.
40. Cotter, *Genesis*, 283.
41. "Tamar's status was thus what is termed *shomeret yavam* ('awaiting the levir') in rabbinic parlance, and any extra-levirate sexual relationship would have been adulterous." Sarna, *Genesis*, 269.

another time indication, "After many days" (Gen 38:12). This marks the next stage of the story when time will slow down until, at the crucial point, narrated time becomes one with real time.

At this point the real action begins. Notably, this is where Tamar takes things into her own hands. Judah makes another journey and the movement downwards to death and instability turns, due to the action of his neglected and forgotten daughter-in-law, and becomes a movement upwards to life and stability. The final death recorded in this story is that of the "wife of Judah, Shua's daughter" (Gen 38:12), the only one for whom Judah apparently mourned. At this point Judah "goes up" with his friend to Timnah, the place of reckoning.

Tamar's Story

Genesis 38:13–23 | The prostitute

The knowledge people possess is important in this story. Anonymous informants tell Tamar that Judah, having completed the period of mourning, "is going up to Timnah to shear his sheep" (Gen 38:13). Suspecting Judah's sexual need and knowing the festive atmosphere surrounding sheep shearing, she "suddenly races into rapid, purposeful action, expressed in a detonating series of verbs."[42] Seeing an opportunity she takes the initiative to right an injustice. Symbolically, Tamar disguises herself, taking off her widow's clothes, putting on a veil, wrapping herself up before sitting in a strategic location, Enaim עינים—the place of the eyes (Gen 38:14a). The Hebrew name makes allusion to the fact that, presumably, only Tamar's eyes were visible.[43] Bos comments, "It is here that the process begins by which Judah will receive his eye opener as to righteousness."[44]

The narrator does not speak of her motivation but, significantly, does reveal that Tamar was now aware of Judah's duplicity, "She saw that Shelah was grown up, yet had not been given to her in marriage" (Gen 38:14b). Coats rightly comments, "The goal of her plan is to secure her right in the *levirate*. That right is not marriage, but the conception of a child."[45] The child (if male) would bring her social and economic security as well as honoring the continuing demands of her relationship to her deceased

---

42. Alter, *Art of Biblical Narrative*, 8.
43. The Hebrew עינים can mean well, spring, or eye.
44. Bos, "Eyeopener at the Gate," 121.
45. Coats, *Genesis*, 274.

husband. Osgood notes that both in Genesis 38 and Ruth, "it is the woman who actively seeks fulfilment of the levirate law,"[46] presumably to secure a future for herself, to give her status in the clan and security in her old age. After all, who else would best care for an elderly widow apart from her own son? The reader is left to draw the conclusion that Tamar's only option is to have a child by Judah.

In taking off her widow's clothes Tamar signals a change in her identity from a woman trapped as a levirate widow-in-waiting to a woman with autonomy. Her change of clothing indicates her intention to disguise herself and trick Judah into thinking she is a harlot.[47] Her identity to Judah remains veiled, "When Judah saw her, he thought her to be a prostitute (זונה), for she had covered her face" (Gen 38:15). Clearly, Tamar wants to trick Judah into having sexual intercourse with her but as Bal points out, "her trick is a response to the trick played against her, not an initiative of trickery."[48] Judah has already defrauded her by letting her languish in her father's house with no intention of giving her Shelah in levirate marriage. Her deception is successful and the reversal continues in that the woman who has been invisible in her father's house is now seen by Judah, who takes her for a prostitute. Without any preliminaries, he bluntly propositions her, "Here, let me come into you" (Gen 38:16). Tamar, just as straightforward in her reply, astutely asks, "What will you give me, that you may come into me?" (Gen 38:16). The narrator then attempts to mitigate Judah's action by emphasizing his lack of knowledge, "for he did not know that she was his daughter-in-law" (Gen 38:16).

Obtaining Judah's means of identification is central to Tamar's risky strategy; essential to her future if she becomes pregnant, dictating the difference between life and death. Narrated time becomes one with real time as the two barter over conditions until Tamar gets what she wants, Judah's seal, cord, and staff, irrefutable evidence of his identity, in lieu of a kid. Tamar has planned things so she can clearly identify the father of any child she might bear as a result of this liaison.

Niditch notes the link between trickery, wisdom, and control, "Successful trickery is also a form of wisdom, requiring forethought, planning, cleverness; it too is an attempt to achieve temporary control of one's

---

46. Osgood, "Early Israelite Society," 356.

47. The Hebrew word זונה is used to denote a woman who offers sexual favors for pay, as such a woman was not under the authority of her father or a husband and therefore free to control her own sexuality. Bird, "Harlot as Heroine," 120.

48. Bal, "Tricky Thematics," 148–49.

environment."⁴⁹ According to Niditch's analysis, trickery is a positive thing, "a form of wisdom." Tamar resorts to deception as the only way out of her situation.⁵⁰ She has indeed acted with forethought and planning, choosing her moment and place, ensuring she has proof of identity. In her new *persona* as a prostitute she exploits the one thing she has reclaimed as her own, her sexuality, while Judah, driven by his desires, foolishly gives her an excessive pledge. At this point in the story it is Tamar who is clearly in control of the situation but her temporary control only lasts as long as it takes to change her clothes. After intercourse, she leaves, resumes the garments of widowhood, returns to her place in her father's house and waits. Having taken the huge risk of going outside in the role of a prostitute, Tamar, in putting on the garments of widowhood, returns to her former role as *persona non grata* inside her father's house. She has done what she can to right a wrong and now God does what he can and she conceives. God blesses Tamar's refusal to have a future as a *persona non grata* dictated to her for it is in the nature of God to honor and free the trapped.⁵¹ In terms of the plot, the movement from death to life has taken place.

GENESIS 38:20–23 | THE PROSTITUTE CANNOT BE FOUND— A COMIC INTERLUDE

Meanwhile, Judah, a man of standing, concerned to recover his credentials, dispatches his friend, Hirah the Adullamite, to deliver a kid to "the woman." "Her namelessness is the narrative's way of emphasising Judah's casual relationship with Tamar."⁵² Unfortunately for Judah "he could not find her" (Gen 38:20), so he has to ask where the "temple prostitute" (קדשה) is. Bird highlights the difference between the two Hebrew words, prostitute (זונה) and temple prostitute (קדשה), noting that sexual inter-

---

49. Niditch, *Prelude to Biblical Folklore*, 105.

50. On the issue of Tamar lying, Prouser argues that deception is a justifiable weapon to enable disadvantaged and less powerful people to gain justice. Prouser, "Truth about Women," 15–28. For a discussion on Old Testament women as tricksters, see also *Semeia* 42 (1998), which contains a series of essays by feminist writers (including Bal noted above). Rahab and Ruth can also be characterized as female tricksters who outwit men.

51. YHWH performs righteous acts (צדקות) and just acts (משפטים) for all the oppressed (Ps 103:6).

52. Hamilton, *Book of Genesis*, 446. Berlin shows that the way in which Tamar is referred to throughout the narrative signals whose point of view is being given. For example in the scene of sexual encounter, Tamar is "her" and "she"; "the name, like Tamar herself, is concealed." Berlin, *Poetics and Interpretation*, 60.

course with a cult prostitute might seem to be more socially acceptable, a religious activity, while sleeping with a common prostitute was purely a commercial deal for gratification. She comments that the "substitution of terms in this passage is not accidental . . . Hirah knows how to handle the situation."[53] The townspeople deny knowledge of her, "No temple prostitute (קדשה) has been here" (Gen 38:21). It is interesting that in a relatively sparse narrative the narrator chooses to repeat this phrase in the friend's report to Judah, "I have not found her; moreover, the townspeople said, 'No temple prostitute has been here'" (Gen 38:22). Alter notes that, in spite of "the strictest economy of means," the Hebrew authors were in the habit of restating material when appropriate.[54] Here the narrator does this to emphasize the point that indeed Tamar was no prostitute but only a wronged woman seeking justice.

There is something comic about this scene and the ineptitude of the two men trying to retrieve Judah's pledge but in the end being outwitted by a woman whom they considered to be a common prostitute. Judah, concerned not to become a laughing stock,[55] lets the matter rest, although *his* identity is now ambiguous. He is justified in his own eyes, "you see, I sent this kid, and you could not find her" (Gen 38:23). Cotter points out, "This is unwitting irony on Judah's part since he had not, in fact, tried at all to make good his pledge to Tamar in her *persona* as his daughter-in-law" (Gen 38:11).[56]

Genesis 38:24–26a | Tamar Is to Be Burned

The third indication of time in the story brings us to its dramatic climax; a turning point that poses a threat to the movement from death to life. "About three months later" (Gen 38:24) (presumably when Tamar's pregnancy begins to show), Judah is told[57] that Tamar his daughter-in-law has been whoring and is "pregnant as a result of whoredom" (Gen 38:24). Without even seeing her, Judah perfunctorily (the Hebrew uses just two

---

53. Bird, "Harlot as Heroine," 125–26.
54. Alter, *Art of Biblical Narrative*, 88.
55. Midrash Rabbah comments that at this point the "Torah laughs at men"; quoted in Dijk-Hemmes, "Tamar and the Limits of Patriarchy," 151.
56. Cotter, *Genesis*, 286.
57. Verse 24 "Judah was told" parallels the report brought to Tamar in v. 13 (see p. 53) where the same phrase is used.

words (הוֹצִיאוּהָ וְתִשָּׂרֵף) orders the harshest of punishments, "Bring her out, and let her be burned" (Gen 38:24c).[58]

There is a double irony at work in the story at this point. With no hesitation, Judah embraced the whore, yet now, again without hesitation, he wants to put to death the one who whored. The father is about to burn his children and the mother of his children. Judah is ignorant of both ironies. Brueggemann comments:

> A striking contrast is established between this man who has standing and status in the community and this woman who stands outside the law and is without legal recourse . . . Clearly, Judah judges Tamar's adulterous actions by a norm very different from the one he applies to himself.[59]

Immediately Tamar is brought out into the public arena although Judah himself is not present (the speed is highlighted by the Hebrew tense, a hophal participle, "she-is-being-taken-out" [Gen 38:25a]). She maintains courageous self restraint until the very last moment when about to be burnt. Then, like Judah and his brothers previously (Gen 37:31–33), she sends evidence to her "father-in-law" (although, unlike the bloodied coat, her evidence is genuine). It is at this point she reveals, "It was the owner of these who made me pregnant" (Gen 38:25). What drama! The reader enjoys the moment as she continues, "Recognize please (הַכֶּר־נָא)[60] whose these are, the signet and cord and the staff." Her words act "Like a trap suddenly springing closed."[61] Judah can do no other than admit ownership. Not only does he recognize his credentials but in doing so he recognizes that Tamar was the unidentified harlot and that she is carrying his offspring. But there is yet another meaning to her plea. Implied in her words is the request that Judah recognize her for who she is; his wronged daughter-in-law. His response shows that he has understood this. It provides the surprise element to the story and its dramatic climax, "She is more righteous than I am" (דקה ממני) (Gen 38:26). This is the crux of the narrative; she has presented convincing evidence. It is at this point that Ju-

---

58. "The Mosaic law fixed the penalty of burning only for the case of a priest's daughter who had become guilty of harlotry (cf. Deut 22:20–24 with Lev 21:9). The usual mode of execution for other cases was stoning." Leupold, *Exposition of Genesis*, 987.

59. Brueggemann, *Genesis*, 309–10.

60. Tamar uses the very phrase, הַכֶּר־נָא used by Judah and his brothers to their father in Gen 37:32.

61. Alter, *Genesis*, 222.

dah "recognizes" his failure to fulfill his obligations; in withholding Shelah from her he has denied Tamar a *levir*. As a consequence, Judah vindicates her action, "since I did not give her to my son Shelah" (Gen 38:26).

How should the phrase צדקה ממני be translated? The stative verb צדק (to be righteous) implies a *state* of righteousness, "she is righteous," rather than referring to righteous *action* taken. However, Reimer notes that the word group "comprises both active and stative meanings: one 'acts rightly', one can 'be righteous.'"[62] In the context of the narrative, the phrase refers to all that Tamar has done in trying to rectify the situation for Judah's family, her dead husband and for herself. In this case both the stative and active meanings apply. Tamar is righteous by virtue of having acted righteously. There is a sense that justice has been served. She has shown herself to be righteous by her actions in enabling her husband's lineage (and thus Judah's lineage) to continue by becoming pregnant by the only available descendant of Abraham, Judah himself.[63] By tricking Judah into acting as her *levir* the injustice of her situation has been resolved.

What is the significance of the comparative ממני? Some have argued that the force of the Hebrew phrase is "she is innocent I am guilty."[64] The phrase could thus be translated "she is in the right as against me." On this understanding the phrase has a judicial meaning in which Judah recognizes Tamar is vindicated. Tamar has not been guilty of wrongdoing, whereas his actions have been wrong.[65] Thus, the phrase is a "comparison of exclusion."[66] However, the phrase can also be read as an inclusive comparative, translated as "she has acted more righteously than I have."[67] On this reading Judah stops short of an admission of guilt or unrighteousness on his part, while acknowledging that Tamar's behavior in what had gone on is more righteous than his. One might ask in what sense in his own

---

62. Reimer, "7405 צדק," 746.

63. Niditch notes, "An unusual adherence to the law of the levirate takes precedence over an incest law." Niditch, "Wronged Woman," 148.

64. Wenham, *Genesis 16–50*, 370.

65. A traditional Jewish commentary takes this view. "And Judah recognized them and said, 'She is in the right. She is pregnant from me, on account of the fact that I did not give her to my son Shelah.'" *Targum Onqelos* Genesis 38:26, in Kugel, *Traditions of the Bible*, 454. Kugel notes that Jewish interpretation considered that Judah's marriage to a Canaanite was sinful (*Testament of Judah* 13:7–8), whereas Tamar, a daughter of Aram (*Jubilees* 41:1, *Testament of Judah* 10:3), was righteous because she did not resort to marriage with a Canaanite (Pseudo-Philo *Biblical Antiquities* 9:5).

66. Reimer, "7405 צדק," 747.

67. Boice, *Genesis*, 46. A slightly different twist is given by Westermann, who translates it as "She is within her rights rather than I." Westermann, *Genesis 37–50*, 48.

eyes has Judah acted righteously? He has told Onan to fulfill his duty as *levir* and acts as a responsible patriarchal father by punishing his errant daughter-in-law when she was found to be pregnant. However, this latter outward action of righteousness merely serves to highlight to the reader the double standard by which Judah operates, a standard that allows him to visit a prostitute with no censure while condemning his daughter-in-law to be burnt. Judah, although outwardly appearing to be righteous, has in fact acted unjustly on a number of occasions in his dealings with his daughter-in-law, whereas Tamar, although outwardly appearing to have prostituted herself, has in fact acted righteously, fulfilling her responsibility as a levirate widow both to Er and to Judah's clan. The duty owed in kinship relationship is subtly emphasized by the narrator's use at this point in the story of the terms daughter-in-law (כלה) (Gen 38:24) for Tamar and father-in-law (חם) (Gen 38:25) for Judah.[68]

Real readers are left to draw their own conclusions about the relative merits of each character. Brueggemann comments, "A contrast is made between the minor offence of Tamar and the major violation of Judah . . . The result is a fresh definition of righteousness, an unexpected assessment of guilt and innocence."[69] This story revolves around the question of what it means to live righteously and, unexpectedly, it is not Judah but Tamar who is the exemplar of a righteous person.

Genesis 38:26b | The Return to Propriety

The final comment made by the narrator to end this section is "And he did not know her again" (Gen 38:26b). The first time the word "know" (ידע) is used for sexual intimacy in this narrative reflects not just an end to any sexual relationship but, as Hamilton points out, "Throughout most of the narrative Judah has not really known Tamar. She is a brother's wife (v. 8), a daughter-in-law (v. 11), a widow (v. 11), a prostitute (v. 15), and a woman (v. 20)."[70] Now Judah has had his "eyes opened" and knows Tamar in a new way. He sees Tamar for who she is and accepts the blame for his ill treatment of her. In acknowledging her as the mother of his children-to-be

---

68. Ziesler reaches a similar conclusion, "In view of the general understanding of family obligations which underlines the story, the meaning is probably not simply 'she is more in the right than I am'—though this is present—but rather, 'she has fulfilled the community obligations better than I have' and therefore is more righteous." Ziesler, *Meaning of Righteousness*, 43.

69. Brueggemann, *Genesis*, 310.

70. Hamilton, *Book of Genesis*, 451.

Judah accepts the justice of her action and receives her back into the clan. The knowledge of Tamar's righteous behavior initiates a change in Judah and in later life he himself will learn to do the right thing; he will offer himself to Joseph in place of Benjamin.[71] Tamar thus becomes the catalyst for Judah's character development.

Genesis 38:27–30 | Judah Regains a Family

The final section of the plot ends where it began, with the birth of Judah's sons, although this time it is Tamar who gives birth to twin boys. The reversal and upward movement towards life started by Tamar's dangerous and unorthodox action is brought to completion. In the wider context of the Genesis narrative, what greater sign of God's blessing on Tamar could there be than twin sons born to Judah? Now that Tamar has reverted to her traditional role as mother inside the home, she no longer has a public presence as an individual, but is referred to by the narrator as "she" and "her." With the birth of the twins the social fabric of the family is repaired and the dilemma is resolved, so it is a sad irony that Tamar herself is neither named nor given any ongoing narrative life beyond the birth of her sons. Judah is absent, as he was for the birth of his second and third sons. Tamar is supported by a midwife. Just as in a later story Rahab will make use of a scarlet cord, so here, the midwife marks Zerah with a crimson thread. However, despite Zerah's hand appearing first, Perez pushes to the front and is born before his brother. Tamar gives birth in a way that recalls the delivery of Esau and Jacob. One of the primary themes that recurs throughout Genesis, the usurpation of the elder by the younger, comes into play as the scene closes.

Androcentric and Feminist Perspectives

Amit argues that "Judah is depicted in this story in a favorable light" and Westermann sees that one consequence of this episode is to portray Judah as "an honourable man."[72] However, I have argued that throughout the narrative Judah is portrayed as less than honorable a number of times but most significantly in his treatment of Tamar, whereas she is shown to be "righteous." Primogeniture left in the hand of "evil" sons and a fearful

---

71. Gen 44:33–34.
72. Amit, *Reading Biblical Narratives*, 92. Westermann, *Genesis 37–50*, 55.

father is unproductive. Their negative response to others threatens life, whereas Tamar's response to others fulfills it and twin sons are born. Judah's one redeeming feature is that he recognizes the injustice of his treatment of his daughter-in-law and consequently the justice of the action she takes.

Another line of traditional interpretation is outlined by Laffey:

> Since the text makes certain that the reader knows this [that it was only after his wife died Judah sought out the harlot], one can only conclude that the author wants to assure the reader of the appropriateness of Judah's sexual act. Finally, Judah made every effort to pay his just debt to the harlot.[73]

But knowledge of Judah's sexual need, while explaining his action in propositioning the woman he thought was a prostitute, hardly makes such action "appropriate." The fact that the reader knows Tamar's identity demonstrates in some senses how inappropriate his act is. Whereas she had been left trapped as a widow in her father's house, Judah, at the first opportunity following his wife's death, seeks out a prostitute. The irony of Judah's effort to pay his debt is missed. Judah attempts to pay his debt to the harlot whilst ignoring the greater debt he owes to the same person, highlighting not the payment of a just debt but the *injustice* of his former action.

Feminist interpreters have pointed out the positive light in which Tamar is portrayed. Bos argues that despite its androcentrism, visible in the lack of condemnation of Judah, the story has a gynocentric bias. "The tone in which the men are discussed, summarily dispatched by God, or acting as if they were in charge and all the while making fools of themselves, points to a gynocentric bias."[74]

However, it could be argued that Tamar is negatively characterized as deceitful. Fuchs comments that depicting women as deceitful has "been among the most successful strategies of traditional patriarchies . . . This may explain the frequent association of women and deception in the Hebrew Bible."[75] Using the story of Rachel (Gen 31) she goes on to outline what she considers typical in biblical tales of female deception, "the suppression of explicit indices of motivation, the suspension of authorial judgement, and the absence of closure."[76] Such patriarchal literary strategies "create the impression that deceptiveness is somehow generic

---

73. Laffey, *Wives, Harlots & Concubines*, 45.
74. Bos, "Out of the Shadows," 48–49.
75. Fuchs, "For I Have the Way of Women," 69.
76. Ibid., 70.

to women."[77] However, what she omits to note is that throughout Genesis the patriarchal fathers are also presented as deceivers; in fact, all the main male characters practice deception. Abraham lies over Sarah's identity, as does his son Isaac over Rebecca. Jacob tricks his brother Esau out of his blessing. Jacob's father-in-law, Laban, tricks him on his wedding night and then, in turn, Jacob tricks him. Jacob's sons inherit their father's failing and trick him over the death of Joseph. Joseph goes on to play a trick on his brothers. Moreover, what Fuchs considers to be typical in biblical tales of female deception is not true of Tamar's story. We have already seen that authorial judgement passed by the narrator on Er and Onan is uncompromising; they are evil in the Lord's eyes (Gen 38:7, 10). In Onan's case God's punishment is explicit; it is because of his mistreatment of Tamar. The narrator shows that Tamar is deceived both by Onan's action and Judah's promise of Shelah, so that she is left in a situation where deception and her sexuality are the only things left to empower her in a powerless situation. Having taken off her widow's clothes, put on a veil and sat down by the roadside, crucially and unusually, the narrator lets the reader see things from Tamar's point of view, "She saw that Shelah was grown up. Yet she had not been given to him in marriage" (Gen 38:14). By this inclusion the narrator strongly implies the motivation for her action in deceiving Judah is to force him (albeit unwittingly) to act as *levir*. Finally, the narrator brings the story to its dramatic and ironic climax when Tamar is declared righteous by the man who had oppressed her. The birth of twin boys with which her story closes signals divine blessing, implied in which is a divine sanctioning of her actions. A more satisfying closure is hard to imagine.

Consequently, in this instance, Fuchs's analysis does not stand. On the contrary, rather than demeaning Tamar as a deceptive woman, Genesis 38 provides readers with a sympathetic portrait of a woman; in gendered terms, it has a gynocentric bias. Within the wider context of the Genesis narrative, it is interesting to note that in the entire book of Genesis, where Abraham is credited with "righteousness" (צדקה) (Gen 15:6), only two people are called "righteous" (צדק)—Noah (Gen 6:9) and Tamar (Gen 38:26).

77. Ibid.

Tamar's Inclusion in Matthew's Genealogy

At the outset it was argued that, to be valid, an intertextual reading must demonstrate a thematic coherence. There are several themes that emerge from Tamar's story that are taken and developed in Matthew's ongoing gospel narrative. I suggest that Matthew names Tamar in the first epoch of the opening genealogy because her story anticipates three important Matthean themes. The first involves a reversal of expectations; it is the theme of the faith of the Gentile outsider who responds more appropriately than the insider and in so doing finds inclusion among God's people. In Matthew's Gospel a number of Gentiles respond to Jesus appropriately with faith and worship, while Jewish insiders are often antagonistic towards him. This theme is introduced in the prologue with the story of the Magi (Matt 2:1–12) and is concluded with the report of the centurion's words at the cross (Matt 27:54). This will be explored in part 2 chapter 9. Secondly, her story is of a person who is both structurally and culturally marginalized; a person, who in spite of her recourse to trickery and posing as a prostitute, is ultimately honored by Judah as being in the right and by God with the birth of twin sons. Throughout Matthew's Gospel Jesus reaches out to and honors those on the margins by touching, healing, and socializing with them. This will also be explored in part 2 chapter 9. Finally, Tamar's story introduces the theme of the importance of women in the purposes of God, since she not only acquires status by bearing a son who Matthew demonstrates is an ancestor of the Messiah but her actions illustrate what it is to be righteous, a key discipleship virtue in Matthew's Gospel. Reference to Tamar's story is the first indication of a positive gynocentric counternarrative that runs throughout Matthew's Gospel, which will be considered in part 2 chapter 10. The theme of righteousness will be discussed here and in part 2 chapter 8.

This text, in an unforgettable way, defines righteousness in the context of relationships. To be righteous is to behave in a way that is appropriate to others, to fulfill the requirements and obligations of a particular relationship. Tamar's story shows that righteousness is not a virtue that an individual possesses in independence from others, nor is it primarily meeting the standards set by forensic norms. It is something one practices in one's relationship with others as a social being. This is in keeping with the broader Hebrew concept of righteousness in the Old Testament. In his classic work, *Theology of the Old Testament*, Eichrodt notes that צדק involves behavior that corresponds to the claims of a relationship and that the term is closely linked to the concept of justice. "The task of righteousness is to render this justice, and the claims which it implies, effective in the proper way, so that the good of all . . . may be safeguarded."[78] Tamar's action both rendered the justice due to her and her deceased husband and effected the good of Judah's clan. Ultimately, the Old Testament's understanding of righteousness is based on Israel's understanding of the righteous character of God. God's righteousness is fundamental to who he is within his being. God's righteousness is expressed in "behaviour proper to some relationship."[79] In the Genesis context, it is expressed within his gracious, covenantal relationship with Abraham and his offspring. In Genesis 38 God is seen to exercise his righteousness in dispensing judgement on both Er and Onan and by the final outcome for Tamar in her reintegration into Judah's clan and the blessing of twin sons. In this instance, God's righteousness is expressed in his execution of justice. God requires his righteousness to be reflected in the righteous behavior of his people. In the story of Genesis 38 a role reversal occurs. Judah, son of Jacob, does not behave in an appropriate manner to his wife, his deceased eldest son or his daughter-in-law, whereas Tamar, the outsider, brought into the family clan but then banished, acts righteously both in relation to her dead husband and ultimately to Judah himself in the bearing of two sons. Her story critiques Judah's actions, which sanctioned her oppression for the sake of a self-serving prudence and propriety.[80] Spina comments on the significance of Tamar's role in the wider purposes of God:

> This outsider, whose legal and social resources were very meager, does more for the future of God's people and therefore the whole world than does the insider Judah, who—theologically speaking—has had everything at his disposal.[81]

Significantly, Tamar is not the only character mentioned in the Matthew prologue who is righteous. A second character flags up the importance of this theme for the ongoing narrative. Joseph, husband of Mary is described as a righteous man. In fact, the first and only thing said of Joseph is that he is δίκαιος (Matt 1:19). Read as an intertext Tamar's story provides a hermeneutical key to this verse.

---

78. Eichrodt, *Theology of the Old Testament*, 241.
79. Ziesler, *Meaning of Righteousness*, 38.
80. Brueggemann, *Genesis*, 311.
81. Spina, *Faith of the Outsider*, 51.

In the context of the prologue, what does being a righteous man mean? France suggests Joseph is righteous because he "is careful to keep the law,"[82] which stated that an engagement must be terminated in a case of adultery:

> As a law-abiding man Joseph would be expected to repudiate his errant fiancée publicly in a trial for adultery... If "righteous" is understood in that sense, therefore, it stands in contrast with rather than as an explanation of his desire to spare her.[83]

Hence France's translation:

> Joseph her husband, because he was a righteous man and yet did not want to expose her to scandal, came to the conclusion that he should break the engagement privately.[84] (Matt 1:19).

On France's reading being a righteous man means strict adherence to the law. However, read in the light of Tamar's story a different meaning emerges.

Joseph's unwillingness to expose Mary is integral to what it means to behave in a righteous manner. On this reading the second clause of the sentence defines the first, "Her husband, Joseph, being a righteous man and unwilling to expose her to public disgrace, planned to divorce her quietly" (Matt 1:24). His righteousness is defined in terms of his relationship to Mary and his concern for her. As one obedient to the commands of the law Joseph decides to sidestep the letter of the law in order not to humiliate Mary. On the basis of a less strict *halakah* he decides to divorce her privately. Beare following this reading opines, "There is no suggestion that *although* he is a just man he is unwilling to stigmatize her; it is precisely by virtue of his righteous character that he shrinks from exposing her."[85] We have noted that Tamar's story demonstrates that righteousness is not to be defined solely in the context of a legal standard but in terms of what it means to live righteously in relationship to someone else towards whom there is an obligation. Consequently, both Joseph and Tamar are righteous individuals; they can consequently be regarded as a gender pair since they provide a double indicator in the prologue that righteousness will be an important theme in Matthew's Gospel.

---

82. France, *Gospel of Matthew*, 51.
83. Ibid.
84. Ibid., 46.
85. Beare, *Gospel according to Matthew*, 68.

Tamar, the practitioner of a risky righteousness, is named by Matthew as a foremother of Christ. Often the four Old Testament women are considered to be included because they foreshadow Mary. However, in keeping with the Messianic focus of the genealogy, I argue that by her inclusion in the genealogy Matthew invites the reader to see the themes in Tamar's story as anticipating the ministry of the Messiah, who is presented in Matthew as the one who teaches and embodies a new righteousness. Tamar points towards the Messiah, who will in his person fulfill all righteousness, and, in doing so, will radically redefine what it is to lead a righteous life. As the righteous Messiah he will bring justice to all those on the margins of society who are mistreated and disenfranchised, including a number of women. Ultimately, he will instruct his disciples to reach out to those outside the boundaries of Israel to include the Gentiles (Matt 28:19). What it means to live righteously is an important theme in Jesus' teaching, a theme that is addressed as a central concern by Jesus in Matthew's Gospel but is not mentioned in the other three Gospels. I will briefly summarize some of the main points that will be further explored in part 2 chapter 8.

Luz notes that the word "righteous" is one of Matthew's key words and "is highly significant in Matthew's Gospel . . . Five of seven instances of this word are found in the Sermon on the Mount, where it constitutes the most important key word apart from 'Father' in reference to God."[86] He goes on to note that these two key words indicate the subject matter of the Sermon on the Mount. If this is the case, the key word "righteous" might recall for the discerning reader the narrative of the first woman named in the genealogy, Tamar and her encounter with Judah, where a definition of "righteous" turns on the comparison between the outwardly apparent righteous behavior of Judah with that of Tamar.

In a crucial text in the Sermon on the Mount Jesus also makes a comparison between two different kinds of righteousness, contrasting the old righteousness of the teachers of the law with the new higher righteousness he calls for from his disciples, "For I tell you, unless your righteousness exceeds that of the scribes and Pharisees, you will never enter the kingdom of heaven" (Matt 5:20). Following the requirements of the law is clearly vital but Jesus indicates that this higher righteousness is something different from mere punctilious attention to the detail of the law.[87] Although the

---

86. Luz, *Theology of the Gospel of Matthew*, 2.
87. Nolland, *Gospel of Matthew*, 224.

religious leaders practice a form of justice/righteousness, it is inadequate.[88] Within this context, Jesus goes on to illustrate what higher righteousness looks like. In six antitheses (Matt 5:21–47) Jesus enumerates how his followers should live *in relation to others* upholding the Torah but redefining, for example, what it is to commit murder or adultery, or to take retaliation, since all must be interpreted in the light of the final antithesis, a love commandment with its relational focus (Matt 5:43–47).[89] The Matthean Jesus is extending a definition of a higher righteousness that is foreshadowed in Tamar's story and also in Joseph's treatment of Mary; righteousness is to be conceived of as right behavior in relation to another, rather than a strict adherence to a legal code with little regard for the individual. This is underlined in the final parable of the fifth and last eschatological discourse (Matt 25:31–46) when those on the king's right are called righteous (Matt 25:37) and are praised for their practical care for the "least of my brothers" in need. In summarizing the law, Jesus calls his disciples to love God first and foremost, flowing from which comes the command to "love your neighbor as yourself" (Matt 22:37–39).

Just as Tamar's action serves to critique Judah's self-serving, outward righteousness that sanctioned oppression for the sake of propriety, so the Matthean Messiah also offers a critique of the righteousness of the scribes and Pharisees, a righteousness that was outwardly impressive (Matt 23:5–7) but that oppressed others (Matt 23:4). He condemns the scribes and Pharisees for concentrating on the *minutiae* of the law but neglecting communal, relational matters of justice, mercy, and faith (Matt 23:23). In its focus on justice in human relationships as the outworking of righteousness, Jesus extends and elaborates the kind of righteousness Tamar's story points towards, the new, higher righteousness that Jesus calls for in the life of his disciples.

What is so notable in the text of Genesis 38 is that the model for righteous behavior is not provided by an upright Jewish patriarch, but a woman, originally an outsider to Judah's clan, who is further marginalized by his mistreatment of her. The significance of this for the ongoing narrative will be explored in part 2.

---

88. Carter, *Matthew and the Margins*, 142.

89. Nolland, *Gospel of Matthew*, 228. Nolland makes this comment on the first antithesis, the murder commandment, but it can be extended to the others.

4

Rahab

Preliminary Remarks

A scarlet thread ties the stories of Tamar and Rahab together, as does the fact that they are both Canaanite women who use trickery to outwit men and gain control of their situation to save their lives and the lives of others. Yet, the setting to Rahab's story is very different to Tamar's. Her story is embedded in the account of the conquest of Canaan by the tribes of Israel led by Joshua. The Joshua narrative seeks to define boundaries, not just in terms of who lives where in the promised land but in terms of who is "in" and who is "out" with regard to the people of God. The book of Joshua is set against the backdrop of the twelve tribes settling in the land and seeking nationhood; Israel has to define her identity.

The Book of Joshua: Defining Identity

Hawk demonstrates that "Joshua is a book about boundaries."[1] His analysis shows that the book of Joshua wrestles with the question of Israelite identity on a number of fronts raising three important questions.

Firstly, is nationhood as the people of God defined simply by "possession of the land" (Josh 1:6, 11)? Claims to land are universally associated with national identity and gaining the promised land is the overriding theme in the book of Joshua.

---

1. Hawk, *Joshua*, xi.

Rahab

Or is Israelite identity defined by behavior expressed in obedience to the laws of Moses? This law was given by God and reiterated by Joshua on the eve of entering the land (Josh 1:7–8). So is religious practice the defining factor to Israel's identity? Religious practice is clearly important. The twelve tribes' first act after crossing the Jordan and before they lay a finger on the inhabitants of the land is to undergo circumcision (Josh 5:2–9) and celebrate the Passover (Josh 5:10).

Or thirdly, is it ethnic separation from the surrounding nations that gives Israel her identity? Acting on the command of Moses, Joshua invokes the ban, חרם, requiring the extermination of everything living that is "Other"—man, woman, child, and animal. This ensures that Israel's "purity" as a nation is enforced. The ban is apparently total, "there was no one left who breathed" (Josh 11:11, 12).

However, the Deuteronomic ideal that pervades the book of Joshua, of Israel's unity bound by covenant to YHWH, with her life shaped by obedience to laws that circumscribe her individual and social life and demand the annihilation of the Canaanites, is challenged at the outset. Alongside epic stories of a nation living in faithful obedience to YHWH who gives amazing victories in battle are stories of a very different kind. These counter stories focus on the particularity of encounters with Rahab, Achan, and the Gibeonites, stories that challenge notions of Israel's unity and distinctiveness.

Hawk's analysis is very helpful is setting the scene to Rahab's story, which demonstrates that Israel's laws have to be lived out in the context of situations that demand redefinition. Polzin notes that in Rahab's story the narrator "chooses the law of the ban to exemplify what is involved when a law is to be interpreted."[2] Rahab's faith and actions demand a modification to the law of ban. Are all the Canaanites to be destroyed and excluded from the Israelite community? Conversely, are all Israelites to be included? Where are the boundary lines to be drawn? The book of Joshua grapples with all these issues.

I note that very early in the Joshua story, Rahab is the first to challenge Israel about how she understands who she is and where the boundaries should be drawn. In relation to Israel, Rahab is an outsider in every sense. She is a Canaanite, a woman, and a prostitute, yet in character Rahab is bold and assertive, both in her dealings with Canaanite royalty and with the Israelite foreign spies. Within a narrative section running from Joshua 2–12 Rahab's story falls into two sections—Joshua 2:1–24 and Joshua 6:22–25. I will first consider chapter 2.

2. Polzin, *Moses and the Deuteronomist*, 115.

Mothers on the Margin?

A Narrative Reading of Rahab's Story— Joshua 2:1–24

The Narrative Structure of Joshua 2:1–24

The narrative of Joshua chapter 2 forms a discrete unit with an introduction (v. 1), a main section (vv. 2–21), that can be broken down further into three parts, and a conclusion (vv. 22–24). The heading given to the Hebrew narrative by the NRSV entitles the chapter "Spies Sent to Jericho." It is the case that on one level this is a spy story about two men sent in to reconnoiter the land in preparation for the assault on Jericho. A breakdown of the narrative might be read in these terms:

INTRODUCTION

Joshua 2:1 | Joshua commissions the spies

MAIN SECTION

Joshua 2:2–7 | The king's delegation
Joshua 2:8–14 | The spies on the roof
Joshua 2:15–21 | The spies escape

CONCLUSION

Joshua 2:22–24 | The spies return to Joshua

Thus, the story can be read in androcentric terms as a spy story that revolves around the affairs of men without reference to Rahab. However, Nelson draws attention to the fact "the primary Rahab story was not really a spy narrative. It only operates inside the framework of one."[3] The spy story is quickly derailed by the difficulties the spies get into and how Rahab helps them. In the account Rahab is the only character who is named and it is she who precipitates the main action and who is the chief protagonist throughout. Seen as Rahab's story another outline emerges:

---

3. Nelson, *Joshua*, 42.

Introduction

Joshua 2:1 | The spies go to the house of Rahab

Main Section

Joshua 2:2–7 | Rahab hides the spies and sets a decoy
Joshua 2:8–14 | Rahab's speech
Joshua 2:15–21 | Rahab provides an escape

Conclusion

Joshua 2:22–24 | The spies return from the house of Rahab

A more balanced outline includes both elements. It is the skilful narrative interweaving of two themes within one plot, the spy story with Rahab's story, which provides drama and intrigue. This story works on a reversal of expectations in which Rahab is contrasted with the spies. Their roles become progressively reversed as the story develops to the point where Rahab's words, repeated verbatim by the spies, provide the incentive for Joshua and the people of Israel to move forward in crossing the Jordan. My narrative headings are inclusive of both themes.

Introduction

Joshua 2:1 | The mission

Main Section

Joshua 2:2–7 | The predicament
Joshua 2:8–14 | An act of faith
Joshua 2:15–21 | The escape

Conclusion

Joshua 2:22–24 | Mission accomplished?

Mothers on the Margin?

Rahab's Story

Joshua 2:1 | The mission

The story starts with Joshua secretly sending out "two spies from Shittim" to "look over the land, especially Jericho" (Josh 2:1). The Hebrew narrators frequently make use of allusion, taking for granted that their audience has a good working knowledge of Israel's own history. The place named Shittim makes intertextual connections with another story that immediately gives this one powerful overtones. It was at Shittim that Israelite men first "began to have sexual relations [prostitute themselves] with the women of Moab. These invited the people to the sacrifices to their gods" (Num 25:1, 2). The warning signs set up by the allusion to the place called Shittim are clear; women of the land are dangerous and lead to apostasy. To make matters worse, the two men disregard Joshua's simple and direct orders to go and view the land. Instead they go directly to Jericho and enter the "house of a woman, a prostitute (זונה) named Rahab (רחב)" (Josh 2:1). In contrast to Rahab, the two men are never named, the narrator throughout the story simply calling them "two men." Rahab's name, meaning wide/broad, hints at her profession and also links her to the broad land of Canaan. In her person she represents the "Other." Hawk comments, "Rahab is a synthesis of all that is most threatening to Israel, a point which the narrator underscores by the names given her: woman, prostitute, Rahab."[4] The reader is fully alerted to expect trouble; surely this woman will lead these two spies astray. Worse still, the spies not only enter her house they "spent the night there" or more literally they lay down (שכב) there (Josh 2:1). Within one introductory verse the narrator has introduced the reader to the setting, Rahab's house, the ostensible plot, a spy mission, and the main players of the narrative—the Israelite spies, who creatively interpret Joshua's command to "view the land," and Rahab, the Canaanite prostitute, of whom nothing of moral courage or insight is expected. As Bird comments, "The prostitute's low social status and low reputation are essential, and related, features [of the story]."[5] Thus the story opens by building on a reversal of expectations.

The undercurrent of sexual innuendo introduced in the first verse by the narrator's use of שכב to lie down, which has strong sexual

---

4. Hawk, *Every Promise Fulfilled*, 61.
5. Bird, "Harlot as Heroine," 130.

connotations, continues throughout the first four verses.⁶ The verb בּוֹא, to enter, is used seven times in rapid succession in verses 1–4 both by the narrator, "So they went and entered the house" (Josh 2:1b), and then by the king's messengers, "Bring out the men who have come to you" (lit. entered you) (Josh 2:3a). Used in conjunction with the even more strongly suggestive שׁכב the narrator, although never specific, gives strong hints of what went on. For what reason would two men on army duty (the LXX says they were young), separated from their families, specifically go to and spend the night at a prostitute's house?⁷ An immediate contrast is set up by the narrator between the unnamed Israelite spies who do the wrong thing and the named Canaanite prostitute, who, as the story unfolds, does the right thing. Confusing signals are being sent out by the narrator. Who is the reader to commend? According to Keil and Delitzsch, "But the Lord so guided the course of the spies, that they found in this sinner the very person who was the most suitable for their purpose."⁸ It stretches a point to legitimize their presence at Rahab's establishment by arguing that it was a result of divine intervention!

Commentators as far back as Josephus⁹ try to ease the situation by making Rahab an innkeeper and this has been picked up by modern commentators, for "where better to get information than a bar?"¹⁰ However, the Hebrew text is quite clear that Rahab is a prostitute (זוֹנה), not an innkeeper. Excuses for the spies have been made on other grounds, "A house like that could be expected to be frequented by men. This probably was the reason why the spies turned in there in order to escape detection."¹¹ Unfortunately for them this proves not to be the case.

---

6. בּוֹא can be used to refer to a man "coming to" a woman for sexual intercourse. Similarly שׁכב lit. to lie down (NRSV "spent the night," v. 2) is ambiguous. To lie with, שׁכב, is a common idiom for sexual intercourse.

7. Were the men assuming that sexual conquest of the land's women was the necessary prelude to the conquest of the land? Brueggemann makes the same connection when he comments, "We treat the land the way we treat women; 'we' being dominant males who are historically owners of both." Brueggemann, *Land*, 174. The text itself hints at this connection in vv. 2 and 3. In v. 2 the king is told the "men have come in here (i.e. Rahab's house) tonight, to explore the land" and in v. 3 the king orders "Bring out the men that have come to you, who came into your house, for they have come in to search out all the land."

8. Keil and Delitzsch, *Joshua, Judges, Ruth, 1 & 2 Samuel*, 34.

9. Josephus, *Antiquities*, 5.1.2.

10. Boling and Wright, *Joshua*, 145.

11. Woudstra, *Book of Joshua*, 69.

Joshua 2:2–7 | The Predicament

In the next verse (Josh 2:2) the king of Jericho is informed (by an unknown person) of the spies' identity, purpose, and whereabouts. The spies' cover has been exposed. The king immediately sends a message to Rahab, "Bring out the men who have come to you, who came into your house, for they have come only to search out all the land" (Josh 2:3). Will she hand over the spies and thereby jeopardize the Israelite mission to "take possession of the land" (Josh 1:11), or will she betray the king's confidence (he never sends men to search her premises)? Within three short verses the narrator has brought the implied reader to a point of dramatic tension centered on Rahab.

Typical of the discontinuity of the Joshua narrative the scene then abruptly shifts to the spies whom Rahab has hidden (Josh 2:4).[12] The sequence of events is unclear as to whether Rahab hides the men in response to the king's demand or has already done so.[13] This, I argue, is a purposeful ploy by the narrator to create further confusion and suspense. Had she known who they were, or was this revealed to her by the king's envoys as she claims? The reader, however, now knows what the king does not; the spies are hidden but, as yet, the reader does not know where. Rahab's response to the king (Josh 2:4, 5) is a clever mixture of truth and lies. She acknowledges the men came to her and lies "the men went out." It is also a ploy to gain time, "Pursue them quickly, for you can overtake them" (Josh 2:5b). Just as in Tamar's story, where the underdog, a female "prostitute," leaves men searching in vain, so here Rahab sends the king's men out of the city, at night, in hot pursuit of the spies. Surely the humor would not be lost on the narrator's audience, especially since readers are told in the next verse (Josh 2:6) that the spies are under their noses, hiding on the roof beneath a pile of flax. Verse 7 follows the pursuers in time all the way to the fords of Jordan.

The narrator finishes this section by pointedly telling readers "as soon as the pursuers had gone out the gate was shut" (Josh 2:7b). The pursuit of the men will not be resumed until verse 22. The episodic nature of Hebrew narrative, switching from one scene to another, as in the previous scene that switched between the king's messengers and the roof, works like a modern film and is used to heighten suspense. The spies are trapped with

---

12. Hawk comments that discontinuity is the "most distinctive feature of the book." Hawk, *Joshua*, xviii.

13. NIV "she had taken"; NRSV "but the woman took." The Hebrew ותקח can be translated either way.

Rahab

no way out, their fate dependent on a Canaanite prostitute. Readers are left with a second point of dramatic tension that again centers on Rahab; will she continue to help them and, if so, how will she get them out of the city now the gate is firmly shut?

Joshua 2:8–14 | An act of faith

Rahab controls the situation. She has risked her life by deceiving the king of Jericho in order to save their lives. She is now in a position to bargain with the spies who are at her mercy. In contrast to her initiative, the spies are passive; they have been sent by Joshua (Josh 2:1), taken and hidden by Rahab (Josh 2:4) and, whereas the king's men are in energetic pursuit, they are now about to go to sleep (Josh 2: 8)! The two phrases in verse 8 introduced by independent pronouns also emphasize the passivity of the spies compared to Rahab's actions, "Before *they* went to sleep, *she* came up to them on the roof" (my italics). Rahab has no intention of letting the men sleep. Butler, enjoying the ironic humor of the narrative, writes, "When the lady of the house finally has time to come to the men in their beds, her bedtime story for them is just what is expected in such an establishment: a confession of religious faith, an act of religious conversion."[14] On a more serious note, what is to be made of Rahab's extended speech (Josh 2:9–13)? She starts with the declaration "I know that the Lord has given you the land" (Josh 2:9). In doing this she expresses what is a recurring theological theme in the book of Joshua; the Israelites will not conquer through their own prowess for the land has been given by YHWH. Two elements of her speech (she speaks of the "dread of you" and "melting hearts") are both features of Israel's holy war ideology and they echo words from the Song of Moses and Miriam, "All the inhabitants of Canaan melted away. Terror and dread fell upon them" (Exod 15:15c–16a). She knows the songs that Israel sang. The fear of "all the inhabitants of the land" she attributes not to the presence of the Israelites but to knowledge of YHWH's act of exodus liberation in drying up the waters of the Red (Reed) Sea. She knows too of the utter destruction wreaked on the kings of Sihon and Og. She is the first in the book of Joshua to vocalize the concept of חרם, the command to devote everything to God by destroying it.[15] In consequence, Rahab

---

14. Butler, *Joshua*, 31.

15. The Hebrew term חרם is notoriously difficult to render in English. The verb is associated with destruction and the noun is used to refer to that which is to be destroyed. "Devote to destruction" is not accurate in all contexts but is the closest

tells the spies, "our hearts failed and there was no courage left in any of us" (Josh 2:11a). Finally, in total contrast to what the reader might expect of a Canaanite prostitute, in the words that parallel Deuteronomy 4:39, Rahab makes a confession of faith in YHWH, "The Lord your God is indeed God in heaven above and on earth below" (Josh 2:11b). Readers might have expected these words from faithful Israelites preparing themselves for the campaign ahead, but from a woman, a prostitute, Rahab? Spina observes that the later Masorete scribes noted in the margins that only Moses (Deut 4:39) and Solomon (1 Kgs 8:23) make the same confession that YHWH is God on the earth below.[16] For the second time confusing signals are being sent out for her confession identifies her with Israel, yet she is a Canaanite under the sentence of death.

Having prepared the ground, Rahab gets to the point and moves from a declaration to a demand, "Now then, since I have dealt loyally (חסד) with you, swear to me by the Lord that you in turn will deal loyally (חסד) with my father's house" (Josh 2:12).[17] Her loyalty towards them in defiance of orders from the king requires a response in kind from them.

Working on the recognition of the importance of the code of hospitality in ancient Israel, Glueck argues that it is as a host to her guests that Rahab shows faithfulness to the spies. He comments, "Rahab showed *ḥesed* and was true to the code governing the relationship between host and guest."[18] However, while duties of hospitality were clearly important, the text implies that the main reason for Rahab's action lies elsewhere. With Sakenfeld, I argue that her loyalty to the spies is primarily consequent on her decision to side with Israel based on her belief, so eloquently expressed to the spies, that YHWH is God.[19]

Glueck goes on to note that חסד can only be practiced between persons who share an ethically binding relationship. By asking the spies to

---

equivalent to the meaning in these texts. See Lilley, "Understanding the Herem," 169–77.

16. Spina, *Faith of the Outsider*, 60.

17. חסד is an important Hebrew word rich with meaning. It is a covenant word. It describes both the steadfast love and mercy God shows towards Israel and also the kindness and loyalty that are called for between humans in their relations towards one another. Notably it describes both an attitude and an action. Because the Hebrew term encompasses a breadth of meaning it is notoriously difficult to translate. Following Sakenfeld, I have chosen to translate it using the English word "loyally" (the NRSV uses "kindly") but recognize this does not fully encompass its meaning. Sakenfeld, *Faithfulness in Action*, 2–3.

18. Glueck, *Hesed in the Bible*, 44.

19. Sakenfeld, *Faithfulness in Action*, 22.

respond to her loyalty with loyalty Rahab is invoking this relationship. She asks that their loyalty be expressed by the deliverance of her family and herself, "deliver our lives from death" (Josh 2:13). Furthermore, she asks them to take an oath and swear by the Lord that they will carry through on their promise and that finally they will give her "a sign of good faith" (Josh 2:12).

The spies wake up to the seriousness of their situation; they are trapped, totally dependent on the loyalty of a foreign prostitute for their lives. With their lives under threat they show no hesitation in breaking the solemn oath that had been given to Joshua to obey him as "we obeyed Moses in all things" (Josh 1:17). They do the unthinkable by entering into what Campbell has suggested is a covenant with Rahab.[20] In the light of the Deuteronomic prohibitions which Joshua reiterates in the first chapter it is all the more surprising that the spies enter so readily into a binding agreement with Rahab that transgresses these laws. Gunn comments, "it is an illegal covenant according to the rules governing the war of occupation, the law of YHWH, the law just mediated by the voice of Moses the servant of God in Deuteronomy, the law that lies at the heart of God's ... exhortation to Joshua at the beginning of his book."[21] It seems that their personal survival is paramount, "Our life for yours!" (Josh 2:14a). Hawk comments, "In contrast to Rahab, there are no words of praise for YHWH on their lips and no acknowledgement of the majestic rule of YHWH. The only words they speak are those necessary to save their lives."[22] However, the spies understand their obligation to reciprocate חסד with חסד. Rahab has saved their lives (and still holds their lives in the balance), so they will save hers. They put one condition on their promise, which perhaps they assume, or hope, that Rahab will not keep, "If you do not tell this business of ours we will deal kindly and faithfully with you," ending limply with "when the Lord gives us the land" (Josh 2:14). The note of conditionality in their remark is in marked contrast both to God's promise that He has given the land (Josh 1:3) and Rahab's initial assertion that "I know the Lord has given you the land" (Josh 2:9). Mention of the land provides the *inclusio* to this extended dialogue.

---

20. See Campbell, "Rahab's Covenant," 243–44.
21. Gunn, "Joshua and Judges," 108.
22. Hawk, *Joshua*, 46.

Joshua 2:15–21 | The Escape

The narrator now gives readers a significant piece of information that is emphasized by its repetition, "her house was on the outer side of the city wall and she resided within the wall itself" (Josh 2:15). Rahab (it is *her* house) actually lives on the boundary line that separates the city from those outside. Until this point the narrator has led readers to believe that this is a closed boundary "for the gate was shut" (Josh 2:7b). Rahab's plan for the men's escape belies this. Just as her faith, wit, and words have led the spies into an agreement that means the boundary between those "inside" Israel and those "outside" is now breached, her actions demonstrate that the boundary of the city wall is porous too, "Then she let them down by a rope through the window" (Josh 2:15).

Her imperatives continue (presumably in hissed whispers) as she issues instructions to the men dangling on the rope, "Go towards the hill country . . . Hide yourselves there for three days, until the pursuers have returned" (Josh 2:16). Several commentators seem puzzled by the story;[23] the conversation "appears to happen at a rather inconvenient time and place."[24] Consequently, Woudstra suggests there is no need to read the story chronologically. Similarly Soggin wants to put verses 17–21 before 15 to avoid "a curious dialogue between the two men who have been lowered from the wall and the woman who remains above."[25] What a lack of imagination and an inability to recognize the wonderfully comic situation set up by the narrator! It is also an arresting visual picture of the power of Rahab in contrast to the helplessness of the men hanging on the end of a rope.

As they get closer to the ground and freedom is within reach, the spies regain a sense of confidence and attempt to add a further number of qualifications to the pact that if not kept would release them from their oath. At the beginning and end of their speech they repeat that is it an oath "that you have made us swear to you" (Josh 2:17, 20). "We are innocent" (נקי) is repeated three times (Josh 2:17, 19, 20) as they seek to lay all responsibility at Rahab's feet (Josh 2:18–20a). They try to weaken the force of the pact by attaching more conditions that might not be fulfilled. Rahab is to tie a crimson cord in the window and gather her family into her house, where they must all stay indoors. Finally, they repeat she must maintain

---

23. E.g., Butler, *Joshua*; Woudstra, *Book of Joshua*; Soggin, *Joshua*.
24. Woudstra, *Book of Joshua*, 16.
25. Soggin, *Joshua*, 42.

her loyalty and not divulge a word to anyone. Rahab readily agrees to this as the men reach the ground. *Their* final action is one of obedience to Rahab, "She sent them away and they departed" (Josh 2:21b). *Her* final action seals the pact, ensuring the protection she and her family will receive if the spies remain faithful to their promise, "Then she tied the crimson cord in the window" (Josh 2:21b).

Joshua 2:22–24 | Mission Accomplished?

The spies heed Rahab's instructions and the narrator follows them as they hide in the hill country for three days, after which they descend, cross over the Jordan and return to Joshua and tell him "all that had happened to them" (Josh 2:23b). *All*, readers wonder? Certainly they pass on one piece of vital information, "Truly the Lord has given all the land into our hands; moreover, all the inhabitants of the land melt in fear before us" (Josh 2:24). Polzin comments, "The authority of these words derives, strangely enough, from their having been uttered not by God, nor by Joshua, but by a non-Israelite and a prostitute at that."[26] Thus, the scene ends with a verbatim report of her words.[27]

The outcome of their spying mission contrasts notably with a previous spying mission to Canaan (Num 13:1) that brought reports that destroyed morale and led the people at the point of entry to the "promised land" to reject the command to go and occupy the land. Deuteronomy, in recalling the event, makes the point forcibly that it was the people's rebellion and lack of faith in YHWH at this juncture that led to forty years of wilderness wanderings. "When the Lord heard your words, he was wrathful and swore: 'Not one of these—not one of this evil generation—shall see the good land that I swore to give to your ancestors'" (Deut 1:34–35). The cause of Israel's faithlessness? The report given by the majority of the spies, "Our kindred made our hearts fail by reporting, 'The people are stronger and taller than we are; the cities are large and fortified up to heaven!'" (Deut 1:28). Israel lost their courage to move forward trusting in YHWH's promise because of the spies' negative, demoralizing report. The reader may wonder what kind of report the spies might have brought back this time had it not been for the faith of a Canaanite prostitute?

What knowledge do the spies return with from their mission? The spies have no information about the lay of the land or of how to breach the

---

26. Polzin, *Moses and the Deuteronomist*, 91.
27. Cf. Josh 2:9.

walls of Jericho; in that sense Rahab has divulged no insider knowledge helpful for a military operation. However, what Rahab has done is confirm to them that YHWH is with his people and will fulfill his promise of the gift of land to them. Her words act as a prophetic oracle of encouragement to trust in YHWH. Her words voice YHWH's words to Israel that will be reiterated later by YHWH to Joshua, "See I have handed Jericho over to you" (Josh 6:2). Rahab's belief that YHWH has given the land into their hands provides Joshua and his people with the courage they need to move forward and cross the Jordan, depicted as a second crossing of the Red Sea (Josh 4:23–24).[28] Ironically, although Rahab is an outsider in every sense, a woman, a prostitute, and a Canaanite, it is her action of חסד towards the spies and her faith in YHWH that enables Israel to take the first steps towards possessing the land. This has implications for Israel's understanding of her nationhood. Joshua 6 demonstrates that Rahab's action forces Israel to reassess their identity at the very point of entry into the promised land.

A Narrative Reading of Rahab's Story—Joshua 6:15–25

Rahab's story is put on hold by the narrator for three chapters as he describes the Israelites' crossing of the Jordan, circumcision, celebration of the Passover, and instructions from "the Lord" about how to capture Jericho. Readers are held in suspense: will Rahab and her family be destroyed or delivered? Will the spies remain true to their word to her, thus compromising the totality of the "things devoted to destruction" (Josh 6:18)? Joshua 6 resumes the story of Jericho with the words "Now Jericho was shut up inside and out" (Josh 6:1), reminding the reader of Rahab's family shut up inside her house. Verses 2–14 describe the instructions for ritual procession around Jericho over six days and Joshua's, the priests', and the warriors' compliance. Rahab's story reaches its resolution in the second half of the chapter.

The Narrative Structure of Joshua 6:15–25

This section divides into two parts. Verses 15–21 focus on the destruction of Jericho but include Joshua's instruction to deliver Rahab. Verses 22–25 describe the deliverance of Rahab but include a reference to the

28. Brueggemann, *Old Testament Theology*, 202.

destruction of Jericho. The structure of the whole is chiastic; a pattern is introduced and then reversed.

Joshua 6:15–21

Joshua 6:15, 16		A destruction of the city
Joshua 6:17		B deliverance of Rahab
Joshua 6:18, 19, 21		A destruction of the city

Joshua 6:22–25

Joshua 6:22, 23		B' deliverance of Rahab
Joshua 6:24		A' destruction of the city
Joshua 6:25		B' deliverance of Rahab

Joshua 6:15–21 | The taking of Jericho

One of the most dramatic scenes in the book of Joshua starts with the report that Joshua and the people make seven circuits around the wall on the seventh day. Resolution of Rahab's story comes at the point of climax on the seventh round. At the moment when the priests blow the trumpets and Joshua commands the army of Israelites, "Shout! For the Lord has given you the city" (Josh 6:16), the narrator inserts a speech from Joshua to the army poised for action. Joshua invokes the law of חרם first mentioned by Rahab to the spies (Josh 2:10c), when he commands, "The city and all that is in it shall be devoted to the Lord for destruction" (Josh 6:17a). All living things and the contents of the city are חרם. The inhabitants of Jericho are "Other"; they are dangerous, different and sinful, toxic to Israel's purity.[29] By reinforcing the Deuteronomic ban, Joshua clearly marks the boundary lines between Israel and all that lives in the city of Jericho.

Apparently, Rahab's fate is sealed. Yet, immediately after, come the words "Only Rahab the prostitute and all who are with her in her house shall live, because she hid the messengers we sent" (Josh 6:17b). Joshua allows for an act of mercy because of Rahab's action. An exception is made that compromises what seems to be an inviolable boundary, a boundary reinforced by his next words, "As for you, keep away from the things devoted

---

29. Cf. Deut 7:4.

to destruction" (Josh 6:18a). The word חרם is repeated in different forms four times in this one verse serving to emphasize the contrast between Rahab's deliverance and the things that have been devoted to destruction. However, even more telling is the contrast between the sparing of Rahab and all who were with her in the terse description of the fall of the city and its destruction (Josh 6:21). Within an *inclusio* of destruction "chains of living beings"[30] are listed; men, women, young, old, oxen, sheep, and donkeys. The verse opens with the words "Then they utterly destroyed" and closes with "with the edge of the sword." As Niditch comments, the "very language forbids the emotions of mercy,"[31] yet mercy is about to be shown.

Joshua 6:22–25 | The taking of Rahab

The public scene of carnage (Josh 6:21) is followed by a scene change that zooms in to a confidential conversation between Joshua and the spies. The ambivalence of his decision to spare Rahab and her family, which, of course, is an infringement of the command just given to "utterly destroy," is implied by his use of words to the spies in private (Josh 6:22). No longer Rahab, she is "the prostitute," "the woman" (Josh 6:22), and the reason for the deliverance of "the woman" and "all who belong to her" is the spies' obligation to an oath they "swore to her" (Josh 6:22). What Joshua describes to Israel as an act of mercy, of חסד, is also privately an act of duty, fulfilling the promise the spies made to her one night on the rooftop of her house, "Our life for yours" (Josh 2:14a).

This time the spies follow Joshua's command correctly:

> So the young men who had been spies went in and brought out Rahab and her father, and her mother, and her brothers, and all who belonged to her and all her kindred, they brought out and set them outside the camp of Israel. (Josh 6:23)

Here another chain of living beings are listed—Rahab, her father, her mother, her brothers, all who belonged to her—all her kindred within an *inclusio* of salvation. The narrator emphasizes that the entirety of Rahab's family is saved by repetition of "all" (כל), both in this verse 23 and in verse 25. But Israel now burns down "all" in the city (Josh 6:24).

The deliverance of Rahab and her family is thus contrasted twice with the annihilation of Jericho. Initially, Joshua's command for her deliverance

---

30. Niditch, *War in the Hebrew Bible*, 28.
31. Ibid., 28.

was embedded in an account of the actions and instructions to destroy the city (Josh 6:15–21). This second time in a reversal, the story of her deliverance is repeated either side of an account of the burning of the city (Josh 6:22–25). "But Rahab the prostitute, with her family and all who belonged to her, Joshua spared" (Josh 6:25). The narrative switch from the destruction of Jericho to the deliverance of Rahab and her family makes the point that her case is an exception to what otherwise is an inviolable rule of total destruction. Even as the "law" of חרם is carried out an exception is being made; an exception won by the courage, wit, loyalty, and faith of a Canaanite prostitute.

The story finishes with an etiological note explaining the presence of a group of Canaanites in Israel. Although "set outside the camp of Israel" (Josh 6:24), presumably because of their ceremonial uncleanness, the narrator concludes with the comment that "She has lived in Israel ever since" (Josh 6:25b).[32] The reason given is that she practiced loyalty (חסד) towards the two young men, "For she hid the messengers whom Joshua sent to spy out Jericho" (Josh 6:25). The narrator strongly implies Rahab's family maintained their identity over the years and although they found a place inside Israel's borders, their position was ambiguous, not outsiders, yet not fully insiders. They were aliens in Israel's midst but nonetheless not excluded from the covenant promises of YHWH. At the crucial moment of the reading of the Law of Moses the narrator notes that, as Joshua renews the covenant, "All Israel, alien as well as citizen were present" (Josh 8:33). In case the point is missed it is reiterated at the end of the passage:

> There was not a word of all that Moses commanded that Joshua did not read before all the assembly of Israel, and the women, and the little ones, and the aliens who resided among them. (Josh 8:35)

The reader knows from chapter 6 that Rahab and her family form part of that alien group and that there is a certain irony in these words. The law of Moses as spelt out in the Deuteronomic text, explicitly forbade that any of the Canaanites should be spared (Deut 20:17–18), yet Rahab, in aligning herself with the Lord of heaven and earth, has secured an exception that grants her a place in Israel's covenantal life.

---

32. NRSV has "her family" but the personal pronoun "she" is stressed in the Hebrew text.

The Contrast with Achan

Achan's story follows on immediately from Rahab's reprieve in chapter 6. In contrast to Rahab, Achan is portrayed as the quintessential Israelite from the pre-eminent tribe of Judah, "Achan, son of Carmi, son of Zabdi, son of Zerah of the tribe of Judah" (Josh 7:1); he is the ultimate insider. Yet, he, as representative of Israel, "broke faith in regard to the devoted things (בחרם)" (Josh 7:1). The narrative places these two stories, which have no explicit connection, side by side in order to make a point. Achan is the mirror image to Rahab, the ultimate outsider. Whereas Rahab secures an exception to the law of חרם for herself and her family, Achan and his family fall under the law of חרם. Achan is seduced by some of the beautiful, valuable things that Joshua declares are חרם, devoted to YHWH. Achan is stoned and burnt along with everything living that is his, "his sons, his daughters, his oxen, donkeys and sheep" (Josh 7:25), as well as all his possessions, including the devoted things. Goldingay notes that "once things are set apart for devoting to YHWH, they become defiling."[33] Achan defiles not just himself and his family but his actions also defile Israel in a way that leads to their defeat in their attempt to take Ai (Josh 7:5). Achan typifies the person who succumbs to the possessive allure of Canaan that Moses warned of in Deuteronomy.[34] The consequence of his decision is death for himself and his family.

The status of Achan and Rahab with regard to Israel is defined not by their ethnicity but by a decision. The two form a narrative gender pair that serves to illustrate that Israel's boundaries are not fixed and that ethnicity does not guarantee a place on the inside. Campbell notes that "Rahab made a *moral* decision to leave the *lo-ammi* and join the *ammi*."[35] Conversely, Achan made an *immoral* decision to disregard the divine command. The text subverts itself and the strict boundaries surrounding Israel delineated by command are redefined by individual choice, both the confessing faith of Rahab (the archetypal outsider) and the violating faith of Achan (the archetypal insider).[36] Hawk rightly observes, "Loyalty to YHWH brings success, identity, and coherence; disloyalty brings failure,

---

33. Goldingay, *Old Testament Theology*, 496.

34. "Do not covet the silver and gold on them, and do not take it for yourselves, or you will be ensnared by it, for it is detestable to the LORD your God. Do not bring a detestable thing into your house or you, like it, will be set apart for destruction. Utterly abhor and detest it, for it is set apart for destruction" (Deut 7:25b–26).

35. Campbell, "Rahab's Covenant," 244.

36. See Spina, *Faith of the Outsider*, 71.

Rahab

disaster, and disintegration."³⁷ Theologically, the point being made is that decision in regard to one's relationship to YHWH is the crucial factor in Israel's identity.

Rahab chooses the Lord and life, "The Lord your God is indeed God in heaven above and on earth below" (Josh 2:11b). For her, there are no boundaries that make belief in YHWH off limits; the whole of the earth is under his sovereign power. She has chosen whom she will serve (Josh 24:15). Rahab's loyalty to YHWH, expressed in her loyalty to the spies, brings her life and gives her an identity and place within the people of God. Her action of חסד consequent on her decision, challenges Israel's boundaries as does the action taken by Achan. Earl argues that not only Rahab and Achan but also the Gibeonites and the aggressive kings are symbolic characters "who embody and exemplify different sorts of responsiveness to YHWH that relates to *structural* level concerns of Israelite identity and relationships with non-Israelites."³⁸ He goes on to opine that the book of Joshua "challenges accepted views of what it is that constitutes Israelite identity . . . Joshua thus demonstrates an openness to the 'outsider' whilst encouraging a searching exploration of the attitudes of those considered to be part of the community."³⁹ I will go on to suggest that a similar rhetoric is at work in Matthew's Gospel and that this is first indicated by the inclusion in the genealogy of three "outsiders" who find a place on the inside in Israel.

חרם and חסד

It is interesting to note that Rahab is the first character in the book of Joshua to give expression to two opposing concepts that underlie Israel's ideology as they enter the land. This ideology is spelt out in Deuteronomy, a perspective that forms the backdrop to the book of Joshua. As Hawk comments, "Deuteronomy constitutes a sort of narrative lens through which the reader may understand the story Joshua tells."⁴⁰ According to the "law" of חרם, possession of the land of Canaan involves not only the taking of the land from its inhabitants but also their total destruction:⁴¹

37. Hawk, *Joshua*, xxi.
38. Earl, *Reading Joshua*, 167.
39. Ibid., 202.
40. Hawk, *Joshua*, xxiv.
41. There is a large amount of scholarly discussion on "the ban" forming part of Israel's war ideology. See Niditch, *War in the Hebrew Bible*, 28–77, and Earl, *Reading Joshua*, 94–112.

> When the Lord your God brings you into the land that you are about to enter and occupy, and he clears away many nations before you—the Hittites, the Girgashites, the Amorites, the Canaanites, the Perizzites, the Hivites, and the Jebusites, seven nations, mightier and more numerous than you—and when the Lord your God gives them over to you and you defeat them, then you must utterly destroy (החרם תחרם) them. Make no covenant with them and show them no mercy. (Deut 7:1-2)

The passage is the first one in the Old Testament to apply the ban to the Canaanites, although Exodus 23:20-33 has expressed the same thought, "They shall not live in your land" (Exod 23:33). The passage spells out the chilling implications for peoples under the ban, devoted to destruction (חרם). Total annihilation is called for; no covenant, no mercy, no intermarriage. The peoples of the land represent the greatest threat to the nation as Israel enters the land. Deuteronomy repeatedly warns that the indigenous peoples threaten Israel's call to uncompromising loyalty to YHWH. Any concession to their ways will cause Israel to turn aside to other gods and contaminate the purity of Israel's devotion to YHWH.

The ban is repeated under instructions for the rules of warfare:

> But as for the towns of these peoples that the Lord you God is giving you as an inheritance, you must not let anything that breathes remain alive. You shall utterly destroy (החרם תחרם) them—the Hittites and the Amorites, the Canaanites and the Perizzites, the Hivites and the Jebusites—just as the Lord your God has commanded, so that they may not teach you to do all the abhorrent things that they do for their gods, and you thus sin against the Lord your God. (Deut 20:16-18)

The peoples of the land threaten to defile and must be destroyed. Anything rendered חרם, therefore, is to be devoted to YHWH, completely off limits as far as the Israelites are concerned. Israel is to be radically separated from the surrounding nations and חרם lays down the boundary lines that are not to be crossed.

Rahab is aware of this ideology; she recalls the utter destruction of the kingdoms of Sihon and Og, paradigmatic events recounted at the beginning of Deuteronomy (Deut 2:26-36; 3:1-7), and she describes the consequent terror of the peoples of Canaan. However, Rahab is determined that, although she is a Canaanite and a prostitute, she will not accept her fate. She takes the decision to protect the spies and confess her faith in YHWH. In spite of the "law" of חרם under which she is condemned to be annihilated, she will plead for mercy, חסד, as a matter of justice, for she has shown mercy. The word חסד is descriptive of what is central to the character of YHWH; his loving kindness or steadfast love that characterizes YHWH's dealings with Israel (Exod 34:6–7). The passage that follows the absolutist condemnation in Deuteronomy 7 is a reminder of this foundational characteristic of YHWH, "Know therefore that the Lord your God is God, the faithful God who maintains covenant loyalty (חסד) with those who love him and keep his commandments" (Deut 7:9). Intuitively, Rahab has understood that YHWH's mercy overwhelms his judgement. Rahab has placed her faith in YHWH and demonstrated it in her חסד towards the Israelite spies. Earl notes that "the way she deals with the spies is interpreted using the fundamental covenant characteristic of חסד, and she appeals to the חסד that she has shown as the basis for her hope."[42] She asks that YHWH's representatives show her the faithfulness and mercy of YHWH. She asks that she and her family will be delivered from death. She depends on YHWH's gratuitous mercy that saves from disaster and destruction,[43] a divine חסד that sustains life.[44] God is merciful. Such divine חסד counteracts God's wrath, limiting its expression. Baer and Gordon comment, "Wrath is a true word, a right word, sometimes an inevitable word . . . But God would not have it his last word. That honor is reserved for his unfailing love (ḥesed)."[45] In appealing to YHWH's covenantal kindness, to his mercy, Rahab realizes a truth that is at the heart of Old Testament theology; that there is a tension between divine judgement and mercy and that divine mercy outweighs judgement. God, it seems, will allow the "law" of חרם to be compromised that his merciful חסד might be demonstrated to one who has shown חסד and thrown herself on his loving kindness.[46]

---

42. Earl, *Reading Joshua*, 126.

43. A mercy to which many Psalms bear witness: Ps 31:7–8, 21–22; 32:10; 57:3–4; 59:10–11; 94:18; 143:12.

44. Cf. Ps 119:88, 149, 159.

45. Baer and Gordon, "2874 חסד," 214.

46. Earl's suggestion that "the story of Rahab may reflect a demanding test case of the interpretation of Deut 7" is in line with my reading of Rahab's story. Earl, *Reading Joshua*, 127.

Feminist Perspectives

A number of scholars have argued that in different ways Rahab's story supports ideological concerns. Rahab thus functions as a mouthpiece for those concerns.

In an article entitled "Inclusion, Exclusion and Marginality in the Book of Joshua" Rowlett has made the observation noted above that Rahab functions "as an obverse image of Achan."[47] She notes that the two stories come back to back in chapters 6 and 7 and that they "illustrate the process of negotiations and exchanges by which insiders may become outsiders and outsiders may become insiders."[48] However, Rowlett's important observation is mitigated by her argument that the stories show "the standard of demarcation turns out to be voluntary submission to the authority structure represented by Joshua and his military men."[49] This supports her contention that the book of Joshua took shape during the reign of Josiah in an attempt to consolidate his kingdom. The book functions "as an encouragement and a threat to its own population to submit voluntarily to the central authority of a government struggling to organize itself."[50] Thus, Rahab becomes an example of obedient submission to authority. Rowlett states, "The men under Yahweh's military command receive homage from Rahab precisely because of their ability to destroy others (like Sihon and Og) in battle."[51]

According to Rowlett's reading of the passage, Rahab's faith in YHWH himself is dissolved into submission to authority structures. However, Rahab certainly never gives homage to the two spies. Her initiative in hiding the spies, borne out of her faith in YHWH, and her control of the situation thereafter are glossed over by Rowlett. She is simply the "Other" who becomes an insider because she accepts structures of control.

Another reading of Rahab comes from a postcolonial feminist scholar Dube.[52] Dube argues that Rahab's story is typical of colonizing literature. She argues Rahab's story follows the model of colonizing literature whereby the colonizer first conquers the women of the land before

---

47. Rowlett, "Inclusion, Exclusion," 21.
48. Ibid., 22.
49. Ibid., 17.
50. Ibid., 23.
51. Ibid., 19–20.
52. Only a very brief consideration of the postcolonial feminist perspective is given here. For a discussion, see Scholz, *Introducing the Women's Hebrew Bible*, 100–121.

Rahab

taking the land itself. Colonizing ideology presents "the targeted groups as womenlike people who require and beseech domination."[53] Once the woman "is met, her affections won, then the land she represents will also be entered and domesticated by the colonizer, or it is at least available for the taking of the colonizer, if so desired."[54] According to Dube Joshua 2 fits this model and therefore Rahab represents the colonized woman who requires and beseeches domination. The spies colonize and conquer Rahab and are then able to enter the land.

However, I argue that contrary to Dube's assertion, Rahab's speech to the spies does not tame her in this way. Her recognition of YHWH's power to take the land does not amount to a desire for domination, but a confession of faith and a pragmatic recognition of the reality of the situation she faces. Theologically speaking she voices the Old Testament belief that land is not owned by any one people's group by rights but is "owned" by YHWH. It is his to give (Josh 2:9) rather than something to be taken. Nor do the spies conquer her, far less win her affections. It is Rahab who dictates the course of events to the invading spies, they are held in her power until she chooses to free them by letting them down the city wall.

Rather than typifying colonizing literature it could be argued that the story of Rahab in Joshua 2 contradicts what might be expected of colonizing literature as defined by postcolonial criticism. In a summary of Said's views, Barry notes that Said argues the "Other" is represented as an anonymous mass of people rather than as individuals making conscious choices.[55] However, Rahab is not just part of an anonymous mass of Canaanites. She clearly is an individual Canaanite with a narratable life history, who has made a conscious choice to align herself with Israel. The text implies this choice has been made before the spies enter the scene. Said also argues that the "Other" seduces and corrupts. The reader might expect her to fulfill the role of the seductive, immoral prostitute assumed of the "Other," yet instead she defines what it is to have faith in YHWH. Rather than corrupting Israel, Rahab's "Otherness" is not condemned. It is as the "Other" that she becomes a source of energy, her faith and actions empowering and enabling for Joshua and the Israelites.

Also working from a postcolonial feminist perspective, McKinlay argues that the "conquest narratives, therefore, may very well be the quite deliberate ideological discourses that put the stamp of distinctive Israelite

53. Dube, *Postcolonial Feminist Interpretation*, 144.
54. Ibid., 76.
55. Barry, *Beginning Theory*, 192–93.

identity upon those who would differentiate themselves from others."[56] Read in this light Rahab becomes an ideological tool in the hand of the Deuteronomist Historian.[57] McKinlay's suspicions are confirmed when Rahab voices Deuteronomistic theology and language, "It seems that once again Israel has taken what was once a folk tale and reshaped it as a tool of its own political ideology."[58] McKinlay argues that the story teller uses an unlikely candidate, a Canaanite prostitute, to reinforce colonizing Israelite ideology. Rahab serves Israel's cause and represents and espouses conformity to those peoples who would differentiate themselves from Israel. Consequently, Rahab "is an Israelite construct and constructed as a pawn of the text."[59]

Apart from serious questions over McKinlay's dating of the text and its composition, I have argued that in defying the ban and demanding loyalty for loyalty, Rahab does not simply voice Deuteronomistic ideology but challenges it. As a Canaanite woman from Jericho devoted to destruction, she pleads for and obtains mercy from Israel's God. Rahab's faith in YHWH to save and her actions of חסד subvert the ban and the boundaries defining Israel. She is neither a tool nor a pawn used for Israel's ideological purposes as justification for the dispossession of her people's land. Although she can be read this way (a reflection of the appalling way the book of Joshua has been used in the past to justify colonial expansion, which Dube and McKinlay understandably and rightly deplore), this does not do justice to the way the text presents her. Neither is Rahab's ethnic identity subsumed by her incorporation into Israel. She and her family retain their identity (Josh 6:25), living under the covenant blessings of YHWH, but outside the camp of Israel (Josh 6:23) as resident aliens (Josh 8:35). In contradiction to Dube and McKinlay's readings I argue that this text portrays Rahab in a positive light. Rahab is a woman who is not compliant but subversive.

Like Tamar's text, this text has a gynocentric bias. To summarize: Rahab is a woman whose marginality within her own society as a prostitute gives her independence denied other women; she owns her own house and is apparently responsible for her father's house too. Her independent status is reflected in her forthrightness in her dealings with the spies and

56. McKinlay, *Reframing Her*, 47.

57. This approach assumes the existence of a Deuteronomist Historian, who compiled existing materials to which were added supplements that supported Deuteronomistic ideology.

58. McKinlay, *Reframing Her*, 44.

59. Ibid., 47.

her determination to secure a place in the land for herself and her family. She is not intimidated by the king's orders to bring the men out but is willing to take a huge risk in hiding them and then providing a way of escape. She is quick witted and intelligent in her response to the king. Her trickery both saves the spies' lives and sends the king's messengers on a foolish chase. But her actions are based on a conviction. Her conviction is not that the two men represent a strong military power; there is no reason the wandering tribes from the wilderness should be able to breach the fortified walls of a well built city. She has reached the conclusion that Israel's God is all powerful, demonstrated in his mighty acts in the miraculous deliverance from Egypt and crossing of the Red Sea. News of the defeat of the kings of Sihon and Og (Deut 2:26—3:7) has reached the inhabitants of Jericho and she describes their reaction, "As soon as we heard it, our hearts failed, and there was no courage left in any of us because of you" (Josh 2:11), yet her actions belie her words. *Her* heart has not failed; and having demonstrated חסד to the spies she challenges them to respond in kind, loyalty for loyalty, and negotiates an agreement that they are honor bound to keep in spite of the fact that it breaches the law of Moses they have sworn to obey. A resourceful and strong woman, she provides the means for the spies' escape, telling them where they can hide for three days ensuring that they will be safe and able to return to Joshua undetected. Her actions, quick-wittedness and faith are contrasted in the narrative both with the gullibility of the king's men and the passivity and silence of the spies. The spies express no praise of YHWH or firm conviction that he has given them the land. Beyond their initial entry to her house they take no initiatives beyond putting conditions on the deal in an attempt to absolve themselves. By the end of the chapter the role reversal between the Israelite spies commissioned by Joshua and the Canaanite prostitute to whom they go is complete. It is Rahab's words of faith, not their own that are reported to Joshua, words of performative power with which the chapter closes.

Rahab's Inclusion in Matthew's Genealogy

What are the themes in the Hebrew narrative of Rahab's story that point to reasons for Matthew's inclusion of her? Read as an intertext to Tamar's story several interesting thematic parallels emerge that suggest why Matthew might have included her along with Tamar and Ruth in the first epoch of the Messiah's genealogy. It was noted at the outset of this chapter that Rahab's story in Joshua 2, like that of Tamar's story, works on a reversal of expectations. Nothing is expected of the Canaanite prostitute, while Israel's future depends on the action of the spies. For a second time the faith of a Gentile outsider is compared favorably with the apparent lack of faith of insiders. Just as the Canaanite outsider Tamar demonstrates what it is to be righteous, so Rahab the *ultimate* outsider (in that she is a Canaanite, female prostitute, among those "devoted to destruction") is the first in the book of Joshua to demonstrate חסד in the decisive action she takes to hide the spies. This confounds all the reader might expect of her; as the paradigmatic outsider she models that which should characterize the insider. As Earl puts it, Rahab "manifests precisely that which characterizes the centre of Israel's identity and existence."[60] This destabilizes the dominant rhetoric of the Joshua narrative that seeks separation from the surrounding peoples and draws into question the boundaries defining the people of God. The comparison between this Canaanite woman and representatives of Israel is underlined by the placement of Achan's narrative directly after Rahab's "salvation" from the destruction of Jericho. In relation to Israel the positions of archetypal outsider Rahab and the archetypal insider Achan are reversed and Rahab finds a place in Israel's covenantal life. This, as has been noted, challenges views of what constitutes Israel's identity as she enters the promised land.

It has been argued by many scholars that Matthew's Gospel is also primarily concerned with the formation of a new identity for the people of God. After a life-time of study Stanton concludes that Matthew's Gospel is a foundation document written to shape the life and community of a new people.[61] Senior concurs, arguing that an "important purpose of the gospel was to address the questions of identity."[62] If this is so, then Matthew's inclusion of Rahab, as with Tamar, in the Messiah's genealogical line gives the discerning reader pause to question the identity of the new community the Messiah will call to himself and the place the faithful Gentile might occupy among the people of God. In chapter 9 I will argue that the Gentile "outsiders" in Matthew's Gospel, such as the Magi, the Roman centurion, and the Canaanite woman all behave as "insiders" in their response to Jesus. Consequently they too challenge the reader's expectations and raise questions over the boundaries defining the people of God and the identity

60. Earl, *Reading Joshua*, 126–27.
61. See Stanton, *Gospel for a New People*.
62. Senior, *Gospel of Matthew*, 84.

Rahab

of those the Messiah will welcome into the kingdom of heaven. In particular, just as the faith of the Canaanite woman in the Joshua text challenges Israel's boundaries so also Matthew includes the story of another notable Canaanite woman of faith who will challenge Israel's boundaries. Like Rahab, the Canaanite woman of Matthew 15 secures an exception that will set a precedent that the new messianic Joshua will follow.[63] Their stories will be read alongside one another in an intertextual comparison in chapter 9.

Another thematic parallel to Genesis 38 is that for a second time Matthew has chosen to include a marginalized woman whose story, far from portraying her as a sinner or sexually scandalous, in fact characterizes her in positive terms; Rahab is a woman of faith and loyalty (חסד). These two characteristics, along with righteousness are key Matthean discipleship virtues and therefore I suggest that her inclusion in the genealogy highlights the role and place of women in the purposes of God making her the second of a trio of women to anticipate Matthew's positive gynocentric counternarrative. Rahab's faith is radical and active. Rahab recognizes the all-powerful nature of the God of heaven and earth and is prepared to put her life (and the lives of her family) on the line. Taking a wager on the mercy and faithfulness of the God of Israel, she invests everything in her agreement with his somewhat unconvincing representatives. Her radical faith—throwing oneself in total dependency on the mercy of God—is the kind of faith that the Matthean Jesus looks for in his disciples and sometimes finds lacking. Twice Jesus remonstrates with his disciples for their lack of faith in a life threatening situation (Matt 8:26; 14:31). Rahab's radical faith has performative power, inspiring Joshua and all of Israel to cross the Jordan and enter Canaan (Josh 2:24; 3:1). Similarly, in Matthew the faith of an individual or group of people is clearly shown to be a component in the availability of Jesus' healing power. Jesus acts in response to people's faith in him, "your faith has healed you" (Matt 9:22), "According to your faith it will be done to you" (Matt 9:29). Conversely, his healing powers are withheld in the case where there is a lack of faith (Matt 13:58; 17:20).

Her faith is a faith that is directed towards the mercy of God and is expressed in merciful actions towards others. It is significant that Rahab's faith is expressed in her חסד, a characteristic fundamental to YHWH and the basis of Israel's hope, on which the covenant between Israel and YHWH is founded.[64] Elsewhere in the Old Testament חסד is one of the

63. Bauckham, *Gospel Women*, 45.
64. Cf. Exod 34:6–7.

three defining characteristics that YHWH requires of those in covenant relationship with him (Mic 6:8). In Matthean terms the covenant term חסד (steadfast love or loving loyalty) is translated into Jesus' call for mercy. Although the Greek word ἔλεος (used to translate חסד) loses some of the strongly covenantal connotations of חסד, the concept in Matthew is directly linked both thematically and semantically to the Old Testament concept of חסד. Davies and Allison comment that in much of Matthew's talk of mercy "there is strict continuity with the OT and Jewish tradition."[65] Of the four Gospels, it is only the Matthean Jesus who teaches about the core value of God's mercy and the need for mercy be demonstrated in the life of his disciples, particularly towards those on the margins (Matt 5:7; 9:13; 12:7; 18:33; 23:23). Notably, Matthew is the only Gospel to state that prostitutes as well as tax collectors will enter the kingdom of God, their gender pairing as "sinners" is found only in Matthew.[66] It is significant, therefore, that two "prostitutes" Rahab and Tamar are both included in the genealogy. Rahab, the trebly marginalized woman, both practices and receives חסד. Like Tamar, her narrative points towards Matthew's interest in those who are marginalized. Her story is illustrative of the mutual obligation involved in the practice of mercy between individuals and how the offering of mercy leads to experiencing the mercy of God. This is a theme that is taken up and developed by the Matthean Jesus. He teaches his disciples in the Sermon on the Mount that if they show mercy to others, God will, in turn, show mercy towards them. "Blessed are the merciful for they will be shown mercy" (Matt 5:7). This is a call for mercy to be shown by all, whether those at the center of society or those on the margins. As Hagner comments, "What the poor and oppressed have not received from the rich and powerful, they should nevertheless show to others." [67] The importance of demonstrating mercy towards others, particularly to those on the margins, in this case tax collectors and prostitutes, is again reiterated in two passages when Jesus is in confrontation with the Pharisees (Matt 9:13; 12:7) where Jesus legitimates his mission by an appeal to the prophetic tradition of Hosea.[68] It is also only the Matthean Jesus who tells the parable of the king who shows mercy to a servant who only deserves his wrath (Matt 18:23–35). Failure to exhibit mercy towards others results in condemnation, seen when the servant fails to forgive the minor debts of

---

65. Davies and Allison, *Matthew 1–7*, 454.
66. Love, *Jesus and Marginal Women*, 85.
67. Hagner, *Matthew 1–13*, 93.
68. Love, *Jesus and Marginal Women*, 151.

his fellow servant. Inclusion of Rahab in the genealogy acts to foreshadow this important Matthean theme and serves to point towards a Messiah who will respond with mercy to those on the margins seeking his help.

5

Ruth

Ruth, Rahab, and Tamar

Ruth is the third woman to be named in the first epoch of Matthew's genealogy. She is the only one of the women from whom a book of the Old Testament is named and who therefore receives sustained attention.

Surprisingly, the character of Ruth has much in common with both Tamar and Rahab.[1] Tamar and Rahab are foreigners, outsiders, and as such might be expected to pose a threat to Israel. Similarly Ruth is a Moabite woman and Moabite women had a reputation in Israel's history; it was sexual relations with the women of Moab that had led Israel astray (Num 25:1-2). All three women at various points find themselves in desperate, life-threatening situations. But against expectations, all three embody virtues that are defining of Israel. Tamar displays righteousness and Rahab and Ruth loyalty (חסד), Rahab to the spies, Ruth to her mother-in-law. Unlike Rahab, however, Ruth's loyalty does not follow confession of faith in YHWH. In fact, it is Ruth's initial demonstration of loyalty to Naomi that leads her to adopt YHWH as "my God" (Ruth 1:16c); her belief is a result of her action of loyalty towards Naomi.

Like Tamar, Ruth has married into an Israelite family, has lost her husband and is childless with no apparent hope of a *levir*. Naomi's concern about her inability to provide security for her daughters-in-law is specifically linked to her inability to provide a *levir*, "Do I still have sons in my

1. For an intertextual reading of Tamar and Ruth, see Wolde, "Intertextuality," 426–51.

womb that they may become your husbands?" (Ruth 1:11b). To remedy the situation, Ruth, like Tamar, places herself in a compromising situation with a man, in order to bring about a happy ending. A number of commentators have noted that the structure of the book itself parallels the story in Genesis 38. Fisch compares the stories of Lot's daughters and Tamar and Ruth all of which exhibit

> the theme of the woman abandoned or widowed and unable, as a result, to continue the line of the generations. And the solution in each case is along the same lines. A father or father-figure becomes responsible for the perpetuation of the family, although the initiative in all three narratives is taken by the widow/daughter herself who secretly or by guile offers herself to the "father."[2]

Ruth, however, is distinctly and uniquely her own person. For the present I wish to address the question of how she is characterized by providing a narrative reading of the text. However, due to its length, I cannot address the complete text in the same detail as I have done before. Necessarily, I will leave many interesting avenues unexplored and focus on the character and person of Ruth as presented by the narrator in relation to the events and people in her story.

A Narrative Reading of Ruth's Story

The Narrative Structure of Ruth

All commentators are quick to note the literary merits of the Ruth narrative. The book of Ruth is a superb short story wonderfully written with "consummate artistry."[3] The narrator is an "artist in full command of a complex and subtle art,"[4] who has carefully structured the plot so that each scene foreshadows and leads onto the next, the whole being a balanced chiasm.[5] If it is assumed this chiasm is a conscious structuring on the part of the implied author, then what reasons might he/she[6] have?

Bailey suggests:

2. Fisch, "Ruth," 429.
3. Trible, *God and the Rhetoric of Sexuality*, 166.
4. Rauber, "Literary Values," 37.
5. As first demonstrated by Bertman, "Symmetrical Design," 165–68.
6. There is some debate as to the possibility of Ruth having been written by a woman because of its gynocentric focus, cf. Bauckham, *Is the Bible Male?*

> When a biblical author is using the inversion principle deliberately he often places the climax in the center. Usually he reinforces this climax by relating it specifically to the beginning and end of the structure. Usually there is a "point of turning" just past the center of the structure. The second half is not redundant. Rather it introduces some crucial new element that resolves or completes the first half.[7]

These observations can be applied to the book of Ruth. The first chapter sets the scene and revolves on Ruth's radical decision to cling to Naomi and leave her homeland. The two middle chapters form the central action of the book where Ruth is the active agent. The climax in both central scenes comes when Ruth's identity is revealed to Boaz and he responds. The "crucial new element" is introduced at Ruth 3:12. Just when the reader thinks all will end happily with Boaz's promise to Ruth to do all that she asks (Ruth 3:11), a complication is introduced in the form of a nearer kinsman-redeemer (גאל).[8] In terms of the plot, the point of turning occurs just past the central two chapters at the beginning of chapter 4 when the situation is resolved (Ruth 4:6). Boaz publicly lays claim to Ruth and in doing so promises to "maintain the dead man's name on his inheritance" (Ruth 4:5). This resolves the theme of emptiness in the first half of the book, bringing fullness to all three central characters, Naomi, Boaz, and Ruth.

Both central chapters 2 and 3 contain five elements that are paralleled in each chapter, the crux of both chapters being when Boaz questions the identity of Ruth and her identity is revealed (c). I follow Linafelt's modified version of Bertram's proposal that the structure of Ruth is a balanced chiasm.[9]

Ruth 1:1–5	A Informal family history (orientated around the tribe and the clan)
Ruth 1:6–18	B Informal kinship ties among women
Ruth 1:19–22	Naomi and the women of Bethlehem
Ruth 2:1–23	C Ruth and Boaz in the field

    a. Exchange between Ruth and Naomi

---

7. Bailey, *Poet & Peasant*, 50.

8. The Hebrew root גאל has been translated variously as nearest kin, kinsman helper, redeemer. I have chosen the phrase kinsman-redeemer as the best approximation to the Hebrew.

9. Linafelt, *Ruth*, xxi.

    b. Ruth goes to the field

    c. *Boaz seeks identity of Ruth, Ruth's identity is revealed*

    d. Boaz deems Ruth worthy, gives her food and protection

    e. Ruth returns and reports to Naomi

Ruth 3:1–18 | C' Ruth and Boaz at the threshing floor

    a. Exchange between Ruth and Naomi

    b. Ruth goes to the threshing floor

    c. *Boaz seeks identity of Ruth, Ruth's identity is revealed*

    d. Boaz deems Ruth worthy, gives her food and protection

    e. Ruth returns and reports to Naomi

Ruth 4:1–13 | B' Formal kinship ties among men

Ruth 4:14–17 | Naomi and the women of Bethlehem

Ruth 4:18–22 | A' Formal family history (orientated around the monarchy)

The points of climax in the central chapters 2 and 3 (Cc and C'c') come when Boaz questions who Ruth is. We, as real readers, are drawn into that same questioning, just who is this Moabite widow who has bound herself to Naomi? The answer given will inform the question of her inclusion in Matthew's genealogy.

Ruth's Story

RUTH 1:1–5 | A MOVE TO MOAB

The story is set "In the days when the judges judged" (Ruth 1:1). In the LXX and the Christian canon the book is placed between Judges and 1 Samuel. Read in this context, it forms a counterpoint to the chaotic corruption of the preceding book of Judges when "everyone did what was right in his own eyes" (Judg 17:6; 21:25).[10]

---

10. In the Jewish canon Ruth is included in the Writings (*Ketubim*). Campbell argues from type of genre and linguistic evidence for an early date around 950–700 BC, Campbell, *Ruth*, 28. This early date would explain the focus on Bethlehem and inclusion of a genealogy in support of the Davidic line. Others have proposed Ruth was written in the period of Ezra and Nehemiah and is a response to the post-exilic laws against intermarriage, e.g., LaCocque, *Feminine Unconventional*, 84–116.

Mothers on the Margin?

In a masterful five verses the narrator introduces readers to a family from Bethlehem, who move to Moab to escape a famine. However, in Moab they experience tragedy after tragedy until "the woman was left without her two sons or her husband" (Ruth 1:5b). Living in Moab spelt death for the men in Naomi's family. This is emphasized by the way the narrator structures the story, interspersing mention of time spent in Moab with death.

Ruth 1:1	a certain man . . . went to live in the country of Moab, he and his wife and two sons.
Ruth 1:2b	They went into the country of Moab and remained there.
Ruth 1:3a	But Elimelech . . . died.
Ruth 1:3b	and she was left with her two sons
Ruth 1:4	These took Moabite wives . . . When they had lived there for about ten years
Ruth 1:5	both Mahlon and Chilion also died.

The upward turn that presumably Naomi had looked for through birth of children after her sons' marriages never happens. Both women remain barren and both sons die. Naomi is left without patriarchal provision, destitute in a foreign country.

Use of allusion by the writer to "invite other texts into play"[11] is important in the Ruth text. Gunn and Fewell opine:

> Negative allusions to Moab as the son of incest (compare the connotation of the term "bastard" in English today), or to Moabite women as those who snared Israelite men who came to eat and drink in Moab (patriarchy habitually blames the women), make Elimelech's foray into Moab to find food a move likely to invite severe condemnation from many in Bethlehem.[12]

To the later Rabbinic mind "it seemed that such a calamity could only have befallen the family as the penalty for their sins."[13] The story of a journey to Moab leading to disaster and death would have been one predicted by any Israelite familiar with their own history.

With the deaths of father and sons, the story seems to end at verse 5 with total disaster for Naomi. The narrator comments, "the woman was

---

11. Gunn and Fewell, *Narrative in the Hebrew Bible*, 163.
12. Ibid., 164.
13. Beattie, *Jewish Exegesis*, 170.

left without her two sons or her husband" (Ruth 1:5). Naomi has a pressing need for economic security. With no male relative to provide for her she will be forced to live as one of the "poor" surviving from hand to mouth. Unexpectedly, there now opens up a space for her and her two daughters-in-law who have been introduced and named amidst the tragedy, "These took Moabite wives; the name of one was Orpah and the name of the other Ruth" (Ruth 1:4). Ruth's introduction identifying her as Moabite and coupling her with Orpah is significant for what follows. The ensuing scene focuses on the three women.

Ruth 1:6–18 | The journey to Bethlehem

Verses 6–7 provide a "transition from a story of men to a story of women, from the land of Moab to the land of Judah, and from narration to dialogue."[14] Naomi hears that the famine in Bethlehem (ironically, the "house of bread") is over, and sets out from Moab with her two daughters-in-law to return to Judah.

Naomi is the first person whose direct speech is reported. It is a speech in rather archaic language fitting to an older person. She opens with the imperative words to her daughters-in-law to "Go! Return each of you to your mother's house" (Ruth 1:8). It ends by her picturing them in the security of a new husband and home. Significantly, she says, "May the Lord deal loyally (חסד)[15] with you, as you have dealt with the dead and me" (Ruth 1:8). The loyalty these two Moabite women have shown to both the three deceased men of the family and Naomi herself is to be a model for YHWH's actions, not the other way round. As Trible points out, YHWH's past action "has meant only famine, dislocation and death . . . Strikingly, the basis upon which Naomi invokes Yahweh's *hesed* is the gracious hospitality of her daughters-in-law."[16] Surprisingly, in spite of Moab's negative connotations for the implied reader, both Moabite women over the years have demonstrated a loyalty to their husbands and Naomi that speaks to her of the covenantal loyalty of YHWH. God's loyalty is something which, from her point of view, has singularly been lacking in her own life since the death of her husband and two sons. In asking YHWH's

---

14. Linafelt, *Ruth*, 7.

15. For consistency I continue to use the English word "loyally" to translate חסד here but the element of kindness, so apparent in Ruth, is missing in the English word "loyally."

16. Trible, *God and the Rhetoric of Sexuality*, 169.

blessing of חסד on them as they return Naomi is asking that YHWH will do for her daughters-in-law what she cannot do, in providing a husband and thus security for them (Ruth 1:9).

Both women remonstrate with Naomi, "No, we will return with you to your people" (Ruth 1:10). Naomi's second longer speech, emphasizing her barrenness and inability to produce more sons for them to marry, convinces Orpah. Naomi has released both daughters-in-law from any further commitment. Orpah's decision is not therefore disloyal, she does the sensible thing and returns. Sakenfeld comments, "Orpah's proper decision helps the narrator to show the reader how extraordinary Ruth's loyalty really is."[17] The narrator reports simply that by contrast, "Ruth clung to her" (Ruth 1:14). It is at this point Ruth becomes an independent figure in the narrative. In contrast to Orpah, she continues to resist her mother-in-law's urging to return.[18]

Naomi's third speech in the chapter addresses Ruth alone and is a final attempt to persuade Ruth to return, "Look, your sister-in-law has gone back to her people and her gods, go back after your sister-in-law" (Ruth 1:15). Ruth's response both defines her intent towards Naomi and defines her in the reader's perception. Her decision is unexpected, unorthodox, and costly. She renounces her family, her national identity, and her gods. As a young, foreign widow with no protection, she resolves to bind herself to a hopeless, bitter, widow who has apparently no means of support even when she returns to Bethlehem. In doing so Ruth sacrifices her chance of security through remarrying in Moab. Her radical decision to align herself with Naomi is an ongoing practical demonstration of the loyalty (חסד) she had already demonstrated in Moab and will continue to show once in Bethlehem. Her speech (the first in the book and therefore significant in placing her as a character in the reader's mind), is a series of succinct

---

17. Sakenfeld, *Faithfulness in Action*, 34.

18. Although a mutual relationship of duty existed among the members of a family in many ancient societies against which the story world of Ruth is set, kinship bonds within ancient Israel were of the utmost importance and the practice of חסד within those bonds in terms of reciprocity was expected of all individuals within the kinship group. The importance of the kinship relationship between Naomi, Ruth and Orpah is emphasized in the narration of the first part of the story where the narrator consistently refers to Orpah and Ruth as Naomi's daughters-in-law (Ruth 1:6, 7, 8) and Naomi calls them "my daughters" (Ruth 1:11, 12, 13). Nonetheless, Naomi makes it clear to both Ruth and Orpah that in their demonstration of חסד they have fulfilled their obligations to her. She cannot reciprocate by providing husbands for them (Ruth 1:11). Therefore, they are free to break their kinship bonds and their responsibility to remain as levirate widows in waiting. Ruth is as free as Orpah to go back to her own people.

statements expressing her חסד towards Naomi. The phrases are repeated, the verbs in the second person and then in the first person.

> Where you go I go
> Where you lodge I lodge
> Your people my people
> Your God my God
> Where you die I will die

Her sheer resolve to go with Naomi whatever the odds, to be with her even beyond death is sealed by an oath (Ruth 1:17b) that leaves Naomi speechless, "When Naomi saw that she was determined to go with her, she said no more to her" (Ruth 1:18). Ruth's fierce loyalty towards this elderly woman is greeted with stunned silence and the narrative moves on.

Ruth 1:19–22 | Arrival in Bethlehem

"So the two of them went on until they came to Bethlehem" (Ruth 1:19). The physical return that had started in Ruth 1:6 continues and is completed in this final episode in chapter 1. Bethlehem is astir with a group of astonished women asking, "Is this Naomi?" (Ruth 1:19). Her response is unequivocal:

> Call me no longer Naomi נעמי (*pleasant*), call me Mara מרא (*bitter*) . . . I went away full, but the Lord has brought me back empty (Ruth 1:20–21)

The contrasting themes of fullness and emptiness running through the first chapter are made explicit and the overriding *leitmotif* of the book is established. Naomi's complaint against God is deeply felt, "the Almighty has brought calamity upon me" (Ruth 1:21). Yet, although she can't see it, she is not totally empty, Ruth is with her.[19] The way in which the narrator refers to Ruth at this point is instructive, "So Naomi returned together with Ruth the Moabite, her daughter-in-law, who came back with her from the country of Moab" (Ruth 1:22). In case the reader misses the significance of the appellation "Ruth the Moabite," the narrator spells it out, "who came back from the country of Moab" (Ruth 1:22). The narrator's comment implies that on her arrival in Bethlehem it is Ruth's foreignness that defines her in the eyes of those living there and not just any foreigner but a Moabite. The criticism of all that was Moabite would surely have

---

19. See Fewell and Gunn, "Son Is Born," 234.

been felt by Ruth under the gaze of the Bethlehemite women, criticism that Naomi, with Ruth allied to her, would have been unlikely to escape.

In one final sentence the narrator finishes one section and points to the next, with a strong hint that the tragic movement of the story is about to turn, "They came to Bethlehem at the beginning of the barley harvest" (Ruth 1:22).

The big surprise of chapter 1 is that this young Moabitess should demonstrate such exceptional loyalty to Naomi. As has been noted, within the wider story of Genesis to 2 Kings, loyalty (חסד) is one of the key characteristics of the covenant-making God of Israel,[20] yet a God who so far in this story, from Naomi's point of view, seems to have been the harbinger of disaster, "the Almighty has brought calamity upon me" (Ruth 1:21c). In contrast, it is Ruth the Moabitess, banned from the congregation of Israel (Deut 23:3), who demonstrates the loving kindness of God to Naomi in a situation where Naomi perceives the Lord "has dealt harshly" (Ruth 1:21b). The next three scenes are an outworking of Ruth's radical commitment to Naomi and a demonstration that behind the events a divine response to her faithful living is being worked out.

Ruth 2:1–23 | Boaz meets Ruth in the barley fields

The next scene starts with an aside by the storyteller that privileges the reader with information unknown to Ruth and overlooked by Naomi, apparently mentally immobile in her grief. Naomi has a kinsman, a "man of substance" (איש גבור) (Ruth 2:1) named Boaz, from the same subclan as Elimelech, a further hint that things might change for the better. However, it takes the initiative and courage of "Ruth the Moabite" to set things in motion for their survival, for the two widows find themselves economically impoverished with apparently no means of support beyond their own resources. The cluster of references to Ruth's Moabite origin (Ruth 2:2; 2:6; 2:22) emphasizes her ethnic, social, and economic marginality as a foreign widow. However, Ruth is able to take advantage of a law (or operative custom) in Israel to provide for the destitute by allowing them to glean fields as they are harvested.[21] "Let me go to the field and glean" (Ruth 2:2) she asks Naomi. Significantly, she voices the hope that she might glean "behind someone in whose sight I may find favor" (Ruth 2:2). It will become apparent that Ruth is putting herself at some risk in order to

20. Cf. Deut 7:12, 1 Kgs 8:23.
21. Cf. Deut 24:19, Lev 19:9–10.

provide for her mother-in-law. She is going out as a young Moabite widow in public, alone. Linafelt points out that her status as a Moabite "connotes something other than vulnerability . . . namely an illicit sexuality."[22]

Naomi speaks to her daughter-in-law for the first time since Ruth countered her command to return to Moab in 1:15, "Go, my daughter" (Ruth 2:2c). In just three Hebrew words the whole chapter is summarized, (she gleaned) וּתְלַקֵּט (she arrived) וַתָּבוֹא (she went) וַתֵּלֶךְ (Ruth 2:3). But there is another dynamic at work in events and the storyteller re-enters to describe it, "As it happened, she came to the part of the field belonging to Boaz, who was of the family of Elimelech. Just then Boaz came from Bethlehem" (Ruth 2:3, 4). A happy coincidence or divine providence? Trible puts it beautifully, "Within human luck is divine intentionality."[23] After polite greetings to his workers, Boaz immediately spots Ruth and asks to whom she belongs, "Truly a patriarchal question."[24] Ruth "belongs" to no one. Boaz's question and the answer provided is the turning point of this chapter since knowledge of Ruth's identity defines Boaz's response.

The servant replies, "She is the young Moabite woman who returned with Naomi from the country of Moab" (Ruth 2:6). Her availability as a young Moabite widow is hinted at and it becomes apparent this could easily make her the subject of sexual molestation. It is not without reason that later Boaz tells his men not to touch her (Ruth 2:9) and that Naomi advises Ruth to stay with Boaz's young women so she won't be bothered elsewhere (Ruth 2:22). The overseer goes on to note her polite request and her unrelenting work in the fields on behalf of her mother-in-law (Ruth 2:7).

The narrator "zooms in" to Ruth and Boaz in the barley field as a long section of dialogue between them takes place, the slow pace of this section conveying both the importance of the meeting and the length of day in the field. Boaz offers Ruth opportunity to glean, protection, and water, as well as advice on gender relations. Falling prostrate to the ground she responds with what Fischer refers to as "exquisite courtesy that would not blur the social differences between the destitute foreign widow and the well-off native."[25] "Why have I found favor in your sight, that you should take notice of me, even I, a foreigner?"(Ruth 2:10).

Boaz's next speech reveals he knows more about Ruth than the reader might have expected. He recognizes the depth of her commitment to her mother-in-law. Trible notes that his words resonate with echoes of

22. Linafelt, *Ruth*, 27.
23. Trible, *God and the Rhetoric of Sexuality*, 176.
24. Ibid.
25. Fischer, "Book of Ruth," 28.

Abraham's migration, "you left your father, mother, and the land of your birth, and went to a people whom you had not known before" (Ruth 2:11). While her actions echo Abraham's call (Gen 12:1), Ruth had received no divine call or promise of blessing.[26]

But now Boaz invokes a blessing on her. "May the Lord reward you for your deeds and may you have a full reward from the Lord under whose wings (כנפים) you have come for refuge" (Ruth 2:12). However, Ruth's "reward" will be dependent on clever planning by Naomi, risk-taking and the use of initiative by Ruth herself and consequent action by Boaz. YHWH's blessing will be worked out through human lives. Ruth responds to Boaz's prayer for her blessing by asking that she might continue to "find favor" with Boaz "even though I am not one of your servants" (Ruth 2:13).

The narrative continues with Boaz's generous (and maybe not entirely altruistic) response that grants her gleaning rites beyond those stipulated by law. This ensures food security for the two widows and also that Ruth stays gleaning in his fields! Underlying his generosity is the sense that Ruth's חסד towards Naomi is being repaid in kind by Boaz. He offers her food and she eats "until she was satisfied and had some left over" (Ruth 2:14). Boaz then organizes his workers to ensure she will take a full shawl of grain home to Naomi. He seems unaware that in providing a secure environment and rich pickings for Ruth to glean, he himself is providing a refuge for her. Ruth completes the hard physical labor of gleaning, threshing and then carrying the grain back to the city. The allusion to fullness and fertility (she brings home seed from Boaz) is reflected in the physical world by her mother-in law's delight over the amount of grain and leftover lunch she brings home. In a patriarchal world, a man must have taken notice of her (Ruth 2:19)! Both women withhold significant information from each other until the last moment; Ruth, that it was Boaz in whose field she gleaned, and Naomi, that "The man is near to us, he is one of our kinsman-redeemers (גאל)"[27] (Ruth 2:20c). For the first time Naomi revises her fate, "Blessed be he by the Lord, whose loyalty (חסד) has not forsaken the living or the dead!" (Ruth 2:20b). The syntax of this sentence in Hebrew (as in English) is unclear. Does the "whose" refer to Boaz or YHWH? Surely the storyteller's point is that it is both; God's loyalty towards Naomi has been expressed through Boaz's generosity towards Ruth, just as earlier

---

26. Trible, *God and the Rhetoric of Sexuality*, 177.

27. A גאל was required to redeem the land of his relative to ensure the property stayed within the kinship group and redeem the relative if they were in financial difficulties, see Lev 25:25.

it had been expressed by Ruth's generosity of spirit in her loyal determination not to forsake Naomi.[28]

Campbell comments:

> Boaz invokes God's blessing upon Ruth only to become himself the agency for the fulfillment of that blessing ... Naomi praises the God who still acts with *ḥesed* because Boaz has so acted, and it will be the *ḥesed* of both Boaz and Ruth which will bring Naomi fulfillment. We can say that persons act as God to one another.[29]

Yet the woman who demonstrated the radical loyalty towards Naomi that earned Boaz's blessing is not a daughter of Israel but "Ruth the Moabitess" (Ruth 2:21). Similarly it is Canaanite Tamar who earns Judah's praise for being in the right (Gen 38:26) and Canaanite Rahab who is praised by Joshua (Josh 6:17).

The added irony of a woman from Moab supplying food for Naomi in the "city of bread" should not be lost. Ruth continues her daily hard labor to supply food as the scene closes with Ruth living and working among women, gleaning through the barley and wheat harvests (Ruth 2:23).

Ruth 3:1–18 | Ruth Meets Boaz at the Threshing Floor

As noted above, chapter 3 is in many ways a counterpart to chapter 2. It opens and closes with conversations between Ruth and Naomi, which surround an extensive encounter between Ruth and Boaz. The crucial difference is that this encounter is private not public, during the night not day, when even the language itself is cloaked in mystery and ambiguity. Ruth is no longer referred to as the Moabite but called "my daughter" by Boaz. The narrator names her "the woman" next to Boaz who is simply called "the man," as they relate to each other as man and woman.

Unlike the previous two chapters, chapter 3 opens with dialogue as Naomi addresses Ruth with two rhetorical questions (as Boaz had done in Ruth 2:8–9). The reader senses that Naomi is picking up the threads of her life again as she refers to the need for security mentioned in Ruth 1:9. The first two verses set the scene. "With her opening words, Naomi thus registers her intentions, alludes to Boaz's potential, and points to an

---

28. The same verb עזב "to forsake" (often used in the context of covenant terminology) is used in Hebrew both in Ruth 2:20 and in Ruth 1:16.

29. Campbell, *Ruth*, 113.

opportune place for matters to develop."³⁰ Naomi goes on to unfold her plan in a series of eight Hebrew verbs and instructs Ruth to wash, anoint herself, put on her best clothes, and go down to the threshing floor (Ruth 3:3a). Significantly she is to conceal herself until Boaz has eaten and drunk. Threshing floors were later associated with prostitution (cf. Hos 9:1). The implication is that within this story world it also held associations with sexual impropriety (Ruth 3:14).

Ruth is then to observe, go, uncover his "feet," and lie down when, finally, Boaz will tell her what to do (Ruth 3:4b). What Naomi asks of Ruth is both calculating and dangerous; the clever plan puts Ruth in a very compromising situation. As Linafelt points out:

> Naomi is sending an unmarried Moabite woman out in the dead of night to lie down next to a (perhaps drunken) man, to uncover that man in some way, and then wait and see what he tells her to do.³¹

Ruth is taking a significantly greater risk than her previous public exposure in the fields to glean. Now she will go to a man in private, on the threshing floor, at night. The reader is given no indication about what Ruth thinks, she simply says, "All that you tell me I will do" (Ruth 3:5b). Does she think it a good or bad plan? Is she surprised at the risk involved? Does she want security in the house of Boaz? Bos points out that readers know "in the past Ruth has not been one to follow directives from her mother-in-law and that her initiatives [not Naomi's] have set events in motion."³² Although the reader is told that Ruth "went down to the threshing floor and did just as her mother-in-law had instructed her" (Ruth 3:6), readers will see that her obedience is supplemented by her own initiative in dealing with Boaz.

To leave the reader in no doubt about the overtones in this encounter, the storyteller uses sexually loaded language throughout this scene. Three Hebrew verbs with *double entendres* are used repeatedly, שכב lie down—eight times,³³ ידע know—three times,³⁴ בוא go into—four times,³⁵ and גלה reveal—twice.³⁶ Finally, the phrase מרגלתיו "place of his feet" has

30. Bos, "Out of the Shadows," 61.
31. Linafelt, *Ruth*, 48.
32. Bos, "Out of the Shadows," 61.
33. Ruth 3:4 three times, 7 twice, 8, 13, 14.
34. Ruth 3:3, 4, 14.
35. Ruth 3:4, 7 twice, 14.
36. Ruth 3:4, 7.

euphemistic overtones.³⁷ Bernstein argues that the language is a literary device used to create the sense of sexual and emotional tension felt by the characters.³⁸ The darkness of the night is reflected in the ambiguity of the text leaving real readers to form their own conclusions about whether intercourse takes place. The *double entendres* point to the sexually provocative nature of Ruth's actions that leave the older man Boaz flustered and confused. I suggest that since within the larger narrative context both Boaz and Ruth are characterized as individuals who live righteously in this case also they continue to remain above reproach.

Ruth waits until Boaz has eaten and drunk and is "in a contented mood" (Ruth 3:7) before she secretly uncovers his "feet" where he is lying at the end of the heap of grain and lies down next to him. Readers are left wondering with Trible, "How will a patriarch of Israel respond to this bold action by a woman from Moab?"³⁹

The crux of this scene (Ruth 3:8–9) comes at midnight when the man stirs and is startled to find a woman lying at his feet. "Who are you?" he asks (Ruth 3:9). This question parallels his question about Ruth's identity put to the overseer (Ruth 2:5). Ruth's answer will direct the outcome of the remainder of the plot. This time, in a very different context, Boaz is caught unawares and Ruth is in control of the situation. Her answer is the turning point of the scene, "I am Ruth, your maidservant." The Hebrew word for maidservant, אמה, used by Ruth here to describe her status stands in contrast to her previous public identification of herself as שפח (Ruth 2:13). The difference is significant as אמה indicates she is eligible for marriage.⁴⁰ However, a hint is not enough and Ruth does not wait for Boaz to tell her what to do. Instead, by way of a request, she tells him; she asks for marriage and protection "Spread your cloak /wing (כנף) over your servant, for you are a kinsman redeemer (גאל)." Her words echo Boaz's comment to Ruth that she has found refuge under the God of Israel's wings (Ruth 2:12). Now she asks Boaz to bring her refuge and security.

The events in chapter 4, consequent to her request, imply that in fact Ruth asks Boaz for two things, for marriage and for redemption. Boaz understands this shown by the consequent action he takes at the city gate.⁴¹

37. In Hebrew "feet" can be a euphemism for a man's genitals or legs, see Linafelt, *Ruth*, 49, and Sasson, *Ruth: A New Translation*, 69–70.

38. Bernstein, "Two Multivalent Readings," 19.

39. Trible, *God and the Rhetoric of Sexuality*, 183.

40. Linafelt, *Ruth*, 54.

41. This assertion touches on a much debated topic revolving around the relationship between marriage, levirate marriage and redemption in Ruth, cf. Beattie, "Ruth

She has combined two requests; firstly that he marry her, "spread your wing over your servant"[42] and act as *levir* to provide a child for Mahlon (Ruth 4:10) and thus, essentially, a son for Naomi (Ruth 4:17). Secondly, she requests that he act as kinsman-redeemer[43] to buy the use of the land left by Elimelech and his sons (Ruth 4:9). Boaz in agreeing to her request essentially agrees to marry her and father a child who will (if male) inherit the use of the land which Boaz will redeem on behalf of Naomi (Ruth 4:5). As Campbell comments, "From the story's point of view, the combination of redemption and levirate marriage is a *presupposition*, and furthermore it is one which this remarkable Moabitess introduces."[44]

Boaz responds with blessing and a recognition of the extent of Ruth's חסד that has been expressed in her request. "May you be blessed by the Lord, my daughter; this last instance of your loyalty (חסד) is greater than the first; you have not gone after young men, whether poor or rich" (Ruth 3:10). Ruth's first initial loyalty to Naomi in the costly sacrifice of leaving her homeland is superseded by her current request. Her request reflects her loyalty both towards her dead husband, Mahlon, and also Naomi. She has chosen to remain as a widow, not going after younger (and more attractive?) men, instead turning to the man she presumes is Naomi's nearest kinsman who will be able to act as a *levir*. She also makes clear her continued commitment to Naomi. The purchase of Naomi's field (which readers discover from Ruth 4:3 is up for sale), will bring Naomi current financial security but also ensure that Elimelech's property will stay in the family and provide an inheritance for any son born to Ruth and Boaz, a son who in turn will provide for Naomi in her old age. While her request for marriage is not contingent on Boaz redeeming Naomi's land she implies they are closely linked and Boaz's consequent action in chapter 4 shows he has understood this. However, he reverses the order of Ruth's request by implying to Mr."So and So" and the elders of the city that he is primarily interested in buying the field (in which he has shown no interest

---

III," 39–48; Sasson, "Issue of Ge'ullāh," 52–64; and Osgood's discussion in Osgood, "Early Israelite Society," 359–64.

42. Cf. Ezek 16:8.

43. Sasson argues that Ruth makes two requests, the first to be taken into Boaz's family (either as a bride or concubine) and secondly that he act to redeem Naomi's land but that his role as redeemer is not linked to acting as a *levir*. I argue that Boaz fulfills a dual role as a גאל both in acting as *levir* and in redeeming Naomi's land, see Sasson, *Ruth: A New Translation*, 83–92.

44. Campbell, *Ruth*, 132.

until now) and that marriage to Ruth (in whom he has shown considerable interest) is a secondary consideration!

Perhaps now Boaz begins to realize that he will be the agent through whom YHWH's loyalty will be repaid to Ruth. Bos comments, "Nowhere in Ruth is the correspondence between human activity and divine activity so clearly put as in 3:9. Divine recompense must be brought into active operation by Boaz."[45]

Ironically, he tells her not to fear (although he was the one who had been unnerved in the middle of the night). He promises he will do all that she has asked, for all recognize that in the outworking of her loyalty to Naomi, Ruth is a "worthy woman" (אשת חיל) (Ruth 3:11b).

However, a complication is introduced at this point (Ruth 3:12) that prolongs the narrative into chapter 4; there is another kinsman redeemer more closely related than Boaz. The matter will have to be addressed in the morning. In the meantime, Ruth lies at his feet until just before daybreak, then leaves "before one person could recognize another, for he said, 'It must not be known that the woman came to the threshing floor'" (Ruth 3:14). Boaz acknowledges the risk to her reputation that Ruth took in coming to him by night on the threshing floor.

The close of the chapter mirrors the close of the previous chapter with Ruth bringing grain home to Naomi. Naomi asks, "How did things go with you, my daughter?" (Ruth 3:16). Ruth's answer focuses on Boaz and fails to tell her mother-in-law about *her* forthright instructions to *him*. Her last words are those reporting Boaz's speech, "Do not go back to your mother-in-law empty handed" (Ruth 3:17b). For the second time Ruth has brought home seed from Boaz for Naomi. Her radical commitment to Naomi, leading to her hazardous actions at the threshing floor, has borne fruit. Will Boaz act? The women are now dependent on men to put into action what Ruth has initiated. Readers have to wait with Ruth to "learn how the matter turns out" (Ruth 3:18). Although Ruth is spoken of and praised by others in chapter 4 this is the last time that Ruth herself speaks and essentially her role as an independent character is over.

Ruth 4:1–13 | Negotiations at the City Gate

The action of the story moves to the public arena of men and now becomes a patriarchal man's story of "acquiring Ruth the Moabite" (Ruth 4:5, 10) as the narrative moves towards its resolution. As Boaz clinches the deal, the

---

45. Bos, "Out of the Shadows," 62.

men of the city invoke the wedding blessing of the Lord on "the woman" (Ruth 4:11) and "this young woman" (Ruth 4:12). Ruth is not named. Asking for fertility they voice patriarchal concerns for the restoration of a male name and line. They recall ancestral mothers from the past, Rachel and Leah, "the two of whom built the House of Israel" (Ruth 4:11), and, more notably, Tamar, who as mother of Perez is the ancestress of the tribe of Judah and thus the matriarch of the local clan in Bethlehem.[46] The men of Bethlehem (unlike some Christian commentators) apparently have no problems with Tamar's history. Linafelt comments that ironically the powerful men of the city recognize their dependence on the fertility of women to provide what they often value the most—children, or more precisely, a male child.[47]

In a single connecting verse, containing just thirteen Hebrew words, much happens. Ruth and Boaz are married and Ruth conceives and gives birth to a son. Although barren for ten years in Moab, in this marriage Ruth does not remain unfruitful. For the first and only time in the story YHWH appears as a character. God, it seems, has heard the prayers of the people and elders at the gate, for omnisciently the narrator reveals "the Lord made her conceive, and she bore a son" (Ruth 4:13). Up to this point God's loyalty has been demonstrated through the characters in their relations with one another. Now, there is a direct divine response to Ruth's faithful living; YHWH's loyalty to Ruth, Boaz, and Naomi is made evident in the birth of a son.

Ruth 4:14–17 | Naomi's Emptiness Is Filled

At this point the gynocentric focus of the narrative returns. Surprisingly, the narrator does not record Boaz's reaction to the birth but reports the words of the women of Bethlehem who acknowledge God's blessing on Naomi (Ruth 4:14). With the birth the narrative reaches its resolution; Naomi's emptiness becomes fullness as she takes the child and "places him on her lap" (Ruth 4:16).

As for Ruth? Her tribute is paid by the women of Bethlehem who focus on Ruth as the bearer of life. Her child will be Naomi's kinsman-redeemer (Ruth 4:14), a restorer and sustainer of life for Naomi (Ruth 4:15). In addressing Naomi they acknowledge that Ruth is the one "who has loved you; she is better to you than seven sons" (Ruth 4:15). They

---

46. Bernstein, "Two Multivalent Readings," 23.
47. Linafelt, *Ruth*, 75.

go on to name the child Obed. Not only the women of Bethlehem, who had ignored Ruth on her arrival, but also the people and elders now fully embrace the Moabitess (Ruth 4:11–12). She is integrated into Bethlehem society as a wife and mother. Ironically, having come in from the margins of society as a wife and mother, her individuality within the narrative is lost, just as Tamar's was.

Ruth 4:18–21 | The Genealogy

By the close of the book, Ruth has become totally invisible in an all male genealogy in which Boaz is the begetter. The story that began with Elimelech and the threat to his line ends with the genealogy of Tamar's son Perez, which lists Boaz as father of Obed (restorer of Elimelech's line), grandfather to David. However, surprisingly, neither Tamar nor Ruth are mentioned. The placing of an all male genealogy at the end of a book that has had a sustained gynocentric bias is strange. In noting this oddity Bauckham argues that

> the genealogy says in effect: "This is how the usual men's perspective views the history of this period of David's ancestors. This is the way you readers are accustomed to thinking of this period. Everything the narrative you have just read has taught you to see as important is here left out."[48]

Possibly Bauckham is right, it is feasible to read the all male genealogy as an ironic commentary on patriarchal perspectives. Alternatively it could be argued that patriarchy has the final say in the book of Ruth.

The ten names in the concluding genealogy of Ruth recur in the first epoch of Matthew's genealogy (Matt 1:2–6) but in his genealogy the two widows, Tamar and Ruth, are included in his annotations, named as foremothers to both David and Christ. Consequently, in contrast to the patriarchal genealogy that provides the epilogue to Ruth, the patriarchy of the genealogy that acts as the prologue to Matthew's Gospel is undermined by the annotations in which a total of four Old Testament women are mentioned as well as Mary, mother of Christ.

---

48. Bauckham, *Is the Bible Male?*, 17. See also his discussion in Bauckham, "Book of Ruth," 29–45.

Feminist Perspectives

In recent years, many women have read Ruth afresh, challenging the dominant male perspective that Ruth exemplifies worthy feminine behavior. Loving, loyal and obedient, docile and submissive, Ruth has also been regarded in Jewish rabbinic commentary as the ideal proselyte and worthy ancestress to David. Bronner has shown that the rabbis added beauty, royal lineage, and modesty to the list,[49] while modern western commentators have read Ruth as an idyllic love story.[50]

However, feminist scholars have read Ruth differently. In 1978, Trible produced a groundbreaking and influential literary feminist reading of Ruth in which she argued that Ruth was a "human comedy" that was suggestive of "a theological interpretation of feminism"[51] in which two women "make their own decisions; they work out their own destinies."[52] Since Trible's work, which drew attention to the independence, commitment, and courage of both Ruth and Naomi, a wide range of feminist commentary on Ruth has been produced, from Bal's psychoanalytical reading (1987)[53] to the more recent radical feminist reading of Fuchs (2003).[54] Many feminist studies have found evidence that Ruth is "a female text."[55] It redefines reality from a female perspective and serves to counteract the patriarchal texts that form the biblical norm. Ostricker argues Ruth is "a text embedded in Scripture that forms a counter-current to certain biblical concepts and motifs, and thereby enriches and deepens the Bible as a whole."[56] Meyers suggests it is a text that "can be heard as Israelite women's language"—a language that provides a gynocentric perspective on everyday life in ancient Israel.[57]

Although many feminist critics have read Ruth as a story about women who determine their futures, subverting and challenging the dominant patriarchal world, a minority have argued that Ruth and Naomi are only upheld in the text because they are working in the interests of patriarchy

---

49. Bronner, "Thematic Approach to Ruth," 157–64.
50. See, e.g., Hubbard, *Book of Ruth*.
51. Trible, *God and the Rhetoric of Sexuality*, 196.
52. Ibid., 195.
53. Bal, *Lethal Love*, 68–88.
54. Fuchs, *Sexual Politics in the Biblical Narrative*, 74–84.
55. Brenner, introduction to *A Feminist Companion to Ruth*, 14.
56. Ostriker, "Book of Ruth," 344.
57. Meyers, "Returning Home," 92.

to continue a male inheritance. For this reason, Fuchs is suspicious of the Ruth text since Ruth gives birth to a son who contributes to the stability of a patrilineal genealogy. "Roles (such as motherhood) will be valorized because of their potential to enhance male dominance."[58] She continues, "this valorization has specific political functions . . . it is well suited to the needs of the patriarchal order. Mother-figures are to be valorized when they go out of their way to re-establish patrilineal disruption."[59] Is Ruth only valorized by the text because she bears a son who will continue the patriarchal line? I consider that the Ruth text is much more nuanced than is implied by Fuchs. The narrative provides two different perspectives on why Ruth is valorized as mother. First and foremost I have argued that the narrator portrays the birth of her son as the continued outworking of Ruth's radical loyalty to Naomi. The birth of her son is depicted by the narrator primarily as providing for Naomi. The male perspective, that "the name of the dead may not be cut off from among his brothers and from the gate of his place" (Ruth 4:10) is given at the city gate by Boaz. Both are presented as equally valid outcomes for motherhood. Although the closing patrilineal genealogy might point in one direction, the Ruth text itself does not suggest that the valorization of motherhood is confined to an enhancement of male dominance but points in quite another direction, her son is Naomi's redeemer.

Following Fuchs, Levine suggests that "the tale might be seen less as a celebration of Ruth's abilities and *chesed* than as a pernicious, exploitative tract."[60] She argues that not only does it suggest that women's principal worth is in producing sons but it shows that Gentile women are "sexually manipulative and therefore dangerous . . . Perhaps Ruth's unconventional actions are acceptable in this book only because she is a Moabite."[61] Such women "should not be fully incorporated into Israel."[62] However, Levine is feeding into the precise rhetoric that is challenged by the book of Ruth. Ruth does not behave as might be expected of a Moabite woman, sexually manipulative and therefore dangerous. Although her visit to Boaz on the threshing floor is extremely unconventional, it is at the behest of her Israelite mother-in-law. The book never implies that such a woman "should not be fully incorporated into Israel" but closes in its celebration of "Ruth

---

58. Fuchs, *Sexual Politics in the Biblical Narrative*, 47.
59. Ibid., 82.
60. Levine, "Ruth," 85.
61. Ibid.
62. Ibid.

the Moabitess" (Ruth 4:10) who, as a Moabitess, is honored and accepted into Boaz's house (Ruth 4:11).

My reading challenges the more radical feminist interpretations but also rejects any reading that minimizes the loyalty, sheer hard labor, risk taking, and initiative that Ruth exercises to provide a secure future for both herself and her mother-in-law.

Ruth's Inclusion in Matthew's Genealogy

By listing Ruth as well as Rahab and Tamar in his annotations, Matthew is reminding the competent reader of stories about three very different but significant foreign women, Gentiles whose faithfulness to Israel's God and her covenant traditions is notable.

Like Rahab, but in a very different manner, Ruth is notable for her loving loyalty. Although the word חסד only occurs three times in Ruth (Ruth 1:8; 2:20; 3:10) it underlies much of what takes place and is one of the main *leitmotifs* of the text. Within the Ruth text it is used to describe the actions of people towards one another and it also describes YHWH, who never appears as a character but who is referred to. Naomi initially uses the word of her daughters-in-law's actions toward her and their deceased husbands in her parting blessing. She also implies that it is high time that YHWH "do steadfast love" (Ruth 1:8), the expectation being, within his commitment to Israel as their God, that he will show loving kindness. Later Naomi sees YHWH's loyalty at work in Boaz's generosity (Ruth 2:20). In the Ruth text divine and human loyalty are closely interconnected.

Whereas in Joshua 2 Rahab's חסד established an ethical commitment between two parties that were not in previous relationship and who were in fact enemies, Ruth's חסד is an expression of loyalty within an established kinship relationship. Yet, Ruth takes her חסד beyond the level of obligation by refusing to leave Naomi and binding herself to her as a levirate widow. Ruth's loving loyalty to Naomi is reflective of the covenant loyalty of YHWH demonstrated in his freely binding himself to his people within the covenant.

Boaz recognizes the extraordinary level of Ruth's loyalty and commitment to her mother-in-law (Ruth 2:11). Ruth's demonstration of חסד forms his perception of this Moabite woman and is the basis on which he shows kindness to Ruth. Ruth continues to act on the basis of חסד when she seeks marriage from Boaz and calls him to his duty as kinsman

Ruth

redeemer (Ruth 3:10). It is her actions of kindness and loyalty in providing for her mother-in-law (in naming them daughter and mother-in-law the narrator continues to emphasize the kinship connections between the two women), that lead the people of Bethlehem to recognize that far from being a threat as a young Moabite widow, she is a worthy woman (Ruth 3:11). Both Ruth and Boaz exhibit what Sakenfeld argues is at the heart of חסד, "deliverance or protection as a responsible keeping of faith with another with whom one is in a relationship."[63] Ruth's generosity and kindness to her mother-in-law, reciprocated in Boaz's kindness to her, ultimately "saves" Naomi from an embittered, poverty-stricken, old age.

As was noted in chapter 4, the Hebrew word חסד represents an important concept in the Old Testament. Like righteousness חסד is a theologically freighted term since it describes not only what is at the heart of the relationship between YHWH and his people but also the essential nature of YHWH's character. The Old Testament throughout its legal, narrative, and prophetic material bears witness that YHWH is compassionate and gracious, slow to anger, abounding in steadfast love (חסד) and faithfulness (cf. Exod 34:67; Num 14:18; Neh 9:17; Ps 86:15; 103:8; 145:8; Joel 2:13; Jonah 4:2).The word is variously translated as steadfast love, faithfulness, loyalty, and loving kindness and covers the description of relationships both on a human level and between the divine and human, particularly in terms of the covenant relationship (Exod 20:6 *et passim*).[64]

Ruth's story demonstrates several aspects of this freighted word חסד. Firstly it illustrates the relational quality of חסד; a deep and faithful commitment to another person that goes beyond mere obligation. Secondly it demonstrates the reciprocal nature of חסד, those who practice loyal kindness in turn receive kindness from others. Finally Ruth's story illustrates the saving quality of חסד that offers help and deliverance to the one in need. Inclusion of her in the genealogy, like that of Rahab, serves to point towards a merciful Messiah and anticipates the trajectory of his teaching, since, as we have seen, mercy is a key discipleship virtue. This Matthean theme will be explored more fully in chapter 8 but to summarize briefly:

The offer of deliverance and help is at the heart of Matthew's presentation of Jesus, the Messiah "will save his people from their sins" (Matt 1:21). In his teaching, healing, and relationships with others Jesus will epitomize the חסד that is at the heart of God. The call for a generous, loving kindness

---

63. Sakenfeld, *Meaning of Hesed*, 233.

64. It occurs 246 times in the Old Testament and a significant amount of scholarly work has sought to define the term from different angles, cf. Glueck, *Hesed in the Bible*; Sakenfeld, *Meaning of Hesed*; Clark, *Word Hesed*.

towards others underlies much of Jesus' teaching in Matthew. He calls his disciples to go the second mile in their treatment of others (Matt 5:41), to love their enemies (Matt 5:44), and in teaching his disciples that those who are merciful will receive mercy (Matt 5:7) Jesus calls all, rich and poor, to be merciful. The discerning reader might be drawn back to the stories of the two women in the genealogy who although themselves are marginalized are prepared to show loyalty and mercy to others.

Furthermore, Ruth's actions foreshadow what Jesus practices and asks for from those who would follow him. In her steadfast commitment to Naomi and the consequent service and risk taking involved, Ruth models the role of a disciple. Ruth is prepared to leave her people, her allegiance to other gods and her "mother's house" behind in order to follow Naomi in utter loyalty. Jesus calls for the same loving loyalty from his disciples both in their treatment of others and also in his calling to follow him. They are called to leave all, including their family and the commitments that family might involve (Matt 8:18–22), and follow him in service (Matt 20:22).

Significantly, Ruth is not a devout Jewish woman but a Moabite, a Moabite woman, who according to Deuteronomic law should be banned from the congregation even to the tenth generation (Deut 23:2–3). Yet, this woman demonstrates the kind of loving kindness and mercy required of God's people. Although she is not an Israelite she, like Tamar and Rahab, behaves in a way that God desires. Consequently, she is accepted and integrated into Bethlehem society and so her life, like that of Tamar and Rahab's, becomes a radical call to inclusivity.

Campbell's comment is relevant here:

> What makes Ruth a true Israelite is that she, like others in the story who are generically Israelites, behaves like one. There is clearly a comprehensive character to such a view. It sees *hesed* as something within the capability of human beings of whatever lineage.[65]

Not only does Ruth's story throw light on the nature of חסד but, like Tamar and Rahab's stories, it challenges conceptions about those who can come under YHWH's wings or, to put it in Matthean terms, can enter the kingdom of heaven. All three women thus challenge Israel's perception of her own identity.

---

65. Campbell, *Ruth*, 82.

Tamar, Rahab, and Ruth

To conclude this investigation of the first three named women in the genealogy I want to summarize my findings.

By now it will be clear that certain common themes are emerging. When read as intertexts to one another, the Hebrew narratives of the three women named in the first epoch of Matthew's genealogy reveal several common themes that are taken up and developed by Matthew in his Gospel.

All three stories are concerned with women who are on the margins. All three are structurally marginalized within the patriarchal worlds in which they exist, not only simply because they are women but more specifically because they are in an anomalous position in terms of their sexuality, since two are levirate widows and one is a prostitute. As a group of women they perform the positive function in the Messiah's genealogy of representing those who are marginalized; it is this group of people to whom, Matthew demonstrates, the Messiah's ministry will be primarily directed. This will be considered in part 2 chapter 9.

Even more notably, all three are also foreign women, originally outsiders to Israel. All three women are contrasted with Israelite male insiders (Judah, the spies, and Boaz), who are challenged and prompted by them to act in line with God's purposes. All three align themselves with YHWH and demonstrate a radical loyalty to his people. Through their faithful behavior they are accepted into the people of God, moving from the margins to a place inside Israel. A dynamic of inclusivity undergirds all three stories. This anticipates the Matthean theme of faithful Gentiles who respond more appropriately to Jesus than Israelite insiders and who consequently find a place in Israel. Significantly, in their Old Testament narratives, Tamar and Ruth become mothers to sons in the redemptive Davidic line. Whilst Rahab's motherhood is not a feature of her Old Testament story, she too is instrumental in Israel's redemptive history. Matthew recognizes this by honoring her with motherhood of a son in the line of the Messiah. As Love notes, the status of the women is ascribed by Matthew because as non-Israelites they are included in Jesus' lineage, but their status is also acquired because although their stories of origin culturally marginalize them "they are, nonetheless, heroines within the great Israelite story."[66] Matthew bears witness that all three mothers occupy a key place in Israel's salvation history.

---

66. Love, *Jesus and Marginal Women*, 104.

Mothers on the Margin?

All three narratives have a gynocentric bias since, unusually for Hebrew narrative, all three women are at some point the main protagonists in the plot who take positive initiatives in situations that threaten death and destruction, to bring about a happy ending. All three episodes start with Israelite men (Judah, the spies, and Elimelech), travelling into foreign territory where things go wrong and death threatens. The three women, all negatively associated with these foreign places, at some point in the plot, all take risky, courageous action on behalf of those from Israel. Their actions bring about a surprising reversal of fortunes that enables a forward movement in God's purposes for Israel. Consequently all three women are portrayed in an affirmative light.

Furthermore, in spite of the scandalous overtones to all three stories that many commentators have in the past been quick to emphasize, all three women are characterized primarily neither in terms of scandalous sexual activity nor in terms of their sinfulness, but by their virtues of righteousness, faith and loyalty. All three women are challenging embodiments of the faithfulness, righteousness, and mercy which characterize YHWH himself and that are central to Israel's identity as the people of God. The women demonstrate virtues that Matthew will show not only foreshadow the character of the Messiah but also are attributes Jesus teaches as vitally important in the lives of his disciples. Part 2 chapter 8 considers further how righteousness, faith, and mercy are all key virtues of Matthean discipleship and how therefore Matthew hints from the outset that women will be included alongside men among the disciples of Jesus. It will be argued in part 2 chapter 10 that they, along with Bathsheba and Mary, are the first indication of a positive gynocentric counternarrative that runs throughout Matthew's Gospel.

Ultimately, the presence of the women in the genealogy is subversive. The three women subvert the norms represented by Israel's fathers in terms of their marginality, ethnicity, and gender. Their inclusion in the Messiah's ancestry is the first indication that the birth of the Messiah will involve a reconfiguration of Israel's identity in these three areas.

But what of Bathsheba and Mary? The next two chapters will consider the two women who are mentioned in the annotations of the second and third epoch of the genealogy.

6

"She of Uriah"

Matthew's genealogical reference to the fourth woman of the Old Testament is startling. Whereas the first three women are named, Bathsheba is given no personal name, but only referred to as Uriah's wife; in this sense she is unnamed.

And David was the father of Solomon by she of Uriah (ἐκ τῆς τοῦ Οὐρίου) (Matt 1:6b)

The shock of the reference to the fact that Solomon's mother did not "belong" to David but to Uriah is compounded by the knowledge that technically this is "incorrect" since Bathsheba was David's wife by the time she conceived and bore Solomon. Clearly, Matthew wants to draw attention to the circumstances surrounding Solomon's birth. I will begin by reviewing the Old Testament narratives where Bathsheba appears.

Bathsheba in the Old Testament

Bathsheba appears in three stories in the Old Testament: the story of adultery, murder-by-proxy, and marriage that lead to Solomon's birth (2 Sam 11–12), the story of a dying king and the question of accession where Bathsheba intercedes on Solomon's behalf (1 Kgs 1:11–31), and her intercession as queen mother before her son Solomon on Adonijah's behalf (1 Kgs 2:13–25). Since Rost's thesis of 1926 in which he argued for the existence of a unified throne succession narrative, running from 2 Samuel 9–20 to 1 Kings 1–2, these chapters, referred to as the "succession narrative," have generally been recognized to be the work of a single author.[1] For a number of years scholars interested in the narrative as story have generally accepted that these chapters form one integral piece of literature that was originally written as a "great and grand story"[2] in which the accession of Solomon (1 Kgs 1–2) is the final outcome of the events between David and Bathsheba in 2 Samuel 11–12. More recently Rost's thesis has been challenged on a number of fronts.[3]

Gunn has pointed out that an analysis of 2 Samuel 9–20 and 1 Kings 1–2 that focuses on David the king in terms of accession, rebellion, and succession is inadequate because it fails to recognize that the key episodes in 2 Sam 11–12 are about David's private life. In his analysis he underlines how the private and political constantly impinge on one another and that this is an important thematic element that Rost's thesis does not take into account.[4]

More recently Keys has argued that the books of 1 and 2 Samuel form a coherent unified whole and that 1 Kings differs from it on grounds of "style, language, content, theological orientation and position."[5] She concludes that 1 Kings is a later work although clearly there is a close link between the two texts. Klement has also challenged Rost's thesis, arguing for the structural unity of 1–2 Samuel. Although on a first reading the closing chapters of 2 Samuel (2 Sam 21–24) seemingly have little to do with the main text, Klement has demonstrated how the pattern of ring structures in the main section of 2 Samuel are thematically linked to the final chapters.[6] Consequently the concluding sections are more integrated with the main text than was previously thought.[7]

The argument that 1 and 2 Samuel are a separate literary work to 1 Kings is supported with reference to Bathsheba. The stylistic narrative treatment of her in 1 Kings is quite different to that of 2 Samuel 11–12, where narrative attention devoted to Bathsheba is minimal.

In 1 Kings Bathsheba is one of the main characters in the plot, interacting with Nathan and David and controlling the dialogue as she

---

1. Rost, *Succession*.
2. Fokkelman, *Narrative Art and Poetry*, 9.
3. See the discussion summarizing the scholastic history by Birch, "First and Second Books of Samuel," 950–54, 1269–71.
4. Gunn, *King David*, 88–110.
5. Keys, *Wages of Sin*, 70.
6. Klement, *2 Samuel 21–24*.
7. See Firth, *1 & 2 Samuel*, 20.

"She of Uriah"

intercedes for her son. Family matters and affairs of state converge as she and Nathan petition the dying king, reminding him of his promise that Solomon should succeed him as king. Through an admirably tactful speech Bathsheba obtains a public affirmation from the bedridden king, "That your son Solomon shall succeed me as king" (1 Kgs 1:30). The central issue revolves around whether or not David has sworn the oath concerning his succession to which Nathan refers (1 Kgs 1:13) and that is the crux of Bathsheba's appeal (1 Kgs 1:17). A number of commentators have wondered whether David ever made such an oath as there is no written record of it. Alter suggests this is "a central ambiguity which the writer surely intends to exploit."[8] Was it just a ploy made up by Nathan but presented in such a way that the king would be convinced he had indeed made such an oath? On this reading Bathsheba manipulates the king in order to save her life and the life of her son. Or had David actually, many years previously, made an oath before Bathsheba within the privacy of his palace?[9] On this reading Bathsheba is holding David to his responsibility to fulfill his promise and commitment to her in much the same way that Tamar with Judah, Rahab with the spies and Ruth with Boaz all held men accountable to fulfill their responsibilities. What can be established for certain from the text is that David responds by taking his responsibility seriously. Having promised to keep his oath to her, he goes on to command Zadok, Nathan, and Benaiah to anoint Solomon immediately as king. Consequently Bathsheba becomes queen mother, treated with respect and deference (see Solomon's treatment of her 1 Kgs 2:19).

It is as a mature woman, with power and prominence as queen mother, that Bathsheba is presented to the reader by the narrator in 1 Kings 2. Her request on behalf of Adonijah for Abishag proves to be her final request, one that results in her son Solomon reigning without rival. The text is unclear as to whether she made the request naïvely or with intent. Either way, she has played a significant role in securing the future of Solomon's "house" in fulfillment of YHWH's promise to David (2 Sam 7:12–13) determining the continuing leadership of the Davidic monarchy at its first crucial transition point.[10]

---

8. Alter, *David Story*, 366.

9. Nathan tells Bathsheba to say, "Didn't the king swear to your maidservant..." (1 Kgs 1:13). Bathsheba says to David, "You swore by YHWH your God to your maidservant..." (1 Kgs 1:17). David replies to her, "As I swore to you by the Lord the God of Israel..." (1 Kgs 1:30).

10. Solvang notes that "Bathsheba's activity as queen mother is consistent with her royal counterparts as glimpsed in extra-biblical sources and is paradigmatic for

Within the 2 Samuel text her presentation is very different. The narrative focus is on David, who is the main protagonist, and Uriah and Joab. In her role as Uriah's wife, Bathsheba is almost entirely passive and she says only two words throughout. Both Fokkleman and Berlin regard her within the narrative as simply an agent, the performer of an action necessary to the plot. The plot calls for adultery and Bathsheba fills that role.

I argue that it is the story in the text of 2 Samuel 11–12, rather than the text of 1 Kings, to which the Matthean narrator is alluding to since in 1 Kings Bathsheba is never referred to as the wife of Uriah. The two stories in 1 Kings introduce her solely as "Bathsheba, Solomon's mother" (1 Kgs 1:11; 2:13) whereas in 2 Samuel 11–12 the narrator refers to her as the "wife of Uriah" four times (2 Sam 11:3, 26; 12:10, 15). Matthew's narrator refers to her in the same way (Matt 1:6). In consequence, in order to address the question of her inclusion in Matthew's genealogy I will address the 2 Samuel story as a discrete literary unit without reference to 1 Kings.

Although Berlin refers to her in the 2 Samuel story as "a complete non-person,"[11] I will argue this is not the case. In Berlin's analysis the level of characterization of an individual is linked to function within the plot. However, Chatman has argued for a more fluid understanding of characterization as an integral process that takes place between the reader and the text. For Chatman characterization is built up from a variety of images.[12] This the text provides. Bathsheba *is* a person in the 2 Samuel story, albeit shadowy and ill defined in terms of her character and motivation. Readers know that she is beautiful (2 Sam 11:2). Readers, unusually in the case of a woman, are also given her patrimony (2 Sam 11:3). Becoming pregnant gives Bathsheba the power to send (as opposed to David's power of sending)[13] a message of two Hebrew words, "I'm pregnant" (2 Sam 11:5)

---

viewing her successors within the biblical text." See her discussion of Bathsheba's role as queen mother. Solvang, *Woman's Place*, 153.

11. Berlin, *Poetics and Interpretation*, 27.

12. Chatman, *Story and Discourse*, 118–19. Bach also uses Chatman's theory as a basis for her examination of the figure of Bathsheba. "Following Chatman's concept of characterization as an integral process of reader and text, I examine the biblical figure of Bathsheba, not as a passive non-person, but first as an object of male sexual fantasy, seen and not heard, and then as a good mother, heard and not seen." Bach, "Signs of the Flesh," 61.

13. One of the notable word usages in these two chapters is the repeated use of the Hebrew root שׁלח. David as king has the power to send and repeatedly sends others to do his bidding e.g., 2 Sam 11:1, 3, 4, 6, 8, 14. In turn Joab sends David news of Uriah's death (2 Sam 11:18, 22) and victory over Rabbah (2 Sam 12:27) Finally, YHWH sends Nathan to David in judgement (2 Sam 12:1). The word is thus a *Leitwort* for these two chapters, binding them together as a whole.

"She of Uriah"

which will propel David into a downward spiral of cover-up, treachery, and murder. An insight into her inner emotional life is provided at the point when readers see her mourning after the death of her husband Uriah (2 Sam 11:26) and needing consolation after the death of her firstborn son by David (2 Sam 12:24). She is the bearer of a second child, Solomon (2 Sam 12:24), and it is as the life bearer of the son who is beloved of the Lord (2 Sam 12:24) that the scene in 2 Samuel closes on the woman who is finally named Bathsheba. However, it is the way in which the crucial opening scene is read (2 Sam 11:1–5), that determines the character of Bathsheba in the reader's eye.

Reading the Gaps in the Text: Differing Perspectives

It has already been noted that in terms of characterization, Hebrew narrative is often ambiguous. The ambiguities are created because typically readers are not told of a character's motives, inner life or intentions. The gaps in the text invite real readers to enter into the web of interpretation, to respond to the text by supplying a character's motives for themselves. We have already seen that vastly different conclusions about the character and nature of the women under discussion can be drawn from different readings of the text. This becomes particularly apparent in Bathsheba's case where readers are told nothing of Bathsheba's thoughts, feelings or motivation in the crucial scene in 2 Samuel 11: 2–5. Commenting on the narrator's reticence in the 2 Samuel 11 narrative, Sternberg notes the central gaps in the plot sequence:

> [The narrator] presents external occurrences alone, deed and words, leaving his agents' inner lives opaque—even though in a dramatic narrative of this type it is precisely the motives and thoughts of the characters that interest the reader most. To understand what is going on, the reader must assume here the existence of emotions, passions, fears, and scheming . . . The narrator himself, however, evades all explicit formulation of hidden thoughts and designs, thus creating the central gaps in the plot sequence.[14]

Consequently this particular narrative has provided biblical commentators (and many others), ample scope for conjecture and hypothesis concerning Bathsheba's character and motivation. Ironically, Sternberg's evaluation

---

14. Sternberg, *Poetics of Biblical Narrative*, 190–91.

of Bathsheba seems to be more influenced by the rabbis than by the text itself. While he has a detailed discussion on gap filling in regard to David, Uriah, and Joab, he ignores Bathsheba. Of her (in a footnote) he writes:

> It is impossible to determine Bathsheba's attitude, though one would not imagine that she showed much resistance . . . The rabbis, ideologically committed to David and his line, argued that it was she who had seduced the king—why else should she have bathed naked on the roof?[15]

Sternberg has allowed his gap filling in regard to Bathsheba to be influenced by ideological rather than textual indicators. Traditionally this has been the case. Blenkinsopp may be taken as a typical example when he opines that Bathsheba's story illustrates the biblical motif of "the Woman who brings Death."[16] Blenkinsopp's views are heavily colored by his reading of Eve as the woman who seduces Adam. He claims that Bathsheba's story strengthens the pattern "according to which death comes through the wiles of a woman."[17] By bathing in sight of the king Bathsheba seduces David and her cry of "I'm pregnant" is "more a cry of triumph than an S.O.S. signal."[18] Bathsheba is one of a number of women who lure men into sin since "this kind of woman seduces the heart."[19]

In consequence over the years Bathsheba has been painted, by artists literally, as the seducer, the one whose provocative naked bathing in sight of King David lured him into sin. As Exum has shown, in paintings and films, Bathsheba's body has become an object of male sexual fantasy.[20]

One implication of reading 2 Samuel 9–20 and 1 Kings 1–2 as a single narrative is that a number of scholars have formed opinions about Bathsheba's characterization in 1 Kings and then read this back into the 2 Samuel story, drawing conclusions about Bathsheba that are highly questionable when the story is considered as a discrete unit. From their reading of 1 Kings they infer that Bathsheba must have manipulated King David from the start. For example, when commenting on the phrase "she came to him" (2 Sam 11:4) Alter comments:

15. Sternberg, *Poetics of Biblical Narrative*, 526n10.
16. Blenkinsopp, "Theme and Motif," 52.
17. Ibid.
18. Ibid.
19. Ibid., 53.
20. See Exum, *Plotted, Shot and Painted*.

> Her later behavior in the matter of her son's succession to the throne (1 Kgs 1–2) suggests a woman who has her eye on the main chance, and it is possible that opportunism, not merely passive submission, explains her behavior here as well.[21]

Nicol explicitly states in his paper "The Alleged Rape of Bathsheba: Some Observation on Ambiguity in Biblical Narrative":

> By permitting this less ambiguous narrative [1 Kings 1] to influence the reading of the other two [2 Samuel 11 and 1 Kings 2] in which there is certainly a rather greater degree of ambiguity, I concluded that the resourcefulness she evidences in it weighs the argument in favour of an interpretation of Bathsheba as a clever and resourceful woman, not just in 1 Kings 1 but in all three stories.[22]

Bathsheba's "resourcefulness" is read as her complicity in the adultery, "Bathsheba's action of bathing in such close proximity to the royal palace was deliberately provocative."[23] Nicol goes on to argue that on the basis of 2 Samuel 11:4 the narrator "has represented her as participating in adultery at a time she had some reason to believe she was fertile."[24] He concludes that as a clever and resourceful woman Bathsheba in marrying David "achieves her goal."[25] I have to question whether a woman living in Israel in the eighth century BC would have known the peak fertility point of her monthly cycle. However, Nicol goes on to raise an important issue: where a narrative is ambiguous, what factors lead commentators to prefer one interpretation over another? He goes on to note that the "total reading of the text must be consistent and coherent," yet he makes no reference whatsoever to 2 Samuel 12, which I shall argue is integral to the narrative unit as a whole and provides an important hint about Bathsheba's complicity or lack of it.

In a much more recent article entitled "Bathsheba Revealed" feminist writer Klein agrees that Bathsheba was "complicit in the sexual encounter."[26] She suggests Bathsheba's main motive was the desire for motherhood but alongside this was the desire to "advance her standing

---

21. Alter, *David Story*, 251.
22. Nicol, "Alleged Rape of Bathsheba," 43.
23. Ibid., 44.
24. Ibid., 51.
25. Ibid., 53.
26. Klein, "Bathsheba Revealed," 51.

in the community."²⁷ Klein works on the assumption that Bathsheba was married to an infertile man and argues that she plans things so that she seduces the king at a time when she is most likely to conceive in the hope that she will fall pregnant. Klein would agree with Blenkinsopp and Nicol that her cry of "I'm pregnant" is one of triumph, not distress. In achieving this she "fulfils her mission to bear sons."²⁸ Klein's thesis is highly improbable. It would seem to be an extremely risky strategy, with the threat of a death sentence for adultery, to seduce a king in order to have a child while her husband is at war and cannot therefore possibly be the father. Surprisingly, Klein reduces Bathsheba, as other commentators have, to the level of a woman who exploits "her sexual allure as a temptress in order to gain her objective."²⁹

Bailey, focusing on the power relations in 2 Samuel 10–12, argues that together David and Bathsheba were complicit in the act of adultery. It is a "story of political intrigue in which sex becomes a tool of politics."³⁰ He suggests that Lot's daughters and Tamar (Gen 38) serve as a "precedent for portraying situations where women engage in sex as a means of improving their status."³¹ In Bathsheba's case, sex is used as a tool to gain political advantage through a co-partnership with David. Bailey surmises that their affair was a result of a planned political alliance between Ahithophel's line and David's line. David's power is consolidated through marriage and the birth of their child.

We have seen that in Tamar's case it was an act of desperation and loyalty to her husband that forced Tamar to exploit her sexuality. Lot's daughters too had little choice in their situation if the family line were to continue. Bailey's conjecture is based on a reading of Genesis 19 and 38 that I find unacceptable. Furthermore in order to work, it involves a questionable amendment of the text of 2 Samuel 11–12 to a position after the Absalom revolt.

Firth also argues that David had political reasons for sleeping with Bathsheba. He bases his argument on the observation that in 2 Samuel 9–20 the function of sexual congress with another man's wife is an attempt to claim authority over a rival.³² On this reading David sleeps with Bath-

27. Ibid.
28. Ibid., 53.
29. Ibid., 54.
30. Bailey, *David in Love and War*, 88.
31. Ibid., 89.
32. Firth, *1 & 2 Samuel*, 416.

sheba, having found out who she is, in order to claim authority from Uriah whom he considers to be his political rival. Bathsheba is not an accomplice in the plan but simply a means to an end. Firth's reading rests on the assumption that Uriah posed a threat to David. However, the big weakness in this argument, a weakness acknowledged by Firth, is that the text never gives reasons as to why David should view Uriah in this way. Firth notes that an initial reading might not support his position, but argues that the disclosure of information at other points of Samuel opens up the possibility he suggests. Like Bailey's argument, it is based on conjecture that has no basis in the immediate text. Furthermore, both Bailey and Firth's readings make the episode of 2 Samuel 11:1–5 redundant. David's sighting of Bathsheba bathing and the notice of Bathsheba's sexual attraction signaled by the narrator's reference to her beauty becomes irrelevant. In both cases, with Uriah at war, David could have simply sent for Bathsheba and slept with her.

In contrast to arguments for political reasons for David's action, several scholars have suggested that David's action is a result of the male lust of an all powerful king and should be seen as rape. Noll writes, "The terse wording of 2 Samuel 11:4 is designed to express a superior's forced imposition upon an inferior, which in modern parlance is rape."[33] Both Ackerman[34] and Gunn[35] have noted the connections between the rape of Tamar in 2 Samuel 13 and David's taking of Bathsheba that precedes it. They argue that Tamar's rape is designed to serve as a mirror image to David's rape of Bathsheba.[36] However, it must be noted that the text in 2 Samuel 13 is clearly more explicit in terms of Tamar's refusal and Amnon's use of force. The rendering of "she of Uriah's" story is much more ambiguous. Nevertheless, I shall argue that a number of narrative clues within the story itself and its broader context point towards David's guilt and Bathsheba's innocence.

Feminist writer Exum goes so far as to accuse the textual narrator of raping Bathsheba. In a chapter entitled "Raped by the Pen," Exum argues that the androcentric biblical narrator violates Bathsheba's character

---

33. Noll, *Faces of David*, 59–60.

34. Ackerman, "Knowing Good and Evil," 49.

35. Gunn writes, "Clearly we are expected to see in chapter 13 a recapitulation of what had gone before in chapter 11." Gunn, *King David*, 98–99.

36. In their closing comments on the story of Amnon and Tamar Cotterell and Turner say, "We are constantly made to look back, to the sexual excesses of David and particularly the Bathsheba episode." Cotterell and Turner, *Linguistics and Biblical Interpretation*, 253.

"in depriving her of voice and in portraying her in an ambiguous light."[37] Since the narrator in 2 Samuel 11:1–5 does not allow the reader to see things from Bathsheba's perspective, the narrator denies her subjectivity and because

> the denial of subjectivity is an important factor in rape . . . the narrator symbolically rapes Bathsheba, and by withholding her point of view, he presents an ambiguous portrayal that leaves her vulnerable to the charge of seduction . . . The narrator who disrobes Bathsheba and depicts her as the object of David's lust is the real perpetrator of the crime against Bathsheba.[38]

Exum is accurate in her observation that, since the reader is not provided with Bathsheba's point of view, her portrayal leaves her open to charges of seduction. However, I will argue that at the crucial moment, the narrator provides the reader with David's point of view (not Bathsheba's) in order to indicate that the impetus and inclination to sleep with Bathsheba comes from David, not her. I contest Exum's view that "the text hints that she asked for it"[39] because she allows herself to be seen. I also reject Exum's claim that the narrator is voyeuristic; no provocative disrobing of Bathsheba takes place and she is simply described as very beautiful in order to explain David's attraction to her. Ironically, Exum's writing is far more voyeuristic than the writing of the biblical narrator whom she accuses of voyeurism.

A Narrative Reading of Bathsheba's Story

Second Samuel 11–12 is a discrete literary unit within the larger cycle of the David story. Brueggemann notes that these two chapters (2 Sam 11–12) depict the key turning point in David's life and are a "pivotal turning point in the narrative plot of the books of Samuel."[40] He comments, "The text is placed at the exact point where the narrative shifts from public triumph . . . to personal pathos, now to be spun out in the narrative that follows."[41] A shift in the portrait of David also comes at this point where the focus changes from David's public to his private life. The former narrative

---

37. Exum, *Fragmented Women*, 171.
38. Ibid., 173–74.
39. Ibid., 189.
40. Brueggemann, *First and Second Samuel*, 271.
41. Ibid., 272.

"She of Uriah"

(2 Sam 5–10) is upbeat, a story of victories and success for David in his public life as Israel's king. The latter chapters, starting with the pivotal incident with Bathsheba, are much more ambiguous and tinged with the tragic effects of sin. In one sense these chapters mark a transition from a life under blessing to a life under curse but that distinction is too rigid for we shall see that with the curse comes blessing too.

Chapters 11–12 are bracketed by reference to the wider political events of the kingdom. The war with Ammon is detailed in the first verse, 2 Samuel 11:1. "They [all Israel] ravaged the Ammonites, and besieged Rabbah" introduces the story and also completes it in 2 Sam 12:26–31. Licht notes, "The external political event of the war with Ammon thus serves as literary framework for the personal events of David's crime and punishment . . . It certainly is a deliberate device."[42] Similarly, Alter comments that the link verse 1 is a "brilliant transition device. It firmly ties in the story of David as adulterer and murderer with the large national-historical perspective of the preceding chronicle."[43] However, as well as tying the external political scene to the private scene of David's downfall, this verse provides the tone for the ensuing events. The Ammonites have been ravaged, a term which foreshadows and hints at what is to follow. Hollywood-type readings of a love story are clearly not in line with the narrative tone set by the opening verse.[44]

The Narrative Structure of 2 Samuel 11–12

Second Samuel 11–12 comprises one narrative unit, framed by the war against the Ammonites, which both introduces the scene between David and Bathsheba and provides a concluding epilogue to the birth of Solomon. Nathan's pronouncement of YHWH's judgement provides the turning point of the narrative.

---

42. Licht, *Storytelling in the Bible*, 136.
43. Alter, *Art of Biblical Narrative*, 76.
44. The Hollywood films *David and Bathsheba* (1951) and *King David* (1985) both portray 2 Samuel 11 as a love story. The passage has been translated by artists and more recently filmmakers visually to portray a naked and shameful Bathsheba as the voluptuous seducer in order to make David less guilty at Bathsheba's expense. See Exum, *Plotted, Shot and Painted*.

2 Samuel 11:1	David sends Joab and all Israel against Ammon
2 Samuel 11:2–5	*David has sexual relations with Bathsheba resulting in pregnancy*
2 Samuel 11:6–13	David attempts and fails to manipulate Uriah
2 Samuel 11:14–25	David orders and achieves the murder of Uriah by proxy
2 Samuel 11:26–27	*The wife of Uriah mourns and becomes David's wife bearing a son*
2 Samuel 12:1–6	The Lord sends Nathan to David with a parable
2 Samuel 12:7–15a	YHWH's judgement on David and his house
2 Samuel 12:15b–23	The Lord strikes the child, in vain David pleads for his life
2 Samuel 12:24–25	*Bathsheba mourns and bears David a son named Solomon*
2 Samuel 12:26–31	Joab summons David against Ammon

Bathsheba's Story

2 Samuel 11:1–5 | David Takes Bathsheba

It is springtime "when kings go out to battle" (2 Sam 11:1a)[45] but, although "David sent Joab with his officers" (2 Sam 11:1b), he himself "remained at Jerusalem" (2 Sam 11:1c). Sternberg has pointed out that this ironic comment by the narrator directs "the reader to view the king (who tarries at home) in ironic contrast to all the others (whom he has sent to make war)."[46] The next verse dispels any ideas the reader might entertain that he had pressing business in Jerusalem because readers are told that David did not get up from his siesta until "late one afternoon" (2 Sam 11:2a). Strolling round on the roof of the palace in the cool of the evening, he catches sight of a woman bathing. The narrator first lets the reader see Bathsheba through David's eyes, "he saw a woman bathing from the roof and the appearance of the woman was very beautiful" (2 Sam 11:2c). David's position on the roof gazing down reflects his status and position of power in relation to the woman bathing below. By letting the reader see

---

45. I follow the MT "kings" rather than the variant reading "messengers."
46. Sternberg, *Poetics of Biblical Narrative*, 194.

the "woman" from David's point of view the narrator subtly implies that both the impetus and inclination for what follows were David's. The narrator gives no indication of what the woman sees, or if she is aware of his gaze. In providing the time of day, place, and situation the narrator implies that it was a particular combination of events rather than any ploy on the woman's part that led to David's catching sight of her. It is impossible to know whether Bathsheba was aware that her courtyard could be seen from the palace roof, nor do readers know whether she was naked as has so often been assumed. Consequently, I do not read the narrative as suggesting that Bathsheba planned to seduce the king from the start by bathing provocatively within sight of the palace roof, as some have argued.[47] Later, her motivation for bathing is provided by the narrator and this reinforces Bathsheba's innocence.

David sends (שלח)[48] someone to find out who the woman is. The report comes back, "This is Bathsheba daughter of Eliam, the wife of Uriah the Hittite" (2 Samuel 11:3b). Bathsheba is a married woman of importance, possibly granddaughter to David's advisor Ahithophel[49] and wife to one of his top fighting men Uriah.[50] The information about the woman's patrimony does not prevent David's action. Knowledge that she is the wife of Uriah the Hittite, who was fighting alongside Joab and all Israel, gives David the opportunity he needs. David doesn't hesitate, for immediately in the next verse "David sent (שלח) messengers and he took her, and she came to him, and he lay with her" (2 Sam 11:4a). The relatively slow pace of the first three verses contrasts with the rapid pace of verse 4. There is no speech or dialogue between the two and the scene is reported with the greatest economy. Brueggemann comments, "The action is quick. The verbs rush as the passion of David rushed. He sent; he took; he lay . . . The royal deed of self-indulgence does not take very long."[51]

---

47. "It cannot be doubted that Bathsheba's action in bathing so close to the king's residence was provocative, nor can the possibility that the provocation was deliberate be discounted." Nicol, "Bathsheba: A Clever Woman?," 360.

48. See p. 124n13, on שלח.

49. See p. 32n36.

50. Cf. 2 Sam 23:34, 39 and 2 Sam 13:39. Uriah the Hittite was one of David's elite warriors. He has a good Yahwistic name—Yahweh is my light—which suggests that, although Hittite, he was born in Israel. McCarter, *II Samuel*, 285.

51. Brueggemann, *First and Second Samuel*, 273.

Five verbal clauses with one inserted circumstantial clause describe the whole scene:

> David sent messengers,
> And took her,
> And she came to him,
> And he lay with her,
> As she purified herself from her uncleanness,
> Then she returned to her house.

The series of active verbs in verses 2 and 3, "and he saw … sent … inquired … sent … took her … lay with her," indicate that the main initiative was David's.[52] But what of Bathsheba in all this? She is the subject of the third verbal clause "she came to him" (2 Sam 11: 4b). Does this imply that, although she was taken, she did not resist? A royal imperative gave her but one option. The king commanded and she complied. Did she know for what purpose she was summoned? As David stands looking down at her, he is the one in control with the power to send for her. Just as earlier David had taken a woman from her husband for his own benefit, "Ishbaal sent and took her (Michal) from her husband" (2 Sam 3:15) so here it is implied the woman had no choice in the matter.

The narrator interestingly waits until after the act of intercourse, disrupting the verbal clauses, to inform the reader why Bathsheba had been bathing, "she was purifying herself from her uncleanness" (2 Sam 11:4c). Her act of bathing was not a deliberate ploy but happened every month (presumably in the same place) as she took a ritual bath, required by the laws of purity, cleansing herself from the "impurity" of menstruation.[53] The difference on this occasion was that the king had time on his hands. The text insinuates David should have been at war with "all Israel." Instead with nothing better to do this particular month, from his vantage place on the palace roof, he sees a beautiful woman and lusts after her. Bathsheba herself was "guilty" of three "sins"; being visible, being a woman and being beautiful. It is ironic that Bathsheba's purity is mentioned directly after the sexual act. This suggests that the narrator is deliberately including the information here in order to set up a contrast between Bathsheba, who is fulfilling her religious obligations, and David who acts sinfully. I concur therefore with Fokkelman's observation:

---

52. Garsiel, "Story of David and Bathsheba," 255.
53. Cf. Lev 15:19–24.

> Opposite the man who is the prey of blind passion stands Bathsheba, and by the contrast her purity receives emblematic aspect.—The text is moreover not at all interested in her possibly having shared the responsibility. It shows her merely as an object of desire, in vv. 2–4, and of David's choice, in v. 27.[54]

Of course, this is an important piece of information in other ways. Readers know that with Uriah on the war front, any child conceived must be David's. The clause is both an ironic comment on David and significant for the progression of the plot.

The narrator gives no indication of Bathsheba's reaction to what has taken place, simply noting that "she returned to her house" (2 Sam 11:4c). There is no evidence that David and Bathsheba had an ongoing relationship, no mutually consenting love affair. Evans comments, "The writers present this not as a great romance but as a rather seedy action on David's part that led to consequences with which he must now deal."[55]

A period of narrated time passes, "a characteristic biblical time-jump through summary from an action to its significant consequence,"[56] weeks during which Bathsheba presumably wondered about the possibility of conception. "The woman (note the impersonal reference) conceived; and she sent (שלח) and told David 'I am pregnant' (הרה אנכי)" (2 Sam 11:5). No clue is given to Bathsheba's state of mind or the tone of her announcement but this time Bathsheba maintains her spatial distance. She is now in a position to "send" a message to David. There is no threat or demand. The two Hebrew words הרה אנכי are enough to nullify David's control of the situation; two key words that are to change forever the Davidic monarchy. Her "sending" holds him responsible. She is not willing to suffer the consequences of their actions alone. Her pregnancy makes her very vulnerable and the power to act for or against her is in David's hands.

In the first five verses three different forms of name are used for Bathsheba, her kinship name (2 Sam 11:3), her proper name (2 Sam 11:3), but most frequently the common female designation אשה. In verse 2 David twice sees a woman אשה and in verse 5 the narrator tells the reader "the woman (אשה) conceived." By contrast, as well as her kinship name, she is given her proper name בת־שבע by an unknown individual in verse 3. However, she remains simply as "the woman" throughout most of the narrative and her proper name is not repeated until the last reference to her in

---

54. Fokkelman, *Narrative Art and Poetry*, 52–53.
55. Evans, *1 and 2 Samuel*, 188.
56. Alter, *Art of Biblical Narrative*, 76.

2 Samuel 12:24. By means of this device the narrator indicates that, from David's point of view at this stage and for most of the narrative, she is not seen as a person, but only as a woman with whom he can satisfy his lust. Finally, in verse 3, she is referred to as "the wife of Uriah the Hittite" אשׁת אוריה החתי. This final designation is the most significant in terms of the narrative plot and it is used of her on three more key occasions to deliberately keep her marital relationship with Uriah to the fore (2 Sam 11:26; 12:10; 12:15b). By constant reference to Uriah the narrator highlights David's guilt. Bathsheba might just be a beautiful woman to David but the reader is reminded that she is Uriah's wife and that in taking her, David transgresses God's commands not to commit adultery or covet another man's wife (Exod 20:14, 17).

2 Samuel 11:6–27; 12:1–25 | The Consequences

David does not leave Bathsheba to face the consequences of their sexual encounter on her own but neither does he admit his moral culpability. Instead he plans a ruse to get Uriah to sleep with his wife and thus divert suspicions of an illegitimate pregnancy. The next two sections (2 Sam 11:6–13; 11:14–25), focus on David's unsuccessful attempts to get Uriah to sleep with his wife and David's consequent murderous instructions carried out by Joab in order that his adultery would be kept secret.[57] The woman plays no part in this story, she remains in "the house" (2 Sam 11:4) and only reappears once her husband has been killed on the battlefield. However, though absent in person, the reader is repeatedly reminded of her presence in the house in the dialogue that occurs between David and Uriah (2 Sam 11:8, 9, 10, 11, 13).

Bathsheba re-enters the story as a widow in mourning, having received news of Uriah's death. Although she is carrying David's baby, it is her status as Uriah's wife that is emphasized by the narrator in 2 Samuel 11:26, where three times her marital relationship is stressed, "When the *wife of Uriah* heard that *Uriah her husband* was dead, she mourned *for her husband*" (my italics). There is no indication that her grief was not genuine and it is the only notice of emotion in the whole chapter. In contrast to the following chapter the emphasis is on *her* loss; David shows no signs of remorse or regret at this point. Following this period, for the second time

---

57. For a fascinating discussion of all the ambiguities of whether Uriah knew what David had been up to and why David summons Uriah to Jerusalem, see Sternberg, *Poetics of Biblical Narrative*, 199–229.

Bathsheba, who is not named, is sent for and brought to David, this time to become his wife, "And when she had gone through the mourning David sent and brought her to his house and she became his wife and she bore him a son" (2 Sam 11:27a). The narrator describes the events in quick, terse phrases. Readers are told nothing of her feelings or reactions to this second occasion when David sends for her (having sent her husband to his death). Berlin writes of verse 11:26–27a, "One and a half cold, terse verses to sum up the condition of a woman who has had an adulterous affair, become pregnant, lost her husband, married her lover, the king of Israel, and borne his child!"[58] Some would argue this is what Bathsheba had been hoping and longing for, to marry the king, her lover and father of her child. Conversely, readers can be appalled that, after the recent loss of the husband she loved, she is forced into a marriage by the man who had taken advantage of her and murdered her husband. Nonetheless, she is not left to languish as a widow carrying a child that has not been fathered by her husband with the possible mortal consequences she would face.[59] In marrying her, David takes responsibility for her and his child. The narrator gives the reader no direct information but the text indicates Bathsheba's vulnerability as a victim of David's sending.

These events are followed by the narrator supplying the reader with a crucial piece of information. The child may be born in wedlock, "But the thing that David had done was evil (וירע)[60] in the eyes of the Lord" (2 Sam 11:27b). Finally, the surface of the David and Bathsheba story is "fractured"[61] by the narrator informing the reader of YHWH's point of view, blame is laid clearly at David's feet. What does "the thing" (הדבר) refer to? Nathan's words of rebuke and pronouncement of judgement on David (2 Sam 12:9–12) make clear that it is *both* his act of adultery *and* the act of murder that are being referred to. Both Bathsheba and Uriah are the innocent victims of David's abuse of power. YHWH has been the silent observer of events and now his judgement on David's actions is about to be pronounced. Just as in Tamar's story YHWH judged and condemned the evil actions of Er (Gen 38:7) and Onan (Gen 38:10) leading to their deaths, so here the narrator explicitly tells us that YHWH has been watching events unfold and these events are evil (רעע) in his eyes. Ironically, this phrase mirrors the words David sent to Joab after the carnage of his

---

58. Berlin, *Poetics and Interpretation*, 26.
59. Cf. Lev 20:10, Deut 22:22.
60. From the root verb רעע indicating moral evil.
61. Sternberg's word, Sternberg, *Poetics of Biblical Narrative*, 190.

men and Uriah's death, "Do not let this matter be evil in your eyes" (2 Sam 11:25). Clearly, David's verdict on events is at odds with YHWH's.

The narrator's insertion of YHWH's point of view demonstrates that the king's power is not absolute; he cannot take a woman and the life of her husband without facing YHWH's judgement. This time it is the Lord who does the sending (2 Sam 12:1) and Nathan confronts David with a parable about a poor man with a treasured, little ewe lamb, "she was like a daughter to him" (2 Sam 12:3b).The force of the parable is directed against the rich man who, reluctant to kill a lamb from his own flocks for a guest, takes the poor man's lamb and kills her. Significantly, the lamb herself is innocent. The denouement of the scene comes after David's furious response towards the rich man's actions as Nathan cries, "You are the Man! . . . you have despised me [the Lord] and have taken the wife of Uriah the Hittite to be your wife" (2 Sam 12:7a, 10b).

Just as the rich man took the lamb belonging to another man for his own use, so King David has taken Bathsheba, who belonged to another man, for his use. The parable spells out David's guilt in taking Bathsheba and Bathsheba's innocence as the poor man's lamb. The parable also serves to indicate that David had violated a relationship between Bathsheba and Uriah that had been deep and endearing. David responds immediately with recognition of his guilt, "I have sinned against the Lord" (2 Sam 12:13a). God in his mercy "puts away" David's sin (2 Sam 12:14), although the consequences of his sinful grasping will have devastating and long term effects (2 Sam 12:10a). However, the baby, it appears, becomes the scapegoat for David's sin (2 Sam 12:14). That the child is the fruit of David's adulterous action is emphasized by the narrator with another reference to Uriah's wife, "The Lord struck down the child that Uriah's wife bore to David, and it became very ill" (2 Sam 12:15b). In the next few verses the reader is shown David's passionate response to the child's illness but, in spite of David's fasting and weeping over seven days, the child dies. Evans is right when she comments on Nathan's words in 2 Sam 12:14, "For modern readers this is one of the most difficult verses in the Bible."[62] Helpfully, Osgood suggests that the child's death was a "severe mercy . . . a token of the divine compassion for Bathsheba in the longer term" as it saved Bathsheba from the dishonor of future palace gossip over the identity of the child's father.[63] The only hint the reader gets concerning the child's mother's feelings is when David, for the first time, shows affection and care

62. Evans, *1 and 2 Samuel*, 190.
63. Osgood, "1 and 2 Samuel," 177.

towards Bathsheba by consoling her. After he has repented and suffered the initial consequences of his sin in the death of their first child, David responds to Bathsheba with comfort. This is reflected through the narrator finally naming her Bathsheba, "Then David consoled his wife Bathsheba, and went to her, and lay with her; and she bore him a son" (2 Sam 12: 24a).

Immediately after tragedy, judgement, and death, a new life is conceived in the womb of the woman Bathsheba, now "his [David's] wife" (2 Sam 12:24a). Dramatically, the birth is marked not by YHWH's anger but by his love. The narrator omnisciently tells the reader that "The Lord loved him" (2 Sam 12:24b). This is reiterated when Solomon is given a second name through Nathan the prophet, Jedidiah (beloved of the Lord). Incredibly life has begun again for this family.

Brueggeman comments:

> The placement of Solomon's birth in the narrative is stunning. Solomon is born so close to the sordidness . . . This God has an amazing capacity to work more life at the border of death.[64]

We have already seen how through the initiative and courage of three women, Tamar, Rahab, and Ruth, God worked "more life at the border of death." Now here, through this fourth woman, God in his grace does the same again.

Yet some have argued that Bathsheba brings not life but death. Gunn, following Blenkinsopp,[65] considers that Bathsheba, like the other women in the book of Samuel, is the bringer of death.[66] On the contrary, I argue death has come because of David's sinful abuse of power, his lustful taking of another man's wife leading to murder. By contrast, it is Bathsheba who is the bearer of life. God chooses to work more life at the border of death through the woman who in the past has so often been marginalized and maligned by biblical interpreters. Of David's many wives it is Bathsheba who is the bearer of the son who will fulfill the divine promise made to David, "I will raise up your offspring after you, who shall come forth from your body and I will establish his kingdom" (2 Sam 7:11). Her son is the child beloved of God who will maintain the line of David until eventually a Messiah will be born.

---

64. Brueggemann, *First and Second Samuel*, 284.
65. See p. 126.
66. Gunn, *King David*, 43.

Mothers on the Margin?

2 Samuel 12:26–31 | Postscript

The final section of this narrative unit doubles back in time and tells readers the outcome of the war against Ammon. In deferring information about victory until this point this story becomes an indirect means of reading the David and Bathsheba story. Sternberg suggests it provides a

> wry counterpoint to the personal doings of the victor. The king has stayed in Jerusalem, others have waged his war, he reaps the fruits of a subordinate's campaign and gives the city his own name: a fitting last note of ironic commentary on the tale of a king who steals a subordinate's wife and sees to it that she "be called after his name."[67]

It provides not only an ironic comment but also an interpretative key. The guilt has already been placed by the narrator fairly and squarely on David's shoulders (2 Sam 11:27b; 12:9). Now here at the end of the story, David's guilt is inferred more subtly. The king acts in a similar way on the political front to the way he had behaved privately; by taking something that he had not earned, nor was rightfully his.

The Inclusion of "She of Uriah" in Matthew's Genealogy

The second section of fourteen generations in Matthew's genealogy would read very smoothly "And David was the father of Solomon . . . and Solomon the father of Rehoboam" (Matt 1:6b–7a) if it were not for the troublesome annotation "And David was the father of Solomon *by the wife of Uriah*" (Matt 1:6b, my italics). Why has the Matthean narrator made reference to her by including her in an annotation at this point? Secondly, why is she only defined as *Uriah's* wife within a context where it would have been much more natural for Matthew to refer to her simply as Bathsheba, or even as *David's* wife, for it was as the wife of David that Bathsheba conceived and bore Solomon. I contend that read as an intertext to 2 Samuel 11–12, reference to "she of Uriah" in the annotations is made for the same reasons as Bathsheba is given that appellation in the 2 Samuel text; to draw attention to David's sinful treatment of both Bathsheba and Uriah and the abuse of his power as king.

---

67. Sternberg, *Poetics of Biblical Narrative*, 196.

"She of Uriah"

Hutchinson makes the strained assertion that Bathsheba is probably cited by Matthew as "the wife of Uriah" because "Mention of 'the wife of Uriah' rather than her name was probably meant to focus attention on Uriah's faith in contrast to that of David."[68] This is to support his argument that the inclusion of the women shows that "at crucial times in Israel's history Gentiles demonstrated more faith than Jews in response to God," hence the faith of Tamar versus that of Judah, Rahab versus the Israelites and Ruth versus that of the judges' generation.[69] However, the Hebrew text makes no mention of either man's faith. The ironic contrast that is set up between Uriah and David is between a man who reveres the rules of war that will not allow for enjoyment with his wife whilst the army is fighting, against the king who has been doing just that; enjoying Uriah's wife.

The rather startling annotation in the genealogy to "she of Uriah" (ἐκ τῆς τοῦ Οὐρίου) serves to remind readers of the story surrounding Solomon's birth; a story tinged with the violation of a woman, betrayal, murder, marriage, and the death of a baby, Solomon's elder brother, a story in which the narrative points to David's guilt and Bathsheba's innocence.

To summarize, this is achieved by the narrative in 2 Samuel in a number of ways. The narrative framing of the story within the military seizure of Ammon points to David's coercive action as does the consequent rape of Tamar by Amnon. Secondly, in the initial scene, Bathsheba is focalized by David, not the other way round, indicating the power to take her and initiative to do so lies with him. This is supported by the narrative where it is David who is primarily the subject of the active verbs, it is David who is the one who sends for Bathsheba and sleeps with her. Bathsheba's innocence is further indicated when she is described as having purified herself just before David sent for her. However most crucial to the interpretation of events is the narrator's comment that it was "the thing that *David* had done" which was "evil in the eyes of the Lord" (2 Sam 11:27, my italics). Finally, Nathan's parable draws parallels with Bathsheba and the innocent lamb taken by force. It is David who is the subject of Nathan's parable, to whom Nathan is sent to declare, "Why have you despised the word of the Lord to do what is evil in his sight? You have struck down Uriah the Hittite with the sword and have taken his wife to be your wife" (2 Sam 12:9). The cumulative effect of these narrative strategies is to draw attention to David's culpability in the abuse of his position and power as king.

---

68. Hutchison, "Women," 160.
69. Ibid.

Turning to her annotation in Matthew's genealogy, attention should be paid to the pattern of the genealogy and her placement within it. It is clearly significant that "she of Uriah" appears at the head of the second epoch. The division of the genealogy into three epochs is reflective of Matthew's ideological understanding of history. Matthew interprets Israel's history in the light of his theological understanding of events. The naming of many generations is not just tracing a line of descent but a tracing of the outworking of God's dealings with his chosen people; a charting of salvation history. By dividing the genealogy into three groups each of fourteen generations, Matthew highlights both the upward and downward train of events in salvation history. The first epoch of fourteen generations from Abraham to King David traces an upward trend from the promises made to Abraham, as the line of Judah by Tamar, continues through the generations, through both Rahab and Ruth, until it reaches its apex in the golden era of King David. Verse 6 is the tipping point. The first period of fourteen generations ends at verse 6a, finishing with the words, "David the king" (τὸν Λαυὶδ τὸν βασιλέα) (Matt 1:6a). Verse 6b opens the second period of fourteen generations. From this point on the trend is downwards until the disastrous events "at the time of the deportation to Babylon" (Matt 1:11). This turning point is indicated in two ways. David is named a second time but no longer as king. More pertinently, he is named as "the father of Solomon by the wife of Uriah" (Λαυὶδ δὲ ἐγέννησεν τὸν Σολομῶνα ἐκ τῆς τοῦ Οὐρίου) (Matt 1:6b). In Matthew's depiction of salvation history David's taking of Uriah's wife and the consequent murder of Uriah is the catalyst for the unraveling of events both within David's immediate family but ultimately the events that led finally to the exile. Matthew's inclusion of "she of Uriah" in the genealogy at this point draws attention to God's punishment of David and consequently others who exploited and misused positions of power and status.

Exile engendered questions over the fulfillment of divine promises made to Abraham and David, promises compromised because of human sin, by Israel failing to fulfill her covenant responsibilities as YHWH's chosen people. In spite of the return from exile, the third epoch does not resolve these issues. Although there is a historic return to the land under Zerubbabel, of which Matthew must have been aware, the narrator frames the third epoch as starting from the disastrous events of the exile and closing with the coming of Christ, "from the deportation to Babylon to the Christ, fourteen generations" (Matt 1:17). No reference is made to the return from exile because the narrator focuses on Christ as the one who will resolve the crisis of the downward spiral of events. Eloff makes the same point:

> By locating the focal point of this third and final epoch in τοῦ Χριστοῦ, Matthew is stating that the problem of the exile and the consequent nonfulfilment of the promises to the patriarchs, to David, and thus to Israel, are only finally resolved with the coming of Jesus.[70]

It is with the birth of the Messiah, son of Abraham and son of David, that the one who will bring salvation comes. The pattern of the genealogy indicates that with the birth of the Messiah salvation history will reach its denouement and God's promises will be fulfilled.

Yet there is an irony here, for it is "she of Uriah" who bears Solomon, chosen by God to continue the line that will lead to the birth of the Messiah, who will "save his people from their sins" (Matt 1:21). The mention of "she of Uriah" in the annotations performs a positive as well as a negative function, drawing attention to the theological truth that is pictured by the ending of her story in 2 Samuel. It is the same theological truth that was evident in Rahab's story. God's mercy outweighs his judgement. In God's economy and grace there is always new life at the borders of death. God's judgement on David's abuse of power followed by David's repentance leads to forgiveness. God's mercy and forgiveness is demonstrated through Bathsheba the abused and marginalized woman who becomes the bearer of Solomon, the one who fulfills God's promise and perpetuates David's line. Theologically her presence alerts the reader to the divine punishment of sin worked out over many generations but more importantly her inclusion points to God's gracious forgiveness that will ultimately be expressed in the saving ministry of the Messiah.

Like Bathsheba, Tamar, Rahab, and Ruth also have significance in relation to divine promises made in the past. By their placement in the first epoch, the Matthean narrator indicates that, just as through Bathsheba the divine promise to David was initially fulfilled, so the divine promise to Abraham that he would become the "ancestor of a multitude of nations" (Gen 17:5) is initially fulfilled in the lives of these three Gentile women who through their faithful living all find a place in Israel. Thus the role of women in salvation history is endorsed both in terms of their motherhood of sons in the redemptive line but also more specifically as those who in various ways were instrumental in the fulfillment of the divine promises

---

70. Eloff, "Ἀπό . . . ἕως," 91.

to the two patriarchs of Israel. In the following chapter it will be argued that similarly, by naming Mary in the closing verse of the genealogy, the Matthean narrator draws attention to the vital importance of her role in salvation history, demonstrating that it is through Mary that the divine promise to both Abraham and David is ultimately fulfilled in the birth of her son, the Messiah.

Finally, it has been noted that the inclusion of first three women in the opening epoch of the genealogy raises questions over Israel's identity in terms of the purity of her lineage, the position of those at the center in relation to those on the margins, and the place of women. Bathsheba's inclusion also serves to raise questions about Israel's identity in relation to the exercise of status and power and the place of those on the margins, including women, in the purposes of God. These are themes that will be taken up by Matthew and developed in the ongoing gospel narrative.

7

Mary

Mary's Relationship to the Four Foremothers

The last woman mentioned in the concluding genealogical annotation is the first woman encountered in the narrative—Mary. She appears at the final point of disruption in the genealogy, its end and climax, as mother of the Messiah (Matt 1:16).

How does she stand in relation to the other mothers of the genealogy? As has been noted, many commentators argue that the four women Tamar, Rahab, Ruth, and Bathsheba, have been included in the genealogy because in some way they foreshadow the fifth and final woman, Mary.[1]

Scandalous and Irregular Unions

Brown in his definitive treatment of the birth narratives states:

> It is the combination of the scandalous or irregular union and of divine intervention through the woman that explains best Matthew's choice in the genealogy . . . Matthew has chosen women who foreshadow the role of Mary, the wife of Joseph.[2]

Just as there was something extraordinary and scandalous in the sexual activity of the four women of the Old Testament, so Mary too is apparently

---

1. See p. 32–33.
2. Brown, *Birth of the Messiah*, 74.

in a scandalous situation, betrothed to Joseph yet expecting a child not fathered by him.

Davies also argues that "readers are intended to notice that each of them behaved in a sexually scandalous way while fulfilling God's purpose . . . Recalling their stories would help prepare readers for the potentially scandalous story about Mary, who became pregnant before she was married."[3] These scholars' emphasis on the common link between the women being their sexually scandalous and irregular unions is problematic because, as has been shown, this is not the emphasis in their Hebrew narratives.

That their sexuality plays a part in all their stories is not denied. Tamar risks her life by posing as a prostitute, whilst for Rahab prostitution is her livelihood. Both attract men—Tamar her father-in-law, Rahab two spies from wandering desert tribes. Both take advantage of the contact to exercise power in an otherwise powerless situation to bring about good. Ruth is encouraged by Naomi to use her female attraction to gain Boaz as a husband and David lusts after Bathsheba's beauty. However, as has been demonstrated, their stories neither condemn them as scandalous nor do they ultimately focus on their sexuality.

Goulder's poem written to explain the women's inclusion in Matthew's genealogy, exemplifies the line of interpretation that has focused on their sexual "irregularities" and has characterized them as morally questionable women.

> Exceedingly odd is the means by which God
> Has provided our path to the heavenly shore—
> Of the girls from whose line the true light was to shine
> There was one an adulteress, one was a whore:
> There was Tamar who bore—what we all should deplore—
> A fine pair of twins to her father-in-law,
> And Rahab the harlot, her sins were as scarlet,
> As red as the thread that she hung from the door;
> Yet alone of her nation she came to salvation
> And lived to be mother of Boaz of yore—
> And he married Ruth, a Gentile uncouth,
> In a manner quite counter to biblical lore:
> And of her there did spring blessed David the King,
> Who walked on his palace one evening and saw
> The wife of Uriah, from who he did sire
> A baby that died—oh, and princes a score:

3. Davies, *Matthew*, 31.

> And a mother unmarried it was too that carried
> God's Son, and him laid in a manger of straw,
> That the moral might wait at the heavenly gate
> While the sinners and publicans go in before,
> Who have not earned their place, but received it by grace,
> And have found them a righteousness not of the law.[4]

When one reads Goulder's little ditty with what impression of these women is one left? Readers should "deplore" the twins Tamar bore to her father-in-law (presumably because Goulder considers they were born of incest). Rahab is the "harlot" whose "sins were as scarlet, | As red as the thread that she hung from the door." Ruth is problematically characterized as "a Gentile uncouth," whose marriage to Boaz was "quite counter to biblical lore." Finally, Bathsheba is "an adulteress" who bore offspring to "blessed David the King." What of the men who were in relation to these women? No mention is made of the spies. Judah, the father-in-law, and Boaz are simply named and David is "blessed." Goulder's verse serves to illustrate how all four women have been read from a western male religious perspective that is quick to link women with sex and sin, while exonerating the men with whom they were in relationship.

If one could ask any of their original Hebrew storytellers to write a poem about the women, one feels it would have a very different tone. Three of them are explicitly praised within their texts: Tamar as "more in the right" (Gen 38:26), Rahab "because she hid the messengers" (Josh 6:17) and Ruth as a "worthy woman" (Ruth 3:11). While Bathsheba does not receive direct praise, her story in 2 Samuel closes with the message from Nathan that her son Solomon is loved by the Lord (2 Sam 12:24, 25). They are never held up to moral censure.

It is quite clear from the narrative analysis in chapters 3–6 that the assumed common factor of scandalous sexual activity in regard to the birth of their sons is not convincing. Although others have argued that Tamar's union was scandalous and incestuous, my analysis has demonstrated that the narrative of Genesis 38 does not represent Tamar's union with Judah in this way. The story highlights her righteousness as she sought to fulfill her obligation to produce an heir for her deceased husband. Rahab is often seen solely in terms of her activity as a prostitute, yet it has been demonstrated that the biblical narrative focuses on her faith in YHWH manifested in her action of חסד in hiding the Israelite spies. Rahab's story in Joshua says nothing about her union with Salmon. Such a union is possibly a creative

---

4. Goulder, *Midrash and Lection*, 232.

act on the part of Matthew, not Rahab. One has to assume she continued as a prostitute to make her union with Salmon scandalous, but of this we know nothing. The reading of Ruth as involved in scandalous sexual activity assumes that she seduces Boaz on the threshing floor. Other scholars have talked of "irregular unions," indicating the irregularity of Boaz marrying a Moabite woman. Within the narrative the birth of her son is not linked with scandal, nor is her marriage seen as irregular. Finally, many have read Bathsheba as a woman who is guilty of seduction and adultery, but it has been demonstrated that the narrative emphasizes David's guilt in the taking of another man's wife; it was not her but his actions that were scandalous and irregular.

To characterize the four women in terms of the scandalous sexual irregularities of their lives, neither does justice to them as women nor does justice to their individual narrated histories. It is disingenuous to suggest that in this way they foreshadow Mary. As we shall see, Matthew's narrative makes it quite clear that Jesus was not born from a scandalous or even irregular sexual union. The narrator informs the reader from the beginning that Mary's pregnancy was from the Holy Spirit. A century ago Heffern pointed out the "sheer impossibility of comparison between them and Mary . . . [A] virgin mother could not be typified by any of the four"[5] and surely this is the most important point in refuting this argument. Matthew's narrative clears Mary of any scandalous sexual activity, in fact, of any sexual activity whatsoever prior to the birth of Jesus.

Divine Irregularity

The second point to Brown's suggestion concerning the reason for the women's inclusion talks of "divine intervention."[6] He defines this as the working out of God's messianic plan in the lives of these women.[7] Witherington extends this idea and turns the argument on its head by focusing not on the women's irregularity but on "divine irregularity," "it is likely these women are included to emphasize 'divine irregularity'—how God can use unusual women and unusual circumstances to produce leaders such as Solomon or Jesus."[8] This, I feel, comes closer to the mark, yet this view still creates a problem in that it regards the women (and not the men)

5. Heffern, "Four Women," 74.
6. See p. 146.
7. Brown, *Birth of the Messiah*, 595.
8. Witherington, *Matthew*, 41.

as "unusual." Also, in the difficult situations portrayed, very little is said initially of God's action. It is *their* initiative in life threatening situations that is ultimately blessed by God in the birth of a child or, in Rahab's case, in deliverance. Their inclusion in the genealogy does indeed bear witness to the fact they all feature in the outworking of the divine plan but to focus on these women as emphasizing divine irregularity is disingenuous. The genealogy bears witness to many stories where God works "irregularly" through the contingencies of human situations, both male and female, to bring about his divine purposes.

Feminist Views

The search for a common theme linking the four women to Mary has taken a very different turn in feminist scholarship. Forming a feminist critique, Wainwright argues that the actions of four women "encode aspects of woman's power. God's messianic plan unfolds in and through such power."[9] Narrative analysis has shown that Tamar, Rahab, and Ruth are all women who show courage and initiative to resolve threatening situations. However it cannot be argued that this is the main characteristic of all four women since it has also been shown that Bathsheba is largely passive. Wainwright comments that "the wife of Uriah comes to David, one of the few actions attributed to her"[10] but this intimates both that Bathsheba is a willing partner and that such action is a positive move in God's purposes, neither of which are the case. It is only as queen mother that Bathsheba exercises power and I have argued that her naming as "she of Uriah" precludes her role as queen mother.

It is in the context of Mary as a social misfit, outside recognized boundaries but with whom nevertheless God identifies, that feminist writer Jane Schaberg finds connections with Tamar, Rahab, Ruth, and Bathsheba. Schaberg writes:

> Mention of these four women is designed to lead Matthew's reader to expect another, final story of a woman who becomes a social misfit in some way; is wronged or thwarted; who is party to a sexual act that places her in great danger; and whose story has an outcome that repairs the social fabric and ensures the birth of a child who is legitimate or legitimated.[11]

9. Wainwright, *Feminist Critical Reading*, 68.
10. Ibid.
11. Schaberg, *Illegitimacy of Jesus*, 33.

As with other commentators who seek to "fit" all four women into ways of foreshadowing Mary, Schaberg's analysis falls short. The categories are so broad and all encompassing that they describe some of the women at some time but never all of them at every stage, least of all Rahab. She is not wronged or thwarted by her situation. On the contrary, one could argue she exploits it to her advantage. It is the spies' presence in her establishment rather than any sexual act that places her in danger as the king demands that she bring the men out. Her story tells us nothing about the birth of a child who is legitimated and her presence in Israel challenges rather than repairs the social fabric.

This chapter will explore how Mary is presented by Matthew and what this might indicate about her relationship to the four Old Testament women, before going on to draw conclusions about the significance of the five women for the gospel narrative.

A Narrative Reading of Mary's Story

Mary in Matthew 1:16–17

As the narrator reaches the end of the genealogy, the pattern A begot B, B begot C is broken again for a final time, at the thirty-ninth use of the verb "to beget." Instead of the anticipated "Joseph father of Jesus," Matthew 1:16 reads "Jacob the father of Joseph the husband of Mary, of whom Jesus was born, who is called the Messiah." A mother has been introduced for the fifth time at the crucial point in the genealogy. However the wording to introduce Mary is different. The most radical discontinuity of all happens at the birth of Christ.[12]

Matthew 1:3	ἐκ τῆς Θαμάρ
Matthew 1:5	ἐκ τῆς Ῥαχάβ
Matthew 1:5	ἐκ τῆς Ῥούθ
Matthew 1:6	ἐκ τῆς τοῦ Οὐρίου
Matthew 1:16	Μαρίας, ἐξ ἧς ἐγεννήθη

Whilst the other four mothers were the object of the preposition ἐκ Mary's name is related to Joseph as a possessive genitive. This displaces Joseph. Joseph is not identified as the father of Jesus but the husband of Mary. He is defined in terms of his relationship to her. Mary, in turn, is

12. Cf. Waetjen, "Genealogy as the Key," 216.

identified as the mother of Jesus. The wording focuses attention on Mary as Jesus' mother. She is introduced with the passive voice for "beget" as the one from whom Jesus is born (ἐξ ἧς ἐγεννήθη Ἰησοῦς) (Matt 1:16). Immediately the reader is aware that this is unusual. It is not Joseph who begets but rather Mary who gives birth, or in the narrator's terms, more passively, from whom the one who is called the Messiah is born. Surprisingly, no father is mentioned. From the start Mary appears to be in an anomalous position. Joseph is her husband, yet not the begetter of her son. She is defined in terms of her motherhood of Christ. The reader is left asking two questions: how did Mary conceive Jesus and how did Jesus become related to Joseph and therefore part of the Davidic line? It will be argued that the ongoing narrative is primarily concerned with providing an answer to these two questions.

Mary in Matthew 1:18–25

a) The narrative structure of Matthew 1:18–25

An outline of the passage demonstrates that almost the entire focus of the scene is on Joseph: his deliberations, the angelic announcement of the birth to Joseph and his obedient response.

Matthew 1:18	A description of Mary's circumstances
Matthew 1:19	A description of Joseph's planned response
Matthew 1:20–21	An angel of the Lord appears to Joseph commanding him to take Mary as wife and announcing the birth of Jesus
Matthew 1:22–23	A fulfillment saying
Matthew 24–25	Joseph's obedient response

Although Mary's motherhood is of vital importance, she herself is not an actor in these scenes. The passage is prefaced with the words, "Now the birth of Jesus the Messiah took place in this way" (Matt 1:18a) but the story does not focus on Mary or the birth itself but on the events surrounding the birth in relation to Joseph. Following Stendahl and others, I suggest these verses are not a birth story but are essentially an explanation of Jesus' origins.

b) Matthew 1:18–25 in relation to Matthew 1:1–17

A firm line is normally drawn under the end of the genealogy in verse 17 and a new heading, such as "The birth of Jesus the Messiah" (NRSV), is added to the biblical text of verses 18–25. However, these verses are providing answers to the questions left hanging by the unexpected wording of verse 16.

Stendahl, in his significant article "Quis et Unde?," argues for the unity of chapter 1 against the position that separates the Matthean birth narrative from the genealogy; verses 18–25 are "the enlarged footnote to the crucial point in the genealogy."[13] He considers that as a whole the first chapter of Matthew answers the question concerning the Messiah—"Who?," its structure centered around personal names. Stendahl makes an important observation. The focus of the narrative is not on the distinctly female experience of giving birth but on providing an explanation of Jesus' Davidic ancestry and divine origins. The narrative explains the break in the expected pattern, which indicates that Jesus, the son of Joseph's wife Mary, is not actually Joseph's son. Together with the genealogy the following verses answer the question *Quis?* (Who?). Jesus is shown to be son of David but also by implication son of God. Helpfully, Brown argues for an extension of Stendahl's outline. He considers that 1:1–17 address the *Quis?* (Who?) of Jesus' identity and 1:18–25 the *Quomodo?* (How?) of Jesus' identity.[14] Following this outline I shall consider the verses that address the "How?" of Jesus' identity.

c) An alternative narrative structure

Kingsbury suggests an alternative to the narrative structure previously outlined that divides Matthew 1:18–25 into alternate voices, that of the narrator directly addressing the (implied) reader followed by the narration of the story.

Matthew 1:18a	Narrator speaks directly to the reader—comment
Matthew 1:18b–21	narration of the story
Matthew 1:22–23	Narrator speaks directly to the reader—comment
Matthew 1:24–25	narration of the story

Kingsbury, in his narrative analysis, argues that each part of the text finds its climax in the citation of a name of Jesus, thus:

---

13. Stendahl, "Quis et Unde?," 74.
14. Brown, *Birth of the Messiah*, 53.

Mary

Matthew 1:18a	|	comment *Messiah*
Matthew 1:18b–21	|	story *Jesus*
Matthew 1:22–23	|	comment *Emmanuel*
Matthew 1:24–25	|	story *Son of David*[15]

Building on Kingsbury's analysis I argue that the fourfold narrative division explicates the Messiah's origins. Explanation is given concerning not only "Who?" Jesus is but "How?" he was conceived and incorporated into Joseph's line.

Matthew 1:18a	|	comment *Messiah* Jesus' origins
Matthew 1:18b–21	|	story *Jesus* Mary—pregnant from the Spirit
Matthew 1:22–23	|	comment *Emmanuel* A virgin shall conceive
Matthew 1:24–25	|	story *Son of David* By adoption

My analysis will proceed under these headings.

Matthew 1:18a | Jesus' Origins

In verse 18a the narrator addresses the narratee in order to provide some answers to the questions left hanging by the cryptic ending of the genealogy. Literally, it reads, "Now of Jesus the Messiah the genesis was thus." (Τοῦ δὲ Ἰησοῦ Χριστοῦ ἡ γένεσις οὕτως ἦν) (Matt 1:18a). The unusual word order in the Greek suggests the emphasis in these verses is on Jesus. There has been some scholarly controversy over how γένεσις should be translated but here it is concerned with origins as in Matthew 1:1 rather than birth.[16] This is supported by the context of these verses, the content of these verses and the chiastic pairing of this phrase with the opening phrase of the Gospel.

1. Context

The verses answer questions raised by the preceding verse 16. They address the problem of the broken link in verse 16. They explain how Jesus came to be formally adopted by Joseph and thus is the "Son of David," the title used by the angel in addressing Joseph (Matt 1:20). The verses

---

15. Kingsbury, "Birth Narrative of Matthew," 159–60.
16. Cf. Waetjen, "Genealogy as the Key," 217; Scott, "Birth of the Reader," 88–89.

also explain the odd use of the passive voice in verse 16 which reverses expectations of another male begetting with the introduction of Mary as the one from whom Christ was born.

2. Content

The content of the following verses say nothing about the actual birth itself even in Matthew 1:25; rather the verses address the circumstances surrounding the birth. In addition, Kingsbury notes that the term "origin" is much broader in scope than birth. It has to do with relationships to mother, father, lineage, and forebears rather than the physical birth itself and this is what is focused on in these verses.[17]

3. Chiasm

This phrase forms a chiasm with the title of the genealogy.

> Βίβλος γενέσεως . . . Ἰησοῦ Χριστοῦ
>
> The book of origin . . . of Jesus Christ Matthew 1:1
>
> Ἰησοῦ Χριστοῦ . . . ἡ γένεσις
>
> Of Jesus Christ . . . the origin Matthew 1:18

The first verse in Matthew's Gospel promises an account of Jesus' origins. Now a narrated account must explain the nature of the Messiah's identity following the odd way the "book of origin" finishes in verse 16. That said, the focus of this current chapter is on Mary, what characterizes her and the role she plays.

Mary—Reading into the Silences

In order to tease out the reality of Mary's situation and to create some sense of her character it will be necessary (as with Bathsheba) to read into the gaps. Feminist critics note the silence in the text that erases the reality of the woman's situation. Fiorenza argues that feminist critics must "find ways to break the silence of the text."[18] It is possible to search for clues and allusions in the text that might indicate the actuality of the woman's position on which the text is silent. It is at this point that reader response plays

---

17. Kingsbury, "Birth Narrative of Matthew," 156.
18. Fiorenza, *In Memory of Her*, 41.

a part. Lapsley argues that an "ethically significant response" depends on the reader being able to empathize with individuals and "the moral complexity of the worlds they inhabit."[19] Using this methodology, brief reflections on Mary and her circumstances will be included in the analysis. Another reading strategy that is used will be to read Mary intertextually, in the light of the young woman of Isaiah 7:14; the fulfillment text in Matthew 1:22–23 invites the comparison.

MATTHEW 1:18B–21 | MARY: PREGNANT FROM THE SPIRIT

The narrator opens the story of Jesus' birth by addressing the reader with these words:

> When his mother Mary had been engaged to Joseph, but before they came together she was found to be with child from the Holy Spirit (Matt 1:18b)

The Greek word μνηστευθείσης (the middle or passive of the verb "to be betrothed") describes the relationship that existed at this point between Joseph and Mary. The story assumes knowledge of the two stage process of marriage that operated within Israelite society at the turn of the eras.[20] The phrase "before they came together" (πρὶν ἢ συνελθεῖν αὐτοὺς) refers not just to their living apart but also to their sexual abstinence. The narrator wants to make it clear that at this stage in their betrothal Joseph has not had intercourse with Mary. However, "she was found to be with child" (εὑρέθη ἐν γαστρί). Another passive used to describe Mary acts to disrupt the story. Mary is found to be with child. Her pregnancy is now known and she is in a threatening situation. Joseph's reaction in 1:19 implies that he understands the situation to obligate, or allow him, to divorce Mary on the assumption that either Mary has committed adultery or that she has been raped. The penalty for the former, according to Deuteronomic

---

19. Lapsley, *Whispering the Word*, 11.

20. Brown cites later rabbinic documents, which describe this two step process to marriage making clear the process that is implicit in the Matthean narrative. The first stage, which this verse refers to, was the consent or betrothal, where a young girl reaching puberty was formally given by her father in a marriage agreement to a man. In the presence of witnesses a bride price was paid and from that point on the girl would have the status of a married woman, the man having legal rights over her. (Note the angel's words to Joseph in Matt 1:20, "Mary, your wife.") However, the wife would continue to live in her father's home for about a year before the second stage of the marriage occurred. The girl would then transfer to her husband's home. Up to this point her virginity would be assumed and any violation would be considered adultery. Brown, *Birth of the Messiah*, 123.

law, was death. A young betrothed woman found to be pregnant before cohabiting with her husband was sentenced to be stoned to death "because she committed a disgraceful act" (Deut 22:20–21). Although there are no records to indicate that this was imposed in first-century Palestine, in the setting of Matthew's story, Mary's pregnancy, violating Jewish law, clearly leaves her exposed and vulnerable.[21]

Matthew's presentation of Mary here invites real readers to reflect on the situation of a frightened, young, pregnant, Jewish girl in rural, first-century Palestine, facing social ostracism, perhaps having to beg to keep herself and her child alive, or even possibly facing death. Interestingly Mary's situation echoes that of Tamar. Tamar, when living in her father's house and promised to a man in marriage, is also found to be pregnant. Her life and the life of the twins she is carrying are threatened by Judah's unequivocal response to the news of her pregnancy, "let her be burned" (Gen 38:24). As yet readers are uncertain of Joseph's response to Mary, he may publicly repudiate her too, thus threatening her life and the life of the child she carries. The lives of both women are held in the balance by the men with whom they are in relation. In both cases the narrator remains silent about the woman's reactions or sentiments, her fears or her courage. Real readers are left to imagine the horror of their situations.

It is at this point that crucially, the omniscient narrator supplies the reader with information about the conception of Mary's child, the child was "from[22] the Holy Spirit" (ἐκ πνεύματος ἁγίου) (Matt 1:18b).

The juxtaposition of the phrase "from the Holy Spirit" with the preceding one, "she was found to be with child," is startling. In the first, suspicion is thrown on Mary and a pervading element of scandal is introduced to the story; Mary is shamed. But now the implied reader is invited to see Mary in a new light; she is honored, her child is from the Holy Spirit.[23] Intertextual allusions abound. The genesis or birth of her child recalls the

---

21. Historically, it is uncertain whether the Jews in Palestine had authority under the Romans in the New Testament period to carry out capital punishment and, if so, whether it was used for cases of adultery.

22. Here I am following the NRSV translation of ἐκ as "from." However, this preposition can also be translated as "by," "of," "by means of" and as the chapter proceeds, I will use these different translations interchangeably to catch the nuance of the phrase.

23. Scott claims that this continues a pattern seen in the narratives of Tamar, Rahab, Ruth and Bathsheba. He argues that "all four women from the point of view of a shame-honor system are tainted sexually . . . Yet despite this shame, these women all have the honor ascribed by the Lord." Clearly I contest this reading and the way in which Scott argues Mary's situation has been foreshadowed in the lives of the four women in the genealogy. Scott, "Birth of the Reader," 87–88.

genesis of creation when the Spirit of God hovered over the face of the waters as God called life into being (Gen 1:2). Now in a second act of non-sexual creation, unique as the creation of the universe, God's Spirit has brought life to Mary's womb. However, although Mary's shame is not allowed to linger for longer than an instant with the reader, Joseph only knows that the woman to whom he is betrothed is expecting a baby he has not fathered. The narrative tension is driven by the disjuncture between Joseph's knowledge and that of the reader. The explanation of Mary's pregnancy in the final words of this verse will not be given to Joseph until the angel tells him (Matt 1:20), but as Brown points out, "Matthew wants the reader to know more than do the characters in the story, so that the reader will not entertain for a moment the suspicion that grows in Joseph's mind."[24]

But readers do not know what Mary knows. Unlike Luke's account, here there is no description of any angelic revelation to Mary and the reader is left to wonder at what point she herself knew of the divine conception. Throughout the narratives of Matthew 1–2 men receive revelation concerning Jesus, in the form of dreams (Joseph and the Magi), or a celestial sign (the Magi) or in the form of scripture, as given to Herod (Matt 2:6). Mary, however, receives no such revelation.

In the next verses (Matt 1:19–21) the androcentric emphasis is on Joseph, his deliberations and his angelic revelation. In a similar way to his Old Testament namesake (the Joseph of Genesis 37–50 whose father is also Jacob), he is a dreamer of important dreams. However, just as Mary was defined by her relationship to her child, Joseph in turn is defined by his relationship to Mary, Joseph is "her husband" (Matt 1:19). Mary's situation continues to be the catalyst for the plot as Joseph considers how he is to resolve the difficult situation presented by her pregnancy. As a righteous man he resolves not to shame her in public but to divorce her quietly.[25] He, not Mary, receives the divine annunciation of Jesus' birth, climaxing in the announcement that she will bear a son Jesus, who will save his people from their sins. He is told specifically not to be afraid to take Mary home as his wife, for the child conceived in her is from the Holy Spirit (ἐκ πνεύματός ἐστιν ἁγίου) (Matt 1:20c). The final phrase of the sentence (variously translated as of/from/though the Holy Spirit)[26] conveys to Joseph

---

24. Brown, *Birth of the Messiah*, 124.

25. See pp. 65.

26. This phrase could also be translated literally "is of a spirit which is holy," the verb "to be" separating holy and spirit and there being no definite article. Matthew does not have a developed pneumatology. Later reflection led to a fuller understanding

what readers already know, that Mary's pregnancy is of divine origin. The angel's message overturns his decision and his perception of Mary for a unique work of the Spirit has taken place in her life.

However, despite the theological significance given to Mary as bearer of the one who will save from sin, Mary as a character does not appear. Although the story does not offer the least clue to Mary's thoughts, actions or character, reflection on her relationship to the Holy Spirit of God, which is implied by the text, yields insights. Matthew witnesses that Jesus was born from Mary (Matt 1:16) by the Holy Spirit (Matt 1:18, 20). The Greek verbs, used to describe this extraordinary happening in verse 16 and 20 are passive (ἐγεννήθη, γεννηθὲν). In other words, use of the passive here indicates that God is the active agent.[27] The use of this stylistic feature is not to sideline Mary but to point away from human activity to the activity of the Holy Spirit. Divine passives are used again later in the Gospel to describe an exceptional event where God is the active agent. In the first three of Jesus' prediction sayings, passives are used to describe an event beyond his death that parallels the events of his conception in its distinctiveness; Jesus will be raised.[28] No reference to the Spirit's activity in the resurrection is made in Matthew's narration but the use of the passive verb by Jesus in talking of events after his death points beyond human activity to the divine. On that occasion the Spirit raised Mary's son. Here, in a unique work of creation, the Spirit and Mary bring to life Mary's son, who is to save his people from their sins.

MATTHEW 1:22–23 | A VIRGIN SHALL CONCEIVE

Matthew's genealogy has already provided the narrator's commentary on Jesus' ancestry and made explicit that the Messiah's roots lie in the Old Testament narrative of God's dealings with his chosen people. Direct commentary is also provided by way of formula-quotations.[29] The intro-

---

of the Holy Spirit as the third person of the Trinity, hence translators supply the definite article (the) and capitalize the words holy and spirit.

27. The *passivum divinum* makes it possible to avoid naming directly the agent of the action of the verb.

28. ἐγερθῆναι (Matt 16:21), ἐγερθήσεται (Matt 17:23; 20:19).

29. Most commentators agree that there are ten such formula quotations, identified by the set introductory formula containing the verb πληροῦν, fulfill, i.e., Matt 1:22–23; 2:15; 2:17–18; 2:23; 4:14–16; 8:17; 12:17–21; 13:35; 21:4–5; 27:9–10. Another quotation uses the synonymous verb ἀναπληροῦν (Matt 13:14–15) and four more stress fulfillment in the introductory formula by using other phrases such as γέγραπται. This

ductory formula in verse 22, "All this took place to fulfill what had been spoken by the Lord through the prophet," is typical of these citations; the first four (five if one includes Matthew 2:5–6, where the introductory formula has been modified a little) falling within the infancy narratives. The quotations are a kind of editorial comment by Matthew who has creatively interpreted Old Testament texts that have lent themselves to the purpose. Their theological importance for Matthew lies in the way they explain how the events of Jesus' life are the fulfillment of God's purposes promised in the Old Testament. The citation from Isaiah 7:14 is intended to show how the birth of Mary's son fulfills scripture. The citation from Isaiah 7:14 uses the LXX version with its explicit reference to a virgin, παρθένος, rather than the MT עלמה that does not refer specifically to a virgin but to a young woman reaching puberty.[30] By citing the LXX version the narrator clearly links Mary's birth from the Holy Spirit to her virginal state.

However, the quotation of Isaiah 7:14 draws another mother into Mary's story. The cracks in the narrative of Matthew's first chapter, which have allowed readers to catch glimpses of five mothers, now widen. Isaiah 7 likewise portrays a young Jewish mother expecting a child in a situation that threatens her life and the life of her child. In the face of imminent danger this young woman gives expression to her faith in God's presence by the naming of her child. What is significant in the context of *her* story (Isa 7:1–17) is not the manner of the child's conception but the name given to the child by his mother. The naming of her child is a sign that points to the undaunted faith of a young girl,[31] who, in spite of the impending threat of war, bloodshed, and death, dares to name her son "God with us" (עמנו אל). Readers of Isaiah learn very little of this young mother, yet her prophetic witness points beyond the confines of her time and place to the birth of another son. The narrator of Matthew's Gospel finds in her naming the resource for naming Christ. The name Immanuel, given in faith by a young mother under mortal threat, is the name given by the Matthean

includes the citation in Matt 2:5–6, as well as 3:3, 11:10 and 26:31.

30. Any discussion of the fulfillment sayings with reference to their usage of Greek and Hebrew must be prefaced with a cautionary note. In the first century there were a great multiplicity of textual traditions of Scripture. There existed not just standardized Hebrew MT and Greek LXX but variant Hebrew traditions, Aramaic targums and a number of Greek translations. When we add to this Matthew's free renderings by Matthew himself then we cannot be sure of his sources.

31. Scholars have debated whether she was the prophetess (Isa 8:3) who bore Isaiah's children (Isa 8:18), or a royal princess/concubine in the court of Ahaz, further speculating that this child might be the king's son Hezekiah. However, the case is unresolved and I prefer to rest with the knowledge that she is a brave young mother.

narrator to Mary's child. It functions to describe the significance of who Mary's child is, emphasized by the translation provided by the narrator, "God is with us" (Matt 1:23).[32] At the close of the Gospel the risen Christ himself recognizes the prophetic power of this naming, for it is with these words that Matthew chooses to end his Gospel, "And remember, *I am with you* always, to the end of the age" (Matt 28:20, my italics). Although the narrator says nothing of Mary's faith or prophetic insight the citation of this verse invites readers to see Mary in the light of this earlier young woman of faith.

Matthew 1:24–25 | By Adoption

The scene returns to the story as Joseph wakes up and in obedience to the angel's command takes Mary as his wife. Although now his wife, Mary's virginal status is emphasized, "he did not know her." The only notice of the birth is given in four sparse words. They include the only active verb used of Mary, "until she gave birth to a son" (ἕως οὗ ἔτεκεν υἱόν) (Matt 1:25). The final phrase of the first chapter addresses the question raised in verse 16 of how Jesus is related to Joseph and, consequently, David. In naming the child Jesus, Joseph acknowledges Mary's child as his legitimate son and consequently Jesus is adopted into the Davidic line[33] but as Anderson points out, in terms of Jesus' origins Matthew bears witness that "Although Jesus is Son of David through Joseph, he is Son of God through Mary."[34]

Matthew 2:1–23 | The Child and His Mother

The second section of Matthew's narrative is concerned with Jesus' geographical place of birth, Bethlehem, and his final destination, Nazareth. In Stendahl's terms the narrator is answering the question "Whence?" The plot development of Jesus' movements—to Egypt, from Egypt, and, finally, to Nazareth—is driven by the threat posed by Herod.

Whereas the narrative in Matthew 1 mainly focused on Joseph's private life, Matthew 2 is a story that revolves almost exclusively around men in the public arena involving politics and power play. King Herod, wise

---

32. See Kupp, *Matthew's Emmanuel* for an extended discussion of the significance of the naming of Mary's child.

33. Brown notes that the Jewish position bases paternity on a man's acknowledgement of a child by naming him. Brown, *Birth of the Messiah*, 139.

34. Anderson, "Matthew: Gender and Reading," 10.

Mary

men from the east and Joseph are the main actors supplemented by the chief priests and scribes of Jerusalem. The focus of all these men is the Christ child. He is searched for and found by the wise men, considered a threat and plotted against by Herod and protectively moved around by Joseph. Yet, always with him is his mother Mary.

In chapter 1 Mary is described as both Jesus' mother and Joseph's wife. In chapter 2 the focus switches to her child; Mary is *his* mother. Like the Madonna and child of medieval paintings, the two are set apart from the other players in the scenes as they unfold. While this chapter refers to Mary only in connection with Jesus, it is also the case that reference to Jesus virtually always involves reference to Mary. As Gaventa points out, "Matthew reflects a powerful connection between the two."[35] As in the first chapter, Mary is a passive figure but in reality her role is crucial. Her child is dependent on her for survival.

Significantly, the narrator reverses the natural order and makes Mary secondary to Jesus. There are five references to the child and his mother:

τὸ παιδίον μετὰ Μαρίας τῆς μητρὸς (Matt 2:11)

τὸ παιδίον καὶ τὴν μητέρα αὐτοῦ (Matt 2:13)

τὸ παιδίον καὶ τὴν μητέρα αὐτοῦ (Matt 2:14)

τὸ παιδίον καὶ τὴν μητέρα αὐτοῦ (Matt 2:19)

τὸ παιδίον καὶ τὴν μητέρα αὐτοῦ (Matt 2:21)

Repeated references to the child and his mother stand in stark contrast to the all-male world of political and military might that dominates the narrative. It is within the context of threat and danger they most frequently appear in the narrative of chapter 2. This is only mitigated by the scene within the house (Matt 2:11) when the Magi find them. The child and his mother are the objects of the actions of others. The Magi see them, fall down, and worship (Matt 2:11). Joseph is commanded by the angelic messenger to "Get up, take the child and his mother . . . flee to Egypt" (Matt 2:13) and then, on Herod's death, to return to the land of Israel (Matt 2:19). And twice, in obedient response Joseph gets up and takes the child and his mother (Matt 2:14, 21). Mary is seen with her child and taken with her child but takes no action herself and says nothing. Readers are left to surmise the consequences for a young mother having to flee at night with her baby and of her reaction to the news of the murder of the children in Bethlehem that must have reached them. Rachel is named to mourn for

35. Gaventa, *Mary*, 43.

these children, for Jeremiah bears witness that Rachel does not forget her children (Jer 31:15) and the narrator cites this verse (Matt 2:18).[36] There is a silence in the text that Rachel's weeping uncovers. In her weeping for those taken into exile are heard the cries of the mothers of Bethlehem wailing for their murdered babies, for "In misfortune, Israel needs Rachel's tears."[37]

Mary and her child are for a second time threatened with death because of their marginalized position. In chapter 1 it is Mary's anomalous position in relation to her pregnancy that appears to threaten her child until Joseph takes her as his wife and adopts Jesus. Now, in this second chapter, it is Herod's threat to her child that threatens Mary. Joseph, the child, and his mother become wanderers and refugees, while those at the static center exercise a ruthless authority. The focus of the narrative after the visit of the Magi is on the angel's interaction with Joseph, who continues to receive divine dreams. While Joseph is the active participant in the drama, he continues to act not on his own initiative but in obedience to the angelic command, the focus of which is the safety and well being of the child and his mother. Gaventa notes that it is not two parents who flee to Egypt protecting the child but Joseph who is ordered to protect the child and his mother.[38] Moses/Exodus/Exile typology all play a part in the story, as Matthew tells it, as the family find refuge in Egypt before finally returning to Israel. Herod's death heralds the final angelic command to Joseph to leave Egypt for Israel with "the child and his mother." Three geographical phrases serve to explain how they went into (εἰς) the land of Israel (Matt 2:21), then into (εἰς) the district of Galilee (Matt 2:22), and ultimately into (εἰς) the city of Nazareth (Matt 2:23). At Nazareth Joseph settles. He will not appear again in this narrative. His adoptive fatherly role of protection has been completed. Jesus will be brought up in Nazareth and will consequently be called a Nazorean. The naming of Jesus parallels the final naming in Matthew's opening chapter dealing with Jesus' origins (Matt 1:25), neatly rounding off the first two chapters of the Gospel.

---

36. Rachel, as mother of Joseph, represented the two northern tribes of Ephraim and Manasseh descended from him. Her second son, Benjamin, became the father of one of the southern tribes. Thus, she represented both Israel and Judah and mourns for their exile.

37. Clément and Kristeva, *Feminine and the Sacred*, 85.

38. Gaventa, *Mary*, 43.

Mary

A Comparison with Luke

A surface reading of the text might suggest Matthew's text allows very little space for the feminine. A comparison with Luke's infancy narrative reinforces this conclusion. One of the most marked differences between the two is the attention given to Mary. In Luke, it is Mary who receives an angelic visitation with news of her child to be. In Luke Mary is God-favored and freely responds in courageous and obedient acceptance (Luke 1:28–38). In Luke Elizabeth's Spirit-inspired words praise Mary as blessed among women, the one who faithfully believes in the fulfillment of God's promises. In response, Mary voices her overflowing worship to God as she sings the Magnificat, bearing witness to the greatness and mercy of the mighty one who lifts up the humble and scatters the proud (Luke 1:39–56). It is in Luke that Mary gives birth to her first born son, wraps him in cloths, and lays him in a manger and Mary who ponders the message angels bring to the shepherds that her son is Savior and Christ (Luke 2:6–19). It is to Mary that Simeon addresses his prophetic words concerning the destiny of her child and her own sorrow (Luke 2:34–35). Finally, it is Mary after her child goes missing in the Temple, who "treasures all these things in her heart" (Luke 2:51).

What greater contrast could there be between Luke's Mary and Matthew's Mary, who takes no action of her own beyond an indirect reference to her giving birth, says nothing, interacts with no one, and is never addressed by humans or angels? No window into her relationship with God or others is opened nor is there any indication given of her inner musings. Bauer comments that in literary terms "strictly speaking, she is not a character" in Matthew's account.[39] In terms of plot analysis Mary, like Bathsheba before her, is merely an agent in the Matthean infancy narrative.

However, to read both Matthew and Luke's accounts as birth stories is to fall into a category error. Clearly this is what Luke's narrative account is about as indicated not only by the content but the context of the account. Luke introduces the birth of Christ by way of the birth of John the Baptist. Mary's extraordinary virgin conception is contrasted with the miraculous but sexual conception of John. By contrast, Matthew's account is not set in the context of another birth story. Matthew's account is not a birth narrative but an account of Jesus' origins. Firstly, it is an explanation of Jesus' human and divine origin, a footnote to the ending of his genealogical book of origins (Matt 1:18–25) and, secondly, it is an explanation

---

39. Bauer, "Kingship of Jesus," 320n39.

of his geographical origins (Matt 2:1–23). Read in this light the narrative emphasis is completely different. It does not focus on Mary or the birth because it is not primarily a birth narrative. A second obvious explanation for Matthew's lack of attention to Mary is that he did not possess the sources available to Luke.[40] Accepting this serves to undergird the notion that Matthew's account is not a birth story.

To complete Matthew's portrayal of Mary brief attention must also be given to two other passages. In similar fashion to Mark and Luke in the narration of Jesus' public ministry Matthew shows little interest in Mary.[41] The Matthean narrator makes only two further references to Mary, both oblique, in which Mary neither speaks nor acts.

Mary in Matthew 12:46–50

As Jesus is speaking to the crowds, his mother and brothers come looking for him, wanting to speak with him. Verses 46 and 47 open with the typically Matthean Semitic "behold" (ἰδού), drawing the reader's attention to his mother and brothers. Mary is placed in the context of her family as mother. Matthew gives no notice of their arrival or indication of their intent.[42] Although Matthew does not imply any negative intent on their part, Jesus' mother and brothers are left standing outside the house in which he is ministering. This is emphasized with a repetition of the information in the report to Jesus that they are waiting outside.[43] Their presence provides an opportunity for Jesus to teach about his true family. A third ἰδού (Matt 12:49), contrasts them with the mixed group of disciples surrounding him. Those who do the will of Jesus' heavenly Father are his brothers, sisters, and mother. Is Jesus thereby rejecting his own mother? It would seem Jesus wants to stress the importance of his new family of disciples rather than disassociate himself from his natural family. It is a matter of priorities; the loyalties to natural kinship family are relativized in the light of God's claims.[44] As readers we do not know what Mary understands of

---

40. See Brown, *Birth of the Messiah*, 244–50, for a discussion of Luke's possible sources.

41. This contrasts with John's Gospel where stories of Mary and her son chiastically frame the gospel narrative (John 2:1–12; 19:25b–27).

42. Cf. Mark 3:21 where Jesus' family want to restrain Jesus thinking he is out of his mind.

43. Some variants omit v. 47.

44. Unconvincingly, Sim argues that since Mary is depicted favourably in the

Mary

Jesus' actions and teaching. Other than that Jesus had brothers we learn nothing new about Mary.[45]

Mary in Matthew 13:54-58

The final reference to Mary (Matt 13:53-58), in which she is named, comes from the amazed reaction of those within his own home town synagogue. It varies very little from Mark's slightly more extended account (Mark 6:1-6a). Knowing Jesus' family background, the townsfolk question Jesus' wisdom and miracles. They know he is the carpenter's son; they also know that his mother is called Mary and that Jesus has brothers and sisters, so they ask, "Where then did this man get all this?" (Matt 13:56). The focus of this episode is on those who "took offense" at Jesus (Matt 13:57), rather than on Mary or his family. As in chapter 12, it is the varying response of people to Jesus that is the focus of the account, not his mother Mary.

Very little is added to Matthew's portrayal of Mary from these two brief references. She remains characterized as a mother but the intimacy implied between the Christ child and his mother in chapter 2, now that Jesus is engaged in his adult ministry, is no longer present. In the final scene in Matthew's Gospel in which she appears in person (Matt 12:46-50), Jesus does not go out to her, nor is she invited in.[46] His concerns within his adult ministry are focused, not on his human family, but on his family of disciples who, at this point, become distinguished from the crowds as those who do the will of the Father.

Matthean birth narratives she also is included in the group of disciples that do the will of their Father. However, the emphasis of the passage is in the contrast (not the similarity) between Jesus' natural family outside and those inside the house listening to his teaching. Sim, *Gospel of Matthew*, 191-92.

45. The Catholic position is that these are cousins.

46. Some have argued that "Mary the mother of James and Joseph" (Matt 27:56) is in fact Mary, the mother of Jesus, because the names James and Joseph appear in the list of Jesus' brothers in Matt 13:55. Mary is consistently referred to as Jesus' mother (cf. Matt 1:18; 2:11, 13, 20, 21; 13:55). It would seem very strange that at the crucial point of Jesus' crucifixion Matthew would name Mary in this way or that she would be called "the other Mary" (Matt 27:61; 28:1).

Feminist Perspectives

A number of feminist scholars, using a variety of methodologies, have provided interpretations of the infancy narrative of Matthew.[47] One of the most radical positions taken by a feminist scholar working from a literary standpoint is that proposed by Schaberg.

Schaberg's Thesis—An Illegitimate Pregnancy?

Schaberg carefully builds up a case arguing that Matthew is not handing down a tradition of divine conception but a tradition of an illegitimate pregnancy that is nonetheless blessed by God "who sides with the outcast, endangered woman and child. God 'acts' in a radically new way, outside the patriarchal norm but within the natural event of a human conception."[48]

She notes the initial silence in Matthew 1:16 concerning Jesus' paternity, a silence that Schaberg claims does not deny the reality of a human father, whom she argues is the missing person, there only being 13 and not 14 generations named in the last section of the genealogy. She goes on to argue that the phrase "of the Holy Spirit," used in the narrator's comment to the reader (Matt 1:18) and by the angel to Joseph (Matt 1:20), in and of itself does not mean that Jesus was conceived miraculously without a human father. She supports this view with the observation that never before in Jewish texts has divine begetting referred to a literal divine conception (e.g., Deut 32:18; Ps 2:7). Therefore the phrase "of the Holy Spirit" should be read in the same way as other previous Jewish texts and consequent Christian texts in which she claims the divine begetting is metaphorical. She uses these arguments to support her view that, in fact, Jesus was fathered by a human male either through extra marital sex, or seduction or rape. Theologically, her point is that, in spite of Mary's illegitimate pregnancy, God is still the one who gave life to her child, thus her child is from the Holy Spirit. She goes on to argue that Jesus' begetting by the Spirit "constitutes him as Son of God in a special sense."[49] She is unclear what this means and why Jesus' begetting of the Spirit should be any different from previous instances of women "metaphorically" begetting by the

---

47. See Schaberg's paper that discusses the work of Ruether, Daly, Schotroff, Corrington, Wainwright, Anderson, and Levine. Schaberg, "Feminist Interpretations," 35–62.

48. Schaberg, *Illegitimacy of Jesus*, 74.

49. Ibid., 67.

Spirit. Schaberg has adopted an *a priori* position that both a human father and God were involved in Mary's conception, "God parents the illegitimate Messiah . . . more profoundly than the unnamed biological father" and then proceeds to argue her case.[50]

However, both the narrator's comment in Matthew 1:18 and the angel's comment to Joseph in Matt 1:20 indicate that they are referring not in some metaphorical way to Jesus' conception but rather are explaining the *agency* of Mary's begetting. The story in Matthew points to something that is unique, a divine begetting that is *not* like others and has never been attested to before (either in Jewish or Greek literature).[51] As Wright comments, "the whole point is that the birth of Jesus was different from other births and so is without parallel."[52] No human father is implicated.

Schaberg goes on to suggest that nothing in the context of Matthew 1 requires us to read Matthew 1:18, 20 in terms of a virginal conception. What of Matthew's use of Isaiah 7:14, his own editorial comment on events? Schaberg claims, "It is agreed . . . that Matthew's interest, like Isaiah's, is not centred on the manner of the child's conception."[53] While it can be argued in its original context Isaiah's interest is not on the manner of the child's conception, we have seen that the rhetoric and context of the text in Matthew indicates that the manner of the child's conception is precisely Matthew's interest. She does allow that the word παρθένος in the LXX "played a role in Matthew's choice of citation,"[54] but only special pleading on Schaberg's part, that Matthew in including the citation from Isaiah 7:14 was not thinking of a virgin conceiving miraculously but of a virgin being seduced or raped,[55] allows her to dismiss this verse.

It must be asked that if Matthew and Luke do not bear witness to a virgin birth, where did the Christian belief in the virgin birth come from? Schaberg's weak response is that, under pressure from the continuing scandal of the illegitimacy tradition, the church after Matthew and Luke "certainly did come up with this belief."[56] How anyone would think up a

---

50. Schaberg, *Illegitimacy of Jesus*, 68.

51. This is also true of Luke whose infancy narrative diverges in so many ways from Matthew's but who significantly agrees on the point that Mary was a virgin (Luke 1:34) and that her pregnancy was attributed to the power of the Holy Spirit (Luke 1:35).

52. Wright, *Real Godsend*, 31.

53. Schaberg, *Illegitimacy of Jesus*, 71.

54. Ibid.

55. Cf. Deut 22:23–27.

56. Schaberg, "Feminist Interpretations," 52.

virgin birth as a plausible explanation for an illegitimate pregnancy and expect it to be believed is hard to imagine.

From a historical point of view it seems likely that the infancy narrative in Matthew was written partly in response to questions that had been raised over Jesus' parentage, his origin as a human being (Matt 1:18–25), and questions raised over his physical location at birth and consequent location in Nazareth (Matt 2:1–23). It may be argued therefore that the narrative was written partly for Christian apologetic reasons to *defend* Jesus against accusations of illegitimacy. Although written claims that Jesus was illegitimate do not surface until the second century AD, in Celsus's anti-Christian polemic (AD 177–180), there is a strong implication in the words of Jesus' opponents in John 8:41 that charges of illegitimacy were circulating from an earlier period.[57]

Schaberg's hermeneutics of suspicion as she reads into the silences of the text have imposed on it a reading that is sophisticated but untenable. While I appreciate her theological point that God sides with the outcast, endangered woman and child, her theory that Matthew is writing about an illegitimate pregnancy honored by God is unsustainable.

Other Feminist Viewpoints

Much more helpfully other feminist scholars have noted how the account of Mary's virginal conception undermines and subverts an androcentric perspective. Wainwright argues:

> From a feminist perspective . . . the account of Mary's conception of Jesus without reference to male begetting could function as a most profound critique of the androcentric perspective of the genealogy.[58]

Although Mary's mothering of Jesus recalls the earlier mothering of those in the Messianic line, Mary's motherhood is unlike that of the foremothers in the genealogy. Mary's virginal conception in a unique way demonstrates that, through his Spirit, God chose to act outside of patriarchal norms of

---

57. Cf. Brown's reconstruction of Celsus's position, taken from Origen's *Against Celsus I*, 28, 32, 69 (ca. AD 248). Brown, *Birth of the Messiah*, 535.

58. Wainwright, *Feminist Critical Reading*, 73. This has also been argued by Jones, who opines that the presence of the women in the genealogy and Jesus' spiritual conception subverts male ideology and patriarchal institutions. Jones, "Subverting the Textuality," 261.

which male begetting is one of the most fundamental. Wainwright goes on to comment:

> A woman who is named παρθένος is with child and the child is named holy. The reproductive power of woman and her role in the birth of the Messiah is affirmed outside of the patriarchal structure.[59]

God, by his Spirit, is not confined to norms. Mary experiences the new creativity of God's Spirit in a way that will forever remind readers of Matthew's story that Christ's unique birth was as a result of God working outside of patriarchal boundaries. Elizabeth Johnson, noting this point, comments, "being 'outside' is precisely where the encounter with the Holy One takes place . . . in her precarious state she helps to birth the work of the Spirit."[60]

Mary in Matthew's Gospel

At the outset it was noted that the textual space given to Mary as a character does not correlate to the importance of her role as mother of Christ. In answer to the question "How is Mary characterized in the Matthean narrative?" the reply is, "Hardly at all." She never speaks or interacts directly with any other character (human or divine). She takes no independent action beyond giving birth. It is only possible to imagine her situation by reading into the silences of the text. In every text where she is mentioned she is portrayed solely in terms of her motherhood. She is a mother on the margins on two counts. Firstly, within the context of the narrative itself Mary experiences a position on the margins carrying a child who has not been fathered by her husband, then having given birth, she is threatened by death and forced to flee with Joseph and the child to Egypt. She is also textually marginalized in Matthew's Gospel. What is so startling in Matthew's account of Mary is the disjuncture between her theological significance as mother of Christ and the narrative space afforded to her as a character. I suggest there are three reasons for this.

Firstly, the text's androcentrism is reinforced by its focus on Jesus. The text of Matthew's Gospel is entirely Christocentric, everything and everyone else is subordinated to the central focus on Jesus the Messiah. Secondly, the emphasis is on divine initiative and command in the events

---

59. Wainwright, *Feminist Critical Reading*, 74.
60. Johnson, *Truly Our Sister*, 238.

related within the infancy narrative. Although Mary plays no active role apart from the act of giving birth, Joseph also does not act on his own initiative but consistently acts in obedience to divine revelation. It is divine revelation that brings about a change in Joseph's perception of Mary, causing him to take her as wife and adopt her son into his family, and divine initiative protects them from Herod's murderous intentions. Mary's passivity is not to sideline her as a character, but is a device used to point to the divine agency in Mary's conception. Finally, I have argued that the infancy narrative is not a birth story but a story of Christ's origins. As such, the focus is not on the human experience of pregnancy, birth and motherhood. In consequence Mary as a character remains in the background.

Nonetheless, her marginalization as a character in no way detracts from the importance of her role. Mary is represented not only as a mother to her son but as *the* mother to the Messiah. She appears as the final person at the climax of the Messiah's genealogy. Her role in the unfolding history of salvation is vital as the one from whom the Christ is born, the one whose child is from the Holy Spirit. The unique relationship between Mary and the Spirit to which the narrative witnesses, plus the supreme significance attached to her son, elevates her. Textually on the margins, her motherhood of the Christ, by the Spirit, brings her into the theological center of Matthew's vision of salvation history; the Messiah is the Son of God through Mary.

We must now address the question of Mary's relationship to the other women in the genealogy.

Mary's Relationship with "She of Uriah"

In chapter 6 it was argued that their genealogical placement at the start and end of the second and third epoch brought Bathsheba and Mary into close relationship. "She of Uriah" is mother to the first son of David in the redemptive line and Mary is mother to the Messiah, the final son of David. Furthermore, it is interesting to note that there are intertextual similarities in the way the texts in 2 Samuel and Matthew 1 present Bathsheba and Mary.

Both Bathsheba in 2 Samuel and Mary in Matthew, in relation to the plot, are merely agents, rather than fully fledged characters. An agent serves to forward the course of events in the plot, their naming enables the reader to relate to them as a character within the story but little else is known about what they think, say or do. Using Chatman's alternative concept of characterization, it has been argued that it is possible to characterize Bathsheba on some level from the 2 Samuel account; however, in Matthew's account, Mary is given no voice at all and the only action she takes, while of incredible significance, is related in one terse phrase, "she bore a son" (Matt 1:25).

However in spite of their limited characterization, the events surrounding the pregnancies of both women form the kernel of the plot in both 2 Samuel 11–12 and Matthew 1:18–25. A kernel event is an event that is integral to the development of the narrative.[61] In other words, there are interesting stylistic similarities in the way that the plot has been constructed that give added significance to both women. It is Bathsheba's conception and her message sent to King David that provides the kernel for the plot in 2 Samuel 11–12. Similarly, it is the discovery of Mary's pregnancy as a betrothed young woman that is the catalyst for the story told in Matthew 1:18–25. So although both women are very much background figures to the main narrative, which in both cases revolves around men, they are important because their pregnancies are the kernel event that precipitates the main narrative interest.

However, it is their pregnancies that place both women on the margins since both carry children not fathered by their husbands. Although both women are insiders to Israel their pregnancies leave them in dangerous positions on the social margins. Nonetheless at the close of their stories both women through marriage become part of the Davidic line by bearing sons of David.

A number of interesting parallels can also be drawn between these sons of David, born of Bathsheba and Mary respectively. Though there are question marks over the circumstances of their births, both are specifically named as "beloved of the Lord." After the birth of Solomon, the narrator omnisciently tells readers that "The Lord loved him" (2 Sam 12:24c). This message is repeated through the prophet Nathan who gives Solomon a second name, Jedidiah, which in Hebrew means "beloved of the Lord"

---

61. Chatman writes, "Kernels are narrative moments that give rise to cruxes in the direction taken by events. They are nodes or hinges in the structure . . . Kernels cannot be deleted without destroying the narrative logic." Chatman, *Story and Discourse*, 53. If one were to delete a kernel event the logic of the plot would not make sense. On the other hand, satellite events are not crucial to the plot. They are minor events that embellish the story but can be deleted without disturbing the logic of the plot. Kernel events do not necessarily take up a large portion of the narrative and conversely satellite events can actually occupy the main portion of the story as it develops from the kernel event.

(2 Sam 12:25). Like Solomon, Jesus is twice named "the Beloved" of God, at his baptism (Matt 3:17) and at the transfiguration (Matt 17:5).

Within the ongoing narrative of 1 Kings, Solomon is a key figure in two ways. Firstly, he asks for and receives wisdom (1 Kgs 3:28; 4:29). In Matthew Jesus is also the one in whom wisdom dwells (Matt 11:18).[62] Secondly, Solomon builds the Temple (1 Kgs 7) in which God chooses to have his name and presence dwell (1 Kgs 8:10, 20). Clear parallels are drawn with both Solomon (Matt 12:42) and the Temple (Matt 12:6) by Jesus in Matthew's Gospel. Jesus claims that in himself something greater than either Solomon or the Temple is here. In his very being Jesus, as Immanuel (Matt 1:23), brings the presence of God to his people.[63] Finally, in Matthew, it is as the Son of David that Jesus is characterized as the one who heals. Kingsbury notes that Matthew directly links the title Son of David with Jesus' activity of healing and it is as Son of David that children greet him as he rides into Jerusalem and enters the Temple (Matt 21:9, 15).[64] As the first son of David to ascend the throne, Solomon points forward to Jesus the greater Son of David. The links between the two are drawn both within the introductory genealogy and within the Gospel as a whole.

The Five Women of the Genealogy: Their Relationship to One Another and Matthew's Gospel Narrative

This chapter commenced with a discussion of various scholars' views on the ways in which the four foremothers of the genealogy relate to Mary. I reject theories that view the women as problematic in some way or that seek to fit the women into one single framework. I further reject the basic premise that assumes the reason for their inclusion is to foreshadow Mary. It has been argued in chapters 3–6 that the primary reason for the inclusion of Tamar, Rahab, Ruth, and Bathsheba as individuals is because in different ways they all point forward not to Mary, but to the Messiah. This is in keeping with the Messianic focus of the genealogy.

---

62. Witherington argues that Matthew's Gospel deliberately presents a sapiential portrait of Jesus that is guided by the Solomonic tradition. Witherington, *Matthew*, 20, 245, 338–89.

63. Although never explicitly stated by Matthew it is implied that in Jesus Solomon's prayer at the dedication of the Temple finds its ultimate fulfillment (1 Kgs 8:13).

64. Kingsbury, "Title 'Son of David,'" 592, 598.

Nonetheless, although I do not consider their foreshadowing of Mary to be the primary reason for their inclusion as individuals, I note that in certain respects they *are* related to Mary in that a common dynamic of marginalization undergirds all their stories. Although the five women are on the margins in a number of different ways, all five women face social exclusion vis-à-vis their status in regard to their sexuality. Tamar and Ruth are levirate widows. They are both in an anomalous situation in that they are part of a kinship group yet not fully integrated because of lack of children. Rahab, as a prostitute, occupies a liminal position, betwixt and between, in that she is neither a virgin in her father's house nor a married woman in her husband's house. As such she is outside the social order. It has just been noted that Bathsheba and Mary are both married women yet are carrying a child not fathered by their husbands. In doing so they are outside the sexual/social boundaries required of them. All five women experience positions of structural marginalization that leave them in threatening situations as outsiders to patriarchal and social norms. It is in this sense that it could be argued that the four women of the Old Testament foreshadow Mary.

Noting this common dynamic of marginalization is important when we come to consider the collective significance of the women for Matthew because not only the first three women but in fact all five women act to represent all who are marginalized, excluded from the centers of political, religious, and social power. All five women experience positions of marginalization that leave them in threatening situations as outsiders to Israel's patriarchal, ethnic, and social norms but all ultimately find a place on the inside. Part 2 chapter 9 will define concepts of marginality before going on to consider two marginalized character groups in Matthew's Gospel. It will explore stories of both the disenfranchised Jew and the Gentile outsider. I contend that the presence of the five women in Jesus' ancestry points towards a Messiah who will welcome all those who are on the margins, both Jew and Gentile, and anticipates the Gospel's inclusive soteriological vision.

In chapters 3, 4, and 5, I have concluded that what characterizes Tamar, Rahab, and Ruth is pivotal to the outcome of their stories. Although they are outsiders to Israel, each woman acts in ways consistent with YHWH's covenantal calling and command to his people, and in so doing each woman finds a place on the inside, within Israel. Their stories anticipate key themes that find their trajectory in the teaching of Jesus; themes of righteousness, faith, and חסד (mercy). In part 2 chapter

8 I will demonstrate that these three virtues are important descriptors of Matthean discipleship, describing character traits which should identify the new people of God Jesus calls to himself. It is significant therefore that these virtues are not foreshadowed by Israelite male figures but by women who are characterized by their marginality and ethnic otherness to Israel. Their inclusion within the Messiah's genealogy challenges Israel's identity and anticipates the importance of the widening of her boundaries in the kingdom that the Messiah inaugurates.

Together, Bathsheba and Mary bracket the period from David to the Messiah. The theological significance of their placement at the head of the second epoch and the close of the third epoch of the genealogy has been noted. However, in contrast to the first three women little can be deduced of their significance in terms of their characterization; in literary parlance both Bathsheba and Mary are agents to the plot rather than fully rounded characters. Chapter 6 has concluded that Bathsheba's inclusion in the genealogy draws attention to David's sinful abuse of power extended over many generations but also to God's gracious promise of salvation in the birth of a Messiah. Her presence additionally raises questions concerning status and the exercise of power among Israel's patriarchs. This chapter has drawn attention to Mary's role in Matthew's account of Jesus' origins. The unique creative work of the Spirit in Mary to bring life to her womb sets her apart, but Matthew's witness to Jesus' divine origins, as Mary enters into motherhood, does not involve any detailed portrayal of Mary who, like Bathsheba remains passive throughout. Nonetheless, without the sexual involvement of a man, the virgin birth acts as a fundamental critique to patriarchy.

As well as a dynamic of marginality bringing the women into a common relationship, the five women obviously relate in terms of gender; very simply all five are female. In what is an androcentric text within a patrilineal genealogy their presence as a group of women is striking. They need not have been included. Luke's very different genealogy has no mention of women. Matthew, however, deliberately honors these women as foremothers and mother to Christ. His inclusion of them highlights that it is through women as well as men that the divine promises have been fulfilled. As a gender group they will be significant in the story of Jesus as Matthew tells it. Their presence in the genealogy intimates to the reader that just as women have played important roles in the past and at the Messiah's birth, women will continue to play important roles both within the lifetime of Jesus and in the eschatological future that the Messiah will inaugurate. Part 2 chapter 10 will argue that the inclusion of the five women in the genealogical annotations serves to establish and indicate that there is a positive gynocentric counternarrative to Matthew's Gospel that both complements and subverts the dominant androcentric gospel narrative. The chapter will go on to explore the other women who make up this gynocentric counternarrative before drawing conclusions concerning what Matthew's Gospel is saying about the role and position of women among those who are disciples of Jesus.

Taken as a collective whole, it is not just the first three women but the presence of all five women in the genealogy that is subversive of Israel's identity. As representatives of the Gentiles, the marginalized, and women, they subvert Israel's understanding of who she is on three levels: her exclusive calling as the people of God, her assumptions about the place of those at the center in positions of power and status, and her patriarchal assumptions about the priority of the place and role of men in the purposes of God. Matthew's inclusion of the five women in the genealogy is the first indication that the birth of the Messiah will bring Israel to a critical point in redefining her identity on all three levels.

Part Two

The Collective Significance of the Women for the Ongoing Gospel Narrative

8

Tamar, Rahab, and Ruth

Aspects of Matthean Discipleship

Part 1 has established that the first three named women of Matthew's Gospel are characterized within their Hebrew narratives not in terms of their sinfulness or scandalous sexual activity but by their virtues of righteousness, faith, and loyalty. This short chapter will argue that righteousness, faith, and loyalty are three central aspects of the Matthean Jesus' teaching in relation to discipleship. It is therefore significant that these themes first appear in the stories of Tamar (righteousness), Rahab (faith and loyalty), and Ruth (loyalty). The naming of Tamar, Rahab, and Ruth in the genealogy highlights and anticipates the importance of these themes as key virtues for Matthew. No attempt will be made to address fully each theme; my purpose is simply to outline the contours of these three virtues in Matthew's Gospel and to demonstrate that all three are key aspects of Matthean discipleship, before drawing conclusions about Matthew's construal of Christian identity. Consequently, it will be shown that there is an intertextual thematic coherence to the readings of the narratives of Tamar, Rahab and Ruth and also to some of Matthew's distinct key themes. Semantically, loyalty translates into the word "mercy" in Greek so the three topics under consideration will be righteousness, faith, and mercy.

Righteousness in Matthew[1]

Part 1 chapter 3 established that Tamar's story in Genesis 38 revolves around an exploration of what it is to be righteous. It has been argued that her story demonstrates that to be righteous has primarily ethical rather than forensic dimensions. Tamar is characterized in Genesis 38 as a woman who acted righteously in relation to those with whom she was in kinship relationship. A similar emphasis can be found in the Matthean teaching on righteousness. Her naming in the introductory genealogy is an indication of what it is to be righteous and that the exercise of righteousness as a theme may well be important in the ongoing gospel narrative. In her story the dramatic force of the narrative also revolves around a reversal of expectations of where righteousness is to be found; this is another theme that is picked up in Jesus' teaching in Matthew's Gospel, particularly in the Sermon on the Mount.

What it means to live righteously is a key concept in Matthew's Gospel. Overman comments, "'Righteousness' emerges as the all-embracing notion for the actions, behavior, and disposition of the disciples and followers of Jesus."[2] At first glance, the theme of righteousness, δικαιοσύνη, might not seem of great importance since the term only occurs seven times.[3] However, frequency of use does not directly correlate to the importance of the concept for Matthew. On each occasion use of the noun δικαιοσύνη is distinctive to Matthew's Gospel. Before looking at each usage of the noun δικαιοσύνη, mention will be made of the usage of the adjective

---

1. A full discussion of the theme of righteousness in Matthew is beyond the remit of this thesis. A much fuller treatment is provided by Przybylski in his book *Righteousness in Matthew and His World of Thought* where he sets out to establish the meaning of both righteousness and the righteous in Matthew's Gospel. However, he rejects the notion that this thesis is based on, that the Old Testament provides the interpretative key to understanding Matthew. Instead, in order to investigate righteousness terminology, he turns to the Dead Sea Scrolls and the tannaitic literature. He concludes that Matthew's concept of righteousness reflects the contemporary Jewish notion that the righteous are those who live in such a way so as to meet the demands God places on them to live according to the law. His overall argument is unconvincing because it is based on a faulty premise and does not do justice to a number of passages in Matthew, particularly Matt 5:6 and 6:33 in which the righteousness to be hungered for ultimately comes from God and is based on God's righteousness. Przybylski, *Righteousness in Matthew and His World of Thought*.

2. Overman, *Matthew's Gospel*, 92.

3. Matt 3:15; 5:6, 10, 20; 6:1, 33; 21:32.

δίκαιος and the verb δικαιόω in Matthew's Gospel that together constitute the Matthean righteousness terminology.[4]

The corresponding adjective δίκαιος occurs more frequently (17 times) than the noun. As we have seen, it describes Joseph (Matt 1:19) in connection with his merciful intentions to divorce Mary quietly. It is often used of those who are praised by Jesus for their upright, righteous behavior but in the following examples Jesus does not elaborate on the content of such behavior (Matt 10:41; 13:17; 13:43; 13:49; 23:35). Elsewhere Jesus clarifies the strongly ethical content of what it is to be righteous. To be righteous is to love your enemies (Matt 5:44-45) and to care for those in need (Matt 25:37, 46). It is also used as a term of contrast, those who are righteous are compared to those who are unrighteous (Matt 5:45) or evil (Matt 13:41-43, 49). The verb δικαιόω occurs twice (Matt 11:19; 12:37) and in both cases carries the sense of "to justify." The first example (Matt 11:19, cf. Luke 7:35) is of particular interest. When accused of gluttony, drunkenness, and mixing with tax collectors and sinners, Jesus argues that wisdom is shown to be right, is justified, and vindicated by her deeds. Jesus' act of wisdom in reaching out to those on the margins challenges the conventional wisdom of the religious teachers on what constitutes righteous behavior. However, it is the seven examples of the noun δικαιοσύνη, used exclusively in Matthew's Gospel, that are decisive in determining the contours of Matthew's thought on righteousness.

John the Baptist is described by Jesus as the one "who came to you in [the] way of righteousness" (Matt 21:32). It is clear from John's preaching that his awareness of the coming kingdom of heaven led to his call for repentance and baptism. This would set people on the path of a restored relationship with God resulting in a changed lifestyle, in other words, the way of righteousness. It is John who heralds and prepares the way for Jesus' ministry. The essence of John's message, "Repent for the kingdom of heaven has come near" (Matt 3:2), is repeated verbatim in Matthew's summary of Jesus' preaching (Matt 4:17). Matthew's presentation of the two men in similar terms emphasizes that they stand in close relationship to one another.[5] In speaking of John, Jesus speaks of his own ministry. He too will show the way of righteousness.

The first words spoken by Jesus in the Gospel, and therefore of special significance, persuade John to baptize because "it is proper for us

---

4. The group of words δικαιοσύνη, δίκαιος, δικαιόω are the equivalent to the Hebrew terminology צדק and צדקה describing righteousness.

5. Further examples are given in Davies and Allison, *Matthew 1-7*, 289.

in this way to fulfill all righteousness" (Matt 3:15). The word "fulfill" is fraught with resonance because of its use in the formula quotations and in the key passage of Matthew 5:17–20, where Jesus says he has come to fulfill the law and the prophets. Jesus in his person and actions is bringing to a fulfillment all that was anticipated in the old dispensation of the law and prophets. Implied in his words to John is the notion that righteousness involves obedience to God's will. In identifying himself with the many Israelites who came seeking a baptism of repentance Jesus fulfills the righteousness to which God calls him. In his relationship with others and in his total obedience to God Jesus, throughout the Gospel, continues to model what it is to live a righteous life. As he goes to his death Jesus is named once again as a "righteous man" (Matt 27:19). Consequently, Jesus' righteousness is defined initially and at the conclusion and climax of his mission in terms of his willingness to be fully identified with those to whom he ministered in obedience to the will of his Father. Just as he fulfills all righteousness, he in turn calls his disciples to a life of righteousness.

It is in the first set of discourse material, as Jesus addresses his disciples in the Sermon on the Mount, that righteousness, as an aspect of discipleship, emerges as a key theme. It is within this sermon that the other instances of δικαιοσύνη all fall.

The fourth beatitude reads, "Blessed are those who hunger and thirst for righteousness, for they will be filled" (Matt 5:6). This corresponds to Luke's second beatitude, "Blessed are you that hunger now, for you shall be satisfied" (Luke 6:21). What is significant is Matthew's addition of what is to be hungered for—righteousness (δικαιοσύνη). This signals that righteousness is an important and distinctive concept in Matthew. In the same way, whereas the Lukan Jesus instructs his disciples to "seek his kingdom, and these things will be added to you" (Luke 12:31), in Matthew the phrase "and his righteousness" (Matt 6:33) is added. All those who are seeking God's kingdom must above all else seek for his righteousness. The righteous are the merciful (Matt 5:7), the pure in heart (Matt 5:8), and the peacemakers (Matt 5:9). For this and other marks of righteousness Jesus warns his followers they will suffer but in their suffering they will be blessed, "Blessed are those who are persecuted for righteousness' sake, for theirs is the kingdom of heaven" (Matt 5:10).

Both of Jesus' sayings in Matthew 5:6 and 6:33 indicate that God's righteousness is a gift to be sought for and received. Yet elsewhere in the sermon, notably in Matthew 5:17–20, it is required and demanded of disciples that in following Jesus they must act righteously in keeping with the commandments of the law (Matt 5:18-19). The tension between the two is maintained by the Matthean Jesus, the virtue of righteousness is both a gift from God and to be lived out in obedience to God's commands. These verses (Matt 5:18-19), which have no parallels in the other Gospels, are foundational for Matthew's understanding of righteousness; Jesus talks about a righteousness that exceeds that of the teachers of the law, "For I tell you, unless your righteousness exceeds that of the scribes and Pharisees, you will never enter the kingdom of heaven" (Matt 5:20). Although the religious leaders practice a form of righteousness, it is inadequate and misdirected. Fundamental to Jesus' criticism of their righteousness is that it is an outward display, "They do all their deeds to be seen by others" (Matt 23:5). Their hypocrisy lies in the fact that their outward public deeds of righteousness do not match up to their interior life (Matt 23:2, 27-29). The higher righteousness Jesus calls for is an advance on both the text of the Torah and traditional interpretations of it. Each of the six points of the law (or traditional interpretations of it) are to do with human interpersonal relationships: anger and reconciliation (Matt 5:21-26), adultery (Matt 5:27-30), divorce (Matt 5:31-32), speaking with integrity (Matt 5:33-37), retaliation (Matt 5:38-42), love for enemies (Matt 5:43-48). Jesus enumerates how his followers should live *in relation to others* through upholding the Torah but redefines what is asked of the disciple in terms of not only their outward action but also their interior life. Nevertheless it is important to note that "The controlling interest is not 'righteousness' *per se*, but being a disciple, which means above all to 'follow' Jesus."[6] Barton's insight is an important reminder that all Jesus' teaching on righteousness must be seen in the context of his call to discipleship.

Underlying Jesus' teaching is a call to a loving response to others, spelt out in the final antithesis where disciples are called to love their enemies (Matt 5:44). A righteous life also involves acts of righteousness towards God envisaged in the three traditional elements of Jewish piety: alms giving, prayer, and fasting (Matt 6:1-18). But Jesus warns that one should not practice one's [acts of] righteousness before others in order to be seen by them (Matt 6:1). The higher righteousness to which Jesus calls his disciples can ultimately only be given as a gift from their heavenly Father as disciples enter into a right relationship with him. Yet the practice of righteousness in daily life is something to which they must aspire, seeking to be perfect and complete (τέλειος) as God is perfect (Matt 5:48).

---

6. Barton, *Discipleship*, 149.

Later in the Gospel, in summarizing the law, Jesus calls his disciples to love God first and foremost, flowing from which comes the command to "love your neighbor as yourself" (Matt 22:37–39). The importance of the love command to be manifest ethically in the life of the disciple is underlined in the final parable of the fifth and final eschatological discourse (Matt 25:31–46) when those on the king's right are called righteous (δίκαιος) (Matt 25:37) and are praised for their practical care for the "least of my brothers" in need. Righteousness must be a demonstrable feature of those who believe in Jesus. It must be lived out in human relationships, in generosity towards others.

Tellingly, Jesus warns the chief priests and elders that the tax collectors and prostitutes will lead the way in the kingdom of God, "the tax collectors and prostitutes are going into the kingdom of God ahead of you. For John came to you in the way of righteousness and you did not believe him, but the tax-collectors and the prostitutes believed him" (Matt 21:31–32). Not only does Jesus redefine the meaning of righteousness, he turns upside-down expectations of where and in whom righteousness might be found. The inclusion of Tamar in the genealogical annotations recalls for the attentive reader her story; a woman in whom righteousness was found and whose story anticipates this important theme in Matthew's Gospel.

Faith in Matthew

In his essay "On the essence of being a disciple" Barth highlights faith as one of the virtues "which are essential to the making of a disciple in Matthew."[7] The first indication that faith is important to discipleship comes in Jesus' address to his disciples in the Sermon on the Mount. In a section on anxiety over the essentials of life—food and clothing, Jesus reprimands them for their lack of faith in God's ability to take care of them, "you of little faith" (ὀλιγόπιστοι) (Matt 6:30). Worry and anxiety are characteristic among people of little faith. Faith is not intellectual assent to a set of teachings but is defined as a quality of trustfulness that is to be directed towards their heavenly Father. Jesus calls his disciples to put their trust in the provision of their heavenly Father who knows all their needs (Matt 6:32). Faith, in this instance, firstly involves recognition of God's willingness and ability to provide for their basic needs. Secondly, faith requires

---

7. Barth, "Matthew's Understanding," 105.

placing their trust in their heavenly Father that he will do so. The Father/child relationship is the basis for a life of discipleship.

The issue of faith is not raised again until chapters 8–9. It is in the context of Jesus' ministry to those on the margins that the faith of individuals comes to the fore. In fact, half of all Matthew's references to faith occur in these two chapters where the faith of individuals seeking healing is a key component in the stories as told by Matthew.[8] The first person to be praised for their faith in Jesus' healing power is not one of the disciples but a Roman centurion whose faith is demonstrated in his request to Jesus, "only speak the word, and my servant will be healed" (Matt 8:8). Jesus is amazed that such faith should be found not within Israel but from an outsider, "In no one in Israel have I found such faith" (Matt 8:10).

The theme of faith in chapters 8–9 continues with the healing of the paralyzed man (Matt 9:1–8). Jesus responds to the man's need of forgiveness having seen the faith of those who brought him (Matt 9:2). In the healing of the two blind men (Matt 9:27–31) Jesus probes them with a question to discover the depth of their faith, on which basis he restores their sight. Sandwiched between these two stories is the story of a ruler who trusts in Jesus to restore life to his daughter (Matt 9:18–19, 23–26) and a woman whose faith has to overcome her understandable reticence to be seen to reach out and touch Jesus (Matt 9:20–22). Jesus recognizes this and responds to her faith with healing, "Take heart, daughter; your faith has made you well" (Matt 9:22). Faith in each case is directed towards Jesus. It is an active reaching out after his mercy and help. In chapters 8–9 those in need, men and women, Jews and Gentiles, consistently demonstrate this kind of faith in their positive response towards Jesus. It is the kind of faith demonstrated by Rahab in the God of Israel and it is the faith for which Jesus seeks in those who would follow him.

It is notable that the one miracle that does not involve healing in these two chapters focuses in particular on the low level of faith among Jesus' disciples in a life threatening situation (Matt 8:23–27). The disciples are identified more specifically as the inner male group of twelve in Matthew 10:1, where a definite distinction is made between "the disciples" and "the crowds" who have also followed Jesus (Matt 4:25) and listened to his teaching (Matt 7:28). Here this inner group of disciples are rebuked by Jesus in the storm. Jesus asks, "Why are you afraid, you of little faith?"

---

8. In his redactional study of the miracle stories in Matthew, Held has demonstrated that sayings about faith form the statement content and climax to the healing miracles in Matthew. See Held, "Matthew as Interpreter," 284–91.

(ὀλιγόπιστοι) (Matt 8:26) before he goes on to demonstrate his authority over the wind and waves. Bornkamm's famous redaction-critical study of this passage notes that, whereas in Mark (Mark 4:35-41) and Luke (Luke 8:22-25) Jesus first calms the storm and then deals with the disciples' lack of faith, in Matthew's account Jesus challenges their lack of faith before he meets their need. "Before the elements are brought to silence, thus in the midst a mortal threat, the word of Jesus goes forth to the disciples and puts them to shame for their little faith."[9] The disciples' lack of faith then becomes central to the miracle. Bornkamm goes on to note that the expression ὀλιγοπιστία is a favorite word of Matthew's. Apart from one reference in Luke 12:28 he is the only gospel writer to use it (Matt 6:30; 8:26; 14:31; 16:8; 17:20). Among Jesus' disciples "it always denotes a faith that is too weak, that is paralyzed in the storm (8.26; 14.31) and in anxiety (6.30; 16.8)."[10] The narrative arrangement of the sequence of events in chapters 8-9 ensures that the little faith of the disciples in the storm stands in contrast to the faith of two individuals on the margins. In two pericopes that precede and follow the stilling of the storm Jesus praises the great faith of the centurion (Matt 8:13) and the faith of the hemorrhaging woman (Matt 9:22). Faith, it seems, is not the preserve of the religious insider, in fact quite the opposite. Those on the margins are people of faith, while Jesus' inner group of disciples are "ones of little faith" who, when in need, are unable fully to trust him to save. The surprising reversal of expectations of where and in whom faith is to be found has been foreshadowed in Rahab's story in which can be seen an anticipation of this theme.

Jesus reprimands his disciples for their lack of faith specifically on three more occasions: when Peter attempts to walk on the water (Matt 14:31); when they doubt Jesus' ability to provide bread (Matt 16:8) and when they have been unable to heal (Matt 17:14-20). On this last occasion, Jesus replies that their failure to heal is "Because of your little faith" (Matt 17:20). The disciple's lack of faith is typical of their faithless (ἄπιστος) generation (Matt 17:17), yet, unlike others, they do have faith, they have followed Jesus thus far. Jesus strongly implies that their "little faith" is immature and needs to grow. He goes on to indicate that in comparison to their minuscule faith, only the tiniest amount of faith, the size of a mustard seed, is needed to move mountains (Matt 17:20). A similar saying is attributed to Jesus in Matthew 21:21. Both sayings are again prefaced by the formula that stresses the importance of what Jesus is about to say,

9. Bornkamm, "Stilling of the Storm," 56.
10. Ibid.

"Truly I say to you," and both deal with the problem of seemingly impossible requests and unanswered prayer. In this case, the image used by Jesus is not simply of moving mountains but complete mountain removal! All things are possible if they have faith and do not doubt (μὴ διακριθῆτε) (Matt 21:21). Here faith is defined in opposition to doubt, the force of the Greek διακριθῆτε in the middle voice is to hesitate or be in two minds rather than a reference to intellectual doubt.[11] Consequently, the faith the Matthean Jesus seeks for is single-minded and of clear intent.

Several aspects of what has been observed in connection with the theme of faith converge in the story of the Canaanite woman. She also shows outstanding faith in Jesus when in need and is the only person outside chapters 8–9 whom Jesus praises for their faith. The discussion of her story in chapter 9 will demonstrate the tenacity of her faith, which, it will be suggested, like Rahab's faith, is in line with the faith of Abraham, Jacob, and Moses in challenging divinity, as well as reflecting the Psalmists' cry for mercy. As a Gentile, in her manner of faith she behaves like a devout Jew, as Rahab did. In her appeal to Jesus as the Son of David she is "in effect confessing him to be the Messiah sent to Israel."[12] Her persistent, importunate faith in Jesus ultimately brings healing for her daughter. Read as intertexts the two Canaanite women bring to the fore the exceptional faith of the outsider.

The final reference to faith in Matthew's Gospel comes when Jesus criticizes the scribes and Pharisees for neglecting "justice, mercy and faith" (Matt 23:23). Significantly, in the parallel saying in Luke Jesus accuses them of neglecting "justice and the love of God" (Luke 11:42) but neither mercy nor faith is mentioned. Carter summarizes the faith that Jesus demands here as an "openness to Jesus which seeks his power, trusting it to overcome obstacles and transform situations of need."[13] While this is a good definition of the faith of those supplicating Jesus, in this instance, I concur with France who suggests that here the meaning is more likely to be faithfulness to God's requirements in line with the justice and mercy required of them.[14] Similarly, Nolland suggests that Micah 6:8 be read as an intertext to this verse, since it also has a list of three items. The first two, justice and mercy parallel Matthew's list in which case faith would be

---

11. It is to be distinguished from the verb διστάζω that is elsewhere used of doubt in Matthew's Gospel (cf. Matt 14:31; 28:17).

12. Kingsbury, "Title 'Son of David,'" 591.

13. Carter, *Matthew and the Margins*, 459.

14. France, *Gospel of Matthew*, 873–74.

analogous to "walk humbly with your God."[15] This would support France's contention and is probably the most helpful reading in this context. Faith here represents a faithfulness that is an ongoing ethical requirement of the disciple in much the same way as the ongoing ethical requirement for a life characterized by justice (which is another aspect of righteousness) and mercy. The call for faithful living points to another aspect of discipleship emphasized in Matthew. Faith is only one side of the equation; faith must be worked out in practice, it must be manifest in action. It is actions that will expose the authenticity of faith. Jesus warns his disciples that "Not everyone who says to me 'Lord, Lord,' will enter the kingdom of heaven, but only the one who does the will of my Father in heaven." (Matt 7:21). Obedience to the Father in doing his will is the evidence of faith in the life of the disciple. Jesus identifies his family of disciples as those who do the will of his Father in heaven. "For whoever does the will of my Father in heaven is my brother and sister and mother" (Matt 12:50). It is the concern of the Lord's prayer that his disciples request that the Father's will be put into effect (Matt 6:10b) and it is a theme that is picked up again in the parable of the father who asks his two sons to work in the vineyard, which is only recorded by Matthew (Matt 21:28–32). Of the two sons it is not verbal compliance that matters but the one who did the will of his father who is praised. Tellingly it is on this basis that Jesus explains that those on the margins, the tax collectors and prostitutes, will go into the kingdom of God ahead of his listeners, the chief priests and elders (Matt 21:32).

To summarize: faith is a fundamental aspect of discipleship in Matthew. Jesus looks for a response of faith among all those who come to him for help. In Matthew's Gospel, characteristically it is those on the margins, women and the outsiders who believe and respond in faith to Jesus, whereas his disciples often lack faith. This reversal of expectations, where faith is found where least expected, has been anticipated in Rahab the prostitute's narrative where her surprising faith in YHWH contrasts with the noticeable lack of faith in the spies. Her faith anticipates the kind of faith Jesus seeks among those who would follow him. It is a faith that reaches out to God, trusting that in his mercy he will respond to those in need. Significantly, Rahab's faith is also a faith that is manifest through action in the demonstration of practical mercy towards others; in Matthean terms she does the will of the Father.

---

15. Nolland, *Gospel of Matthew*, 938.

Mercy in Matthew

Whereas Tamar's story illustrates the theme of righteousness, Rahab and Ruth's stories focus on the theme of loyalty (חסד). It is significant therefore that, like righteousness, mercy is a closely related theme that receives particular attention in Matthew's Gospel. It could be argued that the twin concepts of righteousness and mercy summarize the essence of the ethical outworking of what it is to do the will of the Father.[16] The Matthean Jesus teaches on the importance of demonstrating mercy to others on a number of occasions. This important and distinctive Matthean theme has been foreshadowed in the genealogy by the naming of Rahab and Ruth. The stories of Rahab and Ruth not only foreshadow the importance of mercy as a theme, they illustrate a principle of mercy that is reflected by the Matthean Jesus; mercy given to others results in mercy received. Rahab and Ruth's stories point not only to the reciprocal nature of mercy in human relationships but also to the theological dimensions of a God who is merciful and who responds in mercy towards those who show mercy to others.

Unparalleled in the other Gospels, it is only the Matthean Jesus who speaks of God's mercy and his desire for mercy in the lives of those who follow him. The noun ἔλεος occurs three times in the sayings of Jesus in Matthew's Gospel, twice in Jesus' polemical response to the Pharisees (Matt 9:13; 12:7) and once in Jesus' condemnation of the scribes and Pharisees (Matt 23:23). The adjective ἐλεήμων describes those who are blessed (Matt 5:7) and the verb ἐλεέω is the action called for by the king in the parable of the unjust servant (Matt 18:33).

In Matthew's Gospel the concept of mercy is based on the premise that God is a merciful God; this is demonstrated in the actions of the Messiah towards those in need. On a number of occasions those who come seeking help from Jesus echo the Psalmist's cry for mercy (Matt 9:27; 15:22; 17:15; 20:30, 31). As the merciful Messiah, Jesus interacts with those around him seeking help. In turn, Jesus highlights the need for others to practice mercy. "Blessed are the merciful for they will be shown mercy" (Matt 5:7).[17] The call for mercy is linked back to God's own merciful ways. Although in this saying the future passive (ἐλεήμονος) implies that the emphasis of Jesus' words is not on how other people will respond to the person who is

---

16. Edin convincingly argues that "in Matthew's Gospel, to be righteous is to show mercy." Edin, "Learning What Righteousness Means," 356. Certainly mercy in Matthew can be identified as an aspect of righteousness, just as righteous behavior towards others is considered to be an aspect of חסד in Hosea 6.

17. This saying is not included in the parallel passage in Luke 6:20–23.

merciful but on how they will be rewarded in the future by God, elsewhere in the sermon Jesus makes clear that there is a human response to mercy that responds to like with like, "In everything do to others as you would have them do to you; for this is the law and the prophets" (Matt 7:12).

Twice in Matthew's Gospel (Matt 9:13; 12:7) Jesus quotes words from Hosea 6:6, "I desire mercy, not sacrifice." The citation of Hosea's words by Jesus is unique to Matthew's Gospel. The citation does not occur in the two parallel passages in Mark and Luke that also describe Jesus' dispute with religious leaders,[18] nor does this citation occur elsewhere in the New Testament, indicating that it is particularly important to Matthew, the implied author.

Within the Hosea passage contrast is made between Israel's חסד that is transient, like the morning mist that burns off with the sunrise (Hos 6:4), and the steadfast constant חסד love that YHWH desires, "for I desire loyalty (חסד) and not sacrifice" (Hos 6:6). Israel's loyalty must be founded on the knowledge of God. Without knowledge of God Israel's actions are not characterized by mercy towards her fellow Israelites; on the contrary her behavior becomes evil, "There is no faithfulness or loyalty (חסד) and no knowledge of God in the land. Swearing, lying, and murder, and stealing and adultery break out; bloodshed follows bloodshed" (Hos 4:1–2). By contrast, the love that God requires must be constant in duration and merciful in the treatment of others. Israel's love is not חסד because it is short lived and is not characterized by mercy.[19]

Hosea's words are a key prophetic principle. Mercy, declares the prophet, is of far higher value than ritual sacrifice and religious observance, it is fundamental to covenant loyalty. Twice Jesus quotes this principle when in dispute with the Pharisees over their judgment of others.

The first citation of Hosea 6:6 occurs in the context of Jesus' call of Matthew the tax collector (Matt 9:9–13), "a typical act, expressive of God's mercy among the marginal and constitutive of a new community."[20] The Pharisees witness Jesus eating with Matthew and "many tax collectors and sinners" (Matt 9:10). Criticism is implicit in the Pharisees' question put to Jesus' disciples, "Why does your teacher eat with tax collectors and sinners?" (Matt 9:11). Jesus himself answers the question put to his disciples, starting with a proverb that uses the analogy of a doctor with sick

---

18. The parallel passage to Matt 9:9–13 is Mark 2:13–17, where the quotation from Hosea is missing. It is also missing from Jesus' words in the passages in Mark 2:23–28 and Luke 6:1–6 that parallel Matt 12:1–8.

19. Edin, "Learning What Righteousness Means," 359.

20. Carter, *Matthew and the Margins*, 219.

patients. In his reply he cites Hosea 6:6, "Those who are well have no need of a physician, but those who are sick. Go and learn what this means 'I desire mercy not sacrifice'. For I have come to call not the righteous but sinners" (Matt 9:12–13). The practice of mercy, of kindness and generosity towards others, is of much higher importance than religious observance or outward show of piety; it involves welcoming all, especially those on the margins who are "sick" and in need of help and deliverance. In citing Hosea 6:6 Jesus indicates that although the Pharisees consider themselves to be righteous it is not true righteousness because it lacks mercy. In their opposition to Jesus' eating with tax collectors and sinners they betray their exclusionary attitude towards others. They neither understand nor are able to embrace the inclusive action of Jesus eating with those on the margins of society, which is a manifestation of the mercy and love of God.

The second citation (Matt 12:7) also comes in a polemical response to the Pharisees' criticism. This time their criticism is directed towards Jesus' disciples for picking and eating grain on the sabbath because they were hungry and therefore "doing what is not lawful to do on the sabbath" (Matt 12:2). In his reply Jesus states that their understanding of the law is inadequate (Matt 12:4–5). The Pharisees' condemnation of the guiltless disciples rests on a legalistic interpretation of the law that involved a rigid compliance. This was because, more fundamentally, their understanding of Jesus' identity is inadequate too, "I tell you, something greater than the temple is here" (Matt 12:6). With no knowledge of God their religious observance, like those in Israel at the time of Hosea, is without mercy and without understanding of what is at the heart of what God desires, "If you had known what these words mean, 'I desire mercy, not sacrifice', you would not have condemned the innocent" (Matt 12:7). What is of primary importance to God is his desire for mercy, in this case the provision to meet the basic human need of hunger.

Jesus warns that there are dire consequences for those who do not respond to God's mercy with mercy towards others. Jesus tells the parable, unique to Matthew's Gospel (Matt 18:23–35), of a king who exhibits mercy towards his servant who is in his debt, "out of pity for him, the lord of the slave released him and forgave him the debt" (Matt 18:27). Although released by the king from his large debt, the servant himself refuses to forgive the minor debts of his fellow servant. The king responds, "Should you not have had mercy on your fellow-slave as I had mercy on you?" (Matt 18:33). The king, representative of God, demands the practice of mercy in response to the gratuitous mercy shown. The servant who lacks mercy is called wicked (Matt 18:32).

In summary, Jesus calls his disciples and the religious leaders to practice mercy. This involves the inclusion of all those on the margins, just as Jesus himself showed friendship to "tax-collectors and sinners" (Matt 11:19). The outworking of mercy should be further seen, for example, in the justice of provision of food for the hungry and forgiveness for fellow human beings. Themes of mercy have been explored both in the stories of Canaanite Rahab and Moabite Ruth. Both Gentile women demonstrate mercy to those in need (the spies and Naomi) and in turn receive mercy from others (Joshua and Boaz) and ultimately from God. The rhetoric of the ongoing text of the Gospel suggests that this is one reason for Matthew's inclusion of these two women in his genealogical annotations.

Conclusion

This chapter has explored the idea that the virtues that characterized the first three named women in Matthew's genealogy are some of the key virtues that the Matthean Jesus seeks for among those who would follow him. Given that justice is synonymous with righteousness, these three key components of discipleship are enumerated by the Matthean Jesus when he criticizes the scribes and Pharisees for neglecting the more "weightier matters of the law" (Matt 23:23). Weightier or heavier refers to the essentials, what is really important. The scribes and Pharisees should have practiced "justice, mercy, and faith" (Matt 23:23). Love notes that for Matthew these themes "become for him evaluative criteria for community life governed by the kingdom of heaven . . . The three matters viewed together amplify Matthew's meaning of the highest commandment of love."[21]

Faith is portrayed as an active reaching out to Jesus trusting that in his mercy he will transform situations of need; it is often those on the margins who respond with such faith. Faith is an important element both in the healing miracles and also in Jesus' teaching directed towards his disciples from whom he seeks for a response of faith and a life of faithfulness; a faith that is manifest in doing the will of the Father. Doing the will of the Father, in Matthean terms, can be summarized by Jesus' call to his disciples to lead a life of "higher righteousness." The virtue of righteousness is central to Jesus' teaching in the Sermon on the Mount and is used by the Matthean Jesus as an all embracing term to describe both the outward actions and interior life that should characterize the disciple. The virtue of mercy, an

---

21. Love, *Jesus and Marginal Women*, 235.

outworking of what it is to be righteous, is also considered to be of great ethical importance; it is at the heart of what God desires and is manifest in the inclusive practice of Jesus.

Matthew has named Tamar, Rahab, and Ruth in the genealogy to draw their stories as intertexts into the story of Jesus. The effect of these stories is to foreshadow these three important themes in Jesus' teaching, themes that are descriptors of discipleship in Matthew and point towards the construal of a new identity for the people of God. It is therefore of significance for Matthew's rhetoric concerning the identity of the group of disciples that Jesus will gather to himself that the individuals that demonstrate these virtues are not Jewish male patriarchs but women who are on the margins both ethnically and socially. This calls into question some of the traditional boundaries that gave Israel identity, boundaries of race, social and religious status, and patriarchy. Read as intertexts to Matthew's Gospel it has been noted that Tamar, Rahab, and Ruth's stories indicate that their presence in Messiah's ancestry is subversive of Israel's identity on these three levels. This has implications for three groups of people whom, it will be argued, are significant in Matthew's narration of Jesus' story: those on the margins in Israel, Gentiles, and women. Chapters 9 and 10 will explore the importance of these groups in Matthew's Gospel.

9

Others on the Margin in Matthew's Gospel

Marginality in Matthew

New Testament scholar Duling, using the work of others in the social sciences, defines four different concepts of marginality, which he then applies to antiquity particularly in relation to Matthew's Gospel. The first and most commonly recognized form of marginality is structural marginality. Structural marginality refers "to structural inequities in the social system: some persons are in the center and some are on the periphery." Duling refers to this as *involuntary marginality*. Such individuals aren't able to participate in normative social statuses, their roles and duties. As a result they can't access the material and nonmaterial resources available to those at the center of society. Consequently they "experience themselves as being personally alienated."[1] Those on the margins "are usually the socially and economically disadvantaged or oppressed . . . They are the vast numbers of poor, destitute, and expendable people, as well as women in certain contexts."[2] He notes that "the author of Matthew has great concern for *structurally* marginal persons"[3] and he goes on to list those whom Jesus tells stories about as well as those Jesus encounters:

---

1. Duling, "Matthew and Marginality," 365.
2. Duling, "Ethnicity, Ethnocentrism," 137.
3. Ibid., 138.

forced laborers, day laborers, slaves, tenant farmers, the poor, the destitute in need of alms, eunuchs, ritually unclean, lepers, a woman with a hemorrhage, women who follow Jesus, the diseased and infirm, the blind, the lame, the deaf, the dumb, the deformed, paralytics, demoniacs, epileptics, bandits and prostitutes.[4]

This group of people I refer to in this chapter as marginalized Jews.

Secondly, Duling notes that structural marginal persons also includes those in poorer ethnic populations "whose norms, values, and attitudes contrast with those in the mainstream, or center."[5] In Matthew's terms these would be the Gentile outsiders such as the Canaanite woman. Duling argues that those ethnic outsiders of richer, higher status, such as the Roman military, are part of a subtype of structural marginality he labels as social role marginality. However, in the Palestinian Judean world in which Matthew's narrative is set, all Gentiles whether those of high status or low, rich or poor, are clearly marginalized as ethnic outsiders and I refer to this group as Gentile outsiders.

Ideological marginality refers to those who choose to affiliate with a non-normative group. Duling refers to this as *voluntary marginality* because individuals and groups do this by choice. The ideologically marginalized are separated from the larger society, its statuses and customs, and so they become marginal or liminal but experience close bonding with one another due to their separation. Ideological marginality is "a *desired, visionary marginality, a self-styled, self-imposed liminality*."[6] Duling thinks Matthew's Gospel sets out several groups who represent this form of voluntary marginality, for example the disciples who leave their jobs and homes because choose to follow Jesus. This would therefore also include the women who follow Jesus (Matt 27:55–56, 61; 28:1–10).

The final concept of marginality defined by Duling is cultural marginality. This refers to persons who are condemned to live between two antagonistic worlds without fully belonging to either. They exist in a world with two or more traditions, languages, political loyalties, moral codes or religions, one of which is more dominant. They are caught between two competing cultures and consequently they experience isolation, identity confusion, and alienation. They are culturally marginal because they don't fully assimilate in either culture but are in-between. Building on Duling's

4. Ibid.
5. Ibid., 137.
6. Ibid., 138.

work Love, in his social-scientific analysis of some marginal women in Matthew's Gospel, identifies the Canaanite woman in Matthew's Gospel as culturally as well as structurally marginal.[7]

In the light of this analysis of marginality how do the five women in Matthew's genealogy experience marginalization?

The Women as Representative of the Marginalized in Matthew's Gospel

Part 1 noted that the women of Matthew's genealogy naturally fall into two groups: the three named women in the first epoch extending from Abraham to David, and "she of Uriah" and Mary who stand at the start of the second epoch and at the close of the third respectively. It has been argued that one of the factors that links this eclectic, cross-ethnic group of women was their experience of marginality, of being on the outside.

We have seen that the five women of the genealogy are not only women textually sidelined by patriarchal begetting in Matthew's genealogy but that they are also outsiders in a variety of ways, marginalized within their own social worlds as represented in their stories. A brief review will illustrate this.

Tamar is a Canaanite outsider to the clan of Judah until Judah takes her as wife for Er. Having been brought into Judah's kinship group, she is then intentionally sidelined by Judah as he orders her to return as a widow to her father's house (Gen 38:11). She exists in a state of involuntary marginalization that is both structural and cultural. She is left in her father's house but under the authority of her father-in-law, trapped in levirate widowhood, with no economic or social power, apparently powerless in a world controlled by men. Forced to use her sexuality to create a future for herself, the name of her husband and the clan of Judah, she is acknowledged by Judah to be more in the right than he. Unwilling to fulfill his responsibilities, it is left to the wit and guile of an outsider to repair the social fabric of his clan. She finds a place on the inside with the birth of twin sons. With the inclusion of her and her sons in his genealogy (Matt 1:3), Matthew bears witness that in Tamar's action she brings about the purposes of God. As mother of Perez, Tamar is the bearer of a son directly in line to King David and the Messiah.

---

7. Love, *Jesus and Marginal Women*, 11.

In contrast to Tamar's dependency, Rahab is an independent woman in her own house. Nevertheless, she is, by virtue of her profession as a prostitute, an outsider within Jericho. Narratively this is signaled by the fact that "her house was on the outer side of the city wall" (Josh 2:15). Structurally marginal within her own society, in relation to Israel she is also marginalized in a number of ways. She is a Canaanite, like Tamar, a Gentile outsider to Israel, and furthermore condemned to die along with the inhabitants of Jericho. In spite of occupying this structurally marginal position on two counts in relation to Israel, she decides to align herself with Israel. She confesses faith in the Lord "God in heaven above and on earth below" (Josh 2:11). In doing this she takes on a voluntary marginality that is ideological. It is her faith, resulting in action, which saves the spies and enables Israel's entry into Canaan. This leads to both her and her family's salvation and a place among the people of God but she remains outside the camp and is therefore culturally marginalized living between two worlds. Her faith as an outsider is contrasted both with the hesitancy of the spies and the apostasy of Achan, an ultimate insider within Israel. Matthew honors Rahab's place in Israel with the inclusion of her in his genealogy as wife to Salmon and mother to Boaz, linking her directly to the third named woman in the genealogy, Ruth.

Like Tamar and Rahab, Ruth is also a Gentile outsider to Israel, experiencing an involuntary structural marginality in two ways, as a Moabite woman but also as living as one of the poor in Bethlehem. She takes the unusual step of choosing to remain with Naomi and in doing so, like Rahab, also aligns herself with the God of Israel (Ruth 1:16), choosing a faith that is normative within Bethlehem but experiencing a cultural marginality as a Moabite woman. Like Tamar, she is a levirate widow with no means of support. Along with Naomi, she is among the poor, existing on the margins of society by gleaning. Economically destitute, with apparently no hope for the future, she provides for her mother-in-law physically by bringing seed home from gleaning and socially by bearing the fruit of Boaz's seed in the birth of a son for Naomi. Through marriage to Boaz and the birth of a son, Ruth thereby becomes an insider in Bethlehem society and the Davidic line. Matthew's genealogy honors her, listing her son Obed as grandfather to King David.

It is Tamar, Rahab, and Ruth's notable presence as three Gentile women that alerts the reader to the theme of the marginalized outsider in Matthew's ongoing narrative, yet the two Jewish women are outsiders too.

Although an insider to Israel, Bathsheba is an outsider to David's line, as she "belongs" to Uriah the Hittite. "She of Uriah" lives outside the king's house and remains narratively an outsider throughout most of her story. With child, as a result of David taking her, David's violation leaves Bathsheba in a structurally marginal position outside the legal sexual norms required of her. With power in King David's hands, she suffers the death of her husband before David takes her as wife, incorporating her into the Davidic line. She also suffers the death of her first child before bearing David a son. Although not naming her directly in the genealogy, Matthew nevertheless bears witness that her son Solomon, beloved by the Lord, succeeds David to the throne and is thus in direct line to Jesus the Messiah.

An insider in Israel, Mary, like Bathsheba, is an outsider to the line of David and is textually on the margins in Matthew's birth narrative. As a result of her pregnancy, Mary is also outside the legal sexual norms required of her as a woman, in her case as a betrothed wife, and therefore like Bathsheba is in a structurally marginal position. Through Joseph's obedience to divine command she is brought into David's line through marriage and bears a son who is the ultimate fulfillment of promises made to Abraham and David. Yet her place on the structural margins of society continues as the holy family are forced to flee for their lives to Egypt.

In different ways all five women occupy positions on the margins, yet they are women whom God honors. Consequently they serve to alert the reader to Matthew's rhetorical stance towards those on the margins. By their presence in the genealogy they serve to anticipate the Matthean Messiah's concern for those who are structurally marginalized; excluded by those at the center of political, social, and religious power.[8] They also provide a hint that the future community of disciples the Messiah gathers to follow him will be differently comprised. The initial purpose of this chapter will be to define the outsider in Matthew's narrative world.

---

8. Carter's postcolonial reading of Matthew's Gospel also notes the importance of those on the margins for Matthew. He reads Matthew's Gospel as emanating from the cultural margins of its time, from a group that lived on the periphery of the dominant context of the synagogue community and the Roman imperial system. As such he argues that Matthew's Gospel "*is a work of resistance written from and for a minority of disciples committed to Jesus*." Carter, *Matthew and the Margins*, 2. While I note the same emphasis regarding those on the margins I make no claims about any Matthean community that prompted the writing of the Gospel.

Outsiders in Matthew's Story

The story of a narrative involves not only characters but settings, the environment where events take place and characters interact. Matthew's narrative world is situated in Palestine; it is a story about Jesus, set in the context of Israel. His ministry is located within the traditional borders of Israel and is directed towards his own people. Most of the characters with whom Jesus mixes and interfaces are Galilean or Judean Jews. Fundamentally, in the ethnocentric world of Matthew's Gospel, the outsider is the structurally marginalized Gentile. This is highlighted early on in the prologue material with the entrance of the Magi from the east, clearly Gentile outsiders, who come seeking the new king.

This chapter will focus on three episodes concerning Gentile characters, the Magi (who form a single collective character), the centurion, and the Canaanite woman, as well as making brief reference to the words of Pilate's wife and those of a centurion and his soldiers at the cross. Due to their ethnic origins all these Gentile characters can be categorized as structurally marginal. It will demonstrate that these characters contribute to a defined sub-plot in Matthew's Gospel that develops both his interest in the marginalized and more specifically the theme of the believing Gentile in relation to Christ, a theme that has been foreshadowed in the narratives of Tamar, Rahab, and Ruth.

Gentile Outsiders

Magi 2:1–12

Roman centurion 8:5–13

Canaanite woman 15:21–28

Pilate's wife 27:19

Centurion and the soldiers at the cross 27:54

However, there are other outsiders, the structurally marginalized within Israel, who are outsiders to those at its social, patriarchal, and religious center: women, children, tax collectors and sinners, and the sick. These people are represented by the inclusion of Bathsheba and Mary among the women of the genealogy and will be considered first. I will limit this discussion to those marginalized Jews, other than women, in Matthew chapters 8–9.

Marginalized Jews
A leper 8:2–4
Peter's mother-in-law 8:14–17
A paralytic 9:2–8
A tax collector 9:9
A ruler and his daughter 9:18–9, 23–26
Woman with hemorrhage 9:20
Two blind men 9:27–31
A mute demoniac 9:32–33
Man with a withered hand 12:10
A mute, blind demoniac 12:22
Father and his epileptic boy 17:14–18
Little children [18:1–5] 19:13
Two blind men 20:29

Marginalized Jews

The outsider in Matthew's Gospel is not simply defined by ethnicity. There are numerous Jewish supplicants, both men and women, who are within Israel, yet are involuntarily on the margins, disenfranchised by the power structures of a society which excludes them. It is towards this group that Jesus' ministry is primarily directed as the parallel summary verses of Matthew 4:23 and 9:35 indicate. The table above shows that the majority of the structurally marginalized Jews who encounter Jesus are grouped together in the healing chapters of 8–9, where Matthew has chosen to provide a representative sample of these people and to collect them together in an overview of Jesus' healing ministry.[9] These chapters will form the basis for my discussion of the marginalized within Israel. The chapters assume the central normative figure of the adult, healthy, Jewish male who is able to fully participate in Temple worship and social life. Consequently, not only the Gentile centurion (Matt 8:5–13), but two Jewish women and a child (Matt 8:14–17; 9:18–26), and many Jewish men find themselves marginal-

---

9. Matthew chs. 8–9 comprise a distinct section. Held, Thompson and Kingsbury have all dealt with these chapters as a discrete unit in Matthew. Held, "Matthew as Interpreter," 165–299; Kingsbury, "Observations on the 'Miracle Chapters,'" 559–73; and Thompson, "Reflections," 365–88.

ized, mainly through illness or disability. Even the ruler, in his identification with his sick girl child, becomes one of the marginalized within Israel. In chapter 10 I will consider the accounts of the two women and the ruler's daughter. A cross-section of male Israelite outsiders remains. I will briefly outline their stories in order to illustrate who they are, how they approach Jesus, and his response.

All of the encounters, bar one, are between Jesus and individuals seeking healing either for themselves or on behalf of another. In his famous redaction analysis of the healing miracles in these chapters Held establishes that what is notable in the way Matthew presents each encounter is the emphasis not on the healing itself but on the dialogue of Jesus with the individual seeking help, which invariably focuses on their faith.[10] Held notes that Matthew, in the way he tells the stories, brings Christ to the fore. However, what Held fails to note is that each individual Jesus encounters is also brought to the fore. Kingsbury comments that "through his encounter with the supplicants, the essence of faith is disclosed."[11] The reader is guided into an understanding of both who Jesus is and how they should view each character by the way they react to Jesus and Jesus' response to them.

Marginalized Jews in Chapters 8–9

MATTHEW 8:2–4 | THE LEPER

The first person to approach Jesus after he comes down from his preaching session on the mountain is dramatically introduced, "and behold, a leper" (Matt 8:2). Nolland notes that the dramatic importance of Jesus' encounters with different individuals in these two chapters is marked "by an unusually high concentration of uses of ἰδού."[12] This serves to draw the reader's attention to each healing act. The leper's first action after approaching Jesus is to prostrate himself before Jesus in worship. The verb used to describe his action is προσκυνέω. It is notable that the Matthean narrator uses the verb προσκυνέω much more frequently than either Mark (Mark 5:6; 15:19) or Luke (4:7–8; 24:52). The verb can mean to kneel, bow low or fall at another's feet with respect, or it can mean to fall down in worship. In Matthew προσκυέω is a semi-technical term indicating more

---

10. Held, "Matthew as Interpreter," 165–299.
11. Kingsbury, "Observations on the 'Miracle Chapters,'" 568.
12. Nolland, *Gospel of Matthew*, 348.

than merely human respect; use of the word implies worship. It is used of the Magi (Matt 2:2, 8, 11), a ruler (Matt 9:18), the disciples (Matt 14:33), the Canaanite woman (Matt 15:25), the mother of James and John (Matt 20:20), and the women at the tomb (Matt 28:9); all kneel and worship Jesus.

Significantly the first person in the main narrative section to worship Jesus is a leper, someone totally excluded from society. This leper is a man of faith, he expresses his belief that Jesus can transform his situation, "Lord, if you are willing, you can make me clean" (Matt 8:2b). His hesitation is not over Jesus' ability to heal but his willingness to cleanse a leper. His plea for cleansing draws attention to the fact that his sickness renders him ritually unclean and therefore unable (according to the instructions of Leviticus 13–14) to participate in normal life and worship. Significantly, before responding verbally, Jesus breaks the Levitical taboo. Narrated time becomes one with real time, "having stretched out his hand he touched him" (Matt 8:3). Jesus apparently ignores the ritual consequences of touching the leper, thereby implying that he considers he has not been made unclean by this action. "I am willing. Be cleansed" are Jesus' words, followed by the narrator's comment, "immediately his leprosy was cleansed" (Matt 8:3). Jesus continues by instructing him to fulfill the cultic obligations incumbent on his acceptance back into society, thus ensuring that the outsider will be welcomed back into normal human relations. Jesus' disciples are commanded to do the same in Matthew 10:8.

Matthew 9:2–8 | The Paralyzed Man

This story concerns the dramatic healing of a paralyzed man but the form the story takes focuses not so much on the healing but on the controversy with the scribes concerning Jesus' ability to forgive sins. It is the faith of the paralyzed man's friends to which Jesus responds, although much of Mark and Luke's detail (Mark 2:1–12; Luke 5:17–26), demonstrating the level of their faith, is not alluded to by Matthew. The man himself lies on his mat in the background while Jesus disputes with the scribes. When he forgives the sins of the paralyzed man Jesus comes into direct confrontation, for the first time, with the Jewish religious leaders. The omniscient narrator tells the reader that "some of the scribes said to themselves, 'This man is blaspheming'" (Matt 9:3). Jesus labels such thoughts as "evil" (Matt 9:4). John the Baptist's first words to the Pharisees and Sadducees, "You brood of vipers" (Matt 3:7), are reinforced by Jesus here with the notion that the trait characterizing the Jewish leaders is evil. This atypical healing story does not involve a conversation between Jesus and the supplicant himself; his faith is assumed in his obedient and dramatic response to Jesus' command, "Getting up he went home" (Matt 9:7). What is characteristic of this story is that not only does Matthew portray the positive response of those on the margins to Jesus and Jesus' healing ministry to them, but he also presents a critique of those at the center; the Jewish religious leaders. This theme is repeated in the next incident and the final healing story in chapter 9 of the mute demoniac.

MATTHEW 9:9–13 | THE TAX COLLECTOR

The narrative pattern of chapters 8–9 is broken by a man who, unlike others, does not come looking for Jesus. He is not a supplicant (he is neither sick nor disadvantaged), nor does he approach Jesus wanting to be a disciple (see Matt 8:19–21). Jesus sees him and calls Matthew the tax collector to follow him.[13] The narrative bracketing of tax collectors here with "sinners" (Matt 9:10) makes clear, that within Matthew's narrative world, tax collectors were considered to be of the lowest order, both in religious and moral terms.[14] Yet Jesus takes the initiative, calls Matthew to discipleship and Matthew gets up and follows. Matthew is next found reclining at table with Jesus and his disciples along with other "tax collectors and sinners" (Matt 9:10), a wider group of those on the margins of society of whom Matthew is representative. In choosing to respond positively to Jesus the decisive turning point has occurred and the socially marginalized are welcomed as insiders at table alongside Jesus' disciples. Narratively they are contrasted with the group of Pharisees, who criticize Jesus for his action, for they recognize that in eating with tax collectors and sinners Jesus symbolically welcomes them in. Jesus responds by stating that his mission is one of mercy, specifically aimed towards those on the margins, the ones who are sick, rather than to those who consider themselves healthy (Matt 9:12–13). The healing Jesus brings extends beyond physical healing to spiritual healing "whereby those who had been isolated or excluded are now drawn into the community and partake of its life."[15]

13. Apart from the two sets of brothers (Matt 4:18–22), Matthew is the only individual specifically called to discipleship.

14. Matthew consistently presents tax collectors in this stereotypical negative light (Matt 5:46–47; 9:10–11; 11:19; 18:17; 21:31–32).

15. Senior, *Gospel of Matthew*, 114.

Matthew 9:27–31 Two Blind Men

In this incident, specific to Matthew, Jesus is followed by two blind men who perceive that, as the Davidic son, Jesus is a man of mercy. It is on this basis that they make their appeal. It is notable that throughout the Gospel it is the marginalized who use the title "Son of David" for Jesus. The blind, the dumb, the lame, Galilean pilgrims and the children in the Temple all recognize Jesus to be the Davidic Messiah.

The two blind men are specifically asked by Jesus in the seclusion of the house, "Do you believe that I am able to do this?" "Yes, Lord," they reply (Matt 9:28). Jesus responds to their affirmation of faith by touching their eyes and the third person imperative is used as a performance utterance "according to your faith let it be done to you" (Matt 9:29). Jesus' touch and words in response to their faith bring healing.

Matthew 9:32–34 | The Mute Demoniac

This short pericope describes how a mute demoniac is brought to Jesus. Jesus casts out the demon and the mute speaks to the amazement of the crowds. By contrast, the Pharisees claim, "By the ruler of the demons he casts out demons" (Matt 9:24). Their blasphemous identification of Jesus as demonic as a result of his merciful ministry serves to enforce the characterization of the Jewish leaders as not only misguided, but evil. On this point Kingsbury comments that the "no-accounts" in Israel perceive that Jesus is the messianic Son of David, "As such, they contrast sharply with the crowds and leaders of Israel, for they neither 'see' nor 'confess' this truth."[16]

Conclusion

Those on the margins in Israel form an important character group in Matthew's narrative since it is to them that Jesus' ministry is primarily directed. The leper, the paralyzed and blind, the tax collectors and sinners all experience an involuntary marginality that leaves them personally alienated. They come to Jesus and receive cleansing, forgiveness, acceptance and healing. Their attitude towards Jesus stands in contrast to those Jews at the center holding power and position, the Pharisees, scribes, and Sadducees.

---

16. Kingsbury, "Title 'Son of David,'" 601.

This group blasphemously misconstrue who Jesus is and are consistently critical of Jesus' ministry to those on the margins (Matt 9:3, 11, 24). Those who are outsiders within Israel come recognizing their need, acknowledging Jesus to be Lord and Son of David and, as such, able to help them. Jesus welcomes them, meets their need and by so doing offers them a place on the inside in the kingdom he inaugurates. In doing so he destabilizes Israel's understanding of who she is because his actions critique those at the center holding positions of power and status, hence the antagonism of the religious leaders. God's concern for those who are excluded and disenfranchised is reflected in Jesus' welcome towards those on the margins in Israel. This important theme is foreshadowed by the inclusion of the five women in the genealogy. Their presence in the Messiah's ancestry serves to call into question the place of status and positions of power occupied by Israel's patriarchs. More specifically, it is "she of Uriah" and Mary who represent all those who are structurally marginalized within Israel.

The Gentile Outsiders

Gentiles only feature occasionally in Matthew's story. This might suggest that Gentile characters are of little consequence. However, as Senior points out, "given the narrative world required of the gospels, could Gentiles be anything but 'peripheral' when they were compared to the Jews with whom Jesus interacted?"[17] If we allow that Matthew's narrative world has the actual life of Jesus as its reference point then it follows that the contours of his story follow the contours of the setting in which Jesus lived; Jesus simply would not have had extensive contact with Gentiles. This, of course, is true of all four Gospels. It is also true to say that in comparison to Mark, Matthew downplays certain elements of Jesus' interaction with Gentiles. The Matthean Jesus limits his mission to Israel and consequently the missionary journey to Tyre and Sidon, recounted in Mark, is omitted and the account of his time in Decapolis ends differently. Matthew's story of the Gadarene demoniacs (Matt 8:28–34) has no account of the healed man's desire to follow Jesus or of his proclamation of Jesus in the Decapolis region (Mark 5:18–20); instead the pericope in Matthew ends with people begging Jesus to leave.

However, in other ways Matthew gives much more consideration to the role of Gentiles than Mark does. There are five instances where the

---

17. Senior, "Between Two Worlds," 13.

direct commentary provided by the Matthean narrator demonstrates that the Gospel as a whole has a wider theological vision. It has already been noted that in the opening verse (Matt 1:1) Jesus is named son of Abraham as well as son of David, hinting that the Messiah will fulfill the divine promise to Abraham that he will be a blessing to "all the families of the earth" (Gen 12:3). Secondly, unlike the other gospel writers, the Matthean narrator introduces Gentiles at the earliest possible opportunity by naming Tamar, Rahab, and Ruth, in the first epoch of the genealogy so providing a universalistic outlook from the start. Thirdly, the fulfillment text that prefaces Jesus' public ministry refers to "Galilee of the Gentiles" (Matt 4:15) and, fourthly, this is followed by the summary verses that include "all Syria" and those from Decapolis (Matt 4:24–25) in the crowds who came to Jesus. The final instance of narratological commentary regarding Gentiles comes in another fulfillment quotation, which refers to the Gentiles hoping in his name (Matt 12:21).

Beside direct narratological commentary, there are also six instances where Jesus himself speaks positively of Gentiles or of Gentile inclusion into the kingdom of God. Jesus contrasts the probable, positive reaction of the Gentile cities of Tyre and Sidon (Matt 11:21) and Sodom (Matt 11:23) with the lack of response to his miracles in the Jewish towns of Chorazin, Bethsaida, and Capernaum. Similarly, he also contrasts the positive response of the people of Nineveh to Jonah and the queen of the south to Solomon with the negative response of the Jewish leaders to himself (Matt 12:38–41). Thirdly, the parable of the vineyard (Matt 21:33–44) closes with the warning that the kingdom of God will be given to a people who produce the fruit of the vineyard, strongly implying Gentile inclusion. Fourthly, in the apocalyptic discourse of chapter 24 Jesus foresees a time when the "good news of the kingdom will be proclaimed throughout the world, as a testimony to all nations" (Matt 24:14). Gentiles also feature in the parable of the sheep and goats when "all the nations" (Matt 25:32), are gathered at the final judgement. Gentiles are clearly among the righteous who have cared for those in need (Matt 25:31–45). Finally and crucially, the risen Christ's final words in Matthew commission his disciples to "make disciples of all nations" (πάντα τὰ ἔθνη) (Matt 28:19).[18]

---

18. Matthew's all inclusive phrase πάντα τὰ ἔθνη here refers to the nations as opposed to the Gentiles. Matthew uses ἔθνη alone when speaking of the Gentiles, e.g., Matt 10:5, but the phrase πάντα τὰ ἔθνη is used three times when referring to the whole of humanity, cf. Matt 24:9, 25:32 referred to above. Nolland, *Gospel of Matthew*, 1265–66.

The Character Group of Gentile Believers

Forming an important part of this Gentile theme, which Senior refers to as "a substantial underlying motif of Matthew's Gospel,"[19] are the three stories of Gentiles who respond positively to Jesus—the Magi (Matt 2:1–12), the centurion (Matt 8:5–13), and the Canaanite woman (Matt 15:21–28). Matthew is the only one of the synoptics to include all three stories of the Magi, the centurion, and the Canaanite woman. The Magi are specific to Matthew alone. Mark does not include the centurion's story and in Luke it is diluted since the centurion's face to face encounter with Jesus does not occur because he sends representatives (Luke 7:1–10).[20] Mark gives a different version of the Canaanite woman's story (Mark 7:24–29), whom he refers to as a Syro-Phoenician, and Luke does not include the encounter with the Canaanite woman. All three stories are key in Matthew's Gospel in defining the place of the Gentile outsider in relation to Jesus and conversely Jesus' relationship to them. I argue that the first three named Gentile women of the genealogy foreshadow this important character group. Particular attention will be paid to Matthew's account of the Canaanite woman since her story clearly resonates with Rahab's story and read as an intertext gives added significance to the inclusion of Rahab in the genealogy.

The Magi's Story

a) The narrative structure of Matthew 2:1–12

Following Davies and Allison this story can be divided into six short scenes:[21]

1. Magi arrive from the east looking for the king of the Jews (Matt 2:1–2).

2. Hearing this, Herod asks and discovers from the chief priests and scribes where the Messiah will be born (Matt 2:3–6).

---

19. Senior, "Between Two Worlds," 16.

20. John has an account of a royal official asking Jesus to heal his son (John 4:46–54) but it is unclear whether this is the same incident. In John's story the man twice implores Jesus to come down and heal his son and Jesus rather than being impressed by his faith is disillusioned.

21. Davies and Allison, *Matthew 1–7*, 224.

3. Herod meets with the Magi, ascertains when the star appeared, tells them where to find the child and asks for their cooperation (Matt 2:7–8).
4. The Magi follow the star to Bethlehem (Matt 2:9–10).
5. The Magi worship the child and offer gifts (Matt 2:11).
6. Being warned in a dream not to return to Herod, the Magi depart (Matt 2:12).

The story is set against the backdrop of Jesus' birth (Matt 2:1a). In the second chapter the focus switches from the private events in the life of Joseph and Mary to the public setting of Jerusalem. The main protagonists in the story are the Magi; it opens with their arrival and closes with their departure. They travel to two places. Scenes 1–3 are set in Jerusalem and scene 4 takes them to Bethlehem where scenes 5 and 6 take place. The two locations highlight the vivid contrast between the two kings: Herod in Jerusalem and the child in Bethlehem.

Matthew 2:1–12 | The Magi

In the first verse, having situated the baby Jesus geographically, "in Bethlehem of Judea," and politically, "in the days of Herod the King" (Matt 2:1), the narrator pauses for an instant to ensure the reader witnesses the arrival of the first group of people who come seeking Jesus; they are Gentiles. "Behold, Magi from the east arrived in Jerusalem" (Matt 2:1). No specific mention is made of the fact that the Magi are Gentiles, but they have come from outside, the east, into Jerusalem, here portrayed as the center of religious and political power. It is where Herod is named as king[22] (Matt 2:1) and where he gathers the religious leaders (Matt 2:4). Their entrance is vocal and insistent, "Where is the child who has been born king of the Jews?" (Matt 2:2).[23] The child they are searching for is, by implication, for them the king of another people, king *of the Jews*. A conflict between Herod and the child is immediately set up by the narrator as both are given the title "king."[24] From the outset king Herod and "all Jerusalem"

---

22. Herod the Great, who ruled from 37–4 BC.
23. Their reference to the "king of the Jews" also indicates their Gentile status as this phrase is consistently used by Gentiles in the passion narrative, e.g., Matt 27:11, 29, 37.
24. See Bauer, "Kingship of Jesus," 306–23.

respond negatively; they are "troubled" by news of a new king (Matt 2:3). Their reaction stands in stark contrast to the Magi who have one aim—to worship Jesus (Matt 2:2).

The verb προσκυνέω is used three times within the pericope (Matt 2:2, 8, 11), twice to refer to the response of the Magi to Jesus and once ironically of Herod's so called intended response. Worship is the appropriate response to the person of Jesus and it is significant that the first to respond to Jesus in this way are the Magi, representatives of the Gentile world.[25]

The Magi having followed the star are nevertheless dependent, as Herod is, on the chief priests and the scribes for information about specific divine revelation as to the child's whereabouts. Herod's first action on hearing the threatening news is to call on his religious advisers. The chief priests and scribes' knowledge leads to the second of the fulfillment sayings, detailing Bethlehem as the place of birth. However, their privileged status as insiders to divine knowledge does not lead them to seek and worship Jesus. The narrator clearly aligns them with Herod and all of Jerusalem. In doing so the narrator establishes two groups at Jerusalem's center, one political and one religious, but both of which are opposed to Jesus.

Having publicly inquired of the scribes, Herod now secretly inquires of the Magi the time of the star's appearing, the information he requires in order to carry out his cruel plan. Herod hears their news, receives the divine revelation of Jesus' whereabouts, and understands what his appropriate response should be "so that I also may go and worship him." (Matt 2:8). It is not until verse 16 that the reader learns of Herod's real intention to kill the Christ child. The consequent slaughter of all the infants in Bethlehem and the surrounding area seals the character portrayal of Herod as one who not only opposes the Christ child but who seeks to kill him.

Following Herod's instructions, coming to the house where the child is, the Magi rejoice "with exceeding, great joy" (Matt 2:10). The narrator uses two superlatives to emphasize how great their joy is. Entering the house, they see Jesus and respond, "falling down they worshipped him" (Matt 2:11). The Magi, representatives of the outside pagan world, then offer him gifts.

---

25. It is also significant that the first to respond in worship at the start of the description of Jesus' healing ministry is the leper, representative of the socially marginalized.

This point forms the climax of chapter 2 and the Magi's journey. It provides an example of what Kingsbury calls Matthew's "rhetoric of comprehension," a literary strategy of characterization "whereby he characterizes dramatic persons to show whether, or to what extent, they, in 'seeing' or 'hearing' Jesus amid the events of the story, 'understand' him aright and respond by 'receiving' him and 'doing' God's will as he teaches it."[26] Kingsbury argues that this literary strategy of characterization is consciously used by Matthew to shape the attitude of the reader in their evaluation of characters. In this case the message is clear—the Gentile outsiders respond to Jesus with worship and the offering of gifts while those at the Jewish center of power attempt to destroy the Christ child.

In contradiction to what might be expected, Gentile Magi model the appropriate response to Jesus. In similar fashion, against expectations, Tamar, Rahab, and Ruth, two Canaanites and a Moabite, all respond to their situations in ways that are appropriate for God's people. The theme of a reversal of expectations when Gentile outsiders respond more fully to Jesus than those within Israel continues in the stories of the centurion and the Canaanite woman and, as noted above, on a number of occasions Jesus himself compares a favorable Gentile response to himself and his message with the lack of response from Israel.

The Centurion's Story

The story of the centurion is placed in the first triad of miracles in chapters 8–9. Thematically, the Gentile centurion is aligned with other Jewish supplicants, a leper and a sick woman. The three together occupy positions that from a Jewish point of view makes them outsiders to the cultic center; the leper because of his illness, the centurion because of his ethnicity and Peter's mother-in-law because of her sickness and gender. But what of the Gentile centurion, does his story continue the themes established by the story of the Magi? Crucially, how does he respond to Jesus and in turn how does Jesus respond to him? The outline below shows that dialogue forms the main content of the story.

a) The narrative structure of Matthew 8:5–13

The centurion's story can be divided into four elements with an introduction and conclusion:

---

26. Kingsbury, "Rhetoric of Comprehension," 359.

Matthew 8:5	the setting and approach of the centurion
Matthew 8:6	the centurion's request
Matthew 8:7	Jesus' response
Matthew 8:8–9	the centurion's speech
Matthew 8:10–13a	Jesus' speech
Matthew 8:13b	the conclusion—healing

MATTHEW 8:5–13 | THE CENTURION

Following his descent from the mountain, Jesus enters Capernaum, his home base for ministry, and a centurion approaches him. Unexpectedly for a member of the occupying forces, the centurion abnegates his position of authority in recognition of Jesus, an itinerant Jewish teacher, who is socially his inferior. The centurion comes on behalf of his son,[27] who is paralyzed "in terrible distress" (Matt 8:6). The man beseeches Jesus using the term "Lord" (κύριε) (Matt 8:6). Implicit in the use of the title "Lord" is an acknowledgement of Jesus' power and authority. Jesus' response is immediate, "I will come and cure him."[28] The centurion's faith-filled response, "I am not worthy to have you come under my roof; but only speak the word, and my son will be healed" (Matt 8:8), is qualified by an explanation. The centurion's argument centers around the question of authority. Because he himself is "under authority" (ὑπὸ ἐξουσίαν) (Matt 8:9), he can give orders and expect them to be obeyed. In the same way he expects Jesus can order the sickness to leave. Ironically, he focuses on the limitations of his authority as a military officer. He has no power over sickness and he acknowledges Jesus' greater authority to heal. Jesus' recorded reaction is all the more noteworthy because it is one of the few instances where the narrator provides the reader with an insight into Jesus' emotional state. The reader is told Jesus was amazed by the centurion's words (ὁ Ἰησοῦς ἐθαύμασεν) (Matt 8:10). The word normally describes people's reaction to Jesus (Matt 8:27; 9:33; 15:31; 21:20; 22:22; 27:14) but here, uniquely, it is used to describe Jesus' reaction to someone and that person is not a pious

---

27. ὁ παῖς could be rendered either "son" or "servant" but I consider the former more likely.

28. Jesus' response is ambiguous in the Greek. Ἐγὼ ἐλθὼν θεραπεύσω αὐτόν (Matt 8:7) could be translated "I will come and heal him" or "should I come and heal him?" The first complies and second resists. I have followed the NEB, NRSV translations opting for the first alternative.

Jew but a Gentile centurion. Jesus is amazed by this man on two counts; his ability to grasp the situation (he acknowledges Jesus has the power to heal by verbal command), and the consequent faith he places in Jesus to heal his child. In what is essentially an episode within an episode Jesus turns to address the crowds following him. The formula "Truly I tell you" (Ἀμὴν λέγω ὑμῖν) (Matt 8:10) signals the importance of what Jesus is about to say; the narrator wants the implied audience to sit up and listen! For a Jew the statement is shocking, "In no one in Israel have I found such faith" (Matt 8:10).

Placed so early in the gospel narrative Jesus' words as reported in Matthew are noteworthy. Levine comments "Jesus reverses the expected soteriological conclusion."[29] Jews, unexpectedly, are compared unfavourably to a Gentile. The reversal of expectations continues as Jesus predicts that in the eschatological future a procession of people from east and west will come and dine with the patriarchs. The outsiders who place faith in Jesus will find a place on the inside at the eschatological banquet. Faithful Gentiles will sit alongside faithful Jews at the patriarch's table. Conversely, those insiders who complacently assume they are heirs of the kingdom (in Matthean terms the Jewish leaders and those who consider themselves righteous) will discover themselves on the outside, cast out into a Jewish envisaged hell of outer darkness.

Finally, the reader returns to the waiting centurion as Jesus turns back to him and tells him his faith is rewarded with the granting of his request. "And the son was healed from that hour" (Matt 8:13).

The Matthean Jesus is making a shocking claim for those of Jewish heritage; entry into the kingdom of heaven is not based on Jewish heritage but on faith. France writes, "it is not a simple matter of 'Jews out; Gentiles in.' Rather, we are to think of a reconstitution of the true people of God which is no longer on the basis of racial ancestry, but, as symbolized by the Gentile centurion, on the basis of faith in Jesus."[30] Consequently, the boundaries are redefined.

Tamar, Rahab, and Ruth also challenge Israel's boundaries. All three behave in ways that find them a place in Israel. More specifically, Matthew has chosen to include Rahab as the first in a line of Gentiles in Matthew's Gospel who, in the conviction that God will help them, show exceptional faith. Her story foreshadows what Jesus makes clear is a reality in the kingdom he is inaugurating. An appropriate faith response to Jesus will

---

29. Levine, *Social and Ethnic Dimensions*, 115.
30. France, *Gospel of Matthew*, 319.

in the future enable Gentile outsiders to find a place on the inside in the kingdom of heaven. Conversely, Achan's story is a reminder that those on the inside who behave inappropriately will be excluded. However, it is in the story of the next Gentile character to approach Jesus that the closest parallels with Rahab's story may be found.

b) The centurion and the Canaanite woman

The stories of the centurion and Canaanite woman that Matthew includes in the main section of his Gospel form a gender pair[31] that both complement and contrast with one another. Both Gentiles implore Jesus on behalf of their sick child and both through their exceptional faith receive healing from a distance for their child. However, the Canaanite woman has to work much harder at convincing Jesus to heal, for three reasons. Firstly, Jesus is engaged in a healing ministry towards many individuals in Capernaum when the centurion approaches him. In her case Jesus is outside Israel's borders. He has withdrawn not for ministry purposes, which he sees confined to Israel both geographically and ethnically, but for space and time away from ministry. Secondly, although both are Gentile outsiders to Israel, the woman is trebly marginalized. The centurion has three things in his favor: he approaches Jesus within Israel's border, he is a man who operates in the public realm, and, like Jesus, he is powerful but under authority. Consequently, he is able to draw the comparison between himself as a man operating under authority and Jesus. By contrast, the Canaanite woman is marginalized not only by her ethnicity but by her gender and consequent lack of opportunity to engage publicly with men. She is also put at disadvantage because she lives in Gentile territory. Totally disenfranchised, she stakes everything on Jesus' power to heal. Thirdly, when the centurion makes his request, Jesus makes no theological or ethnic objections to healing his servant whereas Jesus rejects the woman on two counts: on theological grounds, "I was sent only to the lost sheep of the house of Israel" (Matt 15:24) and on ethnic grounds, "it is not right to take the children's bread and throw it to the dogs" (Matt 15:26). Significantly, her story deals with both objections—she argues that an exception does not take away from the children and her faith sees beyond Jesus' self imposed limitations to his ministry. Consequently of the three main Gentile characters in

---

31. On gender pairings in Luke/Acts, see D'Angelo, "Women in Luke," 441–61, and Beirne's consequent work on gender pairings in John's Gospel in Beirne, *Women and Men in the Fourth Gospel*.

Matthew she is the most pivotal since her arguments are key to the ongoing rhetoric of the Gospel with regard to the mission to Gentiles.

The Canaanite Woman's Story

a) The narrative structure of Matthew 15:21–28

The centerpiece of this narrative revolves around the woman's request and the response from Jesus and from his disciples. Following Davies and Allison I divide the narrative into three main sections—the setting, the main section of dialogue, and the conclusion. Davies and Allison note the distinctive arrangement of the dialogue, which is made up of four dyadic units.[32]

Matthew 8:7	Jesus' response
Matthew 15:21–22a	Setting: Jesus goes out into borderland territories. The Canaanite woman comes out.
Matthew 15:22b–28a	Main section of extended dialogue
Matthew 15:22b	the woman's first request (κύριε)
Matthew 15:23a	Jesus' response (ὁ δὲ + ἀποκρίνομαι) *exchange 1*
Matthew 15:23b	the disciples' request
Matthew 15:24	Jesus' response (ὁ δὲ + ἀποκρίνομαι) *exchange 2*
Matthew 15:25	the woman's second request (κύριε)
Matthew 15:26	Jesus' response (ὁ δὲ + ἀποκρίνομαι) *exchange 3*
Matthew 15:27	the woman's third request (κύριε)
Matthew 15:28a	Jesus' response (τότε + ἀποκρίνομαι) *exchange 4*
Matthew 15:28b	Conclusion: the woman's daughter is healed

The short introductory spatial setting and the woman's designation as a Canaanite are important for what follows since both provide narrative clues about how this episode might be read.

In the first three exchanges, when the woman twice makes a request of Jesus, Jesus responds to her in a fashion that puts obstacles in the woman's way. The tension builds until her third request (the 4th exchange). Each time she addresses Jesus as "Lord" (κύριε). Each time Jesus' response is

---

32. Davies and Allison, *Matthew 8–18*, 541.

Others on the Margin in Matthew's Gospel

introduced by ὁ δε. Jesus finally responds positively (introduced by τότε), granting her request.

The conclusion provides the outcome.

b) Rahab and the Canaanite woman

Of all the intertextual echoes between the five women of the genealogy and the presentation of women in the Gospel, the stories of Rahab and this unnamed Canaanite woman present the clearest parallels. By placing Rahab in the genealogy Matthew invites a comparison that is instructive. There are significant intertextual points of reference that can be drawn between them.[33] Both women experience structural marginalization as women in public spaces who are disreputable in some way, Rahab because she is a prostitute and the Canaanite woman because she has a demon possessed daughter. Furthermore both Ringe and Love argue that this woman too was probably a prostitute.[34] Read as an intertext, Rahab's story clearly foreshadows aspects of the story of the Canaanite woman. A brief survey of the structure, setting, and the two characters illustrates the point. Further comparisons will be made as Matthew's story of the Canaanite woman is analyzed.

The story of the Canaanite woman is told in just seven verses (Matt 15:21–28). The narrative outline falls into three sections: an introduction that provides the setting for the story (Matt 15:21–22a), a main section of extended dialogue between the woman and Jesus (Matt 15:22b–28b), and the conclusion (Matt 15:28c). Although Rahab's story (Josh 2:1–24) is much longer, a comparison of the two narrative outlines reveals a marked similarity between the structures of the two stories.

---

33. Two postcolonial feminist writers have also noted the similarities in their stories but their ideological readings have drawn very different conclusions. See Dube, *Postcolonial Feminist Interpretation*. Of the Canaanite woman she writes, "If she is to survive, then, like Rahab and the Gibeonites, she must parrot the superiority of her subjugators and betray her own people and land." Dube, *Postcolonial Feminist Interpretation*, 147. Also McKinlay suggests that both women are colonized in mind and have "been used as a foil, a cog in the ideological agenda." McKinlay, *Reframing Her*, 110. In contrast, I argue that their narrators give them an independence of mind that challenges the dominant ideology of the text.

34. Ringe, "Gentile Woman's Story," 70. Love, *Jesus and Marginal Women*, 153.

Mothers on the Margin?

The Canaanite Woman	Rahab
Setting—Jesus goes into foreign territories and encounters a Canaanite woman. Matt 15: 21–22a	Setting—The spies go into foreign territory and encounter a Canaanite woman. Josh 2:1
Main section of extended dialogue. Matt 15:22b–28a	Main section of extended dialogue. Josh 2:2–21
Conclusion—The woman's daughter is healed. Matt 15:28b	Conclusion—The spies return to Joshua. Josh 2:22–24

Although there are contrasts between their private and public settings, both women's stories take place on borderlands. The main action of Rahab's story takes place within her house, situated in the city wall. Spatially she lives on the borders of the city, reflecting her position socially; she exists on the margins of society as a prostitute. The Canaanite woman's story takes place on the borders of Tyre and Sidon. The rural hinterland from which she comes suggests her poverty as a peasant.

Consequently, the spatial settings where the women are located signal two things, their ethnic otherness and their social status; neither are in positions of power or privilege.

Rahab and the Canaanite woman are the main protagonists within the plots of their stories; they initiate, the spies and Jesus respond. Consequently, the men find themselves in "unusual" situations, in dialogue with a foreign woman. Both women are in desperate circumstances; Rahab under threat of death, the Canaanite woman desperate on behalf of her demon possessed daughter. Both turn to God's representatives for help in spite of their marginalized status as women who are Gentile outsiders of low social status. Both demonstrate unexpected and determined faith in YHWH/Jesus. Both women create a situation from which they can "bargain"; Rahab by hiding the spies on her roof and thus saving their lives, the Canaanite woman by coming out to Jesus and refusing to desist from her cries for mercy until she gains a response. Both plead for the life/lives of another/others with whom they are in close kinship relationship, whose well being is bound up with their own. The women challenge the preconceptions of Jewish men in an extended dialogue where they refuse to accept that they are beyond the compassion of God. Both plead for mercy and, after a narrative build up of tension in which the men put obstacles in their way, finally find mercy for themselves and salvation for their loved one(s). Their stories thus center on the surprising reversal of expectations. Women, outsiders to Israel, express faith and align themselves with YHWH/Jesus. Rahab recognizes the sovereignty and power of YHWH and the Canaanite woman the lordship and healing power of Christ. Both extract an exemption from the ideology that would exclude them from God's blessings and in doing so they challenge the boundaries placed around Israel as the chosen people, thus challenging Israel's exclusivity.

c) An intertextual reading of the Canaanite woman's story

MATTHEW 15:21–22A | SETTING

The episode starts by Jesus withdrawing into the regions of Tyre and Sidon to escape the censure of the Jewish leaders. Matthew's use of the term "he withdrew" (ἀνεχώρησεν) has been used previously to indicate Joseph withdrawing Jesus from danger (Matt 2:14, 22) and Jesus' withdrawal after dispute caused by Jewish political or religious leaders. Likewise, in Matthew 4:12 and 14:13, Jesus "withdraws" after the initial arrest and then death of John the Baptist and he "withdraws" when he learns of the Pharisees' plot to destroy him (Matt 12:15).[35] At this point in the narrative he distances himself from the Pharisees and scribes who have come up from Jerusalem to question him (Matt 15:1) by withdrawing to the Gentile regions of Tyre and Sidon. Jesus' withdrawal to this region is not for mission or ministry but, following the pattern of his previous withdrawals, to seek peace and quiet from the insistent questioning of the Jewish leaders. Thus, his action is not in contradiction to his mission instructions to the twelve, "Go nowhere among the Gentiles" (Matt 10:5). So far his ministry and that of his disciples has been limited to the regions surrounding Galilee. Jesus, apparently, has no intention of ministering to people in a Gentile region. However, Jesus is confronted with human need and has to decide whether

---

35. In its plural form ἀνεχώρησαν the verb has also been used to indicate the Magi avoiding the danger of returning to Herod (Matt 2:12). Good argues that Matthew's seven instances of the motif of withdrawal are a part of a threefold pattern of hostility/withdrawal/prophetic fulfillment. The story of the Canaanite woman fits into this pattern since the outcome of Jesus' dialogue with her fulfills the prophecy of Matt 12:18 and 12:21. Good, "Verb ΑΝΑΧΩΡΕΩ in Matthew's Gospel," 1–12.

he will go beyond the boundaries of his understanding of the exclusive nature of his mission.

The place of Jesus' withdrawal is described by the narrator as the districts of Tyre and Sidon, τὰ μέρη Τύρου καὶ Σιδῶνος. Intertextual allusions are created for the discerning reader. Tyre and Sidon were traditionally linked together in the Old Testament as Gentile cities that were enemies of Israel under divine condemnation.[36] Matthew's allusion to Sidon (Mark has only Tyre (Mark 7:24)), reminds the reader it was the Sidonians who were to be driven out of Canaanite territory by YHWH (Josh 13:6). Further links are made to the Joshua narrative when the woman is introduced. However, Jesus has already questioned the total condemnation of these cities, comparing Tyre and Sidon favourably with Jewish cities who have not repented, stating that eschatological judgement on these Gentiles cities will be "more tolerable" (Matt 11:22). There is ambiguity over the status of the cities of Tyre and Sidon. Like Rahab, the woman comes from a Gentile area apparently under divine judgement; will she too be condemned?

Jesus has not gone to the cities themselves but to the districts or rural areas that are the hinterland to the two cities. Just as Jesus "came out" of Galilee, the woman "comes out,"[37] not from the cities of Tyre and Sidon themselves but from "that region," indicating her poverty as a rural peasant.[38] They meet in the boundary region at the interface of Jewish and Gentile territory where there are tensions.[39] The setting is reflective of the tensive atmosphere of the story in which boundaries are challenged.

The Canaanite woman is introduced by the emphatic phrase καὶ ἰδοὺ γυνὴ Χαναναία. This parallels the phrase that introduced another woman in need καὶ ἰδοὺ γυνὴ αἱμορροοῦσα (Matt 9:20) but this time she is not

---

36. See Ezek 28; Jer 25:22; 27:3; 47:4; Joel 3:4; Zech 9:1–4. Both were important, relatively wealthy Mediterranean coastal cities condemned by the prophets for their arrogance towards YHWH and his people.

37. It is not clear from the Greek construction of the sentence whether Jesus goes towards or into (εἰς) the district of Tyre and Sidon. It is also unclear whether the woman comes out from the region or simply that she comes out into Jesus' path. Wainwright exploits this ambiguity, noting the woman is a "boundary-walker." Using a term borrowed from anthropology she notes the transformations that often take place in "liminal spaces." Wainwright, *Shall We Look for Another?*, 87–88.

38. Carter, *Matthew and the Margins*, 322.

39. Theissen has demonstrated how the story mirrors the cultural, economic and political tensions that existed between Jews and Gentiles on these borderlands between Galilee and Phoenicia. The regions were contested because both Jews and Gentiles had political desires to settle the hinterlands. The land was essential economically because it provided food for the cities. Theissen, *Gospels in Context*, 61–80.

characterized by her illness but by her ethnicity. Whereas in Mark she is referred to as a Syro-Phoenician woman (Mark 7:26), in Matthew's account she is located geographically in more Hebraic terms as "a Canaanite."[40] As has been noted, she is not the first Canaanite woman referred to in the Gospel; her designation drawing attention to another Canaanite woman already named as a foremother to Christ.

MATTHEW 15:22B–28A | THE DIALOGUE

Matthew 15:22b | The Mother's First Cry for Mercy

The two main players in the story meet as the woman comes out and cries out (the verb in the imperfect indicates a continued action), addressing herself directly to Jesus. This is the only time the Matthean narrator reports a woman verbally accosting Jesus in public, Ελέησον με, κύριε υἱὸς Δαυίδ (Matt 15:22b).[41] The Canaanite woman addresses Jesus as "Lord" (κύριε) as she shouts out for mercy, a title that Beare states "is out of place on the lips of a 'Canaanite.'"[42] However, read against the intertext of Rahab's story and her confession of faith in Israel's Lord, it is perhaps not so surprising. Three times in this short dialogue the woman addresses Jesus as "Lord" (Matt 15:22, 25, 27). Use of the title implies that she recognizes Jesus as superior, as someone with more than human healing powers, able to help her in her need. The title "Son of David" (υἱὸς Δαυίδ) (omitted in Mark who has no direct address) is more surprising on the lips of a Canaanite woman with its specifically Jewish connotations. Bauckham points out that with its links to messianic nationalism use of this title designated Jesus as her enemy.[43] The choice of this title for Jesus by the woman implies she acknowledges her outsider (even enemy) status, yet still she pleads for Jesus to have compassion on her, for use of the title is also an expression of faith in the saving power of Israel's Messiah. She is appealing not for herself but on behalf of her daughter, who is tormented by a demon.

Rahab too is an outsider, but much more overtly a designated enemy whom Israel threatens with death. However, this does not prevent her

---

40. This the only time in the New Testament the word is used. In the Old Testament it is often used to identify Israel's enemy.

41. The only other woman to be reported speaking to Jesus is the mother of the sons of Zebedee (Matt 20:20–21).

42. Beare, *Gospel according to Matthew*, 341.

43. Bauckham, *Gospel Women*, 44.

from pleading for mercy from the spies and implicitly from YHWH, to whom she has confessed allegiance. She also pleads not primarily for herself but for those in her father's house, "Spare my father and mother, my brothers and sister, and all who belong to them, and deliver our lives from death" (Josh 2:13). However, the initial positive response Rahab receives from the spies, "Our life for yours!" (Josh 2:14a), is in marked contrast to the response received by this second Canaanite woman.

Matthew 15:23-24 | Jesus' Response

Led by previous encounters, the reader assumes that Jesus will respond with compassion. Thus, the reader is startled by Jesus' reaction—silence, "he did not answer her a word" (Matt 15:23a). There is no parallel in Matthew or the other Gospels to Jesus' non-response to someone pleading for help. The narrator forces the reader to pause and wonder; why the silent rebuttal? Is Jesus' lack of response due to the fact that she is a lone peasant woman making a nuisance of herself in public? Is Jesus therefore attempting to silence her with his silence? Wainwright argues that the woman is defying convention by shouting out in public and in doing so "challenges Jesus to break down gender barriers."[44] It seems there is some truth in her suggestion since Jesus' response to this woman is in stark contrast to the Gentile centurion with whom Jesus readily enters into dialogue (Matt 8:5-13). There is, as Fiorenza puts it, a tension point because the inclusive preaching of the kingdom has met a restrictive point of dominant patriarchal culture.[45] Yet there are other factors involved, as Jesus' verbal response will show.

In spite of Jesus' silence the woman persists. Clearly, the disciples consider her approach to be inappropriate and irritating and they urge Jesus to send her away. The disciples want to send her away without her request being met, just as previously they had urged Jesus to send away the crowds unfed (Matt 14:15). Finally, Jesus speaks. His reply is heard both by the disciples and the woman. It can be read as a verbal rebuke or as an expression of regret acknowledging the constraints of his ministry, either way, it defines Jesus' self awareness of the nature of his mission, "I

---

44. Wainwright, "Voice from the Margin," 139. Elsewhere, in support of the view of the marginal status of the woman in the public arena, she quotes Jeremias, "Eastern women take no part in *public life* . . . accordingly, a woman was expected to remain unobserved in public." Joachim, *Jerusalem in the Time of Jesus*, 359-60, quoted in Wainwright, *Feminist Critical Reading*, 107.

45. Fiorenza, *In Memory of Her*, 121.

Others on the Margin in Matthew's Gospel

was sent only to the lost sheep of the house of Israel" (Matt 15:24). Jesus clarifies that the boundary preventing his response is not primarily one of gender but of ethnicity. Whereas he previously healed in response to a request by the centurion within Israelite territory (Matt 8:5–13), here he makes it clear he has not been sent into Gentile territory for mission, he has only been sent by God to Israel. Significantly, this hard saying, where Jesus refuses the woman on the grounds of his exclusive mission to Israel, is omitted in Mark's account.[46]

Jesus' expression of his understanding of the limitations of his mission is apparently at odds with the view that has already been articulated in direct comment by the narrator. Following a summary section (Matt 12:15–16), the narrator concludes with a fulfillment citation from Isaiah that demonstrates how Jesus' ministry fulfills words from Isaiah 42:1–4, which specifically include ministry to the Gentiles (Matt 12:17–21). This is unusual for in most of the narrative Jesus' and the narrator's ideological positions are virtually identical. Yet here there is a tension created by the temporal axis of the story. Whilst Matthew looks forward to a time when the gospel will be preached to all nations, from Jesus' point of view the time has not yet come for the Gentiles to be incorporated into the flock. Therefore, for a second time Jesus refuses the woman's pleading.

Matthew 15:25 | The Mother's Subsequent Cry for Help

Nevertheless, the woman is a mother; she is desperate with a mother's desperation for her daughter and has the faith to believe that healing can come from Jesus (just as Rahab knew she could only save her family by an appeal to the God of Israel). She will not give up. Although Jesus' response is negative he at least has entered into dialogue with her. She comes and kneels in front of him. Maybe her action is designed to stop Jesus in his tracks, he will now have to step round her to continue on his way, but her posture also involves submission and worship.[47] This time she makes a single direct appeal to Jesus, simply and poignantly she pleads, "Lord, help me" (Matt 15:25).

---

46. Held notes Matthew's version shows "harder and more Jewish traits." Held, "Matthew as Interpreter," 198.

47. The verb προσκυνέω describes her action; see p. 201.

Matthew 15:26 | Jesus' Response

Surely such action will evoke a positive response, yet shockingly and uniquely in the Gospel, for a third time Jesus rebukes her, "It is not fair to take the children's food and throw it to the dogs" (Matt 15:26). Previously, Jesus has had compassion on the crowds and fed the children,[48] now he refuses her plea for the healing of her child and, in the words of this parable, calls her a dog. What are we, as real readers, to make of this?[49] Davies and Allison comment that the "parable" which is "totally devoid of conciliatory overtones, almost inevitably strikes the modern Christian as too off-putting, even cruel, as designed to wound a human heart."[50] Many commentators try to soften the blow. Levine cites and rejects a number of these:

> Jesus was "undoubtedly speaking in a half-humorous tenderness of manner," with "teasing challenge," and with a "twinkle in the eye." Consequently, "we can be quite sure that the smile on Jesus' face and the compassion in his eyes robbed the words of all insult and bitterness." This argument is hardly credible. The Matthean Jesus is a complex figure, but he is not twinkly, and a cajoling response to an individual in desperate circumstances is not humane . . . Nor again does the diminutive "puppy" help; as feminists frequently remark, being called "little bitch" is no improvement to being called "bitch."[51]

Levine is right. It is all too easy somehow to excuse Jesus' words, yet it seems that Jesus' stance regarding the appropriateness of her request is non-negotiable; the food of the kingdom is for the children only. Is he testing the extent of this woman's faith as so often suggested by commentators? Is he simply stating that her request is outside his remit? Is Jesus

---

48. The covenant phrase "the children of Israel" was often used of God's chosen people (see, e.g., Exod 4:22; Deut 14:1).

49. Theissen suggests "Jesus' rejection of the woman expresses a bitterness that had built up within the relationships between Jews and Gentiles in the border regions between Tyre and Galilee." Theissen, *Gospels in Context*, 65. However I do not read Jesus' rejection of her as a result of any bitterness.

50. Davies and Allison, *Matthew 8–18*, 552.

51. Levine, "Matthew's Advice," 32. The first citation in this passage is from McNeile, *Gospel according to Saint Matthew*, 231; the second and third from Richard France, *Matthew* (Tyndale NT Commentaries: Eerdmans, 1987), 247. The final citation is from Barclay, *Gospel of Matthew*, 122. Although the use of the term "bitch" has strong connotations for the modern reader the use of the term dog then was often used to refer to what is inferior and contemptible, see Phil 3:2, Rev 22:15.

using the situation in order to teach his disciples[52] or is he waiting for her to acknowledge Israel's soteriological priority? Wainwright notes that "a three-fold opposition posed by Jesus to the woman's request, which is unique in the Gospel, significantly emphasizes what is at issue in this story, namely, Jesus' mission to the Gentiles and the legitimacy of the woman's request." The reader is left wondering who will yield first.

Matthew 15:27 | The Mother's Third Request

Remarkably, the woman takes the parable and enlarges on it, applying it to herself, "Yes, Lord, yet even the dogs eat the crumbs falling from their masters' table" (Matt 15:27). She willingly recognizes that Jesus, as the master, is the provider of bread and accepts the metaphorical designation of herself as a dog. Nevertheless, significantly in her response, the dog has moved from outside to inside the house. As Perkinson has noted, she shifts the implication from dogs scavenging for bread thrown outside[53] to an internal domestic scene of dogs begging for scraps under the table.[54] Wainwright makes the same point, "She does not accept the dichotomies of insider and outsider . . . but creates a new space that is inside the house and that allows both the children and dogs to be fed within that household."[55] She does not challenge the insult to herself as a Canaanite Gentile, but instead claims a place for herself under the master's table, thus placing herself under Jesus' care. Even the Gentile "puppies" now under the table are deserving of a few crumbs, which is all she is asking for. The children will not be deprived, both can be fed. She has the faith to believe that God's provision is abundant enough to feed children and puppies. The quantity of leftovers from the feeding of the crowds (Matt 14:20; 15:37), specifically noted by the narrator, witnesses to the truth of her observation.[56] Boldly

---

52. Bailey, *Jesus through Middle Eastern Eyes*, 217–26.

53. The Old Testament refers to dogs in terms of wild, scavenging animals, not domestic animals (1 Sam 17:42; 24:14; 2 Sam 9:8; 16:9; 2 Kgs 8:3; Job 30:1; Ps 59:6, 14; Eccl 9:4). I suggest this is the usage here, cf. Matt 7:6, "Do not give what is holy to dogs."

54. Perkinson, "Canaanitic Word," 75.

55. Wainwright, *Shall We Look for Another?*, 87.

56. The tradition of survival by eating the leftovers was institutionalized in Israelite law. The *ger* (foreigner) had the right to glean the leftovers of the harvest (Lev 19:9, 10; Deut 24:19–22). There are echoes here of Ruth's story; she and Naomi survived on Ruth's gleanings.

she claims that here and now this Gentile puppy should be able to receive the benefits of the gospel along with Jewish children.

Matthew 15:28a | Jesus' Response

Her quick wit, which finds her a place under the table, and tenacious faith that demands to be fed, finally elicit the response from Jesus she has been waiting for, "O woman,[57] how great is your faith! Let be done for you as you desire" (Matt 15:28). Like Rahab, this woman has believed and acted on her faith and in so doing finds a place inside under the master's table. Both women are characterized as having faith, persistence, wit, and determination. They are prepared to challenge and claim until their demand for mercy is met. This woman's faith is the decisive factor in Jesus' granting of her request. She too can receive the bread of the kingdom. She is not only given bread but in the presence of Jesus' disciples, from whom she had endured public rebuttal, she receives Jesus' public praise.

Does the Puppy Become a Child?

Pokorný has understood the story to mean that in accepting the bread the woman and her child "receive the status of children."[58] The good news of the story is that "the puppy became a child."[59] On the contrary, the irony and the importance of the story is that it is as a Gentile woman, not as a Jewish convert, that this woman receives healing from Jesus for her daughter.[60] Rahab's story read as an intertext supports this view. Rahab, the ultimate outsider to Israel, like this woman, finds a place on the inside but in so doing maintains her identity. At the close of her story the narrator comments that "She has lived in Israel ever since" (Josh 6:25). There is an etiological element to her story; explanation of Rahab's origins is needed, strongly implying that her "difference" in Israel remained. Similarly the Canaanite woman doesn't become Jewish. The significance of her reinter-

---

57. The use of ὦ before a vocative Ὦ γύναι is very emphatic and is used only one other time in Matt 17:17 in Jesus' reference not to someone's faith but to a faithless generation of Israel.

58. Pokorný, "From a Puppy to the Child," 337.

59. Ibid.

60. Nolland makes a similar observation, "The Canaanite woman becomes a beneficiary . . . not as freshly made Jewess, but as a Gentile." Nolland, *Gospel of Matthew*, 636n217.

pretation of Jesus' parable lies in the fact that both children and puppies can be fed at the master's table; the puppy does not become a child.

Matthew 15:28b | Conclusion: Healing Is Granted

In a concluding comment, the narrator tells us that "her daughter was healed from that hour" (Matt 15:28). The final words almost read like a postscript to the main focus of the narrative, the woman's faith. Just as the centurion's child was healed "at that hour" (Matt 8:13) in response to his "great faith" (Matt 8:10), so this woman's daughter is healed in response to her "great faith" (Matt 15:28a). Yet, unlike the centurion, this Canaanite woman has operated not from a position of male prestige and power within Israel but from a position of female powerlessness on the borders of Tyre and Sidon. Unlike the centurion, she deflects Jesus' refusal to heal three times. With her faith, persistence, and wit she brings Jesus to the point where he extends his healing power to the demon-possessed daughter of a Canaanite woman from Gentile territory. She insists that Jesus put into action now a promise and vision that he has seen for the future but not realized in the present, when Gentiles would be fed at the table (Matt 8:11). Her challenge of faith and boldness finds a response in Jesus that brings about a change. Remarkably, this is the only story in the Gospel in which someone persuades Jesus to change his mind.

Comparison with Mark 7:24-29

A comparison with Mark's report of the incident shows a number of key differences. The first is that instead of giving a shorter, more precise account than that of Mark, which is Matthew's normal style, Matthew here has a fuller account of a healing story. The greater length comes in the dialogue between Jesus and the woman, not in extra details of the healing, indicating that Matthew wants to place emphasis on the verbal interaction between Jesus and this woman.

Mark's setting is different. He locates the story in a domestic environment, in the privacy of a house, whereas Matthew places the story in male territory, an outdoor, public space. This serves to emphasize both the vulnerability and courage of the woman. In Matthew's account she takes the initiative and comes out to Jesus (Matt 15:22), whereas Mark describes how the woman comes into the privacy of a house, bows down, and begs for healing for her daughter but he does not report any direct speech. In

Mark there is no crying out in public or record of the disciples trying to send her away, nor any sense that she has made a nuisance of herself by repeated requests. Love comments that "Mark further softens a potential gender embarrassment by reserving the woman's words to the end of the story and envisaging them as a response to what Jesus says" (Mark 7:27, 28).[61] Consequently, Jesus refuses her three times in Matthew but only once in Mark.

Jesus' theological opposition to this Gentile woman is far greater in Matthew than in Mark. Jesus' comment about the limitations of his mission to the lost sheep of the house of Israel is not reported in Mark. Also the parabolic saying in Mark contains a significant difference, "Let the children *first* be fed" (Mark 7:27). In Mark's story Israel has *prior* rather than *exclusive* claims to Jesus' healing power. In Mark's account it is Jesus, not the woman, who implies there will be leftovers for the dogs. All three of these differences mean that Mark's Jesus is more amenable to feeding the dogs.

In Matthew's account there is a heightened recognition of the person of Jesus by the woman. The woman's direct speech is reported once in Mark, where she too calls him "Lord" but significantly does not use the messianic title Son of David. The recognition of Jesus' importance is further softened in Mark's account because the dogs under the table eat not from their *master's* table but "from the crumbs of the children" (Mark 7:28).

Finally, in Mark the woman's reply earns the response "For saying that, you may go—the demon has left your daughter" (Mark 7:29) but Jesus makes no specific mention of her great faith that is the climax to Matthew's story. Mark's pericope ends with greater detail about the healing; the woman goes home and finds her daughter lying in bed and the demon gone (Mark 7:30).

The main emphasis in Matthew's account stresses the depth of Jesus' resistance and the woman's persistence and, consequently, her great faith. Faith is what Jesus seeks for and is the appropriate response to recognition of who he is. Ironically, both Gentile Rahab and this second Canaanite woman are exemplars of the faith that Jesus hopes to find among his followers but which often appears to be lacking (Matt 14:31; 16:8).

---

61. Love, *Jesus and Marginal Women*, 149.

The Canaanite Woman and the Traditions of Israel

O'Day observes that the Canaanite woman of Matthew's Gospel reflects the traditions of Israel. "When we listen carefully to the woman's daring words, we hear echoes of words that have been spoken from the beginning of Israel's life of faith."[62] O'Day works from a form critical analysis and takes her cue from commentators who note the resemblance between the woman's words and the cries for deliverance in the lament Psalms.[63] She argues that "Matthew has shaped her words to reflect the traditional, candid speech of Jews before their God,"[64] and contends that Matthew consciously uses the form of the lament psalm to shape the text. She outlines the Canaanite woman's words according to the basic constitutive elements of the lament form, arguing that in essence the woman's words are a short lament psalm:

Petition: Have mercy on me

Address: O Lord, Son of David

Complaint: My daughter is severely possessed . . .

Address: Lord

Petition: Help me

Motivation: For even the dogs eat the crumbs . . .

The woman's words do not just reflect the form of Israel's psalms but also their faith. O'Day opines that just as Israel refuses to turn away from God when everything seems stacked against her but rather confronts God reminding him of his promises, so the Canaanite woman "is infused with this same spirit of defiant resistance to despair, and bold faith in God's promises."[65] She too notes the irony of the fact that "This woman, who shows herself to be full heiress of Israel's tradition of lament, is not Jewish at all, but Canaanite,"[66] yet she fails to draw comparisons with Rahab. O'Day's analysis is helpful in noting the similarities with Israel's liturgical

---

62. O'Day, "Surprised by Faith," 118.

63. She notes the similarity between the woman's cry for mercy and Ps 86:16 and in her cry for help Ps 109:26. In the LXX text of the Psalms ἐλέησον is used 17 times in calling for God's help. O'Day, "Surprised by Faith," 119.

64. O'Day, "Surprised by Faith," 122.

65. Ibid., 124.

66. Ibid.

tradition and with all the needy people in Israel who clung to the promises of God, voicing their protest in lament.

A Prophetic Exception

Through the challenge of these two women made bold in their desperation Joshua and Jesus are brought to the point where they make an exception to the ideology that puts a boundary around Israel as the people of God. Both narratives involve a reversal of expectations in which an outsider finds a place on the inside. Consequently, the women present a challenge to the identity of the people of God; what is it that dictates either exclusion or inclusion? Matthew indicates that Jesus' ministry brings this question to the fore once again as a new people of God are called into being by his presence in Israel.

However, unlike Rahab, the exception the Matthean Canaanite woman secures from a second Joshua is one that will set a precedent for the future. Meier has shown that Jesus' action is the prophetic exception,[67] which anticipates his command to the disciples following his death and resurrection. It foreshadows the words "Go therefore and make disciples of all nations" given in the Great Commission by the risen Christ to his disciples (Matt 28:19). Wainwright comments:

> This prophetic action occurs as a result of a dialogue with a woman. The woman stands therefore, as one of the pivotal points in the Matthean narrative and in the whole Matthean vision of the Jesus-event.[68]

Like Rahab, this Canaanite woman refuses to be disqualified from the grace of God and, in doing so, shows a prophetic understanding of the principles of the kingdom of heaven that "people from the west and east" will be accepted on the basis of their faith in Christ alone. The closing verses of the Gospel indicate that this is the goal of salvation history as envisaged by Matthew.

The theme of the faithful outsider, first indicated by the stories of Tamar, Rahab, and Ruth, is once again clearly seen in the story of the

---

67. Meier takes Matt 10:5–6, 15:24 and 28:16–20 as the basis on which to reconstruct Matthew's vision of salvation history. He argues that the public ministry of Jesus was limited to Israel with a few "prophetic exceptions" which point towards Matthew's vision of salvation history. Meier, *Law and History*, 27–30.

68. Wainwright, *Feminist Critical Reading*, 114, referring to Fiorenza, *In Memory of Her*, 138.

Canaanite woman. She completes the trio of the main Gentile characters in Matthew. The accounts of the Magi, the centurion, and the Canaanite woman's response to Jesus establish that all three have correctly comprehended truths about Jesus' identity. He is king of the Jews, to be sought for and worshipped. He is Lord standing in authority over sickness and he is Son of David, who can be convinced to extend his mercy beyond the boundaries of Israel. However, in overcoming Jesus' theological and ethnic reservations the Canaanite woman's story is most significant in establishing Matthew's rhetoric concerning the inclusion of Gentiles into the kingdom of heaven. Matthew's vision calls for a fundamental realignment in understanding concerning what defines the new Messianic people of God. The inclusion of not only Rahab but also Tamar and Ruth in the genealogy subverts the "purity" of the Davidic line and is the first indication that the birth of the Messiah will bring about a crisis in Israel concerning her ethnic identity.

The picture of the believing Gentile is completed by two brief references in the passion narrative to comments concerning Jesus' identity made by Pilate's wife (specific to Matthew's Gospel) (Matt 27:19) and the centurion and his soldiers (Matt 27:54), to whom both Mark and Luke also make reference (Mark 15:38; Luke 23:47).

Pilate's Wife and a Centurion

Gentile depiction, like the portrayal of the Jews, is not monochrome. Most obviously, Pilate and the Roman soldiers both play a part in Jesus' death. It is therefore all the more notable that despite being aligned with Jesus' enemies, Pilate's wife and a Roman centurion and his soldiers, who are detailed to keep guard at Jesus' crucifixion, respond in faith to Jesus. Pilate's wife (Matt 27:19) and the centurion at the cross (Matt 27:54) form a second Gentile character gender pair. They are the only two characters in Matthew's passion narrative who make positive declarative statements concerning Christ. They voice the truth about Jesus in contrast to those around them. Caiaphas the Jewish high priest accuses Jesus of blasphemy (Matt 26:65) and the Jewish religious leaders hurl mocking insults at Jesus as he dies on the cross (Matt 27:41–43). Pilate's wife declares Jesus to be "that righteous man" (Matt 27:19) and, in the moments following Jesus' death, the centurion overseeing Jesus' crucifixion and those soldiers guarding Jesus, state, "Truly this man was God's Son" (Matt 27:54). Their statements are of theological import because taken together they summarize the truth of Jesus' human and divine nature as presented by Matthew. In the midst of hatred and false accusation, poignantly, it is two Gentiles who confess Jesus to be a righteous man and Son of God.[69] Their declarations are the denouement to the theme of faithful Gentiles that was first introduced in the naming of Tamar, Rahab, and Ruth.

Conclusion

This chapter opened by noting the various ways in which all five women of the genealogy experienced positions on the margin as outsiders and that as a group they represented the outsider in Matthew's Gospel. It went on to define the outsider on two levels. Firstly it demonstrated the Gospel's concern for all those marginalized within Israel represented by "she of Uriah" and Mary. Matthew chapters 8–9 show that Jesus' ministry is primarily directed towards those who are on the margins in Israel, many of whom respond to him in faith. Jesus' ministry to the marginalized calls into question those at the center who hold positions of power and authority in Israel, raising the issue of how greatness among the new people of God is to be construed.

Secondly, it traced the theme of faithful Gentiles who also respond positively to Jesus in worship and faith, in recognition of his true nature. They too receive the food of the kingdom. The theme of faithful Gentile outsiders who find a place on the inside is foreshadowed in the stories recalled by the naming of the three women in the first epoch of the genealogy. Most notably the story of Rahab, read as an intertext, foreshadows and points to the importance of the story of the Canaanite women who, although only a minor character, occupies a key place theologically within the Gospel. Her story destabilizes perceptions of Israel's boundaries, demonstrating that the decisive factor in gaining entry into the kingdom of heaven is not ethnicity but faith in Jesus. The presence of all five women in the genealogy is a radical call to inclusivity. They signal that everyone, regardless of their marginal status or their ethnicity, by faith in Jesus, will be able to find a place in the kingdom of heaven.

---

69. Nolland comments, "We are not intended to inquire too closely what the centurion could mean by 'Son of God' . . . The centurion recognizes the presence of deity and has enough evidence to be profoundly convinced that Jesus is bona fide." Nolland, *Gospel of Matthew*, 1220.

10

Women in Matthew's Narrative Life

A Gendered Reading

This final chapter will argue for the narrative importance of the five women's gender. According to the two current main theories for the inclusion of the four Old Testament women their gender has either been considered to be irrelevant (the Gentile argument) or focus on their gender has mostly been negative and limited to their sexuality (the foreshadowing Mary argument). It will be argued that the five women of the genealogy are the first indication of a positive gynocentric counternarrative that subverts the dominant androcentric narrative of the Gospel that is encoded with patriarchal assumptions about the role and place of women. The five women are also the first indication that Christian identity will no longer be construed along patriarchal lines.

In part 1 I challenged the view that placed the four women of the Old Testament in a negative light and concluded that there were positive, not negative reasons, for the inclusion of each woman in the genealogy. Matthew's rhetoric validates these women and the roles they played in salvation history. His positive evaluation reflects the way the Hebrew stories present the women. This is particularly true of the first three named women in the Gospel: Tamar, Rahab, and Ruth. All three are marginalized in a number of ways, most notably by their Gentile origins and their anomalous positions in relation to their sexuality. Nonetheless, they demonstrate righteousness, faith, and mercy and, by so doing, find a place on the inside among the people of Israel. As a group of women who were originally outsiders to Israel, they demonstrate the fulfillment of the promise to Abraham that he will be "the ancestor of a multitude of nations" (Gen 17:4). Concerning "she of Uriah," less can be said of what characterizes her and the role she plays but I have argued that she is portrayed as the innocent victim rather than the seducer or guilty accomplice. Her inclusion in the genealogy highlights David's guilt and the abuse of his power but also points towards God's gracious mercy and forgiveness. It is through Bathsheba that the promise to David is realized of a son through whom YHWH will establish a kingdom (2 Sam 7:12).

I then went on to consider how these women relate to the fifth woman, Mary. In common with them, Mary initially occupies an anomalous position in relation to her sexuality that puts her on the margins. Divine initiative and Joseph's obedient response bring her and her child into the Davidic line and into Joseph's protective care. Although, like Bathsheba, little is said of Mary as a character, Matthew acknowledges the vital role, as mother to Christ, she plays within salvation history. Born of the Holy Spirit, her son fulfills the divine promises made to both Abraham and David.

Their presence as a group of women disrupts the dominant patrilineal genealogy and raises questions about the exercise of power and place of patriarchy in the new identity of the people of God brought about by the birth of the Messiah. In particular, Matthew's witness to the virgin birth functions as the most profound critique of patriarchal ideology and the prologue's androcentric perspective. This chapter will address the following questions: Is there an androcentric focus in the main gospel narrative and, if so, what role do women play? Regarding the women that are mentioned, what characterizes them? Is there a gynocentric counternarrative that continues to validate women and the roles they play in God's purposes, thus subverting the dominant text? Before conducting my own analysis I will summarize the conclusion of two women scholars who, working from a consciously feminist standpoint, have addressed the question of the Gospel's stance towards gender.

Anderson and Wainwright

In her paper entitled "Matthew: Gender and Reading," Anderson explores the symbolic significance of gender in the Gospel. She notes that "the story world embodies patriarchal assumptions";[1] positions of power and status are male, and patriarchal marriage and inheritance practices are assumed (Matt 1:18–25; 5:31–32; 19:1–12; 21:33–43; 22:23–33). She gives a list of examples that illustrate what she calls the "pervasive androcentrism"[2] of the Gospel, including the opening patrilineal genealogy and the focus on Joseph in the birth story. However, she goes on to note the "striking break" in the patriarchal pattern of the genealogy with the inclusion of the five women and that, although the birth story focuses on Joseph in the virgin birth, God acts outside of patriarchal norms. Anderson concludes that "The important roles of women and Jesus' response to women supplicants strain the boundaries of the gospel's patriarchal world view."[3]

The significance of gender in Matthew's Gospel has been explored more fully by Wainwright. She has worked extensively on Matthew's Gospel, providing a number of feminist critical readings that have come out of the foundational work of her PhD dissertation entitled *Towards a Feminist Critical Reading of the Gospel according to Matthew* in which her aim was to highlight and critique "the clearly androcentric perspective encoded within the text."[4] However, like Anderson, she also notes that this perspective is in "tension with a well-developed narrative theme, namely, women's participation in the βασιλεία ministry of Jesus."[5] She goes on to suggest that the dominant androcentric theme and the women's narrative theme are reflective of struggles within the Matthean community where traditional patriarchal perspectives were being challenged by women. Wainwright supposes that women in the Matthean community were involved in what she refers to elsewhere as the "subversive traditioning"[6] process. She claims stories of women were retained by women in the Matthean community and then, at their behest, incorporated by the final redactor into a text that was originally, univocally, androcentric, and patriarchal. Wainwright refers to these stories of women as "fissures" in the text. In spite of the fact that there were two conflicting traditions preserved within the Matthean community, the final redactor includes them side by side to produce the Gospel as we now have it. She concludes that "the

---

1. Anderson, "Matthew: Gender and Reading," 7.
2. Ibid.
3. Ibid., 21.
4. Wainwright, *Feminist Critical Reading*, 150.
5. Ibid.
6. Wainwright, "Gospel of Matthew," 676.

androcentric perspective in the final redaction has prevailed."[7] This she opines "is most clearly apparent at the beginning and end of the gospel story, in the patrilineage of Jesus and his commissioning of the eleven male disciples to a universal mission" and also in the way that the men are given a voice while the women are often left voiceless. Thus, she argues that the stories of women "have become submerged in the androcentric narrative to the point of almost being silenced by it."[8]

While I have found Wainwright's work stimulating and helpful, nonetheless I disagree with both her conclusion and her methodology. In focusing on the final form of the text I challenge the source critical view, accepted by Wainwright, that the final redactor of the Gospel stitched together various different source materials to form the final document. The Gospel is a literary whole. Matthew (like many other writers) is able to hold several different strands in tension within the whole; these tensions are integral to the narrative and give it shape and meaning. Unravel the strands and the whole disintegrates. The implied author of the Gospel is competent and creative, well able to handle apparently conflicting viewpoints in what is a well crafted and carefully constructed narrative. As Levine comments, "Matthew is neither inconsistent nor schizophrenic."[9] The very fact that women are included in the patrilineage of Jesus demonstrates that women and the roles they play are integral to Matthew's presentation of Israel's salvation history that culminates in the birth of Mary's child, the Messiah. Their inclusion signals that, as a category, women form an important group in the gospel story as told by Matthew. To remove them would leave the Gospel without coherence both in terms of the narrative plot and in terms of its overall vision of the Jesus event. Consequently, while the androcentric narrative dominates I argue that there is a positive gynocentric counternarrative that comprehensively subverts and deconstructs the male centered focus of the Gospel. It is this counternarrative that is the focus of this chapter.

A gendered reading of Matthew reveals that in the ongoing narrative there are relatively few stories about women. Occasionally mentioned as present in the crowds (Matt 14:21; 15:38), stories of individual women are mainly confined to the minor characters who come to Jesus seeking help. Power and status lies with the male characters, who have the dominant narrative role and do the speaking. Jesus' main dealings are with the Jewish

---

7. Wainwright, *Feminist Critical Reading*, 323.
8. Ibid.
9. Levine, *Social and Ethnic Dimensions*, 39.

Women in Matthew's Narrative Life

religious leadership and his inner group of disciples. The first named and chosen disciples are all male and the Gospel closes with the eleven male disciples being sent out for mission by the risen Jesus. Jesus' teaching to his disciples and even the wider group of crowds assumes a male audience and perspective (e.g., Matt 5:28, 32) and his sayings and parables are directed towards men.[10]

So the question must be asked, are women among those who follow Jesus? Among Matthean scholars this is a debated issue. Some think that the phrase "the disciples" refers exclusively to Jesus' twelve male disciples.[11] Being a disciple is not just admiring or adhering to certain teachings. Disciples are called by Jesus to follow him (Matt 4:19, 21). This involves a costly response of obedience, yet apparently no women are specifically called by Jesus or named among those sent out on mission (Matt 10:2). However, the inclusion of the first three named women in the genealogy already provides strong hints to the discerning reader that Matthew is indicating that women as well as men are among those who do the will of the Father. Furthermore the inclusion of all five women demonstrates that women alongside men play crucial roles in the unfolding of salvation history. This chapter will explore whether Matthew's positive rhetoric concerning women continues and whether they are included among those who respond to and follow Jesus.

Characters in Matthew's Story

Jesus

The chief protagonist in Matthew's story is without doubt Jesus; he is set apart from all other characters. From his baptism to his death on the cross the narrator tracks his every movement both in public and in private. Jesus' point of view aligned with that of the omniscient narrator is normative because his values reflect the values of his heavenly Father–God (Matt 11:25). It has been noted that the narrator, in the commentary provided by the genealogy, recognizes Jesus to be Christ, the son of David, the son of Abraham (Matt 1:1). He is the one who will save his people from their sins (Matt 1:21), the one who is Emmanuel, God with us (Matt

---

10. See Love, *Jesus and Marginal Women*, 84–92.
11. E.g., Kingsbury, "Verb *Akolouthein*," 56; Love, *Jesus and Marginal Women*, 78–82; Anderson "Matthew: Gender and Reading," 16–17, 20–21.

1:23). Jesus is the Son of God. His unique divine sonship is affirmed at his baptism (Matt 2:17) and transfiguration (Matt 17:5). The twelve disciples themselves finally recognize and confess that Jesus is the Son of God (Matt 14:33; 16:16) as do the Roman soldiers who witness his death (Matt 27:54). Yet titles alone do not tell readers enough; it is only within the context of Jesus' life, as readers hear Jesus teaching and see him healing, that they can judge the authenticity of the titles given. How others react to Jesus, how they construe Jesus' identity is important for the forward movement of Matthew's story, for Jesus evokes many different responses, from the confessions of his divine sonship just noted, to repudiation, condemnation, and denial. The plot and flow of the story revolves around the person of Jesus; from his birth to his passion and death, and beyond.

Other Characters

In his narrative analysis of Matthew's story Kingsbury suggests that the other characters in Matthew's Gospel can be divided into four main groups:[12]

1. the Jewish leaders
2. the crowds
3. the disciples
4. the minor characters

Kingsbury argues that each group has distinctive characteristics and can be treated as a different collective character within the Gospel, each possessing their own set of traits. It is Jesus' response to each group, enhanced by the arrangement of episodes, that guides the reader into an understanding of both who Jesus is and how they should view each group by the way they react to Jesus. The motivation and nature of each group (and individuals who stand out from the group) is made clear in their interactions with Jesus.

The characterization of the Jewish leaders is entirely negative. In contrast, the crowd following and surrounding Jesus remains well disposed towards Jesus for the majority of the time, astonished at his teaching (Matt 22:33) and constantly seeking his healing help. Jesus shows compassion towards the crowds as they follow him from place to place (e.g., Matt 14:14; 15:32). However, their attitude towards Jesus does not remain

12. Kingsbury, *Matthew as Story*, 10–27.

constant. The reader does not know how to evaluate them until the crucial point in the narrative when they side with the Jewish leaders (Matt 27:20), calling for Jesus' crucifixion (Matt 27:23) and taking the responsibility for his death (Matt 27:23).

The disciples, the chosen twelve,[13] are called to leave all, to be followers of Jesus. They listen to his teaching and are observers of what he does. They are sent on mission (Matt 10:1–15) and are called to participate and share in Jesus' ministry. However, they are far from perfect. Although they respond to Jesus in worship and confess he is the Messiah, they often lack faith and misunderstand what Jesus is teaching them. Peter is portrayed as representative of the group. He veers between faith and failure, confessing Jesus to be "the Son of the living God" (Matt 16:16), yet at the crucial moment during Jesus' night time interrogation denying he ever knew him (Matt 26:69–75).

The minor characters are more diverse. Throughout the Gospel there are individuals who appear for a brief time and then usually are not heard of again. Often they are not even named but are referred to as, for example, "the Magi" (Matt 2:1–12), or "a leper" (Matt 8:2), or "a Canaanite woman" (Matt 15:22), or "the centurion" (Matt 27:54). Many of them are supplicants seeking help from Jesus.

The Women

What of the women? Occasionally mentioned as present in the crowds (Matt 14:21; 15:38) women as individuals are found among the minor characters mainly as supplicants, yet their stories are few. As has been noted, the opening chapter of the Gospel, with its focus on Jesus' patrilineal genealogy, indicates that the focus of the Gospel is both Christocentric and androcentric. A brief glance at Matthew's Gospel might lead one to the conclusion that Matthew shows little interest in women. A table listing the named persons (excluding the genealogy) illustrates the point.

---

13. Matthew does not define "the disciples" as the group of twelve men whom Jesus calls out until Matt 10:2.

MOTHERS ON THE MARGIN?

Named persons in Matthew

Matthew 1:16	Joseph
	Mary
	Jesus
Matthew 2:3	Herod (the Great)
Matthew 2:22	Archelaus
Matthew 3:1	John the Baptist
Matthew 4:18	Simon (Peter)
	Andrew
Matthew 4:21	James
	John
	Zebedee
Matthew 9:9	Matthew
Matthew 10:3	Philip
	Bartholomew
	Thomas
	James son of Alphaeus
	Thaddaeus
	Simon the Cananaean
	Judas Iscariot
Matthew 13:55	James
	Joseph
	Simon
	Judas
Matthew 14:1	Herod (Antipas)
Matthew 14:3	*Herodias*
	Philip (Herodian)
Matthew 26:3	Caiaphas
Matthew 26:6	Simon the leper
Matthew 27:2	Pilate
Matthew 27:16	Barabbas
Matthew 27:32	Simon of Cyrene
Matthew 27:56	*Mary Magdalene*
	Mary mother of James and Joseph

Women in Matthew's Narrative Life

Apart from Mary, Jesus' mother, no woman is named (besides Herodias, an indirect opponent of Jesus), until the closing verses of the Gospel when two other Marys are mentioned. The main plot is centered on Jesus and his interaction with his disciples and his increasingly bitter conflict with the Jewish leaders. A surface reading of the Gospel would suggest that women are of little significance or importance in Matthew's telling of the Jesus story. Nonetheless, there are a number of unnamed women characters who appear from time to time in the story of the Messiah. In terms of narrative labeling, all are minor characters. They appear for a brief moment and then disappear. Like other minor characters they are given no ongoing narrative life, yet it will be shown that their significance outweighs their narrative exposure.

In a similar fashion to Hebrew narrative, what can be learnt of a character is mainly discovered through their speech and actions. The Matthean narrator does not offer the reader physical descriptions and allusion to a character's inner thoughts are rare. It is a character's interaction with Jesus and his response to them that is critical in determining the reader's assessment of each individual. Character interaction is used as an important rhetorical device.[14] How each character sees, understands, and reacts to Jesus and how Jesus responds to them leads the reader to determine what kind of character they are.

Another literary device that is used to shape the reader's understanding is comparison. Comparison was a widely used rhetorical strategy which Matthew employs to establish the differences between character groups.[15] Comparison between character groups is invited of the implied reader, as Anderson notes, "because each group interacts with Jesus, the groups also serve as foils for one another. Episodes are arranged so that comparisons and contrasts are heightened."[16] The response of each group to Jesus and Jesus' judgement of the group reveals to the reader both something about the character of the group (sometimes represented by individuals in the group) and something about the character of Jesus. For the purpose of this thesis I will treat the women as a separate group, arguing that they too have their own set of traits and consistency of response towards Jesus.

---

14. Kingsbury's "rhetoric of comprehension," cf. p. 210. Kingsbury, "Rhetoric of Comprehension," 360.
15. See Stanton, *Gospel for a New People*, 83.
16. Anderson, *Matthew's Narrative Web*, 80.

Mothers on the Margin?

Listed below are all the named and unnamed women characters who appear in both the main central section and the final section of passion and resurrection narrative.[17]

Named and Unnamed Women Who Appear in Matthew's Gospel

Women in the main narrative
Mary 1:18 (Jesus' mother, 12:46; 13:55–56)
Peter's mother-in-law 8:14
Woman with hemorrhage 9:20
A ruler's daughter 9:18
Herodias 14:3
Herodias's daughter 14:6
Canaanite woman 15:22
Mother of sons of Zebedee 20:20
Woman who anoints Jesus 26:7
Servant girl 26:69
Another servant girl 26:71
Pilate's wife 27:19

Many women at the cross including
Mary Magdalene 27:56
Mary mother of James and Joseph 27:56

Women at tomb when Jesus buried
Mary Magdalene and the other Mary 27:61

Women at empty tomb
Mary Magdalene and the other Mary 28:1

---

17. I have not engaged with women mentioned in Jesus' teaching nor with the female imagery used in Matthew.

Matthew 3–25 Women in the Main Narrative Section

Women in Matthew 8–9

Following the prologue of chapters 1–2, no women are mentioned again until the narrative passages of Matthew 8–9 where Jesus, having been shown to be a teacher (Matt 5–7), is now portrayed as healer. The majority of the narrative in chapters 8–9 is androcentric, focusing on Jesus' interaction with men; those seeking healing, his disciples, and the religious leaders. However, included are two pericopes concerning Jesus' healing of two women and a girl.

a) The women's stories

MATTHEW 8:14–15 | PETER'S MOTHER-IN-LAW

This story is the last within the first group of three healing miracles in Matthew 8. The healing of Peter's mother-in-law is told succinctly in two verses. She is unnamed but defined socially in terms of her kinship relation in Peter's family. The story has the following narrative structure:

Matthew 8:14a	Jesus comes into the house
Matthew 8:14b	Jesus sees Peter's mother-in-law bedridden and ill
Matthew 8:15a	Jesus touches her hand
Matthew 8:15b	the fever leaves her
Matthew 8:15c	the woman gets up/is raised
Matthew 8:15d	she serves him

The story is simply told. There are just two actors, Jesus the chief actor is the subject of the first three verbs: he entered, he saw, he touched. The healing forms the climax, the fever leaves her and consequently the woman healed becomes the main actor; she gets up and she serves him. The verbs used of both Jesus and the woman are all linked by the use of καὶ, which is repeated five times.

This narrative does not follow the normal pattern of healing stories where Jesus is approached and is asked for healing. In this case on seeing the situation, unusually, Jesus takes the initiative to heal someone. It is the only time in Matthew's Gospel where he does so.[18] This woman's illness is

---

18. The only other two occasions Jesus takes the initiative to heal are recorded in

suffered privately within the confines of her home and, as Jesus enters, the reader sees her through Jesus' eyes; she is bedridden and feverish. In Matthew's Gospel there is no request from the woman herself or another on her behalf. The story stands in contrast to Mark 1:29–31 and Luke 4:38–39, where others enter with Jesus and ask him to heal her. Consequently, attention is deflected in Mark and Luke's account from the woman herself. In Matthew's account nothing is said either by her or by Jesus. He sees her need and responds with a touch of healing. Having got up the woman needs no period of recuperation but is now the one to minister to Jesus. She expresses her gratitude by serving him (διηκόνει αὐτῷ) (Matt 8:15). In Matthew's account it is Jesus alone whom she serves not the "them" of Mark and Luke. On one level the verb διακονέω can be simply read as referring to her service at table but use of the word is suggestive of a deeper meaning. It is Peter's mother-in-law's service to *Jesus* that indicates that her action is of value beyond the immediate serving of food, since "Without exception, Jesus is, in the First Gospel, either the subject or object of διακονέω."[19] Wainwright suggests that the use of the verb διακονέω in its imperfect form "recalls for the reader the angels' service of Jesus after the temptations (Matt 4:11) where it suggested both the symbolic and the ongoing nature of the service."[20]

As the final healing miracle in the first section of chapter 8 (Matt 8:1–17), the story of Peter's mother-in-law prefaces the concluding note by the narrator that summarizes Jesus' healing ministry portraying it as a fulfillment of the words of Isaiah 53:4, words concerning the Suffering Servant "This was to fulfill what had been spoke through the prophet Isaiah, 'He took our infirmities and bore our diseases'" (Matt 8:17).[21] Although Mark 1:32–43 and Luke 4:40–41 both parallel the verse summarizing Jesus' healing ministry (Matt 8:16) neither finish with this fulfillment quotation. Uniquely within the synoptic Gospels, in quoting from Isaiah 53, Matthew presents Jesus' healing ministry as the fulfillment of the mission of the one who is a servant; healing those who are sick is the outworking

---

Luke's Gospel: the widow of Nain's son is raised (Luke 7:11–17) and a crippled woman is healed on the Sabbath (Luke 13:10–13).

19. Davies and Allison, *Matthew 8–18*, 35.

20. Wainwright, *Feminist Critical Reading*, 85. Wainwright also goes on to discuss the three other references to διακονέω in Matthew's Gospel and argues that it is in keeping with the narrative development "that we read διακόνει as indicating a symbolic or religious restoration for the woman." Wainwright, *Feminist Critical Reading*, 86.

21. Davies and Allison note that this verse "contains the only explicit citation of Isa 53 in the synoptics." Davies and Allison, *Matthew 8–18*, 37.

of his servanthood.[22] Although this first story of the healing of a woman in the Gospel is very brief, nonetheless, it is thus significant that Peter's mother-in-law responds to Jesus' healing service to her, by serving Jesus. Jesus himself later teaches his disciples that a willingness to serve others should be a defining feature in the life of a disciple, just as it has been in his own life and ministry for "the Son of Man did not come to be served but to serve" (Matt 20:28). Apart from angels, Peter's mother-in-law, along with the women at the cross (Matt 27:55) are the only ones in Matthew's Gospel who serve Jesus. Matthew's demonstration that it is women who characterize this important virtue is an indication that Matthew's positive rhetoric concerning women, first indicated by the women of the genealogy, is maintained in the ongoing narrative.

MATTHEW 9:18–26 | THE WOMAN WITH A HEMORRHAGE AND THE RULER'S DAUGHTER

The story of the healing miracles of two "daughters" comes as the first account in the final and third set of miracles (Matt 9:18–34). Their stories are intertwined[23] and thus provide a mutual commentary. A comparison with Mark's account (Mark 5:21–43) reveals that, typically, Matthew's account is devoid of the descriptive elements included by Mark. With regard to the woman with the hemorrhage there is no mention of money spent on physicians and her worsening condition, and the intervening scene of the disciples and crowd is omitted. The secrecy of her approach is downplayed and neither her fear of discovery nor Jesus' awareness that power had gone from him is noted. All subordinate characters have disappeared so that only the encounter of Jesus and the woman remains. As Love notes in Matthew's account "the woman is alone with Jesus in an open space,"[24] this maybe implies her lack of family support. Elsewhere, writing about the social context of Matthew's world, Love highlights that a public space

---

22. France notes that rather than using the LXX rendering "He carries our sins and is distressed on our behalf" that understands the servant as the one who deals with his people's sin (the context in which this verse is alluded to elsewhere in the New Testament, cf. 1 Pet 2:24), Matthew provides a literal translation of the MT version of Isa 53:4 that uses the Hebrew words חלי and מכאב for illnesses and diseases, seeing in this "a pointer to Jesus the healer." Whilst Jesus later in the Gospel interprets his service in terms of his passion (Matt 20:28), here it is in a broader context as the healer, that Jesus is the servant of YHWH. France, *Gospel of Matthew*, 322.

23. As they are in Mark 5:21–43 and Luke 8:40–56.

24. Love, *Jesus and Marginal Women*, 124.

is a dangerous location for women subsisting in an agrarian social world where men normally dominated the public discourse.[25] The emphasis in Matthew's account is on her daring faith in Jesus to heal. By contrast the story of the ruler's daughter is situated in both Gospels in a private household setting. However, in Matthew's account it is only Jesus, not the girl's father and mother or his disciples who enter the house. The account in Matthew finishes at the point of healing and peripheral details are not given; Matthew's interest is not in the ruler or those surrounding her but in the girl and her encounter with Jesus.

Jesus is approached by a ruler whose daughter has just died, into this account comes the story of the woman with the hemorrhage.

Matthew 9:18a	Introduction
Matthew 9:18b–19	Jesus is approached and petitioned by the ruler and follows him
Matthew 9:20–22	A woman approaches Jesus from behind, touches his cloak and is healed
Matthew 9:23–25	Jesus comes to the house, turns the crowd away and heals the girl
Matthew 9:26	Conclusion

Since the healing of the woman with a hemorrhage, whom Jesus names as "daughter" (θύγατερ Matt 9:22), interpolates the account of the healing of the ruler's daughter, clearly they are meant to be read alongside each other. Parallels between the two daughters extend beyond their naming. Both are significantly marginalized members of society; the ruler's child because she is a female minor and, in Matthew's account, has died, the woman because she is female and suffering from a ritually unclean health issue. It is implied that she has suffered her hemorrhage for as long as the girl child has lived.[26]

The contrast in the account is provided by the two characters seeking healing from Jesus. Both are people of faith but there the similarities end. They are introduced in similar fashion: "behold a ruler (ἰδοὺ ἄρχων)" (Matt 9:18), "behold a woman (ἰδοὺ γυνὴ)" (Matt 9:20). The first supplicant is defined by his position in society, he is a ruler.[27] He comes in obeisance to Jesus and makes a startling request that Jesus lay his hands on his child, a girl

---

25. Love, *Jesus and Marginal Women*, 62.
26. This is made explicit in Luke's account, cf. Luke 8:42, 43.
27. Mark 5:22 and Luke 8:41 identify him as Jairus, the leader of the synagogue.

Women in Matthew's Narrative Life

who has already died.[28] The ruler pleads, "but come and lay your hand on her and she will live" (Matt 9:18). As Jesus and his disciples follow him, a woman is introduced into the narrative. Although she, like the male ruler, is unnamed, in contrast to him, she is defined by her sickness. The narrator informs the reader that she had been suffering chronic hemorrhages for twelve years. In contrast to the ruler who approaches Jesus face to face and verbally makes his request as he kneels in front of him, she creeps up from behind, saying nothing, but hoping to touch the tassels of his cloak. Matthew (like Luke, contra Mark) emphasizes the minimal nature of her contact with Jesus and consequently the extent of her faith. Also, at this juncture, unusually, Matthew lets the reader know what she is thinking, "If I only touch his cloak, I will be healed (σωθήσομαι)" (Matt 9:21). For the first time in the Gospel a woman's psychological point of view is given. Her inner thoughts reveal the faith in Jesus that her action in touching the edge of his cloak expresses. They also reveal the motive for her action; her desire for healing. Use of the word σωθήσομαι is significant since the Greek verb σώζω has the double sense of to heal and save. It is used by those in Matthew who are in desperate need.[29] In her inner expression of hope for healing she also expresses the hope that she will be saved. As she touches the tassels of his cloak, Jesus seems to be aware of her inward dialogue of faith for his response is immediate; he turns, sees, and speaks. Her action is not condemned. On the contrary, Jesus encourages her, "Take heart" (Θάρσει),[30] and, using a term of endearment only used once in the Gospel by Jesus, he addresses her, "daughter (Θύγατερ),[31] your faith has made you well (ἡ πίστις σου σέσωκεν σε)" (Matt 9:22). Jesus frames her healing in the same terms as used by her in her inner thoughts, indicating that her healing will go beyond the physical to affect her spiritual salvation, as she desires. His words immediately bring healing to her physical body for the narrator tells the reader that the woman was healed "from that hour" (Matt 9:22b).

There is no time to record the woman's response because Jesus is on an urgent errand. As he approaches the ruler's house he encounters a

---

28. In Mark the child is at the point of death (Mark 5:23). The faith of the ruler in Jesus is all the greater in Matthew where he asks Jesus to raise his daughter from death.

29. The disciples are the first to use the expression in the conviction they are about to die, cf. Matt 8:25.

30. Matthew alone has these words to the woman and they echo Jesus' words to the paralyzed man in Matt 9:2, Θάρσει τέκνον.

31. There are faint echoes of Ruth where "daughter" as a term of endearment is used twice by Boaz (Ruth 2:8; 3:10).

crowd of flute players and mourners making a commotion. They are unwelcome and unwanted for Jesus declares, "the girl is not dead but sleeping" (Matt 9:24). The response of mocking laughter from the crowd stands in stark contrast to the faith of both her father and the unknown woman Jesus has just healed. The pericope reaches its finale as Jesus banishes the unbelieving crowd, goes in, and takes the ruler's daughter by the hand. The narrator simply reports that the girl was raised "ἠγέρθη τὸ κοράσιον" (Matt 9:25b). As he takes the girl's hand, she gets up/is raised (ἠγέρθη).[32] In raising the girl by the hand Jesus raises her from the dead. Her return to life alludes to the raising that Jesus himself will experience (Matt 27:64; 28:6, 7). This is the only account Matthew gives of Jesus raising someone from death; significantly that person is not an adult male (cf. Luke 7:11–17; John 11:1–44) but a girl child.

Unlike accounts in Mark and Luke (Mark 5:21–43; Luke 8:40–56) there is no record of any reaction to the healing, readers do not know in what way the girl reacted nor how her family received her back from death. Both stories in Matthew finish at the point of healing. A literal translation reads:

> And was healed the woman from that hour.
>
> "καὶ ἐσώθη ἡ γυνὴ ἀπὸ τῆς ὥρας ἐκείνης" (Matt 9:22b).
>
> . . .and was raised the girl
>
> "ἠγέρθη τὸ κοράσιον" (Matt 9:25b).

Nothing in Matthew's account deflects from the moment of healing Jesus brings to these two daughters.

In closing, the narrator comments that the report of what had happened spread throughout the district (Matt 9:26). This is confirmed by the narrator in a later summary passage. The woman with the hemorrhage's approach has become known and is a model for many who were suffering:

> After the people of that place recognized him, they sent word though out the region and brought all who were sick to him, and begged him that they might touch even the fringe of his cloak; and all who touched it were healed (Matt 14:35–36)

---

32. The aorist passive of the verb ἐγείρω can be translated simply as "she got up." Alternatively, it can be translated "she was raised."

Her narrative importance takes on greater significance in the light of the knowledge that her faith in reaching out to touch the tassels of Jesus' cloak provides an example that many others, who are in need of healing, follow.

b) Feminist perspectives

Scholars often read these two stories in the light of Jewish, levitical, purity laws, as does Anderson, who cites Leviticus 15:25–33 and observes, "The woman with the hemorrhage is ritually unclean."[33] Wainwright also argues that both the bleeding woman and dead girl are pollutants. She writes: "In each of these stories, the female enters the scene as pollutant, outside the boundaries of ritual cleanliness."[34] However, Levine counters Wainwright's observation in noting that "uncleanness is not a disease, and it implies no moral censure; it is a ritual state in which both men and women likely found themselves most of the time."[35]

Levine goes on to note also how "general sickness bleeds over into menstrual issues"[36] when Wainwright also reads Peter's mother-in-law as "a possible pollutant especially if this sickness is connected to her time of ritual uncleanness."[37] Levine is right to note in such cases "not the evangelist but modern scholarship provides us with the Matthean tractate on women."[38] Wainwright also claims that in healing the hemorrhaging woman and young girl, Jesus has broken down two very significant boundaries: gender and ritual cleanliness.[39] Levine points out that the contention that in these stories Jesus is overcoming these barriers is an argument from silence. Correctly, Levine notes that the text itself never mentions questions of purity, neither menstrual or corpse uncleanness is referred to. No one reacts with shock or indignation to the woman touching Jesus' tassels or Jesus taking the dead girl by the hand. However, on this point I side with Wainwright since within the narrative context of chapters 8–9 it is clear that Jesus is breaking down a number of different barriers be they ritual, ethnic, or social, in order to exercise his authority over illness and death. It

---

33. Anderson, "Matthew: Gender and Reading," 11.
34. Wainwright, *Feminist Critical Reading*, 92.
35. Levine, "Discharging Responsibility," 78.
36. Ibid., 72.
37. Wainwright, *Feminist Critical Reading*, 84.
38. Levine, "Discharging Responsibility," 70.
39. Wainwright, *Feminist Critical Reading*, 91.

would therefore be legitimate to infer from the narrative Jesus' willingness to challenge boundaries of ritual and gender.[40]

Levine makes an interesting point on the Christological significance of the two intertwining stories of the woman and girl read as intertexts to Jesus' passion:

> His [Jesus'] physicality is reflected in the depictions of their bodies. The woman suffers, she bleeds, she acts in humility by coming up behind Jesus, she retains her faith but she does not speak. Jesus too will suffer, will bleed, will act in humility, will remain silent and yet retain his faith. Like the ruler's daughter, Jesus is a ruler's son. At the time of his death, he will be surrounded by a commotion, by people who laugh at or mock him. Like the girl, he will die. And, like the girl, he also will be raised from the dead. And the report of this resurrection too will "spread throughout that district."[41]

The woman and girl's bodies thus provide a model for the body of Christ; women's suffering provides the model for the suffering of the Christ, and women's healing provides the model for the resurrection of the Christ.

It can be argued that in different ways the stories of all three females in chapters 8–9 are anticipatory of Christ's passion and resurrection. In her simple act of service Peter's mother-in-law points to the greater and profound service the Messiah will offer in giving his life as a ransom for many. The suffering of the two daughters foreshadows what the Son of Man is destined to physically suffer; he too will similarly suffer in his body, bleed, and die (Matt 16:21; 17:22; 20:17–19). Yet their transformative healing brought about by Christ also foreshadows that fact that suffering and death is not the end of the story; ultimately, by God's power, Christ too will be raised to life and wholeness.

c) Concluding comments on the women of chapters 8–9

Matthew's gynocentric counternarrative, first indicated by the women in the genealogy, is maintained in chapters 8–9. Two pericopes demonstrate Jesus' concern and care towards two sick women and a young girl who has died, and his willingness to cross social, gender, and ritual boundaries in order to heal. Jesus thus brings into question the boundaries existing in

---

40. E.g., Matt 8:1–4 opens with Jesus touching and healing the ritually unclean leper, he then enters into conversation with a Gentile centurion (Matt 8:5–13), and then touches a sick woman (Matt 8:14–15).

41. Levine, "Discharging Responsibility," 87.

Israel. In their interaction with Jesus the women are shown in a favorable light, unlike the male disciples who are chided for their lack of faith (Matt 8:26) and the scribes whom Jesus calls "evil" (Matt 9:4). The significance of their stories outweighs their narrative exposure since in terms of the Gospel's rhetoric of comprehension, as a character group, they are the first in the main narrative section to establish Jesus' affirmative attitude towards women and their positive response to him. One woman serves Jesus, another provides a model of faith in Jesus for others to follow, and a young girl is the only person in Matthew's Gospel to be raised to life by Christ.

Other Women in the Main Narrative Section

MATTHEW 11:1—16:20 | MARY, HERODIAS, HER DAUGHTER, AND THE CANAANITE WOMAN

This section within the main narrative begins and ends with a focus on Jesus' identity. It opens, as did the start of Jesus' public ministry, with John the Baptist who asks, "Are you the coming One or shall we look for another?" (Matt 11:13). It closes, following Peter's confession, with Jesus telling his disciples to remain silent about his identity as Christ (Matt 16:20). In this section a passing reference is made first to Jesus' mother Mary (Matt 12:46–50) and then to his mother Mary and sisters (Matt 13:55–56). However, as has been noted in chapter 7, they are simply foils for, firstly, Jesus' group of disciples gathered around him and, secondly, those in Nazareth who take offense at Jesus. What is important to note here is that in Matthew 12:46–50, when Jesus replies to the question "Who is my mother, and who are my brothers?" Matthew includes the phrase "καὶ ἐκτείνας τὴν χεῖρα αὐτοῦ ἐπὶ τοὺς μαθητὰς" (Matt 12:49), a phrase that does not appear in the parallel passages in Mark 3:31–35 or Luke 8:19–21. Although in all three accounts Jesus is gender inclusive in his response that whoever does the will of his Father is his brother and sister and mother, it is only in Matthew that this group are specifically referred to as Jesus' disciples. This reiterates the point that women are among those who form the family of Jesus' followers. It is the first unequivocal indication that women are among Jesus' disciples and undergirds the positive gynocentric counter-narrative that has been observed up to this point.

It is in this section that people's reaction to Jesus becomes polarized. It is the reaction of various groups—disciples, crowds, Jewish leaders, and supplicants—to Jesus that drives the plot; who is for and who is against?

Political opposition focuses on Herod but includes two women aligned to him. Both are portrayed in a negative light. In opposing John they oppose Jesus for the two men are closely linked. Herod's women are stock characters; the daughter of Herodias being the seducer and Herodias the murderess. However, opposition to Jesus in this section mainly comes from the Jewish leaders as antipathy between Jesus and them becomes more defined. They frequently question him, accuse him of being possessed by Beelzebub and finally seek to destroy him (Matt 12:14). It is in this context that the story of the Canaanite woman is told, the Pharisees and scribes having just questioned Jesus on the tradition of the elders. Her story is located at the center point, flanked by the two accounts of the feeding of the crowds (Matt 14:13–21; 15:32–39).

Matthew 14:13–21	| |	A The feeding of 5,000
Matthew 14:28–33	|	+ a disciple's little faith
Matthew 14:34–36	|	B Jesus heals many
Matthew 15:1–20	|	C The Tradition of the Elders
Matthew 15:21–28	|	The Canaanite woman
Matthew 15:29–31	|	B' Jesus heals many
Matthew 15:32–39	|	A' The feeding of 4,000
Matthew 16:5–12	|	+ the disciples' little faith[42]

This section starts and finishes with Jesus providing bread to meet the physical needs of the crowds and centers on the Canaanite woman's request to be allowed to eat the crumbs under the children's table. This narrative structure leads the reader to compare the surprising, tenacious faith of the Canaanite woman with two occasions when the twelve male disciples are reprimanded by Jesus for their "little faith" following the feeding of the crowds. On the first occasion it is Peter, representative of the twelve, who is chided for his lack of faith (Matt 14:31). On the second occasion Jesus collectively calls the twelve male disciples "Little-faiths" (ὀλιγόπιστοι) (Matt 16:8), because, although they have seen Jesus feed huge crowds twice, they, unlike the Canaanite woman, still failed to have faith in Jesus' provision.

The story of the Canaanite woman is prefaced by a discussion on what defiles; according to Jesus, ritual cleansing of hands is no longer needed (Matt 15:10–20). By placing her story immediately afterwards

---

42. Outline taken from Wainwright, *Feminist Critical Reading*, 101.

the narrator indicates that neither should this Gentile woman be viewed as "unclean."[43] Certainly, as has been more fully explored in the previous chapter, this woman prompts Jesus to reinterpret more than Jewish ritual purity codes since she challenges the boundaries defining his mission. The significance of her story outweighs her narrative exposure because of her challenge to Israel's identity. Her arguments provide both the justification for, and anticipation of, the broadening of Israel's boundaries to include ethnic outsiders. She plays a key role theologically in Matthew's vision of salvation. The narrative also highlights her outstanding faith in Jesus. Her story makes a significant contribution to the positive gynocentric counternarrative already established by the narrator. This counternarrative continues to portray the valuable mutual interaction between Jesus and women, even a Gentile woman from beyond the borders of Israel. The gynocentric counternarrative also continues to critique Jesus' own inner group of male disciples and to subvert the dominant androcentric focus of the main narrative.

Matthew 20:20–23 | The Mother of the Sons of Zebedee

This pericope, coming after the third passion prediction (Matt 20:17–19), is a reminder that the group following Jesus to Jerusalem from Galilee (Matt 17:22) included women as well as men and was not limited to "the twelve" (although this third prediction is specifically addressed to them). It is in the context of Jesus' prediction that he will first be "handed over" (Matt 20:18) to the chief priests and scribes and then "handed over" (Matt 20:19) to the Gentiles to be tortured and killed before being raised, that the next incident concerning a woman occurs. The theme of greatness and status in Jesus' coming kingdom, central to this pericope, is a theme that Jesus has already tackled in response to the disciples' question "Who is the greatest in the kingdom of heaven?" (Matt 18:1). Jesus places a child in their midst, telling his disciples there must be a change in their identity if they are to enter the kingdom of heaven. Greatness is defined neither in terms of wealth nor power but by the most vulnerable member of society—a child. The question is now brought into focus again by the request of a mother. Matthew's portrayal of the disciples has already featured them misunderstanding his teaching on a number of occasions. It is not the male disciples alone who misunderstand Jesus' mission, the mother of the

---

43. Saldarini, *Matthew's Christian-Jewish Community*, 73.

sons of Zebedee also misconstrues the nature of Jesus' kingship. This short pericope involves three sets of characters, the mother, her sons, and Jesus.

Matthew 20:20	Introduction to the mother and sons
Matthew 20:21a	Jesus questions her
Matthew 20:21b	the mother replies with a request
Matthew 20:22a	Jesus questions mother and sons
Matthew 20:22b	all three reply positively
Matthew 20:23	Jesus responds

The woman is unnamed but, like Mary, she is defined in terms of her motherhood. She is the first woman to approach Jesus directly without preliminaries, presumably because she is accompanied by her sons. Both mother and sons are defined in traditional patriarchal terms in relationship to the head of the household, Zebedee. Her two sons are members of the twelve and on their behalf she comes to ask Jesus for a favor. As might be expected for a Jewish mother of that time and culture[44] this mother wants to further the careers of her two sons. Faint echoes of another mother who importunes a king on behalf of her son[45] serve to illustrate the contrast between the power play of the earthly Davidic kingdom and the power of God's kingdom that will be established by way of service and suffering. As all three kneel before Jesus their mother makes a request. Jesus asks simply, "What do you want?" He is willing to consider her request and she comes straight to the point, "Declare that these two sons of mine will sit, one at your right hand and one at your left in your kingdom" (Matt 20:21b). Her request shows that she, like the male disciples, does not understand the nature of the kingdom Jesus will inaugurate. She imagines an earthly kingdom, anticipating Jesus will soon take up royal rule in which he will be seated on the throne with his two principal advisers either side of him. Jesus does not criticize her for her presumption in making the request but points out, "You do not know what you are asking" (Matt 20:22a). Most commentators assume that Jesus turns from the mother and addresses her sons[46] (at this point the verbs become plural), but there is no reason to assume that their mother is not included in the challenge Jesus makes to

---

44. Moltmann-Wendel shows that culturally this woman behaves as a typical mother—she wants to enhance the honor of her sons. Moltmann-Wendel, *Women around Jesus*, 123–26.

45. Bathsheba in 1 Kgs 1:15–21.

46. E.g., Davies and Allison, *Matthew 19–28*, 88.

them. He questions her and her sons about the authenticity of their commitment in following him, "Are you able to drink the cup that I am about to drink?" (Matt 20:22b). That "the cup" is a reference to Jesus' coming passion is made clear in his words at Gethsemane (Matt 26:39). In inviting mother and sons to drink from his cup Jesus calls them to share in his suffering. Their response, "We are able" (Matt 20:22b), is positive but lacks understanding. Maybe the brothers and mother construe Jesus' words to mean the need for some sort of self sacrifice before his earthly kingship can be achieved.

This pericope is followed by the indignant reaction of the other ten disciples which leads Jesus to teach them again about the nature of greatness. For a second time Jesus locates greatness in terms of one who is socially marginal.[47] In the first instance it was a child, on this occasion it is a slave (δοῦλος) (Matt 20:27). Definition of greatness in terms of the powerless, marginalized, and vulnerable requires his disciples to re-envisage what is at the heart of Christian identity. True greatness will be modeled by Jesus, whose servant ministry on behalf of others will lead him to his passion for "the Son of Man came not to be served but to serve, and to give his life as a ransom for many" (Matt 20:28).

Unlike most of the other women in the Gospel, this woman has a continuing place in the narrative; she is mentioned one more time. As events unfold, in company with the other disciples, the two sons of Zebedee, following Peter's lead, express their confidence in their ability to face death with Jesus (Matt 26:35). However, in Gethsemane they are unable even to watch with Jesus. Ironically, they sleep while Jesus wrestles with his "cup" (Matt 26:36–46). Then along with the other disciples they desert him and flee (Matt 26:56). But their mother remains. She is among the group of women who are at the cross looking on from afar (Matt 27:55). From this group, three women are mentioned specifically by Matthew. He alone among the gospel writers includes the mother of the sons of Zebedee. At the scene of the cross she is now drinking the cup of suffering and sorrow (Matt 27:56). In contrast to her sons she has remained faithful to her promise.

Why is the mother of Zebedee's sons included in Matthew's story when Mark excludes her? (Mark 10:35–40). Scholars have puzzled over this apparently unnecessary inclusion in Matthew. Traditionally it has been argued that she is included to put her sons in a better light so that their misguided request is deflected onto her.[48] However, I argue that she

---

47. Carter, *Matthew and the Margins*, 403.
48. Albright and Mann, *Matthew*, 241; Gundry, *Matthew*, 401.

is included for quite the opposite reason. Matthew includes this woman as an example of a mother who, unlike her sons, faithfully follows Jesus. Although her request of Jesus is inappropriate she is not condemned. Instead Jesus challenges her to a deeper level of discipleship. She acts as a foil to her sons because, in spite of her initial lack of understanding, she demonstrates that she is able to drink the cup by following Jesus to the cross. Matthew will show she is not the only woman to do so (Matt 27:55). Her story continues to establish the narrative importance of women as a gender group. The gynocentric counternarrative maintains a critique of Jesus' inner group of male disciples and acts as a corrective to the dominant androcentric focus of this section. Her significance outweighs her narrative exposure because in her actions she exemplifies the kind of greatness the disciples of Jesus are called to; a faithful following and service.

Women's stories in the main narrative section are few but nevertheless significant. Together they support the contention that, as a gender group, women are important and that the positive rhetoric concerning women, first established by the inclusion of the five women of the genealogy, is maintained throughout the main narrative section. Jesus' interaction with these women does not merely "strain the boundaries of the gospel's patriarchal world view"[49] but entirely undermines it. This will be made clearer still in the final section of the gospel narrative.

Matthew 26–28 | Women in the Passion and Resurrection Narrative

The triumphal entry followed by Jesus' eschatological discourse material leads into the final section of Matthew's Gospel, the passion and resurrection narrative (Matt 26–28). Does the narrator occasionally continue to train the spotlight on women at this crucial point in Jesus' life?

On the surface, in keeping with the rest of the narrative, this story revolves around men as Jesus is brought into direct conflict with Jewish and Gentile leaders at the center of power. It opens with the Jewish religious leaders' plot to kill Jesus and closes with the same Jewish leaders continuing to plot against him, even after his death. Into this framework come the dramatic events of Jesus' last meal with his inner group of male disciples, his betrayal and arrest, his trials by the male ruling powers of Israel and Rome, his death by crucifixion at the hands of the soldiers, and

---

49. Anderson, "Matthew: Gender and Reading," 21.

his burial by Joseph. Following his resurrection, the eleven male disciples are given a final commission by the risen Jesus. Yet this all-male cast is intermittently interspersed with stories of women, the first of which is the woman at Bethany. The scene moves abruptly from the palace of the high priest where evil is plotted to the home of a leper where kindness is shown.

The Women's Stories

MATTHEW 26:6–13 | THE WOMAN AT BETHANY

This is the last story recounted in the Gospel of a direct encounter of Jesus with a woman. Matthew like Mark,[50] places the story of the woman at Bethany just after the plot hatched by the chief priests and elders to kill Jesus and before Judas's betrayal, two stories in which men facilitate his death: i.e.,

Matthew 26:3–5	The chief priests and elders conspire to kill Jesus
Matthew 26:6–13	The woman at Bethany anoints Jesus
Matthew 26:14–16	Judas betrays Jesus

The place setting is within the domesticity of the house of Simon the leper but it is the temporal setting, in the last days of Jesus' life as others plot his death, that is the significant factor in this story. The story follows this narrative structure:

Matthew 26:6	the setting, the house of Simon the leper
Matthew 26:7	main action, a woman approaches and pours ointment on Jesus
Matthew 26:8–9	the disciples' question and response
Matthew 26:10–13	Jesus' question and response

The main action is reported briefly and simply, "a woman came to him with an alabaster flask of very costly perfume and she poured it over his head as he reclined" (Matt 26:7). In contrast to the naming of Simon that establishes his identity, the narrator tells readers nothing of who the woman is, or where she has come from. Unlike other minor characters

---

50. In addition to Mark 14:3–9 there are parallels to this story in Jesus' Galilean ministry in Luke 7:36–50 and in John 12:1–8, where it is placed just before Jesus' entry into Jerusalem. However, the stories are markedly different to Matthew's account and a comparison will be limited to Mark.

that approach Jesus, she has not come as a supplicant but with something to give. She has no interior dialogue or external speech; she does not say a word. All the attention is focused on her action as she takes an alabaster jar of expensive ointment and pours it on Jesus' head. The narrator delays the telling of Jesus' response to her by shifting attention to the only other witnesses of her action, the disciples, and allowing the reader to see the scene from their psychological point of view. The arrangement of the narrative dramatically serves to contrast Jesus' reaction to the woman's act with that of the disciples. In Mark's account those who reproach the woman for her action are not named as "the disciples" but rather vaguely referred to as "some" (τινές) (Mark 14:4). The Matthean narrator's specific identification of the disciples as those in opposition to her action serves to paint the disciples in a poor light. Of all people, they might have been expected to understand something of the significance of her act since Jesus has just warned them yet again of his impending death (Matt 26:1–2). They see what she does but don't perceive, as they indignantly remonstrate, "Why this waste?"(Matt 26:8). They regard her action purely in utilitarian terms. From their perspective the ointment could have been sold for a large sum and the money given to the poor (Matt 26:9). They fail to understand both the significance of the woman's action and the significance of this moment in Jesus' life. The narrative implies their complaint was only voiced among themselves and to the woman, but knowing their angry accusations Jesus asks, "Why make trouble for the woman?" (Matt 26:10a). His question serves to shift the focus back to the woman and in an extended passage the narrator gives the reader Jesus' perspective on what she has done (Matt 26:10b–13). His speech has four sections. Sections A and A' assess what she has done for him now and indicates the significance of her action in the immediate future. Sections B and B' assess how her action impacts the future beyond the cross and resurrection.

Matthew 26:10b	A She has accomplished a good work for me
Matthew 26:11	B For you always have the poor with you but you will not always have me
Matthew 26:12	A' By pouring this ointment on my body she has prepared me for burial
Matthew 26:13	B' Truly I tell you, wherever the gospel is proclaimed in the whole world what she has done will be told in memory of her

Matthew 26:10b | A

Jesus calls her action a good deed or a beautiful thing (ἔργον καλὸν), a phrase used in Matthew 5:16 for deeds of discipleship. Her action is therefore an appropriate deed of discipleship shown towards Jesus at a crucial point in his ministry, just two days before he will be handed over (Matt 26:2). What the disciples have thought of as waste and therefore bad Jesus puts into the category of good. Moreover it is something good that has been done *to him*. Spontaneous acts of kindness towards Jesus are rare.[51] The only other human noted as showing Jesus spontaneous kindness is Peter's mother-in-law. This woman's beautiful and intimate act of goodness towards Jesus is the last positive action taken by anyone towards Jesus before his death. From this point on Jesus will face betrayal, false accusations, torture, and crucifixion. Only after his death will kindness be shown again by Joseph of Arimathea whose compassionate action in taking, wrapping, and laying Jesus' body in his own tomb will complete the burial process that this woman has initiated.

Matthew 26:11 | B

Jesus goes on to deal with the disciples' objection by focusing on the importance of the present moment. The poor will always be present but he will not always be with them. His departure is imminent; therefore, for the time being, her lavish gift is entirely appropriate.

Matthew 26:12 | A'

Jesus interprets the woman's action as having great significance because her anointing has taken place in the context of his passion, "By pouring this ointment on my body she has prepared me for burial" (Matt 26:12).

Matthew's very succinct exchange between Jesus and the disciples throws the emphasis in Matthew's account onto Jesus' interpretation of the woman's act of kindness as a burial anointing. As Senior has noted,

> Matthew's rendition of the pericope centers its attention on the symbolic act of the preparation for burial, thereby offering

---

51. Nolland, *Matthew*, 1051. Nolland includes the disciples' initiative in preparing the Passover for Jesus (Matt 26:17–18) and the women who had provided for Jesus (Matt 27:55) but neither acts are necessarily spontaneous.

> a bolder and more explicit presentation of the meaning of the woman's gesture.[52]

Whether or not she knows it, her action is seen by Jesus as prophetic and anticipates what is to come. Later Mark and Luke emphasize the reason the women go to the tomb is to anoint Jesus' body (Mark 16:1; Luke 23:56; 24:1). Matthew omits this. Jesus' anointing at this point is seen by Matthew as a prophetic act. In preparing his body for burial she has performed the task of a disciple for a teacher or a loved one for her beloved.

Matthew 26:13 | B'

Solemnly, Jesus emphatically ends his speech with the words "Truly I say to you" (αμὴν λέγω ὑμῖν).[53] His words are an indirect reproach to his disciples who had condemned her. They anticipate the universality of the risen Christ's command to "make disciples of all nations" (Matt 28:19) because Jesus tells his disciples, "Wherever the gospel is proclaimed in the whole world what she had done will be told in memory of her" (Matt 26:13). This woman's action in anointing Jesus at such a timely moment will have significance beyond the immediate future. Astoundingly her prophetic action will be an element of the proclamation of the good news as it is preached throughout the world. Even more astoundingly, as Wainwright points out, "Jesus does not claim the story in his memory but in hers."[54] Although the account is brief, the symbolic, prophetic significance of her loving response to Jesus as he is about to encounter betrayal, rejection, and death far outweighs her narrative exposure as Jesus himself bears witness.

Matthew 26:14–75 | The Disciples, Peter, and Two Servant Girls

The portrayal of the disciples darkens as Judas agrees to betray Jesus (Matt 26:14–16) and Jesus warns of Peter's denial (Matt 26:31–35). Peter and the sons of Zebedee are repeatedly found sleeping, unable to keep watch with Jesus in the garden (Matt 26:36–46). At the crucial point of Jesus' arrest (Matt 26:47–56) Matthew comments, "all *the disciples* deserted him

---

52. Senior, *Passion Narrative according to Matthew*, 28–29.

53. A phrase that occurs 31 times in Matthew and indicates Jesus is saying something important that he wishes others to understand.

54. Wainwright, *Feminist Critical Reading*, 136.

and fled" (Matt 26:56, my italics).⁵⁵ The all male group of Jesus' disciples are identified by the narrator, this time as those who flee the scene. They will not be present as a group again until they meet with the risen Jesus in Galilee. Consequently, by naming them here, the Matthean narrator draws attention to their absence throughout the scenes of Jesus' crucifixion, death, burial, and resurrection.

Peter is the one exception within the group of Jesus' disciples since he continues to follow Jesus into the courtyard of the high priest (Matt 26:69). As the story moves towards its climax two servant girls act as the catalysts for Peter's denial (Matt 26:69, 71). Although he has followed Jesus to the courtyard, now, in effect, he denies his discipleship. In their accusations the two unknown and insignificant girls speak the truth about Peter whilst Peter lies, denying any knowledge of Jesus the Galilean. The gynocentric counternarrative continues to subvert male claims to truth and to challenge their voices as it does in the next scene too.

Matthew 27:19 | Pilate's Wife

The story continues as the all male patriarchal powers of Israel and Rome combine to destroy Jesus. Among scenes of false accusations and hatred, as was noted in the previous chapter, a passing reference is made to one woman; a Gentile, Pilate's wife. Pilate's wife is not seen in person but the narrator gives voice to her in a message sent to her husband as he is about to pass judgement on Jesus. Like the dreams that warned the Magi and Joseph, a warning dream prompts her to what must have been unusual action in disturbing her husband's judicial activity. Among the male voices of chief priests and elders bringing "many accusations" against Jesus (Matt 27:13), Pilate hears one woman's voice; that of his wife. Just as he is about to pass judgement he is made to pause. "While he was sitting on the judgement seat, his wife sent to him saying, 'Have nothing to do with that righteous man (δικαίῳ ἐκείνῳ), for I have suffered greatly today in a dream because of him'" (Matt 27:19). At a crucial moment in the account, Pilate's wife gives voice to the truth about Jesus.

The dramatic irony of a Gentile woman, wife of Jesus' political enemy, seeking to act as his advocate should not be missed. Mention of her provides a surprising break in the narrative that moves inexorably towards Jesus' death. Why does Matthew alone of the gospel writers mention her? One reason is that she functions in the narrative as an opposite echo to

---

55. Mark is less specific, "they all forsook him and fled" (Mark 14:50).

Herodias. Both women send messages to their powerful husbands but their messages stand in stark contrast to each other. Herodias demands John's death, Pilate's wife seeks to prevent Jesus' death. There are parallels too with another woman's story: Tamar's story. As Tamar is being condemned to be burnt to death, she is declared righteous by the man who has sentenced her to death. In a similar fashion, just as Jesus is about to be condemned to be crucified he is declared to be righteous by the wife of the man in the process of sentencing him. The stories hinge on the great irony that both Tamar and Christ are recognized to be righteous by those in opposition to them as they are being sentenced to death, not that Tamar is a Christ figure, merely that their stories echo one another. Judah's voice prevails but the voice of Pilate's wife is drowned in the din of the crowd, "Let him be crucified" (Matt 27:22, 23). Pilate capitulates and Jesus is flogged, mocked, and crucified. The story of Pilate's wife continues to shape Matthew's gynocentric counternarrative in the final critical scene of Jesus' trial and condemnation. Her narrative importance outweighs her very brief exposure since she alone stands out from among the Jewish religious leaders, the crowds, and even her own husband as the one who tells the truth about Jesus.

Matthew 27:55 | Many Women

As Jesus is crucified and dies in eschatological scenes of darkness and terror, the narrator adds a brief comment that reads as an aside or a postscript to all that had gone on.

> Many women (γυναῖκες πολλαί) were also there, observing (θεωρεοῦσαι) from a distance; they had followed Jesus (ἠκολούθησαν τῷ Ἰησοῦ) from Galilee and had served him (διακονοῦσαι αὐτῷ). Among them were Mary Magdalene, and Mary, the mother of James and Joseph, and the mother of the sons of Zebedee. (Matt 27:55)

The narrator's gaze, which has followed Jesus from baptism, for the first time leaves Jesus as with a loud voice he yields up his spirit (Matt 27:50). It pans across to the temple, then onto the graveyard as the saints rise from their tombs and go into Jerusalem (Matt 27:51–53). Then, it pans back to the cross again and the centurion (Matt 27:54). It finally focuses on a seemingly insignificant group in the distance, a group of many women who were observing all that went on. The narrator goes on to tell the reader that these women, invisible until this moment, have been following Jesus

Women in Matthew's Narrative Life

all the way from Galilee. As well as his male disciples, women had been in the group who had gathered in Galilee and travelled with Jesus to Jerusalem (Matt 17:22). Their presence is a silent rebuke to Peter and the other male disciples who are not present. Their faithfulness is of great importance in the light of the fact that the Matthean Jesus has been abandoned a number of times. First abandoned by his home town (Matt 13:54–58), then by his disciples (Matt 26:56, 69–75), and by the crowds (Matt 27:15–26), finally Jesus feels abandoned by God himself (Matt 27:46). However, this group of many women has not abandoned him; they share in Jesus' death in a way his inner group of twelve male disciples are unable to. Among them is the mother of the sons of Zebedee. The mention of the mother of the sons of Zebedee looks back to the promise she and her sons made to Jesus. Of the three, only she is present as she now comes to realize what it means for Jesus to drink the cup. Her naming is also a reminder to the reader that Jesus interpreted his death in terms of his servanthood on behalf of others (Matt 20:28), and that service must characterize the life of those who follow him. It is therefore significant that the Matthean narrator mentions that, as well as observing and following, the group of women had served him.[56] In doing so they had fulfilled a vital practical role for Jesus but their service also characterizes them as disciples. In fact the two verbs ἀκολουθέω[57] and διακονέω both signify their roles as disciples, as does the reference to Joseph of Arimathea "who was also discipled to Jesus" (ὃς καὶ αὐτὸς ἐμαθητεύθη) (Matt 27:57). The "who was also" refers back to the women, just mentioned, and brackets them together with Joseph as those who are prepared to follow him even beyond death.

Why is it only at the point of Jesus' death that the narrator mentions the many women who had followed Jesus from Galilee? Why wait so long

---

56. Use of the verb διακονέω is significant because up to this point it has only been used three times: of Peter' mother-in-law (Matt 8:15), by Jesus himself (Matt 20:28) and of those who failed to minister to Jesus (Matt 25:44).

57. Kingsbury notes that "to follow" (ἀκολουθεῖν) is often indicative of discipleship in Matthew. Although the verb can be used in a literal sense, e.g., Jesus follows the ruler (Matt 9:19), it is more often employed in a metaphorical sense to describe going after Jesus as his disciple. Kingsbury argues that there are two factors that determine whether the verb should be construed literally or metaphorically. The following of Jesus in discipleship involves personal commitment (Matt 4:19, 21; 9:9) and cost (Matt 4:20, 22; 9:9; 19:28). Using this criterion Kingsbury argues that discipleship is limited to "the disciples," a single character group of twelve men named by Jesus (Matt 10:2). Although Matt 27:55 notes the women had followed Jesus from Galilee (implying cost) and were serving him (implying commitment), unconvincingly Kingsbury argues that the verse "is not meant to characterize them as disciples of Jesus." Kingsbury, "Verb Akolouthein," 56.

to do so? Maybe their narrative sidelining until now is a conscious reflection of the contours of a patriarchal society in which women were a background presence in a society where men functioned in the public realm. Davies and Allison suppose it is because of the women's "relative unimportance for Matthew."[58] On the contrary, I argue that these women are far from unimportant for Matthew. Their presence maintains the gynocentric counternarrative at the climatic moment of Jesus' death. Their significance as women continues to outweigh their narrative exposure because these women are important both as witnesses of Jesus' death and as followers and servants of Jesus. Mention of these women at this point is also important because of the fundamental role two of them are about to play. Matthew 27:55 looks both backwards and forwards. The transitive verb θεωρέω has the cross as its object. Many women are witnesses of Jesus' death but from this group three women are singled out; the mother of the sons of Zebedee and two named women. These two named women, Mary Magdalene and Mary, the mother of James and Joseph, will be named and seen again sitting opposite the tomb as Jesus is buried (Matt 27:61), and then at dawn on the first day of the week as they go to see the tomb and discover, with a little angelic help, that it is empty (Matt 28:1).

MATTHEW 27:61 THE TWO MARYS AT THE TOMB

Verse 27:61 occurs at the central point in a transitional passage that moves the reader from the cross to the tomb. The passage both concludes the passion narrative and introduces the resurrection narrative. Matthew 27:57–66 contains two parallel sections between which there is a single verse, 27:61.

Matthew 27:57	Introduction of main character (Joseph of Arimathea)
Matthew 27:58a	Permission sought of Pilate
Matthew 27:58b	Pilate grants permission
Matthew 27:59–60	Task carried out
Matthew 27:61	*Women witnesses named*
Matthew 27:62	Introduction of main character (Chief priests/Pharisees)
Matthew 27:63–64	Permission sought of Pilate

58. Davies and Allison, *Matthew 19–28*, 637.

Matthew 27:65	Pilate grants permission
Matthew 27:66	Task carried out[59]

The structuring of the narrative serves to heighten the importance of the role the women play as well as contrasting the action taken by Joseph of Arimathea and the Jewish leaders in response to Jesus' death. In the absence of the male disciples, in terms of the plot, the Matthean narrator needs the women to provide the link from the cross to the tomb.

Having described Joseph's compassionate burial of Jesus, the narrator notes the two women at the tomb. For the second time the two women are named, "Mary Magdalene and the other Mary were there, sitting opposite the tomb" (Matt 27:61). They have witnessed Jesus' death (Matt 27:56) and now they witness his burial. The narrator does not describe the women during the intervening period but readers are left to surmise that the two Marys remain at the cross until evening (Matt 27:57) and then wait while Joseph comes and takes down the body. To be present at the tomb the two Marys must have then followed Joseph, presumably witnessing how he wrapped the body in clean linen, laid it in his tomb, and rolled a great stone over the entrance. Finally, readers are also left to wonder how long they remain sitting in mourning after Joseph had left.[60]

The sparsity of the narrative concerning the actions of the women serves to emphasize the importance of their presence in two places, at the cross and at the tomb. It spotlights their role as witnesses to Jesus' death and burial. At this point it becomes clear that stories of women are not just "fissures" in the text but central to the climax of Matthew's plot since it is vital to the narrative that there should be people who witness both Jesus' death and burial. In Matthew's Gospel it is the two Marys who take on these important roles. In doing so they subvert the androcentric focus of the narrative that so far has dominated the account of Christ's death on the cross.

Matthew 28:1–10 | The Two Marys at the Resurrection

The resurrection narrative is set within the following narrative structure:

---

59. Outline taken from Davies and Allison, *Matthew 19–28*, 644; my italics added.
60. Sitting was often a gesture of grief. Davies and Allison, *Matthew 19–28*, 652.

Matthew 28:1	the setting
Matthew 28:2–3	main narrative action—an earthquake, an angel "comes down" rolls back the stone and sits on it
Matthew 28:4	reaction of the guards
Matthew 28:5–7	the angel addresses the women
Matthew 28:8	the women start to leave
Matthew 28:9	Jesus meets them
Matthew 28:10	Jesus repeats the angel's message

The temporal setting of events continues to be important; it is "at the dawning of the first day of the week" that the two women "come to see the tomb" (Matt 28:1). Unlike the women in Mark 16:1 and Luke 24:1 they are not carrying spices. For Matthew, Jesus' anointing has already taken place in Bethany by another woman. The narrator is quite specific that Mary Magdalene and the other Mary went to *see* the grave, Θεωρῆσαι τὸν τάφον (Matt 28:1). The use of the participle θεωρῆσαι (beholding) has already been noted, describing the women as they observed Jesus' death on the cross (Matt 27:55). Now it is used again of the named women as they see the tomb. Internal cross-referencing through the repetition of key words is an important technique employed throughout the narrative. The repeated use of this verb here, the only two times it is used in the Gospel, links the scene of the cross to the empty tomb and emphasizes the importance of the women as eyewitnesses. These two women form the link between Jesus' death, burial, and resurrection. It is these two women who also form the climax to Matthew's gynocentric counternarrative. The importance of this counternarrative is clarified further by what happens at the tomb on the dawning of the first day of the week.

Eschatological phenomena such as darkness and an earthquake accompany the crucifixion. For a second time, there is an earthquake as an angel descends, rolls back the stone, and uncompromisingly sits on it. "An angel of the Lord" (Matt 28:2), clearly a divine messenger, has previously appeared three times to Joseph (Matt 1:20; 2:13, 19) but now in the resurrection narrative the angel appears to the women. His appearance mirrors that of the transfigured Jesus (Matt 17:2). The guards, stationed at the tomb at the request of the chief priests and Pharisees (Matt 27:62–66), are for the moment written out of the script. In contrast to the women, the narrator tells readers they were so frightened they "became like dead men" (Matt 28:4). The angel knows the women are looking for Jesus and

Women in Matthew's Narrative Life

in response tells them, "Do not be afraid." The angel continues, "He is not here, for he has been raised just as he said; come, see the place where he lay" (Matt 28:6). From a divine messenger the two women are the first to hear the news of Jesus' resurrection and they are the only two characters in the Matthean resurrection narrative who are invited to see the empty tomb, vital evidence in the account of Christ's resurrection, as the priests and elders recognize (Matt 28:13). The final part of the angel's message commissions the women to tell Jesus' disciples that he has been raised from the dead (Matt 28:7).

The women are frightened, but, unlike the guards, their fear does not paralyse them for it is accompanied by "great joy." Instead, they run to tell their message. "Suddenly Jesus met them and said 'Greetings!'" (Matt 28:9). As they come unexpectedly face to face with Jesus they recognize him and without hesitation take hold of his feet and worship him. The women's personal encounter with Jesus takes them beyond the message of the angel and the evidence of the empty tomb as a grounding for their conviction that he is risen. In words that mirror the angel's message, for a second time they are told not to be afraid and are commissioned to "go and tell" (ὑπάγετε ἀπαγγείλατε) (Matt 28:10) but this time it is the risen Christ himself who sends them.

Discussion has surrounded the apparently redundant meeting with Jesus in Matthew. The women are already on their way to deliver the message for the disciples to meet Jesus in Galilee, why do they need to be told by Jesus a second time? This element, in a relatively spartan account of the resurrection, brings to the fore four key issues in relation to the women. Firstly, their testimony rests not just on an angelic message and the empty tomb but on an encounter with the risen Jesus. Although many people come to Jesus and meet with him, it is the only time in Matthew's Gospel (or anywhere in the New Testament)[61] that Jesus meets with someone, καὶ ἰδοὺ Ἰησοῦς ὑπήντησεν αὐταῖς (Matt 28:9). The importance of the encounter is emphasized with the emphatic ἰδοὺ. Secondly, the women are the first in the Gospel to meet the risen Jesus and the only ones to unreservedly worship him. It is they, as worshipping believers, who initiate and model the appropriate response to their risen Lord. Thirdly, Jesus meets with the women not to deliver a redundant message but so that he himself, as the risen Christ, can commission the women to "go and tell" (Matt 28:10).[62] Fourthly, whereas the angel had used the title disciples

---

61. Nolland, *Gospel of Matthew*, 1252.
62. Davies and Allison comment that "in Eastern Christianity Mary Magdalene

(μαθηταῖς) (Matt 28:7) this time Jesus tells them to take the message to "my brothers" (τοῖς ἀδελφοῖς μου). Implicit is a word of forgiveness. The women are entrusted with the task of making possible the reconciliation between the risen Christ and his unfaithful disciples.[63]

Their commission surely extends beyond the immediate task of telling the disciples that Jesus has risen and has ongoing significance. If, for a moment, we stray beyond the narrative to the reality of the historical event, Jesus' commission to the women is suggestive of the vital role that the two named women are to play as apostolic eyewitnesses to the resurrection within the life of the early church.[64] In Matthew's Gospel it is solely these two women who can affirm the essentials of the early fourfold Christian kerygmatic confession; that Jesus had died, been buried in the tomb, was risen, and had appeared to them (1 Cor 15:4–5). In Matthew's Gospel there are no male disciples at the cross or at the burial, or at the tomb on the first day of the week, and the risen Jesus only appears to the women at the tomb. In Matthew's Gospel the women's witness is unique. Matthew's account of the women's role at the resurrection is the denouement to the positive gynocentric counternarrative that has subverted the androcentric focus and patriarchal assumptions about the place and role of women throughout the narrative. It does so supremely at this point.

It is assumed in the narrative that the women deliver the message since the concluding scene of the Gospel opens as the eleven disciples go to the mountain in Galilee to meet with Jesus (Matt 28:16). The eleven have both believed and obeyed the women. However, in contrast to the women, their response to the risen Christ is mixed. They also see and worship Jesus, but some doubt (Matt 28:17). The counternarrative's favorable comparison of women with the male disciples of Jesus is maintained to the final closing scene. Were others present? Quite possibly women who had been invisible travelling companions with Jesus to Jerusalem are "invisible participants" here.[65] Matthew does not say, but one thing is certain, the final and only meeting of the risen Christ with his "brothers" is dependent on the testimony of Mary Magdalene and the other Mary. The commissioning of the eleven male disciples to "Go . . . and make disciples" (Matt

---

is . . . 'isapostolos', that is, equal to the apostles." Davies and Allison, *Matthew 19–28*, 637.

63. Wainwright, *Feminist Critical Reading*, 312.
64. Bauckham, *Jesus and the Eyewitnesses*, 48–51.
65. Nolland, *Gospel of Matthew*, 1262.

28:19) is reliant on the prior commissioning of Christ to these women and their obedience in going and telling.

A Sideways Glance

A detailed comparison of women in the passion and resurrection narratives with the other gospel accounts is beyond the remit of this thesis.[66] Suffice it to note that both the other synoptic accounts and John agree that women were present at the cross and witnessed his death (Mark 15:40–41; Luke 23:49; John 19:25). Mark and Luke also agree that women witnessed Jesus' burial (Mark 15:47; Luke 23:55) and all three recount stories of women at the empty tomb (Mark 16:1–8; Luke 24:1–11; John 20:1, 11–18). What is notable is that in Luke and John the women's witness of the empty tomb is not unique, in both Gospels male disciples see the empty tomb too (Luke 24:12; John 20:3–10). Like Matthew, the women in Mark are the only ones to witness the empty tomb (allowing for an ending at Mark 16:8) but they flee from their encounter with the young man dressed in white, terrified, without following the angel's instructions to "Go, tell his disciples" (Mark 16:7). Notoriously, Mark's Gospel ends with the words "they said nothing to anyone for they were afraid" (Mark 16:8).[67]

Concluding Comments

It is notable that throughout chapters 26–28, more clearly than elsewhere in the Gospel, the rhetoric of Matthew's gynocentric counternarrative is established by means of comparison. The women act as foils to the two main male character groups, the Jewish religious leaders and the disciples, and also to Pilate, the representative of Gentile political power. The action of the woman who anoints Jesus is contrasted with the reaction of the disciples towards her. What has been very costly for her in her demonstrative anointing of Jesus makes the disciples angry. What they call "waste" Jesus calls "beautiful" and of supreme value to him. The contrast extends beyond the confines of the story itself as it is placed immediately after the Jewish religious leaders gathering to conspire to kill Jesus and before Judas's concupiscence in obtaining thirty pieces of silver in order to betray

---

66. See Bauckham, *Gospel Women*, 257–310.

67. Horsley also discerns a women subplot in Mark's story that challenges hierarchical models of leadership. Horsley, *Hearing the Whole Story*, 203–25.

Jesus (Matt 26:14–16). The woman's action will be remembered wherever the good news is preached as a lasting memorial to her. Judas's lasting memorial is a burial ground for foreigners bought with the returned "blood money." The narrator breaks frame to note that the burial ground "has been called the Field of Blood to this day" (Matt 27:8).

The women's constancy in having followed Jesus from Galilee to the cross stands in sharp contrast to the failure of the male disciples to be present at Jesus' crucifixion. Having fled the garden the group of disciples do not appear again until the closing scene on a mountain in Galilee. Although Peter remains, ultimately he too repudiates Jesus, his denial contrasting with the truth of the servant girls' accusations. Pilate's conviction of an innocent man contrasts with his wife's recognition of Jesus as "that righteous man" (Matt 27:19) whom Pilate then condemns to death.

In the closing scenes the women at the tomb are juxtaposed with the guards and priests and elders who continue to act in opposition (Matt 28:11–15). The final comparison invited by the text is between the differing reactions of the women and Jesus' eleven remaining disciples to his resurrection appearance.

A Positive Gynocentric Counternarrative

To summarize: it has been demonstrated that there is a positive gynocentric counternarrative running throughout Matthew's Gospel that subverts and deconstructs its dominant androcentric focus and patriarchal assumptions about the role and place of women.

Matthew's rhetorical stance concerning women is established in three ways; firstly, paradigmatically, by the women of the genealogy. They are the first indication that patriarchy will be subverted by the birth of the Messiah. Read as intertexts to the Gospel the five women establish the narrative tone concerning women as a gender group, setting the terms of reference that guide the implied reader's response towards women in the ensuing gospel narrative.

Secondly, Matthew's narrative rhetoric concerning women is established in the way Jesus interacts with women and their response to him. In the telling of their stories any peripheral detail is stripped away to leave the reader to focus on the interaction between Jesus and each woman he encounters. Thirdly, the placement of the women's stories in the sequence of events also plays a part in establishing the overall narrative rhetoric. By placing stories of women alongside stories of Jesus' male disciples and the

Women in Matthew's Narrative Life

religious rulers, comparison and contrast with these other male character groups is invited.

The way a book ends is very important to the interpretation of the whole. The ending of a book often resolves issues, explains its meaning and ties up the plot. It has been noted that the prologue of chapters 1–2 and the passion and resurrection narrative of chapters 26–28 frame the Gospel, providing a beginning and an ending to the account of the life of Christ.

With regard to Matthew's gynocentric counternarrative, it has been noted that attention is drawn to women at the beginning and end of the Gospel because, unusually, they are named. Comparison is reinforced by the happy coincidence that Jesus' mother and the women at the tomb are all named Mary. Like Jesus' mother, the two Marys only appear briefly and without introduction. Like her, they have no direct or internal speech. Yet here the similarity ends. In chapters 1 and 2 attention is directed towards Joseph. Mary remains passive. At the beginning of the Gospel it is Joseph who, in accord with patriarchal traditions of divine dealings with men, is the one who on three occasions receives divine angelic revelation and subsequently takes the actions asked of him. Significantly at the end of the Gospel, unlike Mary the mother of Jesus, the two Marys who come to the tomb and encounter Jesus are not passive but active. This time, contrary both to patriarchal expectations of God dealing with men and patriarchal norms of men carrying out important tasks, the gender roles are reversed. A series of active verbs are used for the two Marys; observing (Matt 27:55), sitting (Matt 27:61), coming and looking (Matt 28:1), departing and running (Matt 28:8), approaching, grasping, worshipping (Matt 28:9), and, finally, going (Matt 28:10). It is not Jesus' male disciples who meet with the risen Lord at the tomb but the two Marys. Women are given priority as recipients of revelation and entrusted to take the message to men. The gynocentric counternarrative ends by deconstructing and subverting all patriarchal norms as women take center stage in the closing scenes at the tomb and both meet with the risen Jesus and take the message of his resurrection and reconciliation to his eleven disciples. At the close of his Gospel Matthew is saying something profound about the role of women in the new order brought about by the death and resurrection of Christ. Christian identity will no longer be construed in terms of male hierarchy and dominance. Women will take their places alongside men in a discipleship of equals.

Matthew's positive gynocentric narrative deconstructs the text. This chapter has demonstrated that both its dominant androcentrism and patriarchal ideology is critiqued within the text itself; the text subverts itself. When one turns one's gaze away from the center to the margins, a number of women come into view and a positive ideological gynocentric stance is discovered that validates women and the roles they play in relation both to Jesus and to Matthew's overall vision of salvation.

11

Conclusion

Mothers on the Margin?

Matthew's Call to Conversion

At the outset of this dissertation it was noted that the way a piece of narrative begins is important because it sets the scene for what is to follow, providing hints and clues about what the story will be about and how the reader might interpret it. Matthew's opening genealogy introduces the reader to the Messiah but also to the Gospel as a whole. It is notable among other things for its inclusion of five women in the annotations; five mothers who are on the textual margin of the genealogy.

This dissertation is titled with a question that demands an answer. The question can be read in two ways depending on inflection of voice. The interrogative could refer to the identity of the mothers—is it mothers who are on the margin? Alternatively it could question where they are situated—are they on the margin?

In part this dissertation has been a response to both these questions. Firstly, what of the five mothers? The narratives of the first four women, Tamar, Rahab, Ruth, and "she of Uriah," are intertexts that are drawn by the Matthean narrator into the story of Jesus. A close narrative reading of their varied stories in chapters 3–6 has led to the conclusion that there is much more to these women than simply their motherhood. This is not to demean their significance as mothers (although it is not a feature of Rahab's story), but to point out that both their Old Testament narratives and the ongoing rhetoric of Matthew's text suggests that they are included for reasons beyond Matthew wanting to acknowledge women's roles as mothers in Jesus' ancestral past. The narratives that contain the stories of Tamar, Rahab, and Ruth provide particularly rich material for reflection in the light of their inclusion at the start of Matthew's Gospel. By reading their stories as intertexts to Matthew's Gospel the meaning potential of both texts is altered and new meanings emerge as the two are compared. These women's lives, as portrayed in their stories in Genesis 38, Joshua, and the book of Ruth, give content to characteristics of righteousness, faith, and חסד and these find their trajectory in the teaching of Jesus in Matthew. Chapter 8 has demonstrated that these virtues are key descriptors of Matthean discipleship and consequently Christian identity, since they are virtues that the Matthean Jesus seeks for among his followers. It is therefore significant that these virtues of righteousness, faith, and חסד, characteristics that are also central to Israel's identity as the covenant people of God, are displayed by these three women, women who are structurally marginalized both by their status within society and because they are ethnic outsiders to Israel. Their lives both within their Old Testament narratives and read as intertexts to Matthew's Gospel therefore become a radical call to inclusivity; a call to a re-envisioning of the identity of the people of God. Taken as a group, within the opening epoch of the genealogy they are the first indication of the fulfillment of the divine promise to Abraham that Israel's identity will broaden to include the nations. Even more significantly, chapter 9 has argued that they point forward to a Matthean Messiah who will welcome all those on the margins.

The inclusion of these particular three women, Tamar, Rahab, and Ruth, is also notable for other reasons. From a feminist perspective, all three narratives, unusually, have a gynocentric focus. My analysis has demonstrated they were women who all faced danger and death but who refused to acquiesce passively to what might seem the inevitable. Instead they used what resources they had at their disposal, be it their wit, intelligence, sexuality, or sheer physical labor, actively and courageously to pursue life both for themselves and others. In so doing all three aligned themselves with the God of Israel and demonstrated a radical loyalty to his people, challenging and prompting the male insiders to act in line with God's purposes. It has been argued that along with Bathsheba and Mary their stories set the narrative tone concerning women as a gender group.

Mothers on the Margin?

Chapter 10 has demonstrated how Matthew's positive rhetoric concerning women is maintained in the ongoing gospel narrative in what I have labeled a positive gynocentric counternarrative. This also has implications for the identity of the new people of God in terms of the place and role of women.

The inclusion of "she of Uriah"—Bathsheba, at the start of the second epoch of Matthew's genealogy is notable since her designation as "she of Uriah" would seem to be significant. It was argued in chapter 6 that this draws the narrative in 2 Samuel 11–12 as an intertext into Matthew's narrative, since there she is also named "she of Uriah." In contrast to the first three named women it was noted that her character is much less well defined and, due to the ambiguity of the Hebrew narrative, her story in 2 Samuel has been the subject of much discussion concerning whether she planned to seduce David or to what extent David took advantage of her. It was concluded that a number of textual indicators point to her innocence. Within her Hebrew narrative, having been mistreated by David, not least in the murder of her husband, Bathsheba is very much a mother on the margin. Additionally it was concluded that her placement in the genealogy is significant because it draws attention to God's judgement of sin in salvation history and to his gracious promise of mercy and forgiveness that is brought to fulfillment in the life and ministry of the Messiah. Like Tamar, Rahab, and Ruth, she is a symbol of hope, since through her, at the borders of death, God brings new life into being. Like the first three women, she is on the margin in a number of ways but, as the genealogy bears witness, becomes a central player in the purposes of God.

Of the five women chapter 7 has shown it is Mary who is most clearly characterized solely in terms of her motherhood. Beyond that, the reader learns nothing more about Mary as a character in her own right since Matthew's focus lies elsewhere in an explanation of Jesus' origins. Nonetheless, Matthew's witness to her divine conception of the Messiah through the Holy Spirit sets her apart as a mother and as a woman who experiences the work of the Spirit in a unique way. However, she stands in close relation to Bathsheba as indicated by their placement in the genealogy; both are mothers to sons of David, carrying sons who are the fulfillment of divine promise. Similarities exist in a number of other ways not least because both women are insiders to Israel yet are on the margins because of the child they are carrying. Ultimately, both women, like the first three women, are accepted and find a place on the inside within the Davidic line.

It has been argued in chapter 7 that there is a common dynamic of structural marginality underlying all five women's stories and that this reflects Matthew's concern for the variety of structurally marginal people Jesus encounters. The five women in the genealogy serve to represent all those who are on the margins, all who are disenfranchised and excluded from centers of social, political, and religious power both inside and outside Israel. But their stories also have an underlying dynamic of inclusion that brings into focus the question of who is on the outside and who is on the inside in Israel and what factors dictate either inclusion or exclusion. This is highlighted particularly in Rahab's story, where questions are raised concerning the boundaries defining Israel's identity as she enters the promised land, questions which chapter 9 has shown are paralleled in many ways by the story of the Canaanite woman in Matthew's Gospel. An observation made by Earl on Rahab in his book *Reading Joshua as Christian Scripture* is helpful. Earl notes that in the tradition of Christian interpretation there has been a tendency to focus on the "conversion" of Rahab.[1] He goes on to observe that although in one sense this is true, since she is incorporated into Israel, it is not Rahab's conversion that her story is about but Israel's.

> Rahab's confession is not portrayed as deriving from a "moment of conversion," and her character is not portrayed as changing or developing in the story. Rather, what changes is the way in which she is categorized and perceived by the community of Israel, for she does not change. It is the status that Israel accords to her that changes. In a sense it is *this community* (Israel) that undergoes conversion, in its perception of its own identity and boundaries.[2]

Earl's observation can be extended to Tamar and Ruth, since what is true of Rahab is also true of them. Neither Tamar nor Ruth are dynamic characters. They do not undergo a significant change or development in character. Rather what changes is the perception of Tamar by Judah and of Ruth by Boaz and the people of Bethlehem, based on Tamar and Ruth's manifestation of righteousness and loving loyalty respectively. In both cases it is the status that Israel accords to Tamar and Ruth that changes and brings about a conversion. Like Rahab's encounter with Israel, this conversion affects Israel's perception of her identity and the boundaries she places around herself. While the same cannot be argued of the roles

---

1. Earl, *Reading Joshua*, 145–46.
2. Ibid., 147.

played by Bathsheba and Mary in bringing about a conversion of perception, nevertheless, they also are mothers on the margin who become central to the purposes of God and the fulfillment of divine promise. In their cases it is divine intervention that brings about a conversion in both David and Joseph. Their inclusion in the Messianic family tree serves to deconstruct both the patriarchy and status represented by the fathers of the genealogy and, consequently, they also bring into question the nature of the identity of Israel.

Inclusion of the five women in the Messiah's ancestry is subversive of the perceived "purity" of the Jewish line and raises questions about positions of power and the exercise of patriarchy in the purposes of God. Their inclusion in the ancestry of the Messiah is the first hint that the Gospel will deconstruct an understanding of the new Messianic people of God in the frames of reference traditionally associated with Israel; ethnic otherness, patriarchy, and social/religious status. In other words, the presence of these women in the genealogy is the first indication that the birth of the Messiah will bring about a crisis in Israel's identity in terms of ethnicity, marginality, and gender.

The rhetoric of the Gospel suggests that Matthew wants to bring about a conversion of understanding as to who constitutes the people of God in the Messianic era. How is Christian identity to be construed?

Chapter 8 has argued that while the Matthean Jesus looks for a response of faith among his disciples, a verbal declaration of his Lordship must be lived out in a life of faith that is manifested in obedience to the will of the Father. Jesus' call to a "higher righteousness" is all embracing. It describes both the outward actions and interior life that should characterize the disciple who does the will of the Father. Mercy is a closely related theme that is also distinct to Matthew's Gospel. The Matthean Jesus teaches that the practice of mercy towards others is at the heart of what God desires, since it is mercy they have received from God. Read as intertexts to Matthew's Gospel Tamar, Rahab, and Ruth challenge notions of identity since they show that outsiders are capable of demonstrating righteousness, faith, and mercy. The practice of these virtues is not restricted to those within Israel. Conversely, those inside might not be displaying "fruit worthy of repentance" (Matt 3:8). It is misguided to rely on ethnicity to find a place in the kingdom of heaven. "Do not presume to say to yourselves, 'We have Abraham as our ancestor'" (Matt 3:9), John the Baptist warns the Pharisees and Sadducees, and this theme is continued in Jesus' encounter with the centurion where he warns "the heirs of the kingdom will be thrown into outer darkness" (Matt 8:12).

Mothers on the Margin?

Responsiveness to Jesus in faith and worship is one of the yardsticks by which Christian identity is measured in the Gospel. Chapter 9 has shown this is consistently modeled not by the insiders, the Jewish religious leaders, but by outsiders with whom they are contrasted, both those on the margins in Israel and Gentiles. Within Israel it is the leper, the paralyzed, the blind and the sick who seek out Jesus. It is this group of supplicants along with tax collectors and sinners to whom Jesus' ministry is primarily directed. Their response is invariably one of faith in Jesus, whom they recognize to be Lord and Son of David, able to help them in their need. The Matthean group of Gentiles—the Magi, the centurion, the Canaanite woman, Pilate's wife, and the centurion at the cross—are notable because although they are outsiders to Israel they also recognize and acknowledge Jesus' true identity. While the Magi and centurion model the appropriate response of worship and faith, it is the Canaanite woman's story which in the context of this discussion is the most arresting, because she is marginalized on all three counts: by ethnicity, social status, and gender. Jesus is challenged by her response to his hesitation and rewards her great faith by letting her eat the children's bread as she finds a place inside the house. Like Rahab, she challenges Israel's identity and, together with the other Gentiles, brings into question the notion of who is on the outside and conversely who is on the inside in the kingdom of heaven Jesus is inaugurating.

Finally, in chapter 10 it has been argued that the presence of the five women of the genealogy subverts the patriarchal lineage of the Messiah. The women are the first indication that Christian identity will no longer be construed along patriarchal lines. The woman-focused narrative continues, forming a positive gynocentric counternarrative that runs throughout Matthew's Gospel and subverts both the androcentrism and patriarchy of the dominant text. The virgin birth functions as the most profound challenge to patriarchy but it is not until the close of the Gospel that two women emerge from the margins to take center stage as eyewitnesses to the death, burial, and resurrection of the Messiah. Along the way there are a number of women whose brief narrative presence as minor characters is outweighed by the significance of their response to Jesus. In particular it is notable how women take on vital roles of discipleship in the absence of men in the passion and resurrection narratives. The apostolic commission of the risen Jesus to the two Marys seals the notion that Christian identity is to be gender inclusive; a discipleship of equals. Notably women are the first to worship the risen Christ, just as the Gentile Magi were the first to respond in worship in the prologue and the marginalized leper the first in the main narrative section.

To conclude: the mothers on the margin in Matthew's genealogy are the first indication that Matthew's Gospel is concerned with the construal of a new identity for the people of God. This is an identity that is based on responsiveness to Christ lived out in relationship with others. Matthew indicates that Jesus' new community of disciples will include those on the margins, women, and Gentile outsiders in an ἐκκλεσία (Matt 18:17) of disciples who have responded in faith and worship to Jesus and seek to live out their faith in righteousness and mercy. It is an identity that is not dictated by ethnicity, social status or gender but by a faith in Jesus that is embodied in a Christlikeness expressed in righteous living, in doing the will of the Father. Matthew's call to conversion is a call that needs to be heard afresh by each generation. It is just as important today, as when Matthew was written, that the Church responds to the challenges to Christian identity presented both in the narratives of the five women of the genealogy and Matthew's ongoing gospel narrative.

Bibliography

Ackerman, James S. "Knowing Good and Evil: A Literary Analysis of the Court History in 2 Samuel 9–20 and 1 Kings 1–2." *Journal of Biblical Literature* 109 (1990) 41–60.
Ackerman, Susan. *Warrior, Dancer, Seductress, Queen: Women in Judges and Biblical Israel*. Anchor Bible Reference Library. London: Doubleday, 1998.
Albright, William F., and Christopher S. Mann. *Matthew*. Anchor Bible 26. New York: Doubleday, 1971.
Alkier, Stefan. "Intertextuality and the Semiotics of Biblical Texts." In *Reading the Bible Intertextually*, edited by Richard B. Hays et al., 3–21. Waco: Baylor University Press, 2009.
Allison, Dale C., Jr. *The New Moses: A Matthean Typology*. Minneapolis: Fortress, 1993.
Alter, Robert. *The Art of Biblical Narrative*. London: Allen & Unwin, 1981.
———. *The David Story: A Translation with Commentary of 1 and 2 Samuel*. London: Norton, 1999.
———. *Genesis: Translation and Commentary*. London: Norton, 1996.
Amit, Yairah. *Reading Biblical Narratives: Literary Criticism and the Hebrew Bible*. Minneapolis: Fortress, 2001.
Anderson, Arnold A. *2 Samuel*. Word Biblical Commentary 11. Dallas: Word, 1989.
Anderson, Janice C. "Mary's Difference: Gender and Patriarchy in the Birth Narratives." *Journal of Religion* 67 (1987) 183–202.
———. "Matthew: Gender and Reading." *Semeia* 28 (1983) 3–27.
———. *Matthew's Narrative Web: Over and Over and Over Again*. JSNT Supplement Series 91. Sheffield: Sheffield Academic, 1994.
Ashley, Kathleen M. "Interrogating Biblical Deception and Trickster Theories: Narratives of Patriarchy or Possibility?" *Semeia* 42 (1988) 103–16.
Aune, David E., ed. *The Gospel of Matthew in Current Studies*. Cambridge: Eerdmans, 2001.
Bach, Alice. "Signs of the Flesh: Observations on Characterization in the Bible." *Semeia* 63 (1993) 61–79.
———, ed. *Women in the Hebrew Bible*. London: Routledge, 1999.
Bacon, Benjamin W. *Studies in Matthew*. London: Constable, 1930.
Baer, David A., and Robert P. Gordon. "2874 חסד." In *New International Dictionary of Old Testament Theology and Exegesis*, vol. 2, edited by Willem A. VanGemeren, 211–18. Carlisle, UK: Paternoster, 1996.
Bailey, Kenneth E. *Jesus through Middle Eastern Eyes: Cultural Studies in the Gospels*. London: SPCK, 2008.
———. *Poet & Peasant and Through Peasant Eyes: A Literary-Cultural Approach to the Parables in Luke*. Grand Rapids: Eerdmans, 1983.
Bailey, Randall C. *David in Love and War: The Pursuit of Power in 2 Samuel 10–12*. JSOT Supplement Series 75. Sheffield: Sheffield Academic, 1990.

Bibliography

Bal, Mieke. *Lethal Love: Feminist Literary Readings of Biblical Love Stories*. Indiana Studies in Biblical Literature. Bloomington: Indiana University Press, 1987.

———. "Tricky Thematics." *Semeia* 42 (1988) 133-55.

Barclay, William. *The Gospel of Matthew*. Vols. 1 & 2. New Daily Study Bible. Edinburgh: Saint Andrew, 2005.

Bar-Efrat, Shimon. *Narrative Art in the Bible*. JSOT Supplement Series 70. Sheffield: Almond, 1989.

———. "Some Observations on the Analysis of Structure in Biblical Narrative." *Vetus Testamentum* 30 (1980) 154-73.

Barry, Peter. *Beginning Theory: An Introduction to Literary and Cultural Theory*. Manchester: Manchester University Press, 1995.

Barth, Gerhard. "Matthew's Understanding of the Law." In *Tradition and Interpretation in Matthew*, edited by Gunther Bornkamm et al., 58-164. London: SCM, 1963.

Barth, Karl. *Church Dogmatics*. Vol. 1.2, *The Doctrine of the Word of God*. Translated by G. T. Thomson and H. Knight. 1932-1938. Edinburgh: T. & T. Clark, 1956.

Barton, Stephen C. *Discipleship and Family Ties in Mark and Matthew*. SNTS Monograph Series 80. Cambridge: Cambridge University Press, 1994.

Bauckham, Richard. "The Book of Ruth and the Possibility of a Feminist Canonical Hermeneutic." *Biblical Interpretation* 5 (1997) 29-45.

———. *Gospel Women: Studies of the Named Women in the Gospels*. London: T. & T. Clark, 2002.

———. *Is the Bible Male? The Book of Ruth and Biblical Narrative*. Grove Biblical series. Cambridge: Grove, 1996.

———. *Jesus and the Eyewitnesses: The Gospels as Eyewitness Testimony*. Cambridge: Eerdmans, 2006.

Bauer, David R. "The Kingship of Jesus in the Matthean Infancy Narrative: A Literary Analysis." *Catholic Biblical Quarterly* 57 (1995) 306-23.

———. "The Literary Function of the Genealogy in Matthew's Gospel." In *Treasures New and Old: Recent Contributions to Matthean Studies*, edited by Mark A. Powell and David R. Bauer, 451-68. SBL Seminar Papers. Atlanta: Scholars, 1996.

———. *The Structure of Matthew's Gospel: A Study in Literary Design*. JSNT Supplement Series 31. Sheffield: Almond, 1988.

Beare, Francis W. *The Gospel according to Matthew: A Commentary*. Oxford: Blackwell, 1981.

Beattie, Derek R. G. *Jewish Exegesis of the Book of Ruth*. JSOT Supplement Series 2. Sheffield: Sheffield Academic, 1977.

———. "Ruth III." *Journal for the Study of the Old Testament* 5 (1978) 39-48.

Beirne, Margaret M. *Women and Men in the Fourth Gospel: A Genuine Discipleship of Equals*. London: T. & T. Clark, 2004.

Bellis, Alice O. *Helpmates, Harlots and Heroes: Women's Stories in the Hebrew Bible*. Louisville: Westminster John Knox, 1994.

Berlin, Adele. "Characterization in Biblical Narrative: David's Wives." *Journal for the Study of the Old Testament* 23 (1982) 69-85.

———. *Poetics and Interpretation of Biblical Narrative*. Sheffield: Almond, 1983.

Bernstein, Moshe J. "Two Multivalent Readings in the Ruth Narrative." *Journal for the Study of the Old Testament* 50 (1991) 15-26.

Bertman, Stephen. "Symmetrical Design in the Book of Ruth." *Journal of Biblical Literature* 84 (1965) 165-68.

Beyer, Hermann W. "διακονέω." In *Theological Dictionary of the New Testament*, vol. 2, edited by Gerhard Kittel, translated by Geoffrey W. Bromiley, 81–89. Grand Rapids: Eerdmans, 1964.

Bhabha, Homi K. "Signs Taken for Wonders." In *Literary Theory: An Anthology*, 2nd ed., edited by Julie Rivkin and Michael Ryan, 1167–84. Oxford: Blackwell, 2004.

Birch, Bruce C. "The First and Second Books of Samuel: Introduction, Commentary and Reflections." In *The New Interpreter's Bible*, vol. 2, *Numbers, Deuteronomy, Introduction to Narrative Literature, Joshua, Judges, Ruth, 1 & 2 Samuel*, edited by Leander E. Keck, 947–1383. Nashville: Abingdon, 1998.

Bird, Phyllis A. "The Harlot as Heroine: Narrative Art and Social Presupposition in Three Old Testament Texts." *Semeia* 46 (1989) 119–39.

———. "Images of Women in the Old Testament." In *The Bible and Liberation: Political and Social Hermeneutics*, edited by Norman K. Gottwald, 252–88. Maryknoll: Orbis, 1983.

———. "'To Play the Harlot': An Inquiry into an Old Testament Metaphor." In *Gender and Difference in Ancient Israel*, edited by Peggy L. Day, 75–94. Minneapolis: Fortress, 1989.

Blenkinsopp, Joseph. "Theme and Motif in the Succession History (2 Sam. 11:2 ff.) and the Yahwist Corpus." Supplements to *Vetus Testamentum* 15 (1965) 44–57.

Blomberg, Craig L. "Matthew." In *Commentary on the New Testament Use of the Old Testament*, edited by Greg K. Beale and Donald A. Carson, 1–109. Grand Rapids: Baker, 2007.

Boice, James M., *Genesis*. Vol. 3. An Expositional Commentary. Grand Rapids: Baker, 1999.

Boling, Robert G., and G. Ernest Wright. *Joshua: A New Translation with Introduction and Commentary*. Anchor Bible 6. New York: Doubleday, 1982.

Boring, M. Eugene. "The Gospel of Matthew: Introduction, Commentary, and Reflections." In *The New Interpreter's Bible: New Testament Articles, Matthew, Mark*, vol. 8, edited by Leander E. Keck, 87–505. Nashville: Abingdon, 1995.

Bornkamm, Gunther. "The Stilling of the Storm in Matthew." In *Tradition and Interpretation in Matthew*, edited by Gunther Bornkamm et al., 52–57. London: SCM, 1963.

Bornkamm, Gunther, et al. *Tradition and Interpretation in Matthew*. London: SCM, 1963.

Bos, Johanna W. H. "An Eyeopener at the Gate: George Coats and Genesis 38." *Lexington Theological Quarterly* 27 (1992) 119–23.

———. "Out of the Shadows: Genesis 38; Judges 4:17–22; Ruth 3." *Semeia* 42 (1988) 37–67.

Bredin, Mark. "Gentiles and the Davidic Tradition in Matthew." In *A Feminist Companion to the Hebrew Bible in the New Testament*, edited by Athalya Brenner, 95–111. Sheffield: Sheffield Academic, 1996.

Brenner, Athalya, ed. *A Feminist Companion to Genesis*. Feminist Companion to the Bible 2. Sheffield: Sheffield Academic, 1993.

———. *A Feminist Companion to Ruth*. Feminist Companion to the Bible 3. Sheffield: Sheffield Academic, 1993.

———. *A Feminist Companion to Samuel & Kings*. Feminist Companion to the Bible 5. Sheffield: Sheffield Academic, 1994.

———. *A Feminist Companion to the Hebrew Bible in the New Testament*. Sheffield: Sheffield Academic, 1996.

Bibliography

———. *I Am . . . : Biblical Women Tell Their Own Stories*. Minneapolis: Fortress, 2005.

———. Introduction to *A Feminist Companion to Ruth*, edited by Athalya Brenner, 9–18. Sheffield: Sheffield Academic, 1993.

Bronner, Leila L. "A Thematic Approach to Ruth in Rabbinic Literature." In *A Feminist Companion to Ruth*, edited by Athalya Brenner, 146–69. Sheffield: Sheffield Academic, 1993.

Brown, Raymond E. *The Birth of the Messiah: A Commentary on the Infancy Narratives in the Gospels of Matthew and Luke*. New updated ed. Anchor Bible Reference Library. London: Yale University Press, 1993.

———. "*Rachab* in Mt 1,5 Probably Is Rahab of Jericho." *Biblica* 63 (1982) 79–80.

Brueggemann, Walter. *David's Truth in Israel's Imagination and Memory*. Philadelphia: Fortress, 1985.

———. *First and Second Samuel*. Interpretation Bible Commentary. Louisville: Westminster John Knox, 1990.

———. *Genesis*. Interpretation Bible Commentary. Atlanta: Westminster John Knox, 1982.

———. *The Land: Place as Gift, Promise, and Challenge in Biblical Faith*. 2nd ed. Overtures to Biblical Theology. Minneapolis: Fortress, 2002.

———. *Old Testament Theology: An Introduction*. Library of Biblical Theology. Nashville: Abingdon, 2008.

Burridge, Richard A. *What Are the Gospels: A Comparison with Graeco-Roman Biography*. SNTS Monograph Series 70. Cambridge: Cambridge University Press, 1992.

Bush, Federic W. *Ruth/Esther*. Word Biblical Commentary 9. Waco: Word, 1996.

Butler, Trent C. *Joshua*. Word Biblical Commentary 7. Waco: Word, 1983.

Calvin, John. *A Commentary on Genesis*. Translated and edited by John King. 1847. Geneva Series Commentary. London: Banner of Truth, 1965.

Campbell, Edward F., Jr. *Ruth: A New Translation with Introduction, Notes and Commentary*. Anchor Bible 7. New York: Doubleday, 1975.

Campbell, Ken M. "Rahab's Covenant." *Vetus Testamentum* 22 (1972) 243–44.

Carson, Donald A. "Matthew." In *The Expositor's Bible Commentary*, vol. 8, edited by Frank E. Gaebelein, 1–599. Grand Rapids: Zondervan, 1984.

Carter, Warren. "Kernels and Narrative Blocks: The Structure of Matthew's Gospel." *Catholic Biblical Quarterly* 54 (1992) 463–81.

———. "Matthew 4:18–22 and Matthean Discipleship: An Audience-Orientated Perspective." *Catholic Biblical Quarterly* 59 (1997) 58–74.

———. *Matthew and the Margins: A Sociopolitical and Religious Reading*. Maryknoll: Orbis, 2000.

Chatman, Seymour. *Story and Discourse: Narrative Structure in Fiction and Film*. Ithaca: Cornell University Press, 1978.

Childs, Brevard S. *Introduction to the Old Testament as Scripture*. Philadelphia: Fortress, 1979.

———. *Isaiah*. Old Testament Library. London: Westminster John Knox, 2001.

Chrysostom, St. John. *St. Chrysostom: Homilies on the Gospel of St. Matthew*. Edited by Philip Schaff. Nicene and Post-Nicene Fathers 10. http://www.ccel.org/ccel/schaff/npnf110.i.html.

Clark, Gordon R. *The Word Hesed in the Hebrew Bible*. JSOT Supplement Series 157. Sheffield: Sheffield Academic, 1993.

Clément, Catherine, and Julia Kristeva. *The Feminine and the Sacred*. Translated by Jane Marie Todd. European Perspectives. New York: Columbia University Press, 2001.

Clines, David J. A. *Ezra, Nehemiah, Esther*. Grand Rapids: Eerdmans, 1984.

———. "Story and Poem: The Old Testament as Literature and as Scripture." *Interpretation* 34 (1980) 115–27.

Coats, George W. *Genesis, with an Introduction to Narrative Literature*. Forms of the Old Testament Literature 1. Grand Rapids: Eerdmans, 1983.

———. "Widows Rights: A Crux in the Structure of Genesis 28." *Catholic Biblical Quarterly* 34 (1972) 462.

Corley, Kathleen E. "Jesus' Table Practice: Dining with 'Tax Collectors and Sinners,' including Women." In *Society of Biblical Literature Seminar Papers 1993*, edited by Eugene H. Lovering, 444–59. Atlanta: Scholars, 1993.

Cotter, David W. *Genesis*. Berit Olam: Studies in Hebrew Narrative & Poetry. Collegeville: Liturgical, 2003.

Cotterell, Peter, and Max Turner. *Linguistics and Biblical Interpretation*. London: SPCK, 1989.

Crosby, Michael H. *House of Disciples: Church, Economics, & Justice in Matthew*. Maryknoll: Orbis, 1988.

Cross, Frank M. "A Response to Zakovitch's 'Successful Failure of Israelite Intelligence.'" In *Text and Tradition: The Hebrew Bible and Folklore*, edited by Susan Niditch, 99–104. Atlanta: Scholars, 1990.

D'Angelo, Mary R. "Women in Luke–Acts: A Redactional View." *Journal of Biblical Literature* 109 (1990) 441–61.

Darr, Kathryn P. *Far More Precious than Jewels: Perspectives on Biblical Women*. Louisville: Westminster John Knox, 1991.

Davies, Margaret. *Matthew*. Sheffield: Sheffield Academic, 1993.

Davies, William D., and Dale C. Allison Jr. *A Critical and Exegetical Commentary on the Gospel according to Saint Matthew*. Vol. 1, *Introduction and Commentary on Matthew 1–7*. International Critical Commentary. Edinburgh: T. & T. Clark, 1988.

———. *A Critical and Exegetical Commentary on the Gospel according to Saint Matthew*. Vol. 2, *Commentary on Matthew 8–18*. International Critical Commentary. Edinburgh: T. & T. Clark, 1991.

———. *A Critical and Exegetical Commentary on the Gospel according to Saint Matthew*. Vol. 3, *Commentary on Matthew 19–28*. International Critical Commentary. Edinburgh: T. & T. Clark, 1997.

Deines, Roland. "Not the Law but the Messiah: Law and Righteousness in the Gospel of Matthew–An Ongoing Debate." In *Built upon the Rock: Studies in the Gospel of Matthew*, edited by Daniel M. Gurtner and John Nolland, 53–84. Cambridge: Eerdmans, 2008.

Dijk-Hemmes, Fokkelien van. "Tamar and the Limits of Patriarchy: Between Rape and Seduction." In *Anti-Covenant: Counter-Reading Women's Lives in the Hebrew Bible*, edited by Mieke Bal, 135–56. JSOT Supplement Series 81. Sheffield: Almond, 1989.

Dube, Musa W. *Postcolonial Feminist Interpretation of the Bible*. St. Louis: Chalice, 2000.

Duling, Dennis C. "Ethnicity, Ethnocentrism, and the Matthean Ethos." *Biblical Theology Bulletin* 35 (2005) 125–42.

———. "Matthew and Marginality." *HTS Theological Studies* 51 (1995) 358–87.

Earl, Douglas S. *Reading Joshua as Christian Scripture*. Journal of Theological Interpretation Supplement Series 2. Winona Lake, IN: Eisenbrauns, 2010.

Bibliography

Edin, Mary H. "Learning What Righteousness Means: Hosea 6:6 and the Ethic of Mercy in Matthew's Gospel." *Word & World* 18 (1998) 355–63.

Eichrodt, Walter. *Theology of the Old Testament*. Vol. 1. London: SCM, 1961.

Eloff, Mervin. "Ἀπό . . . ἕως and Salvation History in Matthew's Gospel." In *Built upon the Rock: Studies in the Gospel of Matthew*, edited by Daniel M. Gurtner and John Nolland, 85–107. Cambridge: Eerdmans, 2008.

Emerton, John A. "Judah and Tamar." *Vetus Testamentum* 29 (1979) 403–15.

Esser, Hans H. "Mercy." In *New International Dictionary of New Testament Theology*, vol. 2, edited by Colin Brown, 594–97. Exeter: Paternoster, 1976.

Evans, Mary J. *1 and 2 Samuel*. New International Biblical Commentary, Old Testament Series. Carlisle, UK: Paternoster, 2000.

Exum, J. Cheryl. *Fragmented Women: Feminist (Sub)versions of Biblical Narratives*. JSOT Supplement Series 163. Sheffield: Sheffield Academic, 1993.

———. "'Mother in Israel': A Familiar Figure Reconsidered." In *Feminist Interpretation of the Bible*, edited by Letty M. Russell, 73–85. Oxford: Blackwell, 1985.

———. *Plotted, Shot and Painted: Cultural Representations of Biblical Women*. JSOT Supplement Series 215. Sheffield: Sheffield Academic, 1996.

Fewell, Danna N. "Feminist Reading of the Hebrew Bible." *Journal for the Study of the Old Testament* 39 (1987) 77–87.

Fewell, Danna N., and David M. Gunn. *Gender, Power, and Promise: The Subject of the Bible's First Story*. Nashville: Abingdon, 1993.

———. "'A Son Is Born to Naomi': Literary Allusions and Interpretation in the Book of Ruth." In *Women in the Hebrew Bible*, edited by Alice Bach, 233–39. London: Routledge, 1999.

Fiorenza, Elisabeth S. *But She Said: Feminist Practices of Biblical Interpretation*. Boston: Beacon, 1992.

———. *In Memory of Her: A Feminist Theological Reconstruction of Christian Origins*. 2nd ed. London: SCM, 1995.

———. "The Will to Choose or to Reject: Continuing Our Critical Work." In *Feminist Interpretation of the Bible*, 125–36. Oxford: Blackwell, 1985.

Firth, David G. *1 & 2 Samuel*. Apollos Old Testament Commentary 8. Nottingham: Apollos, 2009.

Fisch, Harold. "Ruth and the Structure of Covenant History." *Vetus Testamentum* 32 (1982) 425–37.

Fischer, Irmtraud. "The Book of Ruth: A Feminist Commentary to the Torah?" In *Ruth and Esther*, edited by Athalya Brenner, 24–49. Feminist Companion to the Bible, Second Series 3. Sheffield: Sheffield Academic, 1999.

Fokkelman, Jan P. "Genesis." In *The Literary Guide to the Bible*, edited by Robert Alter and J. Frank Kermode, 36–55. Cambridge: Harvard University Press, 1987.

———. *Narrative Art and Poetry in the Books of Samuel*. Vol. 1, *King David (II Samuel 9–20 and I Kings 1–2)*. Studia Semitica Neerlandica 20. Assen: Van Gorcum, 1981.

———. *Narrative Art in Genesis: Specimens of Stylistic and Structural Analysis*. Assen: Van Gorcum, 1975.

———. *Reading Biblical Narrative: An Introductory Guide*. Translated by Ineke Smit. Louisville: Westminster John Knox, 1999.

Forster, Edward M. *Aspects of the Novel*. London: Penguin, 2005.

Foucault, Michel. *Power/Knowledge: Selected Interviews and Other Writings 1972–1977*. Sussex: Harvest, 1980.

France, Richard T. "The Formula-Quotations of Matthew 2 and the Problem of Communication." *New Testament Studies* 27 (1980-81) 233-51.
———. *The Gospel of Matthew*. New International Commentary on the New Testament. Grand Rapids: Eerdmans, 2007.
———. *Matthew: Evangelist and Teacher*. Exeter: Paternoster, 1989.
Freed, Edwin. *The Stories of Jesus' Birth: A Critical Introduction*. Sheffield: Sheffield Academic, 2001.
———. "The Women in Matthew's Genealogy." *Journal for the Study of the New Testament* 29 (1987) 3-19.
Fuchs, Esther. "'For I Have the Way of Women': Deception, Gender, and Ideology in Biblical Narrative." *Semeia* 42 (1988) 68-83.
———. "The Literary Characterization of Mothers and Sexual Politics in the Hebrew Bible." In *Women in the Hebrew Bible*, edited by Alice Bach, 127-39. London: Routledge, 1999.
———. *Sexual Politics in the Biblical Narrative: Reading the Hebrew Bible as a Woman*. JSOT Supplement Series 310. London: Sheffield Academic, 2003.
———. "Status and Role of Female Heroines in the Biblical Narrative." In *Women in the Hebrew Bible*, edited by Alice Bach, 77-84. London, Routledge, 1999.
Fymer-Kensky, Tivka. "Deuteronomy." In *The Women's Bible Commentary*, exp. ed., edited by Carol A. Newsom and Susan H. Ringe, 57-68. Louisville: Westminster John Knox, 1998.
Garland, David E. *Reading Matthew: A Literary and Theological Commentary on the First Gospel*. London: SPCK, 1993.
Garsiel, Moshe. "The Story of David and Bathsheba: A Different Approach." *Catholic Biblical Quarterly* 55 (1993) 244-62.
Gaventa, Beverley R. *Mary: Glimpses of the Mother of Jesus*. Edinburgh: T. & T. Clark, 1999.
Glueck, Nelson. *Hesed in the Bible*. Cincinnati: Hebrew Union College Press, 1967.
Goldingay, John E. *Isaiah*. New International Biblical Commentary. Peabody, MA: Hendrickson, 2001.
———. *Models for Interpretation of Scripture*. Carlisle, UK: Paternoster, 1995.
———. *Old Testament Theology*. Vol. 1, *Israel's Gospel*. Downers Grove: InterVarsity, 2003.
Goldsmith, Martin. *Matthew and Mission*. Carlisle, UK: Paternoster, 2001.
Good, Deirdre. "The Verb ΑΝΑΧΩΡΕΩ in Matthew's Gospel." *Novum Testamentum* 32 (1990) 1-12.
Good, Edwin M. *Irony in the Old Testament*. Biblical Literature Series. Sheffield: Almond, 1981.
Gordon, Robert P. *1 & 2 Samuel: A Commentary*. Exeter: Paternoster, 1986.
Gottwald, Norman K. *The Tribes of Yahweh: A Sociology of the Religion of Liberated Israel 1250-1050 B.C.* London: SCM, 1980.
Goulder, Michael D. *Midrash and Lection in Matthew*. London: SPCK, 1974.
Gourevitch, Philip. *We Wish to Inform You That Tomorrow We Will Be Killed with Our Families*. London: Picador, 2000.
Gow, Murray D. *The Book of Ruth*. Leicester: Apollos, 1992.
Gray, John. *I & II Kings*. 2nd ed. Old Testament Library. London: SCM, 1970.
———. *Joshua, Judges and Ruth*. New Century Bible Commentary. London: Nelson, 1967.

Bibliography

Green, Barbara. "The Plot of the Biblical Story of Ruth." *Journal for the Study of the Old Testament* 23 (1982) 55–68.

Greenstein, Edward L. "Reading Strategies and the Story of Ruth." In *Women in the Hebrew Bible*, edited by Alice Bach, 211–31. London: Routledge, 1999.

Greidanus, Sidney. *The Modern Preacher and the Ancient Text: Interpreting and Preaching Biblical Literature*. Leicester: InterVarsity, 1988.

Guardiola-Sáenz, Leticia A. "Borderless Women and Borderless Texts: A Cultural Reading of Matthew 15:21–28." *Semeia* 78 (1997) 69–81.

Gundry, Robert H. *Matthew: A Commentary on His Literary and Theological Art*. Grand Rapids: Eerdmans, 1982.

———. *The Use of the Old Testament in St. Matthew's Gospel with Special Reference to the Messianic Hope*. Supplements to *Novum Testamentum*. Leiden: Brill, 1967.

Gunkel, Herman. *Genesis*. Mercer Library of Biblical Studies. Macon, GA: Mercer University Press, 1997.

Gunn, David M. "Joshua and Judges." In *The Literary Guide to the Bible*, edited by Robert Alter and J. Frank Kermode, 102–21. Cambridge: Harvard University Press, 1987.

———. *The Story of King David, Genre and Interpretation*. JSOT Supplement Series 6. Sheffield: Sheffield Academic, 1978.

Gunn, David M., and Danna N. Fewell. *Narrative in the Hebrew Bible*. Oxford Bible Series. Oxford: Oxford University Press, 1993.

Gurtner, Daniel M., and John Nolland, eds. *Built upon the Rock: Studies in the Gospel of Matthew*. Cambridge: Eerdmans, 2008.

Hagner, Donald A. *Matthew 1–13*. Word Biblical Commentary 33a. Nashville: Nelson, 1993.

Hamilton, Victor P. *The Book of Genesis: Chapters 18–50*. New International Commentary on the Old Testament. Grand Rapids: Eerdmans, 1995.

Hanson, Anthony T. "Rahab the Harlot in Early Christian Tradition." *Journal for the Study of the New Testament* 1 (1978) 53–60.

Hare, Douglas R. A. *Matthew*. Interpretation Bible Commentary. Atlanta: Westminster John Knox, 1993.

Harrington, Daniel J. *The Gospel of Matthew*. Sacra Pagina 1. Collegeville: Liturgical, 1991.

Harris, J. Gordon, et al. *Joshua, Judges, Ruth*. IBC. Carlisle, UK: Paternoster, 2000.

Hauerwas, Stanley. *Matthew*. SCM Theological Commentary on the Bible. London: SCM, 2006.

Hawk, L. Daniel. *Every Promise Fulfilled: Contesting Plots in Joshua*. Louisville: Westminster John Knox, 1991.

———. *Joshua*. Berit Olam: Studies in Hebrew Narrative & Poetry. Collegeville: Liturgical, 2000.

Hays, Richard B. *Echoes of Scripture in the Letters of Paul*. New Haven: Yale University Press, 1989.

———. "The Liberation of Israel in Luke-Acts: Intertextual Narration as Countercultural Practice." In *Reading the Bible Intertextually*, edited by Richard B. Hays et al., 101–17. Waco: Baylor University Press, 2009.

Hays, Richard B., et al. *Reading the Bible Intertextually*. Waco: Baylor University Press, 2009.

Heffern, Andrew D. "The Four Women in St. Matthew's Genealogy of Christ." *Journal of Biblical Literature* 31 (1912) 69–81.

Heil, John P. "Significant Aspects of the Healing Miracles in Matthew." *Catholic Biblical Quarterly* 41 (1979) 274–87.
———. "The Narrative Role of the Women in Matthew's Genealogy." *Biblica* 72 (1991) 538–45.
Held, Heinz J. "Matthew as Interpreter of the Miracle Stories." In *Tradition and Interpretation in Matthew*, edited by Gunther Bornkamm et al., 165–299. London: SCM, 1963.
Hendrickson, William. *The Gospel of Matthew*. Edinburgh: Banner of Truth, 1974.
Hill, David. *The Gospel of Matthew*. New Century Bible Commentary. London: Oliphants, 1972.
———. "On the Use and Meaning of Hosea VI. 6 in Matthew's Gospel." *New Testament Studies* 24 (1977) 107–19.
Honig, Bonnie. "Ruth, the Model Emigrée: Mourning and the Symbolic Politics of Immigration." In *Ruth and Esther*, edited by Athalya Brenner, 50–74. Feminist Companion to the Bible, Second Series 3. Sheffield: Sheffield Academic, 1999.
Horsley, Richard A. *Hearing the Whole Story: The Politics of Plot in Mark's Gospel*. Louisville: Westminster John Knox, 2001.
Horst, Pieter W. van der. "Tamar in Pseudo-Philo's Biblical History." In *Feminist Companion to Genesis*, edited by Athalya Brenner, 300–304. Feminist Companion to the Bible 2. Sheffield: Sheffield Academic, 1993.
Howell, David B. *Matthew's Inclusive Story: A Study in the Narrative Rhetoric of the First Gospel*. JSNT Supplement Series 42. Sheffield: Sheffield Academic, 1990.
Hubbard, Robert L., Jr. *The Book of Ruth*. New International Commentary on the Old Testament. Grand Rapids: Eerdmans, 1988.
Humphries-Brooks, Stephenson. "The Canaanite Women in Matthew." In *A Feminist Companion to Matthew*, edited by Amy-Jill Levine, 138–56. Sheffield: Sheffield Academic, 2001.
Hutchison, John C. "Women, Gentiles, and the Messianic Mission in Matthew's Genealogy." *Bibliotheca Sacra* 158 (2001) 152–64.
Irenaeus. *Against Heresies*. http://www.newadvent.org/fathers/0103.htm.
Jeansonne, Sharon P. *The Women of Genesis*. Minneapolis: Fortress, 1990.
Jeremias, Joachim. *Jerusalem in the Time of Jesus: An Investigation into Economic and Social Conditions during the New Testament Period*. London: SCM, 1969.
Jerome. *The Fathers of the Church: St. Jerome, Commentary on Matthew*. Translated by Thomas P. Scheck. Patristic Series 117. Washington: Catholic University of America Press, 2008.
Johnson, Elizabeth A. *Truly Our Sister: A Theology of Mary in the Communion of Saints*. London: Continuum, 2005.
Johnson, Marshall D. *The Purpose of the Biblical Genealogies*. London: Cambridge University Press, 1969.
Jones, John M. "Subverting the Textuality of Davidic Messianism: Matthew's Presentation of the Genealogy and the Davidic Title." *Catholic Biblical Quarterly* 56 (1994) 256–72.
Josephus. *Antiquities of the Jews*. http://www.ccel.org/j/josephus/works/JOSEPHUS.HTM.
Joy, Morny, and Penelope Magee, eds. *Claiming Our Rites: Studies in Religion by Australian Women Scholars*. Adelaide: Australian Association for the Study of Religions, 1994.

Bibliography

Keener, Craig S. *Matthew*. IVP New Testament Commentaries 1. Leicester: InterVarsity, 1998.

Keil, Carl F., and Franz Delitzsch. *Joshua, Judges, Ruth, 1 & 2 Samuel*. Commentary on the Old Testament 2. Grand Rapids: Eerdmans, 1982.

Keown, Gerald L., et al. *Jeremiah 26-52*. Word Biblical Commentary 27. Nashville: Nelson, 1995.

Keys, Gillian. *The Wages of Sin: A Reappraisal of the "Succession Narrative."* JSOT Supplement Series 221. Sheffield: Sheffield Academic, 1996.

Kidner, Derek F. "Isaiah." In *New Bible Commentary: 21st Century Edition*, 4th ed., edited by Gordon J. Wenham et al., 629-70. Leicester: InterVarsity, 1994,

Kingsbury, Jack D. "The Birth Narrative of Matthew." In *The Gospel of Matthew in Current Study*, edited by David E. Aune, 154-65. Cambridge: Eerdmans, 2001.

———. "The Figure of Jesus in Matthew's Story: A Rejoinder to David Hill." *Journal for the Study of the New Testament* 25 (1985) 61-81.

———. *Matthew as Story*. Philadelphia: Fortress, 1986.

———. *Matthew: Structure, Christology, Kingdom*. London: SPCK, 1976.

———. "Observations on the 'Miracle Chapters' of Matthew 8-9." *Catholic Biblical Quarterly* 40 (1978) 559-73.

———. "The Rhetoric of Comprehension in the Gospel of Matthew." *New Testament Studies* 41 (1995) 358-77.

———. "Structure of Matthew's Gospel and His Concept of Salvation-History." *Catholic Biblical Quarterly* 35 (1973) 451-74.

———. "The Title 'Son of David' in Matthew's Gospel." *Journal of Biblical Literature* 95 (1976) 591-602.

———. "The Verb *Akolouthein* ('to Follow') as an Index of Matthew's View of His Community." *Journal of Biblical Literature* 97 (1978) 56-75.

Kittel, Gerhard, and Gerhard Friedrich. *Theological Dictionary of the New Testament*. Translated and abridged by Geoffrey W. Bromiley. 1933-1973. London: Paternoster, 1985.

Klein, Lillian R. "Bathsheba Revealed." In *Samuel and Kings: A Feminist Companion to the Bible*, edited by Athalya Brenner, 46-64. Feminist Companion to the Bible, Second Series. Sheffield: Sheffield Academic, 2000.

Klement, Herbert H. *2 Samuel 21-24: Context, Structure and Meaning in the Samuel Conclusion*. Bern: Lang, 2000.

Kugel, James L. *Traditions of the Bible: A Guide to the Bible as It Was at the Start of the Common Era*. London: Harvard University Press, 1998.

Kupp, David D. *Matthew's Emmanuel: Divine Presence and God's People in the First Gospel*. SNTS Monograph Series 90. Cambridge: Cambridge University Press, 1996.

LaCocque, André. *The Feminine Unconventional: Four Subversive Figures in Israel's Tradition*. Minnesota: Fortress, 1990.

Laffey, Alice L. *An Introduction to the Old Testament: A Feminist Perspective*. Philadelphia: Fortress, 1988.

———. *Wives, Harlots & Concubines: The Old Testament in Feminist Perspective*. London: SPCK, 1990.

Lambe, Anthony J. "Genesis 38: Structure and Literary Design." In *The World of Genesis: Persons, Places, Perspectives*, edited by Philip R. Davies and David J. A. Clines, 102-25. JSOT Supplement Series 257. Sheffield: Sheffield Academic, 1998.

Bibliography

Lapsley, Jacqueline E. *Whispering the Word: Hearing Women's Stories in the Old Testament*. Louisville: Westminster John Knox, 2005.

Larkin, Katrina J. A. *Ruth and Esther*. Old Testament Guides. Sheffield: Sheffield Academic, 1996.

Leupold, Herbert C. *Exposition of Genesis*. Vol. 2, *Chapters 20–50*. Grand Rapids: Baker, 1979.

Levine, Amy-Jill. "Discharging Responsibility: Matthean Jesus, Biblical Law, and Hemorrhaging Woman." In *A Feminist Companion to Matthew*, edited by Amy-Jill Levine, 70–87. Sheffield: Sheffield Academic, 2001.

———. "Matthew." In *The Women's Bible Commentary*, exp. ed., edited by Carol A. Newsom and Susan H. Ringe, 339–49. Louisville: Westminster John Knox, 1998.

———. "Matthew's Advice to a Divided Readership." In *The Gospel of Matthew in Current Studies*, edited by David E. Aune, 22–41. Cambridge: Eerdmans, 2001.

———. "Ruth." In *The Women's Bible Commentary*, exp. ed., edited by Carol A. Newsom and Susan H. Ringe, 84–90. Louisville: Westminster John Knox, 1998.

———. *The Social and Ethnic Dimensions of Matthean Salvation History*. Studies in the Bible and Early Christianity 14. Lewiston, NY: Mellen, 1988.

Licht, Jacob. *Storytelling in the Bible*. 2nd ed. Jerusalem: Magnes, 1986.

Lilley, J. P. U. "Understanding the Herem." *Tyndale Bulletin* 44 (1993) 169–77.

Linafelt, Tod. *Ruth*. Berit Olam: Studies in Hebrew Narrative & Poetry. Collegeville: Liturgical, 1999.

Lohr, Charles H. "Oral Techniques in the Gospel of Matthew." *Catholic Biblical Quarterly* 23 (1961) 403–35.

Longman, Tremper. *Literary Approaches to Biblical Interpretation*. Foundations of Contemporary Interpretation. Grand Rapids: Academie, 1987.

Longstaff, Thomas R. W. "What Are Those Women Doing at the Tomb of Jesus? Perspectives on Matthew 28:1." In *A Feminist Companion to Matthew*, edited by Amy-Jill Levine, 196–204. Sheffield: Sheffield Academic, 2001.

Love, Stuart L. *Jesus and Marginal Women. The Gospel of Matthew in Social-Scientific Perspective*. Cambridge: Clarke, 2009.

Lucas, Leopold. *The Conflict between Christianity and Judaism: A Contribution to the History of the Jews in the Fourth Century*. Translated from the German edition published Berlin, 1910. Warminster: Aris & Phillips, 1993.

Luther, Martin. *Genesis*. Luther's Works. Vol. 7. St. Louis: Concordia, 1965.

Luz, Ulrich. "The Disciples in the Gospel according to Matthew." In *The Interpretation of Matthew*, edited by Graham E. Stanton, 98–128. London: SPCK, 1983.

———. "Intertexts in the Gospel of Matthew." *Harvard Theological Review* 97 (2004) 119–37.

———. *Matthew 1–7: A Commentary*. Translated by James E. Crouch. Hermeneia. Minneapolis: Fortress, 2007.

———. *The Theology of the Gospel of Matthew*. Translated by J. Bradford Robinson. New Testament Theology. Cambridge: Cambridge University Press, 1995.

Lyke, Larry L. "What Does Ruth Have to Do with Rahab? Midrash *Ruth Rabbah* and the Matthean Genealogy of Jesus." In *The Function of Scripture in Early Jewish and Christian Tradition*, edited by Craig A. Evans and James A. Sanders, 262–84. Sheffield: Sheffield Academic, 1998.

Marguerat, Daniel, and Yvan Bourquin. *How to Read the Bible Stories: An Introduction to Narrative Criticism*. Translated by John Bowden. London: SCM, 1999.

Bibliography

Matera, Frank J. "The Plot of Matthew's Gospel." *Catholic Biblical Quarterly* 49 (1987) 233–53.

———. "The Prologue as the Interpretative Key to Mark's Gospel." *Journal for the Study of the New Testament* 34 (1988) 3–20.

Matthews, Victor H., et al., eds. *Gender and Law in the Hebrew Bible and the Ancient Near East*. JSOT Supplement Series 262. Sheffield: Sheffield Academic, 1998.

McCarter, P. Kyle, Jr. *II Samuel: A New Translation with Introduction, Notes and Commentary*. Anchor Bible 9. New York: Doubleday, 1984.

McKane, William. *A Critical and Exegetical Commentary on Jeremiah*. Vol. 2, *Commentary on Jeremiah XXVI-LII*. International Critical Commentary. Edinburgh: T. & T. Clark, 1996.

McKay, Heather A. "Only a Remnant of Them Shall Be Saved." In *A Feminist Companion to the Hebrew Bible in the New Testament*, edited by Athalya Brenner, 32–61. Sheffield: Sheffield Academic, 1996.

McKenzie, Steven L. *King David: A Biography*. Oxford: Oxford University Press, 2000.

McKinlay, Judith E. *Reframing Her: Biblical Women in Postcolonial Focus*. Sheffield: Sheffield Phoenix, 2004.

McNeile, Alan H. *The Gospel according to Saint Matthew*. 1915. Reprint, London: Macmillan, 1961.

Meier, John P. *Law and History in Matthew's Gospel: A Redactional Study of Matthew 5:17-48*. Analecta Biblica 71. Rome: Biblical Institute Press, 1976.

———. "Salvation History in Matthew: In Search of a Starting Point." *Catholic Biblical Quarterly* 37 (1975) 203–15.

Meyers, Carol. "Returning Home." In *A Feminist Companion to Ruth*, edited by Athalya Brenner, 85–114. Feminist Companion to the Bible 3. Sheffield: Sheffield Academic, 1993.

Minear, Paul S. *Matthew: The Teacher's Gospel*. London: Darton, Longman & Todd, 1984.

Miscall, Peter D. *1 Samuel: A Literary Reading*. Bloomington: Indiana University Press, 1986.

Mitchell, Gordon. *Together in the Land: A Reading of the Book of Joshua*. JSOT Supplement Series 134. Sheffield: Sheffield Academic, 1993.

Moi, Toril, ed. *The Kristeva Reader*. Translated by Seán Hand and Léon S. Roudiez. Oxford: Blackwell, 1968.

Moloney, Francis J. *Woman, First among the Faithful*. London: Darton, Longman & Todd, 1985.

Moltmann-Wendel, Elisabeth. *The Women around Jesus*. London: SCM, 1982.

Morris, Leon. *The Gospel according to Matthew*. Pillar New Testament Commentary. Leicester: InterVarsity, 1992.

Mounce, Robert H. *Matthew*. New International Biblical Commentary. Peabody, MA: Hendrickson, 1993.

Mussies, Gerard. "Parallels to Matthew's Version of the Pedigree of Jesus." *Novum Testamentum* 28 (1986) 32–47.

Nelson, Richard D. *Joshua: A Commentary*. Old Testament Library. Louisville: Westminster John Knox, 1997.

Nicol, George G. "The Alleged Rape of Bathsheba: Some Observations on Ambiguity in Biblical Narrative." *Journal for the Study of the Old Testament* 73 (1997) 43–54.

———. "Bathsheba: A Clever Woman?" *Expository Times* 99 (1988) 360–63.

Bibliography

Niditch, Susan. *A Prelude to Biblical Folklore: Underdogs and Tricksters.* Urbana: University of Illinois Press, 2000.

———. *War in the Hebrew Bible: A Study in the Ethics of Violence.* Oxford: Oxford University Press, 1993.

———. "The Wronged Woman Righted: An Analysis of Genesis 38." *Harvard Theological Review* 72 (1979) 143–49.

Nielsen, Kirsten. *Ruth.* Old Testament Library. Louisville: Westminster John Knox, 1997.

Noll, Kurt L. *The Faces of David.* JSOT Supplement Series 242. Sheffield: Sheffield Academic, 1997.

Nolland, John. "The Four (Five) Women and Other Annotations in Matthew's Genealogy." *New Testament Studies* 43 (1997) 527–39.

———. "Genealogical Annotations in Genesis as Background for the Matthean Genealogy of Jesus." *Tyndale Bulletin* 47 (1996) 115–22.

———. *The Gospel of Matthew: A Commentary on the Greek Text.* New International Greek Testament Commentary. Cambridge, UK: Eerdmans, 2005.

Nowell, Irene. "Jesus' Great-Grandmothers: Matthew's Four and More." *Catholic Biblical Quarterly* 70 (2008) 1–15.

O'Day, Gail R. "Surprised by Faith: Jesus and the Canaanite Woman." In *A Feminist Companion to Matthew*, edited by Amy-Jill Levine, 114–25. Sheffield: Sheffield Academic, 2001.

Osgood, S. Joy. "Early Israelite Society and the Place of the Poor and Needy: Background to the Message of the Eighth Century Prophets, 2 vols." PhD diss., University of Manchester, 1992.

———. "1 and 2 Samuel." In *The IVP Women's Bible Commentary*, edited by Catherine C. Kroeger and Mary J. Evans, 153–83. Downers Grove: InterVarsity, 2002.

Osiek, Carolyn. "Reading the Bible as Women." In *The New Interpreter's Bible*, vol. 1, edited by Leander E. Keck et al., 181–87. Nashville: Abingdon, 1994.

Ostriker, Alicia S. "The Book of Ruth and the Love of the Land." *Biblical Interpretation* 10 (2002) 343–59.

———. "A Triple Hermeneutic: Scripture and Revisionist Women's Poetry." In *A Feminist Companion to Reading the Bible*, edited by Athalya Brenner and Carole R. Fontaine, 164–89. Sheffield: Sheffield Academic, 1997.

Overman, J. Andrew. *Matthew's Gospel and Formative Judaism: The Social World of the Matthean Community.* Minneapolis: Fortress, 1990.

Pardes, Ilana. *Countertraditions in the Bible: A Feminist Approach.* Cambridge: Harvard University Press, 1992.

Patte, Daniel. *The Gospel according to Matthew: A Structural Commentary on Matthew's Faith.* Philadelphia: Fortress, 1987.

Perkinson, Jim. "A Canaanitic Word in the Logos of Christ: Or the Difference the Syro-Phoenician Woman Makes to Jesus." *Semeia* 75 (1996) 61–85.

Petter, Donna. "Foregrounding of the Designation 'ēšet 'ûriyyâ haḥahittî in II Samuel XI–XII." *Vetus Testamentum* 54 (2004) 403–7.

Phipps, William E. *Assertive Biblical Women.* Westport, CT: Greenwood, 1992.

Pokorný, Petr. "From a Puppy to the Child: Some Problems of Contemporary Biblical Exegesis Demonstrated from Mark 7.24–30/Matt 15.21–8." *New Testament Studies* 41 (1995) 321–37.

Bibliography

Polzin, Robert M. *Moses and the Deuteronomist: A Literary Study of the Deuteronomic History*. Pt. 1, *Deuteronomy, Joshua, Judges*. Bloomington: Indiana University Press, 1993.
Powell, Mark A. "The Plot and Subplots of Matthew's Gospel." *New Testament Studies* 38 (1992) 187–204.
Preuss, Horst D. *Old Testament Theology*. Vol. 2. Edinburgh: T. & T. Clark, 1992.
Prouser, O. Horn. "The Truth about Women and Lying." *Journal for the Study of the Old Testament* 61 (1994) 15–28.
Provan, Iain W. *1 Kings*. New International Biblical Commentary. Carlisle, UK: Paternoster, 1995.
Przybylski, Benno. *Righteousness in Matthew and His World of Thought*. SNTS Monograph Series 41. Cambridge: Cambridge University Press, 1980.
Quinn, Jerome D. "Is 'PAXÁB in Mt 1,5 Rahab of Jericho?" *Biblica* 62 (1981) 225–28.
Rad, Gerhard von. *Genesis*. Old Testament Library. London: SCM, 1972.
Rauber, Donald F. "Literary Values in the Bible: The Book of Ruth." *Journal of Biblical Literature* 89 (1970) 27–37.
Reimer, David J. "7405 צדק" In *New International Dictionary of Old Testament Theology and Exegesis*, vol. 3, edited by Willem A. VanGemeren, 744–69. Carlisle, UK: Paternoster, 1996.
Rendsburg, Gary A. "David and His Circle in Genesis XXXVIII." *Vetus Testamentum* 36 (1986) 438–46.
Rhoads, David M. "Jesus and the Syrophoenician Woman in Mark: A Narrative-Critical Study." *Journal of the American Academy of Religion* 62 (1994) 343–75.
Ricouer, Paul. *Interpretation Theory: Discourse and the Surplus of Meaning*. Fort Worth: Texas Christian University Press, 1976.
Ringe, Sharon H. "A Gentile Woman's Story." In *Feminist Interpretation of the Bible*, edited by Letty M. Russell, 65–72. Oxford: Blackwell, 1985.
Rosenberg, Joel. "1 and 2 Samuel." In *The Literary Guide to the Bible*, edited by Robert Alter and J. Frank Kermode, 122–45. Cambridge: Harvard University Press, 1987.
Rost, Leonhard. *The Succession to the Throne of David*. Translated by Michael D. Rutter and David M. Gunn. 1926. Historic Texts and Interpreters in Biblical Scholarship. Sheffield: Almond, 1982.
Rowland, Christopher. *Christian Origins: An Account of the Setting and Character of the Most Important Messianic Sect of Judaism*. 2nd ed. London: SPCK, 2002.
Rowlett, Lori. "Inclusion, Exclusion and Marginality in the Book of Joshua." *Journal for the Study of the Old Testament* 55 (1992) 15–23.
Russell, Letty M., ed. *Feminist Interpretation of the Bible*. Oxford: Blackwell, 1985.
Sakenfeld, Katharine D. *Faithfulness in Action: Loyalty in Biblical Perspective*. Overtures to Biblical Theology 16. Philadelphia: Fortress, 1985.
———. "Feminist Perspectives on the Bible and Theology: An Introduction to Selected Issues." *Interpretation* 42 (1988) 5–18.
———. *The Meaning of Hesed in the Hebrew Bible: A New Inquiry*. Harvard Semitic Monographs. Missoula, MT: Scholars, 1978.
Saldarini, Anthony J. "Absent Women in Matthew's Households." In *A Feminist Companion to Matthew*, edited by Amy-Jill Levine, 157–70. Sheffield: Sheffield Academic, 2001.
———. *Matthew's Christian-Jewish Community*. London: University of Chicago Press, 1994.

Sarna, Nahum M. *Genesis: The Traditional Hebrew Text with the New JPS Translation.* JPS Torah Commentary. Philadelphia: Jewish Publication Society of America, 1989.

Sasson, Jack M. "The Issue of Ge'ullāh in Ruth." *Journal for the Study of the Old Testament* 5 (1978) 52–64.

―――. "Ruth." In *The Literary Guide to the Bible*, edited by Robert Alter and J. Frank Kermode, 320–28. Cambridge: Harvard University Press, 1987.

―――. *Ruth: A New Translation with a Philological Commentary and a Formalist-Folkorist Interpretation.* London: John Hopkins University Press, 1979.

Savran, George. "1 and 2 Kings." In *The Literary Guide to the Bible*, edited by Robert Alter and J. Frank Kermode, 146–64. Cambridge: Harvard University Press, 1987.

Schaberg, Jane. "Feminist Interpretations of the Infancy Narrative of Matthew." *Journal of Feminist Studies in Religion* 13 (1997) 35–62.

―――. *The Illegitimacy of Jesus: A Feminist Theological Interpretation of the Infancy Narratives.* Biblical Seminar 28. Sheffield: Sheffield Academic, 1995.

Schneider, Michael. "How Does God Act? Intertextual Readings of 1 Corinthians 10." In *Reading the Bible Intertextually*, edited by Richard B. Hays et al., 35–52. Waco: Baylor University Press, 2009.

Scholz, Susanne. *Introducing the Women's Hebrew Bible.* Introductions in Feminist Theology 13. London: T. & T. Clark, 2007.

Scott, Bernard B. "The Birth of the Reader." *Semeia* 52 (1990) 83–102.

Scott, J. Julius, Jr. "Gentiles and the Ministry of Jesus: Further Observation on Matt 10:5–6; 15:21–28." *Journal of the Evangelical Theological Society* 33 (1990) 161–69.

Scott, J. Martin C. "Matthew 15.21–28: A Test-Case for Jesus' Manners." *Journal for the Study of the New Testament* 63 (1996) 21–44.

Seebass, Horst, and Colin Brown. "Righteousness." In *New International Dictionary of New Testament Theology*, vol. 3, edited Colin Brown, 352–58. Exeter: Paternoster, 1978.

Seitz, Christopher R. *Isaiah 1–39.* Interpreters Bible. Louisville: Westminster John Knox, 1993.

Senior, Donald P. "Between Two Worlds: Gentile and Jewish Christians in Matthew's Gospel." *Catholic Biblical Quarterly* 61 (1999) 1–23.

―――. "Directions in Matthean Studies." In *The Gospel of Matthew in Current Studies*, edited by David E. Aune, 5–21. Cambridge: Eerdmans, 2001.

―――. *The Gospel of Matthew.* Interpreting Biblical Texts. Nashville: Abingdon, 1997.

―――. *Matthew.* Abingdon New Testament Commentaries. Nashville: Abingdon, 1998.

―――. *The Passion Narrative according to Matthew: A Redactional Study.* Bibliotheca Ephemeridum Theologicarum Lovaniensium 39. Leuven: Leuven University Press, 1982.

Sim, David C. *The Gospel of Matthew and Christian Judaism.* Edinburgh: T. & T. Clark, 1998.

Skinner, Matthew L. "'She Departed to Her House': Another Dimension of the Syrophoenician Mother's Faith in Mark 7:24–30." *Word & World* 26 (2006) 14–21.

Smit, Peter-Ben. "Something about Mary? Remarks about the Five Women in the Matthean Genealogy." *New Testament Studies* 56 (2010) 191–207.

Soggin, J. Alberto. *Joshua.* Old Testament Library. London: SCM, 1972.

Bibliography

Solvang, Elna K. *A Woman's Place is in the House: Royal Women of Judah and Their Involvement in the House of David*. JSOT Supplement Series 349. London: Sheffield Academic, 2003.

Spina, Frank A. *The Faith of the Outsider: Exclusion and Inclusion in the Biblical Story*. Grand Rapids: Eerdmans, 2005.

Stanley, Christopher D. "The Rhetoric of Quotations: An Essay on Method." In *Early Christian Interpretation of the Scriptures of Israel*, edited by Craig A. Evans and James A. Sanders, 44–58. JSNT Supplement Series 148. Sheffield: Sheffield Academic, 1997.

Stanton, Graham N. *A Gospel for a New People: Studies in Matthew*. Edinburgh: T. & T. Clark, 1992.

———, ed. *The Interpretation of Matthew*. 2nd ed. Edinburgh: T. & T. Clark, 1995.

Steinberg, Naomi. "Israelite Tricksters, Their Analogues and Cross-Cultural Study." *Semeia* 42 (1988) 1–13.

Stendahl, Krister. "Quis et Unde? An Analysis of Matthew 1–2." In *The Interpretation of Matthew*, 2nd ed., edited by Graham N. Stanton, 69–80. Edinburgh: T. & T. Clark, 1995.

Sternberg, Meir. "Biblical Poetics and Sexual Politics: From Reading to Counterreading." *Journal of Biblical Literature* 111 (1992) 463–88.

———. *The Poetics of Biblical Narrative: Ideological Literature and the Drama of Reading*. Indiana Studies in Biblical Literature. Bloomington: Indiana University Press, 1985.

Streussy, Marti J. *David: Biblical Portraits of Power*. Carolina: University South Carolina Press, 1999.

Tatum, W. Barnes. "The Origin of Jesus Messiah (Matt 1:1, 18a): Matthew's Use of the Infancy Traditions." *Journal of Biblical Literature* 96 (1977) 523–35.

Theissen, Gerd. *The Gospels in Context*. Edinburgh: T. & T. Clark, 1992.

Thompson, William G. "Reflections on the Composition of Mt 8:1–9:34." *Catholic Biblical Quarterly* 33 (1971) 365–88.

Trible, Phyllis. "Depatriarchalizing in Biblical Interpretation." *Journal of the American Academy of Religion* 41 (1973) 32–48.

———. *God and the Rhetoric of Sexuality*. Overtures to Biblical Theology. Philadelphia: Fortress, 1978.

———. *Texts of Terror: Literary-Feminist Readings of Biblical Narratives*. Minneapolis: Fortress, 1984.

Vanhoozer, Kevin J. *Is There a Meaning in This Text? The Bible, the Reader, and the Morality of Literary Knowledge*. Leicester: Apollos, 1998.

Waetjen, Herman C. "The Genealogy as the Key to the Gospel according to Matthew." *Journal of Biblical Literature* 95 (1976) 205–30.

Wainwright, Elaine M. "The Gospel of Matthew." In *Searching the Scriptures*, vol. 2, *A Feminist Commentary*, edited by Elisabeth S. Fiorenza, 635–77. London: SCM, 1995.

———. " The Matthean Jesus and the Healing of Women." In *The Gospel of Matthew in Current Studies*, edited by David E. Aune, 74–95. Cambridge: Eerdmans, 2001.

———. *Shall We Look for Another? A Feminist Rereading of the Matthean Jesus*. Bible and Liberation Series. Maryknoll: Orbis, 1998.

———. *Towards a Feminist Critical Reading of the Gospel according to Matthew*. Berlin: de Gruyter, 1991.

———. "A Voice from the Margin: Reading Matthew 15:21-28 in an Australian Feminist Key." In *Reading from this Place*, vol. 2, *Social Location and Biblical Interpretation in Global Perspective*, edited by Fernando F. Segovia and Mary A. Tolbert, 132-56. Minneapolis: Fortress, 1995.

Walsh, Jerome T. *1 Kings*. Berit Olam: Studies in Hebrew Narrative & Poetry. Collegeville: Liturgical, 1996.

Watson, Francis. *Text and Truth: Redefining Biblical Theology*. Edinburgh: T. & T. Clark, 1997.

———. *Text, Church and World: Biblical Interpretation in Theological Perspective*. Edinburgh: T. & T. Clark, 1994.

Wegner, Judith R. *Chattel or Person? The Status of Women in the Mishnah*. Oxford: Oxford University Press, 1988.

Wenham, Gordon J. *Genesis 16-50*. Word Biblical Commentary 2. Dallas: Word, 1994.

Weren, Wim J. C. "The Five Women in Matthew's Genealogy." *Catholic Biblical Quarterly* 59 (1997) 288-305.

Westermann, Claus. *Genesis 37-50: A Commentary*. Translated by John J. Scullion. Minneapolis: Augsburg, 1986.

Wilkins, Michael J. *Discipleship in the Ancient World and Matthew's Gospel*. 2nd ed. Grand Rapids: Baker, 1995.

Williams, James G. *Women Recounted: Narrative Thinking and the God of Israel*. Sheffield: Almond, 1982.

Wilson, Lindsay. *Joseph, Wise and Otherwise: The Intersection of Wisdom and Covenant in Genesis 37-50*. Paternoster Biblical Monographs. Carlisle, UK: Paternoster, 2004.

Wilson, Robert R. *Genealogy and History in the Biblical World*. London: Yale University Press, 1977.

Witherington, Ben. *Matthew*. Smyth & Helwys Bible Commentary. Macon, GA: Smyth & Helwys, 2006.

Wolde, Ellen van. "Intertextuality: Ruth in Dialogue with Tamar." In *A Feminist Companion to Reading the Bible: Approaches, Methods and Strategies*, edited by Athalya Brenner and Carole Fontaine, 426-51. Sheffield: Sheffield Academic, 1997.

Woudstra, Marten H. *The Book of Joshua*. New International Commentary on the Old Testament. Grand Rapids: Eerdmans, 1981.

Wright, N. T. *Matthew for Everyone*. Pt. 1, *Chapters 1-15*. London: SPCK, 2002.

Wright, Nigel G. *The Real Godsend: Preaching the Birth Narrative in Matthew and Luke*. Abingdon: Bible Reading Fellowship, 2009.

Yee, Gale A. "Fraught with Background: Literary Ambiguity in 2 Sam 11." *Interpretation* 42 (1988) 240-43.

Zakovitch, Yair. "Humor and Theology or the Successful Failure of Israelite Intelligence: A Literary-Folkloric Approach to Joshua 2." In *Text and Tradition: The Hebrew Bible and Folklore*, edited by Susan Niditch, 75-98. Atlanta: Scholars, 1990.

Ziesler, John A. *The Meaning of Righteousness in Paul*. SNTS Monograph Series 20. Cambridge: Cambridge University Press, 1972.

www.ingramcontent.com/pod-product-compliance
Lightning Source LLC
Chambersburg PA
CBHW061431300426
44114CB00014B/1629